Developing and Evaluating Security-Aware Software Systems

Khaled M. Khan
Qatar University, Qatar

Information Science
REFERENCE

Managing Director:	Lindsay Johnston
Editorial Director:	Joel Gamon
Book Production Manager:	Jennifer Romanchak
Publishing Systems Analyst:	Adrienne Freeland
Assistant Acquisitions Editor:	Kayla Wolfe
Typesetter:	Henry Ulrich
Cover Design:	Nick Newcomer

Published in the United States of America by
Information Science Reference (an imprint of IGI Global)
701 E. Chocolate Avenue
Hershey PA 17033
Tel: 717-533-8845
Fax: 717-533-8661
E-mail: cust@igi-global.com
Web site: http://www.igi-global.com

Library of Congress Cataloging-in-Publication Data

Developing and evaluating security-aware software systems / Khaled M. Khan, editor.
    pages cm
  Summary: "This book provides innovative ideas and methods on the development, operation, and maintenance of secure software systems and highlights the construction of a functional software system and a secure system simultaneously"-- Provided by publisher.
  Includes bibliographical references and index.
  ISBN 978-1-4666-2482-5 (hardcover) -- ISBN 978-1-4666-2483-2 (ebook) (print) -- ISBN 978-1-4666-2484-9 (print & perpetual access) (print) 1. Computer networks--Security measures. 2. Computer software--Development. 3. Computer security. I. Khan, Khaled M., 1959- editor of compilation.
  TK5105.59.D48 2013
  005.8--dc23
                                2012023337

British Cataloguing in Publication Data
A Cataloguing in Publication record for this book is available from the British Library.

The views expressed in this book are those of the authors, but not necessarily of the publisher.

Table of Contents

Section 3
Standard Security Functions

Detailed Table of Contents

Section 1
Software Development Process

Chapter 1

This paper describes results and reflects on the experience of engineering a secure web based system for the pre-employment screening domain. In particular, the paper presents results from a Knowledge Transfer Partnership (KTP) project between the School of Computing, IT and Engineering at the University of East London and the London-based award winning pre-employment company Powerchex Ltd. The Secure Tropos methodology, which is based on the principle of secure by design, has been applied to the project to guide the development of a web based system to support employment reference and background checking specifically for the financial services industry. Findings indicate the potential of the methodology for the development of secure web based systems, and support the argument of incorporating security considerations from the early stages of the software development process, i.e., the idea of secure by design. The developed system was tested by a third, independent to the project, party using a well known method of security testing, i.e., penetration testing, and the results provided did not indicate the presence of any major security problems. The experience and lessons learned by the application of the methodology to an industrial setting are also discussed in the paper.

Chapter 2

The Service-Oriented Architecture paradigm (SOA) is commonly applied for the implementation of complex, distributed business processes. The service-oriented approach promises higher flexibility, interoperability and reusability of the IT infrastructure. However, evaluating the quality attribute security of such complex SOA configurations is not sufficiently mastered yet. To tackle this complex problem, the authors developed a method for evaluating the security of existing service-oriented systems on the architectural level. The method is based on recovering security-relevant facts about the system by using reverse engineering techniques and subsequently providing automated support for further interactive security analysis at the structural level. By using generic, system-independent indicators and a knowledge base, the method is not limited to a specific programming language or technology. Therefore, the method can be applied to various systems and adapt it to specific evaluation needs. The paper describes the general structure of the method, the knowledge base, and presents an instantiation aligned to the Service Component Architecture (SCA) specification.

Chapter 3

Shamal Faily, University of Oxford, UK

Ivan Fléchais, University of Oxford, UK

Despite existing work on dealing with security and usability concerns during the early stages of design, there has been little work on synthesising the contributions of these fields into processes for specifying and designing systems. Without a better understanding of how to deal with both concerns at an early stage, the design process risks disenfranchising stakeholders, and resulting systems may not be situated in their contexts of use. This paper presents the IRIS process framework, which guides technique selection when specifying usable and secure systems. The authors illustrate the framework by describing a case study where the process framework was used to derive missing requirements for an information security policy for a UK water company following reports of the Stuxnet worm. The authors conclude with three lessons informing future efforts to integrate Security, Usability, and Requirements Engineering techniques for secure system design.

Chapter 4

Yudis Asnar, University of Trento, Italy

Fabio Massacci, University of Trento, Italy

Ayda Saidane, University of Trento, Italy

Carlo Riccucci, Engineering Ingegneria Informatica S.p.A, Italy

Massimo Felici, Deep Blue, Italy

Alessandra Tedeschi, Deep Blue, Italy

Paul El-Khoury, SAP Research, France

Keqin Li, SAP Research, France

Magali Séguran, SAP Research, France

Nicola Zannone, Eindhoven University of Technology, The Netherlands

Designing secure and dependable IT systems requires a deep analysis of organizational as well as social aspects of the environment where the system will operate. Domain experts and analysts often face security and dependability (S&D) issues they have already encountered before. These concerns require the design of S&D patterns to facilitate designers when developing IT systems. This article presents the experience in designing S&D organizational patterns, which was gained in the course of an industry lead EU project. The authors use an agent-goal-oriented modeling framework (i.e., the *SI** framework) to analyze organizational settings jointly with technical functionalities. This framework can assist domain experts and analysts in designing S&D patterns from their experience, validating them by proof-of-concept implementations, and applying them to increase the security level of the system.

Jostein Jensen, Norwegian University of Science and Technology, Norway
Martin Gilje Jaatun, SINTEF, Norway

Model Driven Development (MDD) is by many considered a promising approach for software development. This article reports the results of a systematic survey to identify the state-of-the-art within the topic of security in model driven development, with a special focus on finding empirical studies. The authors provide an introduction to the major secure MDD initiatives, but the survey shows that there is a lack of empirical work on the topic. The authors conclude that better standardization initiatives and more empirical research in the field is necessary before it can be considered mature.

Afonso Araújo Neto, University of Coimbra, Portugal
Marco Vieira, University of Coimbra, Portugal

When deploying database-centric web applications, administrators should pay special attention to database security requirements. Acknowledging this, Database Management Systems (DBMS) implement several security mechanisms that help Database Administrators (DBAs) making their installations secure. However, different software products offer different sets of mechanisms, making the task of selecting the adequate package for a given installation quite hard. This paper proposes a methodology for detecting database security gaps. This methodology is based on a comprehensive list of security mechanisms (derived from widely accepted security best practices), which was used to perform a gap analysis of the security features of seven software packages composed by widely used products, including four DBMS engines and two Operating Systems (OS). The goal is to understand how much each software package helps developers and administrators to actually accomplish the security tasks that are expected from them. Results show that while there is a common set of security mechanisms that is implemented by most packages, there is another set of security tasks that have no support at all in any of the packages.

Section 2
Formal Techniques and Tools

Jan Durand, Louisiana Tech University, USA
Juan Flores, Louisiana Tech University, USA
Nicholas Kraft, University of Alabama, USA
Randy Smith, University of Alabama, USA
Travis Atkison, Louisiana Tech University, USA

This paper describes a research effort to use executable slicing as a pre-processing aid to improve the prediction performance of rogue software detection. The prediction technique used here is an information retrieval classifier known as cosine similarity that can be used to detect previously unknown, known or variances of known rogue software by applying the feature extraction technique of randomized projection. This paper provides direction in answering the question of is it possible to only use portions or subsets, known as slices, of an application to make a prediction on whether or not the software contents are rogue. This research extracts sections or slices from potentially rogue applications and uses these slices instead of the entire application to make a prediction. Results show promise when applying randomized projections to cosine similarity for the predictions, with as much as a 4% increase in prediction performance and a five-fold decrease in processing time when compared to using the entire application.

In this paper, the authors propose a formal logic technique to protect information systems. As the widespread use of computer systems grows, the security of the information stored in such systems has become more important. As a security mechanism, authorization or access control ensures that all accesses to the system resources occur exclusively according to the access polices and rules specified by the system security agent. Authorization specification has been widely studied and a variety of approaches have been investigated. The authors propose a formal language with modal logic to specify the system security policies. The authors also provide the reasoning in response to system access requests, especially in situations where the security agent's knowledge base is incomplete. The semantics of this language is provided by translating it into epistemic logic program in which knowledge related modal operators are employed to represent agents' knowledge in reasoning. The authors demonstrate how this approach handles the situation where the security agent's knowledge on access decision is incomplete. The proposed mechanism effectively prevents unauthorized and malicious access to information systems.

The Extensible Markup Language is susceptible to security breaches because it does not incorporate methods to protect the information it encodes. This work focuses on the development of a formal language that can provide role-based access control to information stored in XML formatted documents. This language has the capacity to reason whether access to an XML document should be allowed. The language, $A^{xml(T)}$, allows for the specification of authorisations on XML documents and distinguishes itself from other research with the inclusion of temporal interval reasoning and the XPath query language.

Security is an important and challenging aspect that needs to be considered at an early stage during software development. Traditional software development methodologies do not deal with security issues and so there is no structured guidance for security design and development; security is usually an afterthought activity. This paper discusses the integration of XP with security activities based on the CLASP (Comprehensive Lightweight Application Security Process) methodology. This integration will help developers using XP develop secure software by applying security measures in all phases and activities, thereby minimizing the security vulnerabilities exploited by attackers.

Wesam Darwish, The University of British Columbia, Canada
Konstantin Beznosov, The University of British Columbia, Canada

This paper analyzes access control mechanisms of the Enterprise Java Beans (EJB) architecture and defines a configuration of the EJB protection system in a more precise and less ambiguous language than the EJB 3.0 standard. Using this configuration, the authors suggest an algorithm that formally specifies the semantics of authorization decisions in EJB. The level of support is analyzed for the American National Standard Institute's (ANSI) specification of Role-Based Access Control (RBAC) components and functional specification in EJB. The results indicate that the EJB specification falls short of supporting even Core ANSI RBAC. EJB extensions dependent on the operational environment are required in order to support ANSI RBAC required components. Other vendor-specific extensions are necessary to support ANSI RBAC optional components. Fundamental limitations exist, however, due to the impracticality of some aspects of the ANSI RBAC standard itself. This paper sets up a framework for assessing implementations of ANSI RBAC for EJB systems.

Alastair Nisbet, Massey University, New Zealand
M. A. Rashid, Massey University, New Zealand

Secure Key Deployment and Exchange Protocol (SKYE) is a new encryption Key Management Scheme (KMS) based on combination of features from recent protocols combined with new features for Mobile Ad Hoc Networks (MANETs). The design focuses on a truly ad hoc networking environment where geographical size of the network, numbers of network members, and mobility of the members is all unknown before deployment. Additionally, all key management is performed online making it distinct from most other implementations. This paper attempts to describe the process of development of the protocol and to more thoroughly discuss the simulation software design used to evaluate the performance of the proposed protocol. Simulation results show that security within the network can be increased by requiring more servers to collaborate to produce a certificate for the new member, or by requiring a higher trust threshold along the certificate request chain. SKYE works well within the limitations set by entirely online network formation and key management.

Matteo Avalle, Politecnico di Torino, Italy
Alfredo Pironti, INRIA, France
Davide Pozza, Teoresi Group, Italy
Riccardo Sisto, Politecnico di Torino, Italy

This paper presents JavaSPI, a "model-driven" development framework that allows the user to reliably develop security protocol implementations in Java, starting from abstract models that can be verified formally. The main novelty of this approach stands in the use of Java as both a modeling language and the implementation language. The JavaSPI framework is validated by implementing a scenario of the SSL protocol. The JavaSPI implementation can successfully interoperate with OpenSSL, and has comparable execution time with the standard Java JSSE library.

This paper serves to systematically describe the attempts made to forge fingerprints to fool biometric systems and to review all relevant publications on forging fingerprints to fool sensors. The research finds that many of the related works fail in this aspect and that past successes could not be repeated. First, the basics of biometrics are explained in order to define the meaning of the term security in this special context. Next, the state of the art of biometric systems is presented, followed by to the topic of security of fingerprint scanners. For this, a series of more than 30,000 experiments were conducted to fool scanners. The authors were able to reproduce and keep records of each single step in the test and to show which methods lead to the desired results. Most studies on this topic exclude a number of steps in producing a fake finger and fooling a fingerprint scanner are not explained, which means that some of the studies cannot be replicated. In addition, the authors' own ideas and slight variations of existing experiment set-ups are presented.

Many initiatives exist that integrate e-health systems on a large scale. One of the main technical challenges is access control, although several frameworks and solutions, like XACML, are becoming standard practice. Data is no longer shared within one affinity domain but becomes ubiquitous, which results in a loss of control. As patients will be less willing to participate without additional control strategies, patient consents are introduced that allow the patients to determine precise access rules on their medical data. This paper explores the consequences of integrating consent in e-health access control. First, consent requirements are examined, after which an architecture is proposed which incorporates patient consent in the access control service of an e-health system. To validate the proposed concepts, a proof-of-concept implementation is built and evaluated.

Preface

INTRODUCTION

The popularity of the first collection of the *Advances in Engineering Secure Software series*, entitled, "Issues and Challenges in Security-Aware Software Development" (Khan, 2012), has prompted us to compile this second collection of the series. Our first collection emphasizes on two objectives of security-aware software development, namely, software assurance and security assurance in the light of the development process. It also provides a detailed account on these two aspects. However, this book focuses mainly on three types of major ingredients for security-aware software development. It looks back some of the development of various processes, tools, techniques and security functions that took place last one decade since the inception of security-aware software engineering paradigm. The paradigm basically started in late 1990s with the goal of developing appropriate software engineering process and techniques, in addition to standard security functions, that could ensure constructing secure software products.

The two terminologies *security-aware software* and *secure software* are often used interchangeably. The core idea of this paradigm is to integrate security concerns with all phases in the software development process from requirements to testing and deployment. Such a process not only deals with technical aspects of secure software engineering, but the management aspects of software security should also be addressed. The development of security-aware software is mainly based on software engineering principles focusing on technical as well as managerial aspects of software security along with systems functionalities. The US department of Homeland Security initiated this with the title, 'Build Security in' that essentially advocates this idea (Homeland security).

The issue of security-aware software development was raised by researchers as well practitioners in late 1990s because security has been often treated as an afterthought, delayed to post-deployment phases of the software development process. Worst, security issues are delegated to systems administrators at the deployment as well as maintenance stages. Security-aware software development has emerged as a fundamental concern. Standard security mechanisms such as authentication, access control and encryption are definitely necessary for protecting information and software, but they do not provide end-to-end assurances. Incorporating security into the entire software development process is definitely challenging. It is proposed in (Erl, 2005) that services software should be developed in three ways in order to ensure security: top-down approach, bottom-up approach, and agile approach -- one has to consider security throughout all these three approaches.

The process of developing security-aware software involves many issues, from security policy formulation, security requirements modeling, developing security architecture, integrating security requirements with functionalities, testing verification and validation, and finally assurances that the end product is secure. If we classify these into broader categories, we find that the main research thrust on security-aware software systems revolves around the following three major areas:

- Software development process
- Formal techniques and tool
- Standard security functions

The relationship among the above three is summarized in Figure 1. This figure shows that a security-aware software development process should be based on software development process, formal techniques, and standard security functions. Secure software can be produced by integrating security functions, appropriate formal techniques into various phases of the development lifecycle. Various phases in the development process are associated with different specific techniques and tools. For example, the requirements analysis phase is supported by logic based techniques, the coding is supported by almost all formal techniques. The list of the techniques outlined in the figure is just an example. Similarly, requirements analysis, design, coding and deployment phases should be integrated with the standard security functions. Again, the list of the standard security functions is not complete, it just shows some examples of security functions. More research work is needed in order to identify the appropriate tools and techniques, standard security functions, and their relationships with various phases in the software development process. We now briefly discuss each of the three ingredients in the following sections.

Figure 1. Major ingredients of security-aware software development process

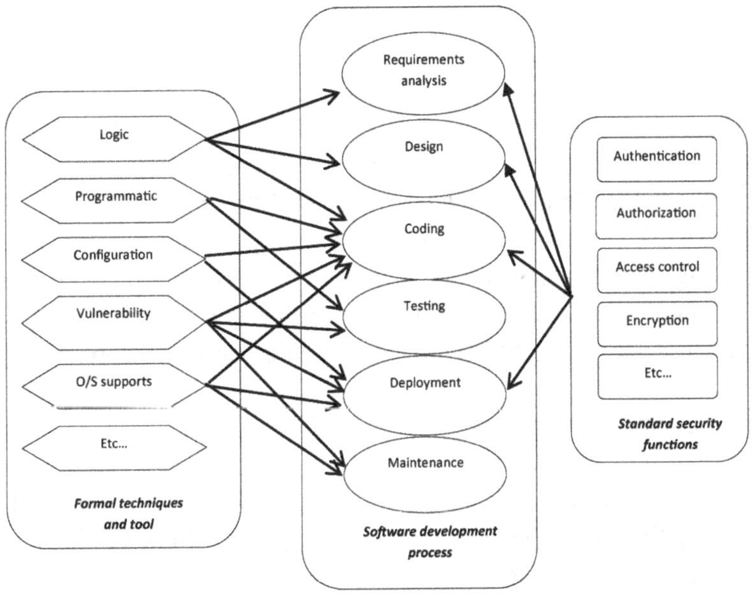

Integration with Software Development Process

The secure software development process involves the distinct tasks and procedures in the development cycle that are used to analyze, design and construct a software product. It has been argued that to achieve security-aware software, we need to address software security throughout the entire lifecycle of the software development process (Khan, 2012). A single task or procedure would unlikely produce security-aware software. Modern software systems are mainly intended to support highly complex business processes and interactions with other systems. While capturing, modeling and reflecting these complex processes in software systems is a challenging task, addressing security concerns of businesses in the software poses even greater challenges. In this context, security-aware software modeling definitely requires a holistic and collaborative approach. At the process level, considerable research activities have been reported in the literature. More notably, the integration of security requirements into UML for secure software modeling and analysis has been developed by several researchers. All these works are centered around UML notations.

Most of these attempt to extend UML in order to incorporate security concerns in the functionality. Probably for the first time, a Framework for Network Enterprise utilizing UML notations to describe a role-based access control (RBAC) model was proposed in (Epstein & Sandhu, 1999). It uses UML to represent RBAC. A similar work, the representation of access control such as MAC and RBAC using UML, was also proposed in (Shin & Ahn, 2000; Ray et al., 2003). An extension of UML, called UMLsec proposed in (Jurjens, 2002a; Jurjens, 2002b) focuses more on multi-level security of messages in UML interaction diagrams (namely sequence and state diagrams). Similarly, in another work called SecureUML (Lodderstedt et al., 2002), the authors introduce new meta-model components and authorization constraints expressed for RBAC.

The main objective of most of these attempts is to extend UML in order to incorporate security concerns in the functionality. Similar work on the extension of UML use cases to include security requirements is reported in (Siponen *et al.*, 2006). Another extension of UML was proposed in (Basin et al., 2009) in order to model security properties such a way that could be evaluated against hypothetical run-time instances such as static analysis regarding users and permissions. A proposal for systematically verifying and validating non-temporal and authorization constraints via UML's Object Constraint Language (OCL) is proposed in (Sohr, K. et al., 2008). The work reported in (Doan et al., 2010) also proposes an approach to integrate access control into UML for modeling and analysis of secure software systems.

Another interesting area of addressing security at the process level is the business process model. The business process model could capture security functions during the modeling phase such as reported in (Baskerville, 1988; Herrmann & Pernul, 1999; Backes *et al.* 2003; Mana *et al.* 2003; D'Aubeterre *et al.* 2008). In most of these works, security requirements are incorporated into the business process model.

Although, several UML based process models have been proceed, unfortunately, we do not have many reports on how successful these are in practice, in real world software development. It would be much interesting to see that these are being used in the industry in order to develop security-aware software.

Formal Techniques and Tools

This area involves research in finding tools and techniques such as programming level constructs, formal approach, application of artificial intelligence, logic based approach, vulnerability detections and mitigations, etc. The enforcement and verification of security policies at the low level software components is definitely a challenging task. There are several techniques used to ensure security of software systems. At the technique level, several research fronts are active in accommodating security issues at the low level programming units and logic of the program flows. Researchers have been exploring ways in which programming languages can be used to ensure that application software correctly enforces its security policies. This type of research work typically focuses on the enforcement of access control policies, data provenance tracking, information disclosure policies, and various forms of information flow policies in the program (Swamy et al., 2008b). Programming languages enable programmers to specify security policies and reason about that these policies are properly enforced in the program (Swamy et al., 2008a). One of the programming approaches to verify the correct enforcement of policies is to encode them as information flow policies for programs.

Research on programming languages demonstrates that security concerns can be dealt with by using both program analysis and program rewriting as powerful and flexible enforcement mechanisms. The security typed programming languages can allow programmers to specify confidentiality and integrity constraints on the data used in a program, and the compiler could verify that the program satisfies the security constraints (Zdancewic, 2002).

Another technique used for security-aware software is logic based approach that provides powerful expressiveness for the specification of security properties and the reason about security functions such as reported in (Fernandez, et al. 1989; Das, 1992; Fagin et al., 1995; Jajodia et al. 2001; Bertino et al. 2003). The logic based approach also provides reasonable flexibility for capturing security requirements. The predicates and rules of logic based language are used for expressing and evaluating authorization policies. A logic formalism has enough capability to specify, reason about and enforce access control polices in software systems.

Answer set programming, a logic based approach, is also being used to express and verify access control polices of a system. The applicability of the knowledge representation and reasoning languages such as logic programming for the design and implementation of a distributed authorization system is becoming promising. Researchers use answer set programming to deal with many complex issues associated with the distributed authorization along with the trust management approach (Wang, 2005). Formal authorization language based on semantics of answer set programming can express non-monotonic delegation policies unambiguously. The expressive power of such languages can represent the delegation with depth, separation of duty, partial authorization, and positive-negative authorizations. The logic based approaches could be used in security requirements analysis and specification during the systems development process. A design decision on security associated with systems functionality could also be reasoned about using logic based programming.

The application of logic based solution as well as programming features to the development of security-aware software looks promising.

Standard Security Functions

Standard security functions such as encryption, access control, authentication etc. are also required to ensure security-aware software systems. These functions ensure that security design and policies are adequately implemented and enforced as planned. Security functions are essential for the development of security software products. More research activities are required in order to identify ways how various security functions could be integrated or deployed at the micro level computing units in the software. It includes finding techniques on how various sophisticated security functions could be employed at data level as well as method level. It is also equally important to ensure that employing various security functions at the low level programming units would not degrade the usability of the system. There is a need for a balance between usability and the use of excessive visible security functions in a software system.

CHALLENGES

The research community has not come yet with any particular methods, tools, techniques and a process that will guarantee secure software construction. The following challenges still remain to be tackled:

- Security-aware software development needs a standard process agreed by all stakeholders such as software engineers, security experts and tool developers. There is no standard process that can be used as a de facto standard. The research communities as well as professional bodies such as IEEE Computer Society, NIST, etc. have not agreed on any single process for the development of secure software. Perhaps, there is none. It is also not realistic to expect that a single silver bullet will enable us to develop security-aware software without obstacles.
- We also need to catalogue various tools and techniques developed so far for security software. The catalog should clearly specify which tool or technique solves which specific problem, their performance rating, etc. An integration framework is required in order to show which tools and techniques are appropriate for which phases in the development process. A clear mapping of integration between tools/techniques and development phases is desperately needed.
- It is still an open question on how to measure the strength of software security in a continuous scale as opposed to a binary 'secure' 'not secure' values. How could we ascertain that system A is more secure than system B? We can envision a security metrics based approach that could forecast the relative security strength (or weakness) of a software product. A very few research work has been reported in this area so far. In other words, how do users know that a piece of software or its units are secure?
- An important security requirement of service oriented software such as cloud computing is that the software learns nothing about the input data, or the computed results of clients. The software can process clients' data without seeing them, as well as without comprehending the meaning of the output data. This goal should be achieved without employing extensive cryptographic techniques.
- We also need more techniques on how to compose different security policies during the integration of two software units in order to achieve a functionality. The composition of security policies in a dynamic software integration time is a challenging research task. It involves identifying contradictions between two participating security policies in a service composition, resolving these conflicts automatically, and so on.
- Another challenging issue still remains unsolved – certification of software from security bugs. We need techniques that would enable software developers to specify achieved security in the software. The claimed security properties could be independently verified by third party certifying authorities. Once certified, software security properties could not be altered and the certificate cannot be tampered.
- Finally, addressing the issue of trust in a software system is a big challenge. We need to find ways that could enable users to decide if software is trustworthy, if it is, how much etc.

ORGANIZATION OF THE BOOK

The chapters of this book are grouped around the three major ingredients of secure software engineering process that have already been discussed earlier. This collection presents total fifteen chapters, and they are grouped into three parts:

- **Section 1:** Software Development Process
  - Chapters 1-6
- **Section 2:** Formal Techniques and Tools
  - Chapters 7-10
- **Section 3:** Standard Security Functions
  - Chapters 11-15

CHAPTER ABSTRACTS

Chapter 1 reports the results on an experience of developing a secure web based system for a financial service industry using the Secure Tropos methodology. The findings of the experiment demonstrate the effectiveness of the methodology for the construction of secure web based systems. It further supports the notion that incorporating security considerations from the early stages of the software development process promotes the idea of secure by design. The developed system was tested by an independent entity using penetration testing. The testing results indicate no presence of any major security problems. This chapter basically demonstrates how the application of a software engineering methodology could support the notion of secure by design. The chapter also shows that the proposed methodology is flexible enough to apply in other application domains.

Chapter 2 presents a method for evaluating the security properties of service-oriented systems at the architectural level. The method attempts to recover security properties of the system by using reverse engineering techniques. It also provides automated support for further security analysis at the structural level. The proposed method is based on system-independent indicators and a knowledge base. It is independent form any specific programming language or technology. The method is flexible enough for adapting in various application systems. The chapter also describes a prototype tool that implements the methods, and the associated knowledge base. It argues that the knowledge base allow flexible refinement and adaptation of existing evaluation rules, and addition of new security aspects to the analysis. It also supports reusability of security expertise obtained from past evaluations, and offers fine-tuning capabilities using its weighting scheme.

Chapter 3 proposes a process framework, called IRIS (Integrating Requirements and Information Security), which provides guidance for the selection of technique when specifying security requirements in order to achieve secure software systems. The chapter demonstrates the applicability of the proposed framework by presenting a case study where the process framework was used to derive missing security requirements for an information security policy for a UK water company. It concludes with three lessons informing future efforts to integrate Security, Usability, and Requirements Engineering techniques for secure system design. The chapter argues that without a better understanding of how to deal with security and usability concerns at an early stage of the systems development, the design process may not achieve the security goals of the system.

Chapter 4 reports an experience with a European Union project in designing security and dependability patterns. It uses SI* framework, an agent-goal-oriented modeling framework in order to analyze organizational settings together with technical functionalities. This chapter demonstrates how a framework could assist domain experts in designing security and dependability patterns, validating them by proof-of-concept implementations, and applying them to increase the security level of the system. It also shows how SI* framework has been used by industries for capturing security and dependability patterns, and how patterns can be applied to achieve a sufficient level of security in the system. The proposed patterns have been used in various application contexts such as air traffic management, e-Health smart systems, etc.

Chapter 5 presents the results of a systematic survey to identify the state-of-the-art model driven development (MDD) focusing on security. The survey was carried out in order to find out how research communities deal with security in model driven development. The chapter addresses three issues: what are the major scientific initiatives describing automatic code generation from design models within the context of security in MDD, what empirical studies exist on the topic, and what are the strengths of the evidence that security aspects can be modeled as an inherent property and transformed to more secure code. It provides an introduction to the major secure model driven development initiatives and suggests that there is a lack of empirical work on the topic. It calls for standardization and more empirical research in this area.

Chapter 6 proposes a methodology based on a comprehensive list of security mechanisms for detecting database security gaps. The security mechanisms are derived from widely accepted security best practices. The methodology is intended to be used for gap analysis of security features which have been extracted from seven software packages composed by widely used applications, including four DBMS engines and two Operating Systems (OS). The main objective of the study is to find how each software package actually helps developers and administrators to achieve their systems security goals. The chapter concludes with interesting results showing that while there is a common set of security mechanisms that are supported by most software packages, however, there are some important security issues that are not supported at all by any of these packages.

Chapter 7 reports on a research effort that uses executable slicing as a pre-processing aid to improve the prediction performance of rogue software detection. The prediction technique used in this work is an information retrieval classifier that applies the feature extraction technique of randomized projection in order to detect previously unknown, known or variances of known rogue software. This approach extracts particular sections or slices from potentially rogue software, and uses these slices to make a prediction. It demonstrates optimal results of a 4% increase in prediction performance and a five-fold decrease in processing time when compared to using the entire application for the prediction. It concludes that a better malicious software classifier can be predicted by applying an executable slicing technique as a pre-processing step to the technique of randomized projection.

Chapter 8 propose a modal logic based approach to protect information system. The logic is used to specify and enforce security policies. The chapter provides the reasoning technique in response to the system access request especially in the situation where the grant access request is incomplete. The semantic of the language is provided by translating the language into epistemic logic program. The chapter demonstrates its applicability with a good number of realistic examples. It is expected that the proposed mechanism could be able to prevent unauthorized access to information systems more effectively. The chapter argues that the language has a strong expressive power to describe a variety of complex security requirements and policies.

Chapter 9 proposes a formal language which can provide role-based access control to information stored in XML documents. The proposed language has the capacity to reason about whether access to an XML document should be allowed or not. The language constructs allows systems designers to specify authorisations on XML documents. The inclusion of temporal interval reasoning and the XPath query language in the language constructs is rich enough to support the specification of authorization features in XML formatted documents. The language basically can be used to define a security policy base capable of specifying all access rights in the scope of an XML environment. The semantics of the language is provided through its translation into a logic program, namely Answer Set Programming (ASP). The chapter shows the application and expressive power of the language with a case study.

Chapter 10 discusses the integration of XP with security functions based on the CLASP (Comprehensive Lightweight Application Security Process) methodology in order to enable software developers using XP to construct secure software. CLASP provides a structured way to address security issues throughout the software development lifecycle. The proposed integration is basically based on interweaving the XP core practices with CLASP security best practices. The chapter argues that security measures should be applied in all phases in the development process. The claims are that this integration could possibly minimize the security vulnerabilities exploited by attackers. It is expected that the integration of XP with security functions enables software developers build more secure software. The proposed approach for extending XP with security complements with CLASP security activities.

Chapter 11 analyzes access control mechanisms of the Enterprise Java Beans (EJB) architecture and defines a configuration of the EJB protection system. It claims that the proposed configuration is less ambiguous than the EJB 3.0 standard. It presents an algorithm that formally specifies the semantics of authorization decisions in EJB. The chapter examines the level of support for the American National Standard Institute's (ANSI) specification of Role-Based Access Control (RBAC) components and functional specification in EJB. It concludes that the EJB specification does not adequately supports the Core ANSI RBAC. This paper finally proposes a framework for assessing implementations of ANSI RBAC for EJB systems.

Chapter 12 attempts to describe the process of development and testing of a new encryption key management protocol for highly dynamic and ad hoc networks. The proposed protocol is called Secure Key Deployment and Exchange (SKYE). It also discusses the simulation software design paradigms used to evaluate the performance of the proposed protocol. The research work demonstrates that the network security can be increased by requiring more servers to collaborate in order to generate a certificate for the new member, or by requiring a higher trust threshold along with the certificate request chain. Three different locations for servers relative to other nodes have been experimented with. It concludes with experimental evidence that the location of nodes designated as servers within the network has an impact on the likelihood of a successful issuance of a certificate.

Chapter 13 primarily presents a model-driven development framework, namely JavaSPI, that allows the user to reliably develop security protocol implementations in Java. It supports a range of modeling activities ranging from the development of abstract models to the verification of models formally. Java is used as both a modeling language and the implementation language. The proposed JavaSPI framework is validated for its applicability by implementing a scenario of the SSL protocol. The chapter also claims that the framework could be successfully interoperated with OpenSSL, and has comparable execution time with the standard Java JSSE library.

Chapter 14 presents a systematic study describing various attempts made to forge fingerprints to fool biometric systems. The chapter reviews a comprehensive number of relevant publications on forging fingerprints to fool sensors. It introduces the basics of biometrics in order to define the meaning of the term security along with the state of the art of biometric systems. It focuses on security of fingerprint scanners. It reports that a series of more than 30,000 experiments have been conducted to fool scanners. The experiments demonstrate that fingerprint scanners are not that easy to be deceived as the other research works suggest. The chapter provides a good deal of data to convince the reader that fingerprint scanners are secure, and cannot be fooled that easily. This work is believed to store public confidence on finger print scanners.

Chapter 15 explores the consequences of integrating patient electronic consents in e-health access control by examining requirements. Based on the analysis, it proposes an architecture incorporating patient consent in the access control service of an e-health system. The work examines various options for representing patient consents, and investigates how to incorporate their directives into the access control decision process. The legal requirements concerning patient are introduced. The chapter proposes a format for representing patient consents, and suggests on how to govern them in their lifecycle. It also presents a policy evaluation algorithm and a reference authorization architecture that incorporates patient consents. The reference architecture is based on the extension of the XACML authorization model. An prototype of the proposed architecture and its evaluation with a case study is also presented.

CONCLUSION

The collection of these chapters embodies a wealth of research outputs and ideas in secure software development. The book is suitable for researchers, graduate students, as well as practitioners. It is expected that this collection promotes the concepts of security-aware software development to a wider community comprising software engineers, security designers, researchers and beyond. I believe that the above line up of chapters with various flavors would generate enough interests in this topic. These chapters are expected to cover the three major ingredients of security-aware software development that have been outlined in this preface. The focus of each chapter varies from chapter to chapter ranging from hard technology to high level description of different ideas. Some chapters are based on complex mathematics, some are on logic, and few are based on operating system products. I am sure this book will satisfy readers from all areas of security-aware software development.

Khaled M. Khan
Qatar University, Qatar

REFERENCES

Alghathbar, K., & Wijesekera, D. (2003). AuthUML: A three-phased framework to model secure use cases. *Proceedings of the Workshop on Formal Methods in Security Engineering: From Specifications to Code*, (pp. 77-87).

Backes, M., Pfitzmann, B., & Waidner, M. (2003). Security in business process engineering. In *Proceedings of 2003 International Conference on Business Process Management, Lecture Notes in Computer Science vol. 2678*, (pp. 168-183). Springer.

Baskerville, R. (1988). *Designing information systems security*. New York, NY: John Wiley & Sons.

Bertino, E., Catania, B., Ferrari, E., & Perlasca, P. (2003). A logical framework for reasoning about access control models. *ACM Transactions on Information and System Security, 6*(1), 71–127. doi:10.1145/605434.605437

D'Aubeterre1, F., Singh, R., & Iyer, L. (2008). Secure activity resource coordination: Empirical evidence of enhanced security awareness in designing secure business processes. *European Journal of Information Systems, 17,* 528–542.

Das, S. K. (1992). *Deductive databases and logic program*. Addison-Wesley.

Doan, T., Demurjian, S., Michel, L., & Berhe, S. (2010). Integrating access control into UML for secure software modeling and analysis. *International Journal of Secure Software Engineering, 1*(1). doi:10.4018/jsse.2010102001

Epstein, P., & Sandhu, R. (1999). Towards a UML based approach to role engineering. *Proceedings of the 4th ACM Workshop on Role-based Access Control*, (pp. 75-85). ACM Press.

Erl, T. (2005). *Service-oriented architecture (SOA): Concepts, technology, and design*. New Jersey: Prentice Hall.

Fagin, R., Halpern, J. Y., Moses, Y., & Vardi, M. Y. (1995). *Reasoning about knowledge*. MIT Press.

Fernandez, E. B., France, R. B., & Wei, D. (1995). A formal specification of an authorization model for object-oriented databases. *Database Security, IX: Status and Prospects*, (pp. 95-109).

Herrmann, G., & Pernul, G. (1999). Viewing business-process security from different perspectives. *International Journal of Electronic Commerce, 3*(3), 89–103.

Homeland Security. (2012). *Build security in – Setting a high standard for software assurance*. Retrieved January 29, 2012, from https://buildsecurityin.us-cert.gov/bsi/home.html

Jajodia, S., Samarati, P., Sapino, M. L., & Subrahmanian, V. S. (2001). Flexible support for multiple access control policies. *ACM Transactions on Database Systems, 29*(2), 214–260. doi:10.1145/383891.383894

Jurjens, J. (2002a). *Principles for secure systems design*. Ph.D. Dissertation, Oxford University Computing Laboratory, Oxford University.

Jurjens, J. (2002b). UMLsec: Extending UML for secure systems development. *Proceedings of UML, Springer LNCS, Vol. 2460*, (pp. 1-9).

Khan, K. (2012). *Issues and challenges in security-aware software development*. Hershey, PA: IGI Global.

Lodderstedt, T., et al. (2002). SecureUML: A UML-based modeling language for model-driven security. In *Proceedings of UML, LNCS, Vol. 2460*, (pp. 426-441). Springer.

Mana, A., Montenegro, J. A., Rudolph, C., & Vivas, J. L. (2003). A business process-driven approach to security engineering. *Proceedings of the 14th International Workshop on Database and Expert Systems Applications*, (pp. 477-481). Prague.

Ray, I., et al. (2003). Using parameterized UML to specify and compose access control models. *Proceedings of the 6th IFIP Working Conference on Integrity and Internal Control in Information Systems*, (pp. 115-124). ACM Press.

Shin, M., & Ahn, G. (2000). UML-based representation of role-based access control. *Proceedings of the 9th International Workshop on Enabling Technologies: Infrastructure for Collaborative Enterprises*, (pp. 195-200). IEEE Computer Society.

Siponen, M., Baskerville, R., & Heikka, J. (2006). A design theory for secure information systems design methods. *Journal of the Association for Information Systems*, *7*(8), 568–592.

Swamy, N., Corcoran, B., & Hicks, M. (2008a). FABLE: A language for enforcing user-defined security policies. In *Proceedings of the IEEE Symposium on Security and Privacy*, Oakland.

Swamy, N., & Hicks, M. (2008b). Verified enforcement of stateful information release policies. In *Proceedings of the ACM SIGPLAN Workshop on Programming Languages and Analysis for Security*.

Wang, S., & Zhang, Y. (2005). A formalization of distributed authorization with delegation. In *Proceedings of the 10th Australian Conference on Information Security and Privacy, LNCS 3574,* (pp. 303-315).

Zdancewic, S. (2002). *Programming languages for information security.* PhD thesis, Cornell University.

Section 1
Software Development Process

Chapter 1
Secure by Design:
Developing Secure Software Systems from the Ground Up

Haralambos Mouratidis
University of East London, UK

Miao Kang
Powerchex Ltd., UK

ABSTRACT

This paper describes results and reflects on the experience of engineering a secure web based system for the pre-employment screening domain. In particular, the paper presents results from a Knowledge Transfer Partnership (KTP) project between the School of Computing, IT and Engineering at the University of East London and the London-based award winning pre-employment company Powerchex Ltd. The Secure Tropos methodology, which is based on the principle of secure by design, has been applied to the project to guide the development of a web based system to support employment reference and background checking specifically for the financial services industry. Findings indicate the potential of the methodology for the development of secure web based systems, and support the argument of incorporating security considerations from the early stages of the software development process, i.e., the idea of secure by design. The developed system was tested by a third, independent to the project, party using a well known method of security testing, i.e., penetration testing, and the results provided did not indicate the presence of any major security problems. The experience and lessons learned by the application of the methodology to an industrial setting are also discussed in the paper.

1. INTRODUCTION

The application of ICT to the financial services industry can support the automation of a number of functions, which are crucial for the further development of the sector, such as the management of pre-employment screening, coordination of financial teams, compliance with relevant regulations and analysis of financial data. The credit crunch and the events of the last couple of years meant that the financial services industry is faced with large changes and as such the development

DOI: 10.4018/978-1-4666-2482-5.ch001

of software systems to support the financial services industry and peripheral sectors introduces a number of new challenges and difficulties.

Security is arguably one of the most crucial and necessary features of software systems that support the financial services industry and an acceptable financial software system may under no circumstances endanger the risk of monetary lose and the leakage of relevant sensitive (private or otherwise) data.

In software engineering practice the usual approach is to perform the analysis, design and implementation of a software system without considering security, and then add security as an afterthought (Devanbu & Stubblebine, 2000; Mouratidis et al., 2006). Nevertheless, recent research has shown that such approach introduces a number of problematic areas and it leads to security vulnerabilities that are usually identified after the implementation and deployment of the system. Since at this point it is quite expensive to redevelop the system to completely overcome such vulnerabilities, the usual approach is to "patch" some of these vulnerabilities as they are identified. However, this is not an acceptable standard for the development of high risk software systems software systems (Blobel & France, 2001; Mouratidis, 2004).

The last few years, it has been widely argued, especially within the requirements engineering (Haley et al., 2006; Basin et al., 2003; Hermann & Pernul, 1999) and information systems (Devanbu, 2000; McDermott & Fox, 1999; Mouratidis & Giorgini, 2006) research communities, that the number of security vulnerabilities could be reduced if security is considered from the early stages of the development process, i.e., a Secure by Design (SbD) approach is employed to support the development of secure software systems. Generally speaking, Secure by Design, within the context of software engineering, means that the software has been designed from the ground up to be secure. In academia, this practice is mostly known as secure software systems engineering or

software engineering for secure systems amongst other terms. Our work is not the only effort at integrating security considerations into software engineering practices and methods. Security requirements frameworks have been proposed (Haley et al., 2006; Mead, 2006) for security requirements elicitation, specification and analysis. On another line of work, the behaviour of potential attackers is used to model security (Lamsweerde & Letier, 2000; Lin et al., 2003). Works have also been presented that extended use cases with respect to security analysis (Hermann & Pernul, 1999; Alexander, 2003). In addition, a large number of efforts are focused on extending existing methods and languages for software systems development (Basin et al., 2003; McDermott & Fox, 1999). Apart from the academic works, industry has also started to recognize the advantages of developing software systems following the Secure by Design principles. Microsoft has introduced the Security Development Process (http://www.microsoft.com/security/sdl/) while IBM has long supported the idea of introducing security as part of the development process (http://www-01.ibm.com/software/rational/announce/innovate/secure.html). McAfee and Citrix Systems have recently announced that they are focused on providing virtual desktops with products that are "secure by design" in order to protect large enterprises from the changing security landscape as employees are increasingly using mobile devices to access corporate resources (http://www.siliconrepublic.com/strategy/item/18252-citrix-and-mcafee-release/).

Nevertheless, empirical studies on the use of secure software systems engineering methodologies have so far been limited. In fact, as far as we are aware, an industrial case study on using a methodology that supports the idea of secure by design from the early requirements stages and throughout the development stages has not been published so far. This paper aims to contribute to this gap by presenting and discussing the application of a software engineering methodology, which supports the idea of secure by design by incorporating the analysis of security considerations from the early stages of the development system, to the development of a web based system for the financial services industry. Our findings from this project indicate the potential of the methodology for the development of secure web based systems, and they support the argument of incorporating security considerations from the early stages of the system development process, i.e., the idea of secure by design. The security of the developed web based system was tested using penetration testing techniques run by an independent to the project party. On the other hand, the paper describes in the form of questions and answers our experience and the lessons learned by this project.

This paper is structured as follows. Section 2 discusses some of the challenges of Secure Software Systems Engineering and provides some requirements for a software engineering methodology to support the integration of security analysis. Section 3 provides information on the background of the project discussing the project setting, aims and the main challenges. Section 4 describes the methodology used and it reports on the main outputs of its application to the Powerchex system. Section 5 reflects on our experiences by discussing the lessons learned, while Section 6 concludes the paper.

2. CHALLENGES OF SECURE SOFTWARE SYSTEMS ENGINEERING

This section discusses the challenges faced in Secure Software Systems Engineering, along with a set of requirements for a methodology to support Secure Software Systems Engineering.

Challenges

1. Developers, who are not security specialists, usually need to develop software systems that require knowledge of security;

2. Security is widely influenced by the environment in which the system resides. However, the environment can be unreliable and change rapidly;

3. Security needs to be considered in the context of the system development taking into account limited resources and high constraints;

4. Security is an issue that crosses many different research and practice areas. As such different security terms are understood differently in different domains. A typical example is that security solutions, such as encryption and authentication, are sometime considered security requirements. As a result, there is an abstraction gap that makes the integration of security concerns into the software engineering process more difficult;

5. It is difficult to define together security and functional components and at the same time provide a clear distinction. For instance, which components are part of the security architecture, and which ones are part of the functional specification;

6. It is difficult to move from a set of security requirements to a design that satisfies these requirements, and also understand what are the consequences of adopting specific design solutions for such requirements;

7. It is difficult to get empirical evidence of security issues during the design stage. This makes the process of analysing security during the design stage more difficult;

8. It is difficult to fully test the proposed security solutions at the design level;

9. Lack of automated tools to support a secure by design process.

Requirements for Methodology

1. Must allow novice security developers to successfully consider security issues during the analysis and the design of software systems;

3

2. Must employ the same concepts and notations during the whole development process in order to provide a common analysis foundation;
3. Must support the explicit definition of the applicability of the security process within its stages;
4. Must be clear and well guided;
5. Must define together security and functional requirements but also provide a clear distinction;
6. Must allow developers to identify possible conflicts between security and other functional and non-functional requirements, early in the process;
7. Must allow developers to analyse security requirements and base design solutions on such an analysis. In other words, it should allow developers to explore different architectural designs according to the identified security requirements;
8. Must allow developers to validate the developed security solution at design stage.

It is worth noting that the above set of requirements is not meant to be an extensive or static list but rather a set of minimum sets that each methodology should demonstrate.

3. PROJECT BACKGROUND

The project is an active collaboration between the School of Computing, IT and Engineering at the University of East London and Powerchex Ltd. It is funded under the Knowledge Transfer Partnership (KTP) programme, which is Europe's leading programme helping businesses to improve their competitiveness and productivity through the better use of knowledge, technology and skills that reside within the UK knowledge base (http://www.ktponline.org.uk) [i.e., academic institutions].

Powerchex specialises in pre-employment screening services for the UK financial services sector. The company's Unique Selling Point (USP) is based on a novel, labour-intensive, distributed screening-process reducing turnaround time of the pre-employment screening service from 20 business days, provided by competitors, to 5 business days. Powerchex clients, who include some of the largest financial institutions in the UK and worldwide, send details of job applicants to Powerchex, who then performs a number of pre-employment screenings, ranging from full background checks to individual checks such as credit search, criminal record search, address verification and academic and professional qualification verification.

A number of professionals from Powerchex were involved in the project ranging from the company's Managing Director (MD), the Operations Manager (OM), the Financial Manager (FM), the Quality Manager (QM), a number of Screeners and the Technical Development Manager (TDM). There was also involvement from various software engineers employed either by Powerchex's service providers (e.g., IT infrastructure, online and in house servers) or by Powerchex's clients IT departments. Our initial analysis and the discussions with these stakeholders indicated that the current system demonstrates a number of problems:

- Labour intensive and prone to errors, costly and not readily scaleable and therefore lacking the capacity to deal with the volume of work required for the expansion of Powerchex;
- Not secure enough; the financial sector deals with large amounts of sensitive and private data and therefore security is the number one concern for major banks;
- Cannot readily incorporate any additional services for clients (current or future);
- Not conducive to staff retention (i.e., repetitive tasks with little reward).

As such the main challenge was to develop a system that will support faster and more efficient screening process, with less errors; Reduce the cost of operation by enlarging the number of screening applications that can be simultaneously handled; Support the collection and analysis of important data, leading to improved operational activity; Ensure the provision of secure services and of the security of the screening process; Support the provision of additional services and functionality for existing and new clients (e.g., electronic submission of applications for checking) as well as being a tool for attracting new clients (e.g., providing a psychometric testing option).

Moreover, a main requirement is that the security of the system must withstand various attack tests that Powerchex's Clients will perform before the system is in operation.

Based on the above challenges and the variety of the team involved in the project and in particular the different knowledge of software development and/or ITC in general, the main four requirements for the selection of the appropriate methodology were:

1.   To follow the Secure by Design idea and incorporate security considerations from the early stages of the development process;
2.   To employ concepts that are easily understood by software engineers as well as stakeholders that are not familiar with software development;
3.   To enable the analysis of security in various stages of the development process;
4.   To enable the validation of the developed system at design stage.

To achieve these, we decided to use the Secure Tropos methodology which includes (1) a modeling language that is based on concepts, such as actor, goal, plan, resource, security constraint, attacker and attack, which are easily understood even by no ITC savvy stakeholders; (2) a security-aware process that introduces security analysis

from the early stages of the development process; (3) and an automated tool that supports the analysis of security at different level and in various stages of the development process.

4. SECURE BY DESIGN DEVELOPMENT OF POWERCHEX'S PRE-EMPLOYMENT SYSTEM

4.1. Secure Tropos

4.1.1. Modelling Language

The Secure Tropos methodology (Mouratidis, 2004) is based on the principle that security should be considered from the early stages of the development process and not added as an afterthought.

The modeling language of Secure Tropos is based on the concept of Security Constraint. A Security Constraint is a specialisation of the concept of constraint. In the context of software engineering, a constraint is usually defined as a restriction that can influence the analysis and design of a software system under development by restricting some alternative design solutions, by conflicting with some of the requirements of the system, or by refining some of the system's objectives. In other words, constraints can represent a set of restrictions that do not permit specific actions to be taken or prevent certain objectives from being achieved. Often constraints are integrated in the specification of existing textual descriptions. However, this approach can often lead to misunderstandings and an unclear definition of a constraint and its role in the development process. Consequently, this results in errors in the very early development stages that propagate to the later stages of the development process causing many problems when discovered; if they are discovered. Therefore, in the Secure Tropos modelling language we define security constraints, as a separate concept. To this end, the concept of security constraint has been defined within the context of Secure Tropos as:

A security condition imposed to an actor that restricts achievement of an actor's goals, execution of plans or availability of resources. Security constraints are outside the control of an actor. An actor (Bresciani et al., 2004) represents an entity that has intentionality and strategic goals within the software system or within its organisational setting. Within a network of actors, which is usually the case in large software systems with multiple stakeholders, one actor might depend on another actor for a *goal*, a *plan* or a *resource*. A goal (Bresciani et al., 2004) represents a condition in the world that an actor would like to achieve. In other words, goals represent actor's strategic interests. A plan represents, at an abstract level, a way of doing something (Bresciani et al., 2004). The fulfillment of a plan can be a means for satisfying a goal. As such, different (alternative) plans, that actors might employ to achieve their goals, are modeled enabling software engineers to reason about the different ways that actors can achieve their goals and decide for the best possible way. A resource (Bresciani et al., 2004) presents a physical or informational entity that one of the actors requires. The main concern when dealing with resources is whether the resource is available and who is responsible for its delivery. To model goals, plans and resources that are security crucial, the modeling language extends the original definition of goal, plan and resource by introducing *secure goals, secure plans and secure resources*. A secure goal represents a strategic interest of an actor with respect to security. In the Secure Tropos context, strategic interest means a course of action that an actor needs to follow to satisfy one or more security constraints. The satisfaction of one or more security constraints by a secure goal is defined through a *Satisfies* relationship. It is worth stating that a secure goal does not define operational details of how a security constraint can be satisfied, since operational alternatives can be considered. A *secure plan* represents a particular way for satisfying a secure goal. In the context of Secure Tropos, this means a specific and defined action that an actor executes to operationalise

a secure goal. A *secure resource* is defined as an entity that is security critical for the system under development. To support the modeling of an actor depending on another actor for a secure goal, secure plan and/or secure resource, Secure Tropos introduces the idea of *Secure Dependency*. A Secure Dependency introduces one or more Security Constraint(s) that must be fulfilled for the dependency to be valid.

To support the analysis and evaluation of the developed security solution, the modeling language supports the modeling of security attacks. An *attack* is an action that might cause a potential violation of security in the system (this definition has been adopted by Matt Bishop's definition of a computer attack). Within the context of an attack, an *attacker* represents a malicious actor that has an interest to attack the system. As described above, an actor has intentionality and strategic goals within the system. In the case of an attacker, the intentionality and strategic goals are related to breaking the security of a system and identifying and executing threats. *Threats* represent circumstances that have the potential to cause loss; or problems that can put in danger the security features of the system. In order to understand the threats that an attacker introduces to the system, it is important to have clear knowledge of the security capabilities of the system. A *secure capability* represents the ability of an actor to achieve a secure goal, carry out a secure plan and/or deliver a secure resource.

4.1.2. Process and Tool Support

To support the requirements for a security-aware methodology identified in the previous section, we developed an iterative process that takes advantage of the Secure Tropos modeling language in the context of four different models. The process, which starts at the early requirements stage and it covers up to detailed design, is one of identifying the security requirements of the software system, transforming these requirements to a design that satisfies them and validating the developed system with respect to security. The process is supported by a number of modeling activities (Mouratidis, 2004), which result in clear models. These models are described.

The methodology is also supported by an automated tool. The tool, called secTro (http://sectro.securetropos.org/), is a platform independent analysis and modelling tool that supports the development and analysis of the methodology's models. The tool has been developed following an iterative approach and it is based on JAVA. In particular, the tool allows developers to model the system under development and its environment and it supports the capture of properties of the various models, and of their components. These are represented as XML type specifications and can be then fed into tools that support the analysis of the security properties of the system under development such as the UMLsec set of tools. The UMLsec set of tools (http://ls14-www.cs.tu-dortmund.de/main2/jj/umlsectool/index.html) generate logical formulas formalizing the execution semantics and the annotated security requirements. Automated theorem provers and model checkers automatically establish whether the security requirements hold. If not, a Prolog-based tool automatically generates an attack sequence violating the security requirement, which can be examined to determine and remove the weakness. This way we encapsulate knowledge on practical security engineering as annotations in models or code and make it available to developers who may not be security experts. Since the analysis that is performed is too sophisticated to be done manually, it is also valuable to security experts.

4.1.3. Models

- **Security Analysis Model (SAM):** A Security Analysis Model supports the understanding of the social dimension of security by considering the social issues, of the system environment, which might affect its security. In doing so, the environment in which the system will be operational is analysed with respect to security. The model enables software system developers to understand the security concerns of each actor and model these concerns with appropriate security constraints. In particular, the model allows software engineers to model the various actors along with their strategic and security needs; and to identify for each actor security constraints. Further analysis is then taking place to examine the security constraints imposed on individual actors and identify any related secure goals, plans and resources that assist in satisfying those security constraints.

Figure 1 shows a limited view[1] of the Powerchex Security Analysis Model. In particular, the model captures the main actors of the system environment along with their goal dependencies and security constraints. The *Client* actor depends on *Powerchex to Screen Employment Candidates*. This goal dependency however introduces a security constraint for Powerchex to *Comply with Relevant Privacy Laws*. In order for Powerchex to perform the relevant checks, information is needed from the Applicant. This is provided through a pre-employment screening form that the Applicants need to fill in and send to *Powerchex*. Once *Powerchex* has this form, the screening process can start. *Powerchex* is imposed a security constraint to *Secure the Applicant Data* as part of the *Receive Filled in Form* dependency.

To perform the relevant checks, Powerchex depends on a number of search providers as well as the Financial Services Authority (FSA). Relevant security constraints have been identified based on these dependencies as shown in Figure 1. For example, Screener 1 Team depends on *Online Service Providers* to *Obtain Relevant*

Figure 1. Security analysis model

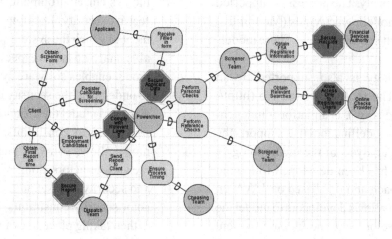

Searches. However, *Online Services Providers* are imposed with security constraints such as *Allow Access Only to Registered [to their service] Users.*

Once the environment of the system has been analysed and modeled, that information is fed to the System Security Requirements Model.

- **System Security Requirements Model:** This model allows the capturing and analysis of the technical dimension of security and how this translates to security requirements for the system. It allows a deeper understanding of how the system under development can support goals to be fulfilled, security constraints to be operationalised, secure plans to be performed and availability of security related resources. In the Systems Security Requirements Model the system is introduced, as another actor, and its security constraints are furthered analysed until a set of security requirements based on these security constraints are derived. In particular, the system is allocated all the relevant goals and dependencies identified in the previous model along with the relevant security constraints. By using standard software engineering analysis

techniques, such as means-end and decomposition, along with automated tool support the information captured in this model is the definition of the system's security requirements enhanced with a set of security constraints, along with the system's security goals and entities that allow the satisfaction of the security requirements of the system.

With respect to the Powerchex System, the information captured by the Security Analysis Model provides a number of security constraints that Powerchex and its relevant actors need to satisfy. For example, see Figure 2, the main goal of the *System* is to support the *Automated Application Process*. In doing so, a number of goals are identified that support the achievement of that root goal. Two of these goals are: *Manage Client Information* and *Requests and Supports Checks Registration and Monitoring*.

Through such analysis a number of security constraints are identified and imposed to the system such as *Keep Applicant Information Secure, Secure Information Access, Keep Searches Secure* and *Produce Proof of Relevant Searches* Further analysis of these security constraints results in the identification of a number of security require-

Figure 2. System security requirements model

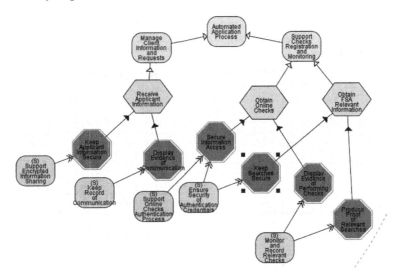

ments for the system such as *Support Encrypted Information Sharing, Keep Record of Communication, Ensure Security of Authentication Credentials* and *Monitor and Record Relevant Checks.*

• **Secure Components Specification Model:** The main aim of this model is to define the architecture of the system with respect to its security requirements. To achieve this, the Secure Components Specification model consists of Secure Capability Diagrams and UMLsec Deployment Diagrams (Jürjens, 2004). This combination allows us to determine the general architecture and the components of the system, and model the security properties of the data structures and architecture. The translation between Secure Tropos diagrams and UMLsec diagrams is taking place following a set of transformation rules (Mouratidis et al., 2006) and with the aid of the automated tools pro-

vided. The Secure Tropos tool produces XML code from the corresponding Secure Tropos models, while the UMLsec tool accepts XML input.

Moreover, the constraints associated with UMLsec stereotypes are checked mechanically, based on an XMI representation of the UML models and using sophisticated analysis engines such as model-checkers and automated theorem provers. The results of the analysis are given back to the developer, together with a modified model, where the weaknesses that were found are highlighted.

Figure 3 provides an example of an UMLsec Deployment Diagram illustrating the physical allocation of part of the Powerchex System related to the *Support Encrypted Information Sharing* security requirement. The Applicant submit their information through a secure channel (information is transmitted encrypted using SSLv3). The system performs appropriate checks to ensure that correct

Figure 3. Physical allocation of the system for applicant registration

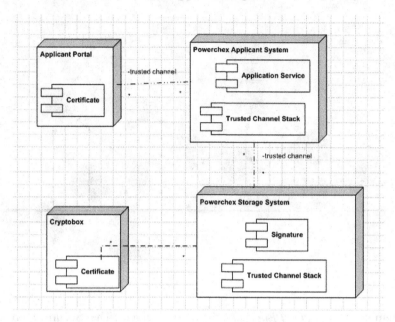

certificates have been provided and once that is ensured the relevant information is registered.

On the other hand, Secure Capability Diagrams are used to analyse specific security related ca-

pabilities of the system. For example, Figure 4 illustrates a Secure Capability Diagram for the *Applicant Search Request* sent by a *Client* to *Powerchex*. When a client submits a request to

Figure 4. Secure capability diagram for applicant search request

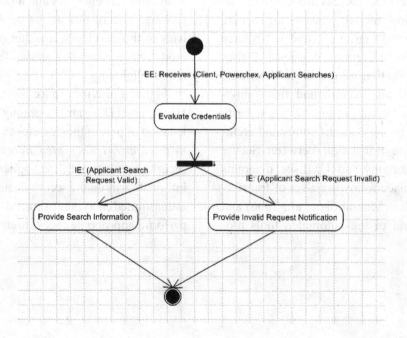

the Powerchex system to provide information about a particular applicant's searches, the system verifies the relevant requests and if the certificates provided are valid it provides the information.

Security Attack Model

The Security Attack Model enables us to test the developed solution against potential attacks at the design level. Initially, we develop scenarios to assist in the identification of relevant attack situations and potential vulnerabilities in the system. For this reason, Security Attack Scenarios (Mouratidis & Giorgini, 2007) are employed. A Security Attack Scenario (SAS) is defined as an attack situation describing the actors of the software system and their secure capabilities as well as possible attackers and their goals. It identifies how the secure capabilities of the system prevent (if they prevent) the satisfaction of the attackers' goals. A security attack scenario involves possible attacks to an information system, a possible attacker, the resources that are attacked, and the actors of the system related to the attack together with their secure capabilities.

To support uniformity throughout the security process, we use the same concepts as in the Security Analysis Model. In particular, an attacker is depicted as an actor who aims to break the security of the system. The attacker intentions are modeled as goals and tasks and their analysis follows the same reasoning techniques as in the Security Analysis Model. Scenarios are derived by identifying potential attacks to the security features of the system identified in the Secure Components Specification Model.

For the Powerchex system, our analysis identified the following categories of attacks as first described by Stallings (1999):

1. **Interception:** In which an unauthorised party, such as a person, a program or a computer, gains access to an asset. This is an attack on privacy.

2. **Modification:** In which an unauthorised party not only gains party to but also tampers with an asset. This is an attack on integrity.
3. **Interruption:** In which an asset of the system is destroyed or becomes unavailable or unusable. This is an attack on availability.

Figure 5 illustrates a simple interception security attack scenario for the Powerchex system. The attacker's main aim is to attack the Applicant Information (Private Information) transmitted between the Powerchex System (Internal System Agent) and a Client (External Agent). However, the analysis in the previous stages have resulted in the introduction of Enryption and Decryption processes and the creation of a secure channel that helps towards that type of attack.

Moreover, with the aid of automated theorem provers and using the information from the security attack scenarios together with the physical allocation of the system components (as defined in the previous model) we are able to investigate further these attacks.

We use UMLsec tools for this analysis. In general, when invoking the tool with the UMLsec models, a security attack scenario is included as an input, and the tool generates the input for the automated theorem prover. The input specifies the assumptions on the initial knowledge of the attacker and the attack conjecture, in first-order logic. An example of this information is shown in Box 1.

The automated theorem prover that is called by the UMLsec tool framework then investigates whether the attack conjecture can be derived from the logical formulae formalizing the assumptions on the system and the adversary. The output from the automated theorem prover is then interpreted by the UMLsec tool, and its interpretation regarding the security requirements under analysis are provided to the user.

Taking into account the information from the interception scenario modeled with the aid of the security attack scenarios process, a potential attack to the Powerchex system involves an attacker listening to the messages sent between the system

Box 1.

```
%-------- Attackers Initial Knowledge -----------
input_formula(previous_knowledge,axiom,(knows(conc(k_ca, conc(conc(id_a,
conc(k_a, eol)), conc(inv(k_a), conc(sign(conc(id_a, conc(k_a, eol)), inv(k_
ca)), eol)))))))).
%---------------------- Conjecture -----------------------
input_formula(attack,conjecture,(
knows(sign(conc(id_p, conc(id_a, conc(m_nt, conc(nt, eol)))), inv(k_p))))).
```

and the Clients (man-in the-middle-attack). As a result, the communication underlies the following threats: (1) The intruder intercepts all the messages sent between objects. She/He can save them for analysis and further use; (2) Messages can be deleted by the intruder, so that the receiver is not able to get a specific message; (3) The intruder is able to insert messages into the communication between objects; (4) By combination of these threats, the intruder is able to manipulate messages. Such threat can be avoided by using an additional encryption mechanism for transmitting permission certificates. For this reason, for the Powerchex system we have employed an appropriate secure protocol. After invoking the automated theorem

prover, with the above information, the UMLsec tool reported that the attack conjecture is not derivable from the axioms, which means that the protocol is secure with respect to the threat scenario and the security requirements that were considered.

5. LESSONS LEARNED

In this sub-section we discuss all the lessons learned from the application of the methodology. We employed a questions/answers format following similar evaluations found in the literature (Jürjens et al., 2008).

Figure 5. Example of security attack scenario representation

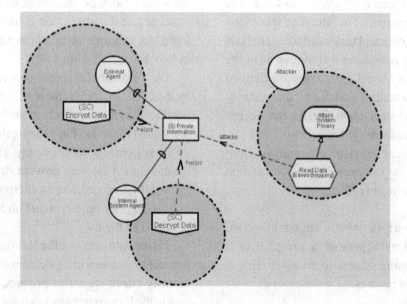

5.1. Lessons Related to Software Engineering Practice

How the Approach is Perceived by Software Engineers?

The majority of the models are created using the secure Tropos modelling language. Such language is based on the i* (Yu, 1995) and Tropos (Bresciani et al., 2004) notation and concepts that although are not widely popular to software engineers – such as for example UML concepts and notation- they are well known in the requirements engineering area. As such we expect that an initial effort is required to understand these concepts and familiarise with the relevant notation.

The project included a number of software engineers with different skills. None of them was familiar with the Secure Tropos modelling language and notation. Introductory sessions took place to familiarise the engineers with the methodology. The feedback received was that the concepts and models are easy to understand. A number of questions were raised about some of the notation used and about the scalability of the models. Moreover, as indicated in the previous sections, a number of UMLsec models are used at the later stage of the approach. In general, these were easily understood since they are mainly based on UML, with which all the software engineers were familiar.

Did You Encounter Any Problems With The Development Of The Models?

As discussed in previous sections, the tool supports an automated consistency check of the developed models with the aid of a pre-defined set of consistency rules. However, during the project we encountered some issues related to inconsistent models. This was mainly the case because the implementation of the consistency rules to the tool was not properly executed. A manual inspection of some of the models indicated that the inter-model rules were enforced by the tool properly but there were some issues with the outer-model rules, which resulted in problems with the consistency of the Secure Components Specification Model and the Attack Scenarios Model. This was the case because these models were created using information from previous models, which use the secure tropos modelling language together with UMLsec concepts and diagrams. As the concepts and notations of these two approaches are different, a number of issues were present that the initial set of consistency rules (Mouratidis, 2004) did not anticipate. A set of guidelines and steps were developed (Mouratidis et al., 2006) to support the correct integration and eliminate the inconsistencies.

Another issue encountered was the scalability of the models. Due to the complexity of the case study, the models developed were very large and that made their development and analysis very difficult. It is worth mentioning however, that the software engineers acknowledged that this is not just an issue with this specific approach but it is an issue found in a number of relevant approaches.

Did You Come Across Any Unexpected Obstacles On The Application Of The Approach On Any Of The Case Studies?

The application of the approach to the case study did no yield any unexpected obstacles. As discussed above, there were some inconsistencies between the models due to some errors on the guidelines, but we were expecting something like this since this was the first time our approach was applied to such complex system and to that specific domain. On the other hand, once these inconsistencies were solved, the methodology worked as expected and we were able to analyse the environment of the system in terms of its security, transform this analysis to a design, and validate the design.

Does the Application Of The Methodology Guarantee The Development Of A Totally Secure Software System?

It is widely accepted that no software systems can be considered to be 100% secure. We share this view, and we do not claim that the application of our methodology guarantees the development of totally secure software systems. On the other hand, we argue that the application of our methodology assist in the development of a system that is more secure than a system that has been developed by a methodology that does not consider security. This argument is mainly supported by experimental findings of the penetration testing and the validation of the security solution, where we identified initial vulnerabilities that the methodology helped us to analyse further and resolve. Moreover, this claim can also be supported by theoretical arguments. First of all, the methodology allows the consideration of both the technical and social aspects of security and therefore allows developers to obtain, from very early in the development process, a clear understanding of any potential security vulnerabilities that might raise from the interplay of the two security aspects. By identifying such vulnerabilities early in the development process, developers are given the opportunity to proper analyse them and find ways to overcome them. Moreover, the methodology allows the consideration of the organisational environment for the modelling of security issues, by facilitating the understanding of the security needs in terms of the real security needs of the stakeholders, and then it allows the transformation of the security requirements to a design that is amenable to formal verification with the aid of automatic tools. This introduces a well structured approach to support the idea of secure by design. In addition, the production of models that integrate security concerns, as opposed to the production of models without security concerns, allows developers to (1) reason in a conclusive way and by taking into account simultaneously the general requirements of the system together with the security requirements and therefore identify any conflicts; (2) develop a extensive and precise security-aware documentation, something that it is required by common security standards, such as the Common Criteria (http://www.commoncriteriaportal.org/).

Does The Methodology Require Security Expertise?

Not all software engineers involved in the project had extensive security training and knowledge. They had however a basic security knowledge. By applying our approach to the case study it became obvious that because of the integration of security analysis into the software engineering process, some extra effort and knowledge is required from software engineers to familiarise with the security concepts, and the process of considering security requirements from the early stages of the development process. Because of this, we expect that our approach will be an attractive option to software engineers looking to develop security-critical systems rather than a general option for any software system development.

5.2. Specific Case Study Related Lessons

How Appropriate Is The Methodology For The Development Of Secure Financial Service Software Systems?

We found the approach appropriate for the project. We believe that the appropriateness of the methodology lies on the fact that it allows us to analyse in a unified framework both the social and the technical dimensions of security. Another important issue for software systems used for the financial services industry is the need to consider in detail any privacy requirements of the system. Our approach allows developers not only to elicit the privacy requirements imposed to the system by the various stakeholders and users, but also by its environment (for instance data sharing laws and rules of a country). Such requirements are subsequently used to determine the architecture of the system and also to analyse whether the developed system is protected against a number of various security scenarios at design stage.

How The Application Of The Methodology Helped To Improve The Security Of The PowerChex System?

The methodology allowed us to identify the security requirements of the systems early in the development process and motivate the development of an architecture that meets these requirements. Then, with the aid of appropriate automations, we were able to check whether the security requirements are satisfied or not. For example, our analysis indicated the need to ensure a strong session management. Strong session management ensures an authenticated user has a cryptographically secure association with his session. To support that issue, our analysis indicated the need to randomise session identifiers to an appropriate size and use extensive available characters. It also indicated the need to automatically time out after 1 hour when the applicant is completing the form and after 10 minutes when the applicant is viewing the submitted form. The session data should be stored in encrypted and self-deleted cookies. Our analysis also helped to identify measurements to reduce vulnerabilities based on Cross-site scripting (XSS) and SQL Injection. In particular, we identified that this issue can be avoided by designing the system to filter all user inputs, e.g., silently strip certain punctuation characters, keywords in script languages and keywords in SQL languages to avoid SQL injection.

What was the Perception Of The Non-It Savvy Participants Of The Methodology's Concepts And Models?

In their majority, they found the concepts of the methodology easy to understand and use. This is particularly true of the concepts employed during the initial models (Security Analysis Model and System Security Requirements Model) i.e., these models that require maximum interaction with the potential system users. The feedback we received stated that it is easy to understand concepts such as actors, goals, plans, security constraints and attackers. This is mainly due to the association of these concepts to real life concepts that are widely used in everyday life. On the other hand, similar to the software engineers, concerns were raised about the potential complexity of the models, especially as the analysis of the system progresses and the models are becoming larger.

5.3. Penetration Testing

The system was tested by third party security expert companies performing penetration testing (Wilhelm, 2009) by simulating attacks from malicious sources. The penetration tests performed automated security scannings of the system, followed by manual attack tests and non-technical attacks to identify any vulnerability in the system. In particular, the tests were based on a "black-box" approach, which assumes no access to the system source code or internal details about the system. The tests were conducted both from the point of view of an anonymous internet-based attacker, and from the point of view of legitimate users of the service. The tests examined, amongst others, the following areas of the system: Network services are securely configured; Externally visible backdoors; URL parameters or hidden fields manipulation; System access out of sequence or without required authorization; Use of cookies; Uploaded data to the system is handled safely; Data validation; Secure authentication; Secure session management; Strong encryption is used; Appropriate error handling is performed.

To test the application's security, the third party company performed the following attacks:

Source Code

It was unable to decompile the application's source code which was also compiled with debugging information excluded (which could reveal the file names and paths on the system where it was built).

Anonymous Access and Information Leaks

The application developed is served entirely over secure HTTPS, with connections to the HTTP version of the site being immediately redirected to the corresponding HTTPS URL.

The results found that no comments or information that would be useful to an attacker were found in the source code of the publicly available application pages.

The third party company also entered various SQL meta-characters into the username and password fields of the login form and was unable to provoke any error messages. This indicates that the inputs are encoded correctly and so the login form is not susceptible to SQL injection. And the username and password are never echoed back to the user and therefore the login form is not vulnerable to cross-site scripting attacks.

Login and Session Management

The results found that usernames and passwords supplied by the application appear to be randomly generated and highly secure with characters contained upper and lower case letters, numbers and punctuation. And it is highly unlikely that an attacker would be able to gain access to a confidential page.

Authorisation

It has been not possible to log in using one user's URL and another user's credentials. Attempting to access a URL not associated with a user results in a "Not Found" error page.

Data Handling

Punctuation characters were all removed from inputs, so a user could not construct a cross-site scripting attacks (XSS) attack by entering a string such as </textarea><script>alert('XSS')</script>.

SQL meta-characters and expressions were also submitted, but in all cases the data were handled correctly and it was unable to construct an SQL injection attack.

The official report received about the penetration testing[2] indicated that no sensitive information is leaked from the system, and that relevant security mechanisms enforce the security policies and requirements of the system.

6. RELATED WORK

In recent years, a considerable number of works with the desire to introduce security considerations during the various stages of the software systems development process have been presented in the literature. Anton et al. (2004) propose a set of general taxonomies for security and privacy, to be used as a general knowledge repository for a (security) goal refinement process. Schumacher and Roedig (2001) apply the pattern approach to the security problem by proposing a set of patterns, called security patterns, which contribute to the overall process of security engineering. Although useful, these approaches lack the definition of a structured process for considering security. A well defined and structured process is of paramount importance when considering security during the development stages of software systems.

On the other hand, a number of researchers model security by taking into account the behaviour of potential attackers. Van Lamsweerde and Letier (2000) use the concept of security goals and anti-goals. Anti goals represent malicious obstacles set up by attackers to threaten the security goals of a system. Crook et al. (2002), introduce the notion of anti-requirements to represent the requirements of malicious attackers. Anti-requirements are expressed in terms of the problem domain phenomena and are satisfied when the security threats imposed by the attacker are realised in any one instance of the problem.

Similarly, Lin et al. (2003), incorporate anti-requirements into abuse frames. The purpose of abuse frames is to represent security threats and to facilitate the analysis of the conditions in the system in which a security violation occurs. An important limitation of all these approaches is that security is considered as a vague goal to be satisfied whereas a precise description and enumeration of specific security properties is still missing.

Differently, another "school of thinking" indicates the development of methods to analyse and reason about security based on the relationships between actors (such as users, stakeholders and attackers) and the system. Liu et al. (2003) analyse security requirements as relationships amongst strategic actors by proposing different kinds of analysis techniques to model potential threats and security measures. Although a relationship based analysis is suitable for reasoning about security, an important limitation of existing approaches is that each of them only guides the way security can be handled within a certain stage of the software development process.

Another direction of work is based on the extension of use cases and the Unified Modelling Language (UML). In particular, McDermott and Fox (1999) adapt use cases to capture and analyse security requirements, and they call the adaption an abuse case model. An abuse case is defined as a specification of a type of complete interaction between a system and one or more actors, where the results of the interaction are harmful to the system, one of the actors, or one of the stakeholders of the system. Similarly, Sindre and Opdahl (2005) define the concept of misuse case, the inverse of use case, which describes a function that the system should not allow. They also define the concept of mis-actor as someone who intentionally or accidentally initiates a misuse case and whom the system should not support in doing so. Jurgens et al. (2004) proposes UMLsec, an extension of the Unified Modelling Language (UML), to include modelling of security related features, such as confidentiality and access control. Lodderstedt et al. (2002) also extend UML to model security. In their work, they present a security modelling language called SecureUML. They describe how UML can be used to specify information related to access control in the overall design of an application and how this information can be used to automatically generate complete access control infrastructures. An important limitation of all the use-case and/or UML related approaches is that they do not support the modelling and analysis of security requirements at a social level but they treat security in system-oriented terms. In other words, they lack models that focus on high-level security requirements, meaning models that do not force the designer to immediately go down to security requirements.

7. CONCLUSION

This paper presents our experiences from the application of a Secure by Design software engineering methodology to the development of the Powerchex System. Our findings indicate that the use of our approach supported the development of a software system that meets its security requirements and it has withstand penetration tests performed by an external to the project party. Our experience on the other hand also indicated some issues for consideration, such as potential complexity of the models, and resolving these issues is our aim for future work.

Although this paper presents the application of our approach to the financial services industry domain, we believe that the approach is applicable to the development of security-critical systems for domains such as telecommunications and health care. Depending on the application domain and the security focus of that particular domain, minor modifications might be necessary. Nevertheless, we believe that the methodology is flexible enough to allow such modifications with minor effort.

REFERENCES

Alexander, I. (2003). Misuse cases: Use cases with hostile intent. *IEEE Software*, *20*(1), 58–66. doi:10.1109/MS.2003.1159030

Anton, A. I., & Earp, J. B. (2004). A requirements taxonomy for reducing web site privacy vulnerabilities. *Requirements Engineering*, *9*(3), 169–185. doi:10.1007/s00766-003-0183-z

Basin, D., Doser, J., & Lodderstedt, T. (2003). Model driven security for process oriented systems. In *Proceedings of the 8th ACM Symposium on Access Control Models and Technologies*, Como, Italy.

Blobel, B., & France, R. A. (2001). A systematic approach for analysis and design of secure health information systems. *International Journal of Medical Informatics*, *62*(2).

Bresciani, P., Giorgini, P., Giunchiglia, F., Mylopoulos, J., & Perini, A. (2004). TROPOS: An agent oriented software development methodology. *Journal of Autonomous Agents and Multi-Agent Systems*, *8*(3), 203–236. doi:10.1023/B:AGNT.0000018806.20944.ef

Crook, R., Ince, D., Lin, L., & Nuseibeh, B. (2002). Security requirements engineering: When anti-requirements hit the fan. In *Proceedings of the 10th International Requirements Engineering Conference* (pp. 203-205).

Devanbu, P., & Stubblebine, S. (2000). Software engineering for security: A roadmap. In *Proceedings of the International Conference on the Future of Software Engineering* (pp. 201-211).

Haley, C. B., Laney, R., Moffett, J. D., & Nuseibeh, B. (2006). Arguing satisfaction of security requirements. In Mouratidis, H., & Giorgini, P. (Eds.), *Integrating security and software engineering: Advances and future visions* (pp. 16–43). Hershey, PA: Idea Group. doi:10.4018/978-1-59904-147-6.ch002

Hermann, G., & Pernul, G. (1999). Viewing business-process security from different perspectives. *International Journal of Electronic Commerce*, *3*, 89–103.

Jürjens, J. (2004). *Secure systems development with UML*. New York, NY: Springer.

Jürjens, J., Schreck, J., & Bartmann, P. (2008). Model-based security analysis for mobile communications. In *Proceedings of the International Conference on Software Engineering* (pp. 683-692).

Lamsweerde, A., & Letier, E. (2000). Handling obstacles in goal-oriented requirements engineering. *IEEE Transactions on Software Engineering*, *26*(10), 978–1005. doi:10.1109/32.879820

Lin, L., Nuseibeh, B., Ince, D., Jackson, M., & Moffett, J. (2003). Introducing abuse frames for analysing security requirements. In *Proceedings of the 11th IEEE International Requirements Engineering Conference*, Monterey, CA (pp. 371-372).

Liu, L., Yu, E., & Mylopoulos, J. (2003). Security and privacy requirements analysis within a social setting. In *Proceedings of the 11th International Requirements Engineering Conference* (pp. 151-161).

Lodderstedt, T., Basin, D., & Doser, J. (2002). SecureUML: A UML-based modelling language for model-driven security. In J.-M. Jézéquel, H. Hussmann, & S. Cook (Eds.), *Proceedings of the 5th International Conference on the Unified Modeling Language* (LNCS 2460, pp. 426-441).

McDermott, J., & Fox, C. (1999). Using abuse case models for security requirements analysis. In *Proceedings of the 15th Annual Computer Security Applications Conference* (pp. 55-64).

Mead, N. R. (2006). Identifying security requirements using the security quality requirements engineering (SQUARE) method. In Mouratidis, H., & Giorgini, P. (Eds.), *Integrating security and software engineering* (pp. 44–69). Hershey, PA: Idea Group.

Mouratidis, H. (2004). *A security oriented approach in the development of multiagent systems: Applied to the management of the health and social care needs of older people in England*. Unpublished doctoral dissertation, University of Sheffield, South Yorkshire, UK.

Mouratidis, H., & Giorgini, P. (Eds.). (2006). *Integrating security and software engineering: Advances and future visions*. Hershey, PA: Idea Group. doi:10.4018/978-1-59904-147-6

Mouratidis, H., & Giorgini, P. (2007). Security attack testing (SAT)-testing the security of information systems at design time. *Information Systems*, *32*(8), 1166–1183. doi:10.1016/j.is.2007.03.002

Mouratidis, H., Jürjens, J., & Fox, J. (2006). Towards a comprehensive framework for secure systems development. In E. Dubois & K. Pohl (Eds.), *Proceedings of the 18th International Conference on Advanced Information Systems Engineering* (LNCS 4001, pp. 48-62).

Schumacher, M., & Roedig, U. (2001). Security engineering with patterns. In *Proceedings of the 8th Conference on Pattern Languages for Programs*, Chicago, IL.

Sindre, G., & Opdahl, A. L. (2005). Eliciting security requirements with misuse cases. *Requirements Engineering*, *10*(1), 34–44. doi:10.1007/s00766-004-0194-4

Stallings, W. (1999). *Cryptography and network security: Principles and practice* (2nd ed.). Upper Saddle River, NJ: Prentice Hall.

Wilhelm, T. (2009). *Professional penetration testing: Creating and operating a formal hacking lab*. Oxford, UK: Syngress.

Yu, E. (1995). *Modelling strategic relationships for process reengineering*. Unpublished doctoral dissertation, University of Toronto, Toronto, ON, Canada.

ENDNOTES

[1] To support easier understanding, we have decided to limit the number of actors, dependencies and security constraints shown in the Security Analysis Model.

[2] For security issues, we are not allowed to make the results of the penetration test widely available.

This work was previously published in the International Journal of Secure Software Engineering, Volume 2, Issue 3, edited by Khaled M. Khan, pp. 23-41, copyright 2011 by IGI Publishing (an imprint of IGI Global).

Chapter 2
Security Evaluation of Service–Oriented Systems Using the SiSOA Method

Christian Jung
Fraunhofer Institute for Experimental Software Engineering, Germany

Manuel Rudolph
Fraunhofer Institute for Experimental Software Engineering, Germany

Reinhard Schwarz
Fraunhofer Institute for Experimental Software Engineering, Germany

ABSTRACT

The Service-Oriented Architecture paradigm (SOA) is commonly applied for the implementation of complex, distributed business processes. The service-oriented approach promises higher flexibility, interoperability and reusability of the IT infrastructure. However, evaluating the quality attribute security of such complex SOA configurations is not sufficiently mastered yet. To tackle this complex problem, the authors developed a method for evaluating the security of existing service-oriented systems on the architectural level. The method is based on recovering security-relevant facts about the system by using reverse engineering techniques and subsequently providing automated support for further interactive security analysis at the structural level. By using generic, system-independent indicators and a knowledge base, the method is not limited to a specific programming language or technology. Therefore, the method can be applied to various systems and adapt it to specific evaluation needs. The paper describes the general structure of the method, the knowledge base, and presents an instantiation aligned to the Service Component Architecture (SCA) specification.

INTRODUCTION

Service-oriented software architectures (SOA) promise enhanced reusability, interoperability, and flexibility for the implementation of business processes in information systems. However, this increase in flexibility and versatility comes at a price: it aggravates software quality assurance. The distributed, inhomogeneous, and often non-transparent nature of service building blocks stemming from different organizational domains is a supplementary constraint for the reliable

DOI: 10.4018/978-1-4666-2482-5.ch002

determination of software quality attributes, especially those that are global properties of the overall SOA system, such as safety or security. Although technical standards such as the Web Services Security Specification (OASIS, 2010) exist, SOA systems are still vulnerable to many basic threat types.

Security is an overarching quality concern that requires adequate treatment at a holistic system level. It cannot be handled effectively by analyzing the security issues only at source code level, especially not in a manual manner. To better keep track of the global security characteristics and to survey the logical security design of a system, all security-related information should be assessed in the context of a more abstract, structural level of the fundamental system architecture. Security-related information refers to system characteristics that can have a positive or negative impact on the system's security, such as code locations where security functions (e.g., authentication, encryption, integrity check) are called or where configuration parameters controlling these functions are defined. We claim that architectural views provide an adequate point of view for the security assessment of complex software systems.

In a SOA, all components have to be analyzed in their current configuration. However, the number of components, their changing orchestration and the distributed nature of SOA systems often renders a manual analysis impracticable.

System behavior, especially the dynamic security characteristics of the system in its entirety, is hard to obtain if the relevant information is scattered across many SOA components and their respective design artifacts.

In an earlier publication (Antonino, Duszynski, Jung, & Rudolph, 2010), we presented SiSOA (»Security in Service-oriented Architectures«), an assessment method for collecting security-related system properties and presenting them in architectural views for efficient evaluation. SiSOA comprises three phases: Extraction, Identification, and Analysis of security properties, as shown in

Figure 1. The Extraction phase uses static analysis and standard reverse engineering techniques to gather security-related information from the system under evaluation. This information from source code, configuration, and policy files is abstracted and generalized in the subsequent Identification phase, and displayed in architectural views. Abstraction is based on security rules from a knowledge base. In the final Analysis phase the abstracted and generalized information is interactively assessed, augmented, and evaluated by the human inspector. To this end, the inspector is guided through different views where potentially harmful security issues as well as positive security features are marked. A more detailed description of SiSOA, especially of the Extraction and Identification phases together with technical details, can be found in Antonino, Duszynski, Jung, and Rudolph (2010).

In this article, we explain the SiSOA method and show how the knowledge base fits into our SiSOA methodology. In addition, we briefly describe our prototype tool that implements SiSOA including the knowledge base and provides support for semi-automatic security evaluation of SOA systems. This includes the description of our security estimation values: severity and credibility.

MODEL EXTRACTION

The purpose of the Extraction phase is to create a model of the analyzed system that stores all basic information necessary for further analysis steps. This model is called system model; it is constructed by using reverse engineering techniques (Chikofsky & Cross, 1990). The system model contains information about diverse software artifacts such as classes, packages, relations between classes or packages, and any other structural information that may potentially contribute to further security analysis. The input for building the model is the source code of the evaluated system and some

Figure 1. Overview of the SiSOA approach

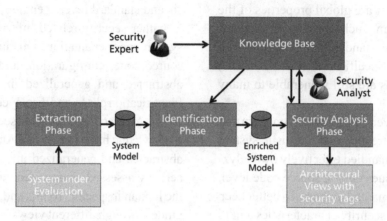

complementary artifacts such as SOA configuration files.

The system model is based on the Eclipse Modeling Framework (EMF) (Steinberg, Budinsky, Paternostro, & Merks, 2008). In our prototype implementation, we reuse two existing EMF models: One is from Apache Tuscany (Davis, 2009; Laws, Combellack, Feng, Mahbod, & Nash, 2011; The Apache Foundation, 2011), a Service Component Architecture (SCA) (OSOA, 2011) implementation; the other is from SAVE (Duszynski, Knodel, & Lindvall, 2009), an Eclipse-based tool for the analysis of software architecture that has been developed at Fraunhofer IESE and Fraunhofer CESE. The SCA model of Apache Tuscany provides higher-level information about services and policies implemented in the analyzed system, while the SAVE model provides lower-level information, for example, about Java classes, methods, and their dependencies.

The information stored in the system model is extracted from the source code and configuration files of the analyzed system. Extraction of class-level information is performed by a customized Java parser, while service-specific information is provided by the application programming interface of the Tuscany framework.

We augmented these EMF models with a connector model that relates the elements of the reused models to each other and adds additional information not included in the original models. After the linking and integration of the partial models, the system model is complete and can be used as input in the Identification phase.

KNOWLEDGE BASE

Basically, the knowledge base is a tree structure for storing security-related information that helps to reveal and assess security properties of a software system, and for relating these properties to fundamental security goals. Several hierarchical levels are used for structuring the information. These levels reflect the Identification and Analysis phases, respectively (Figure 1). The Identification phase (see Section »Identification«) is supported by implementation- and technology-dependent information at the bottom of the hierarchy, whereas the Analysis phase (see Section »Example of a Security Analysis«) uses abstract security goals and indicators forming the top level of the knowledge base hierarchy. The model hierarchy comprises three main levels:

- Tagging rules form the lowest level of the knowledge base. They describe which security related artifacts (e.g., security-related import or call relations, annotations, exceptions, access relations) must be present in a specific part of the system so that a security property can be tagged, and how to derive new security tags based on existing tag constellations. A security tag is a marker that represents a security issue or feature, for instance, the use of cryptographic functions. Tagging rules consist of one or more security tags and subordinate artifacts (i.e., security-related information extracted from the system that triggered the tag assignment).

- At an intermediate level the indicator mapping interconnects security indicators that are human-readable and checkable with referring security tags.
- At the top of the hierarchy abstract security knowledge is represented by security goals as root nodes, which are decomposed into corresponding security indicators.

The knowledge base has to be built by security experts, using insights gained from previous security analyses. For reusing the stored security information, the knowledge base expresses the information in a generalized way, especially in the highest abstraction layer. It may also contain system-specific goals, indicators, or tagging rules, or it can be tailored to individual needs of a security audit. The identification and abstraction process is semi-automatic because new security tags can be added manually to the knowledge base, and existing security tags may be modified by user intervention. The remainder of this section describes the three levels of the knowledge base in more detail.

Tagging Rules

Each security tag is represented as a tree structure (see layers 3 and 4 in Figure 4). This tag tree can be either a »basic« tree where the leaves represent concrete characteristics that can directly be found in the system model during the Extraction phase—so-called security artifacts. Alternatively, the tree can be a »complex« tree combining existing security tags to a new tag at a higher level of abstraction. In the latter case, the leaves of the security tag tree are other security tags. It is also possible to have mixed structures (tags and security artifacts as tree nodes). Logical operators (OR, XOR, AND, NOT) are used to link the subordinate trees that define the overall tag specification.

To structure tags that address similar kinds of security properties (e.g., »DES-encrypted« and »AES-encrypted«) and to simplify their interpretation, the knowledge base defines multiple tagging levels. For example, the tags »DES-encrypted« and »AES-encrypted« can be connected by an OR operator to constitute a more general »encrypted« tag. We can basically distinguish between two tag types. On the one hand, there are tags depending on programming languages or technologies; on the other hand, there are more general tags that aggregate the technology-dependent tags into more abstract, technology-independent concepts.

Every security tag has a predefined application target, which can be a system component such as a class, a service, an interface, or a composite. A security rule will only apply if all its security artifacts (or subordinate security tags, respectively) appear within the scope of their respective application target. Since it is possible to create rules that combine security tags into a new security tag, higher-level security tags that span different targets are promoted to a more general target scope (e.g., from class to service) as required.

When specifying tagging rules, the connections between security artifacts and security tags are weighted. The weighting adds to modeling security knowledge more accurately. Weights reflect the significance of security artifacts that imply a specific security tag, that is, their discriminatory power with respect to the security issue at hand. Weights have to be estimated by a security expert who can judge the impact of an artifact on the security property reflected by the tag. Based on these weights, severity and credibility estimation values are calculated as follows.

Severity calculations determine the quality of the security tagging rule itself. A rule's severity is defined as a pair of values: the first is the sum of weights of all supporting security artifacts; the second value is the median of these weights. Thus, the severity (pair of values) is a static measure, independent of the system under evaluation. Hence, whether a security artifact actually occurs in the evaluation target does not influence the severity calculation.

The rationale behind this metric is as follows: Given an existing tagging rule, additional supportive information appended to the rule (e.g., an additional call relation artifact) should increase the overall severity of the security tag, that is, our confidence in the discriminatory power of the underlying tagging rule. This is expressed by the first value. Its scale is ordinal, which means that only the ordering relation between the values of different tags is significant, but not their difference.

To calculate the first value of the severity for tag rules, the following rules must be applied:

- **OR:** The value of an OR group is calculated as the sum of all subordinated weightings.
- **XOR:** The value of a XOR group is calculated as the average of all subordinated weightings. We have chosen the average, because only one of the subordinated parts should be relevant for the tag assignment.
- **AND:** The value of an AND group is calculated as the sum of all subordinated weightings (same as for an OR group).
- **NOT:** The value of an NOT group is calculated as the sum of all subordinated weightings (same as for AND and OR groups).

The second severity value, the median, assures that a security artifact with high weights has stronger impact on the overall severity than a number of low-weight security artifacts (e.g., one security artifact weighted with five has the same impact as five security artifacts weighted with one for the first severity value, but differs in the resulting median calculation). The median reflects the distribution of the weights in the tagging rule. If there are only a few very high weights and a lot of low weights, then a low median will result. Thus, the median is an additional attribute characterizing the quality of the security tagging rule, i.e., its predictive power to find security indicators.

An example weighting including a calculated severity value pair is shown in Figure 2. Applying the calculation rules for the severity on this example works as follows: To obtain the first value of the severity pair, we first calculate the average of the weights in the XOR sub-trees. For the XOR on the left, node 3 and node 4 yield value 3.5 (the average of their weights, 4 and 3, respectively); for the XOR on the right, the weight of node 8 must be averaged with the weight or the OR-connected nodes 6 and 7, which is the sum of their individual weights, 3 and 4, yielding an average of $(1 + 7) / 2 = 4$. Finally, we sum up these average values with the weights of the remaining nodes 1, 2, and 5, obtaining value 16.5 for the first severity parameter. The second part of the severity value pair is the overall median, which has a value of 3 in this case. Thus, the severity for this example tag is (16.5, 3).

Credibility reflects the probability that a tag is correctly assigned to a system component. Contrary to the severity calculation, the credibility value depends only on the security artifacts that are actually present in the system under evaluation (or not present, respectively, in case of a NOT operator). It is a dynamic measure of the tag quality. Credibility is defined as the ratio of the sums of weights of detected security artifacts to the sum of weights of all possible security artifacts (i.e., the maximum weight sum that can be obtained if all contributing factors that collectively imply the tag were actually present in the system). High credibility indicates that the security artifacts of the evaluation target strongly

Figure 2. Severity example

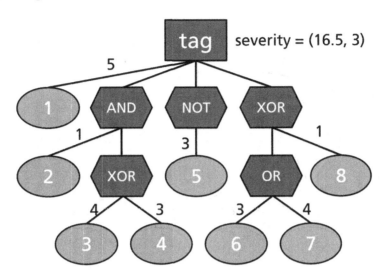

support the tag: The system fully matches the tagging rule from the knowledge base for this specific tag.

The credibility of a tagging rule is calculated as follows:

- **OR:** All weights of the elements in an OR group affect the overall credibility. They are summed up to the denominator. The weights of all elements that are actually present in the system under evaluation are summed up to the numerator.
- **XOR:** If one subordinated element of a XOR group is found, only the weight of this element will be added to the denominator and the numerator. Thus, all absent elements in an XOR group can be ignored. If no element or more than one element in an XOR group is present in the abstract model, the average weight of the subordinated elements of this group is used for the calculation of the denominator, but the value of the numerator is set to 0.
- **AND:** All weights of the elements in an AND group affect the overall credibility. They are summed up to the denominator. If

and only if all elements can be found, they are also added to the numerator.

- **NOT:** All weights of the elements in an NOT group affect the overall credibility. They are summed up to the denominator. The weights of all elements not found in the evaluated system are summed up to the numerator.

An example for the credibility calculation is shown in Figure 3. In our example, nodes 1, 2, 4, and 7 (drawn in dark green) represent security artifacts that actually occur in the system under evaluation, while nodes 3, 5, 6, and 8 (drawn in light orange) represent security artifacts missing in the system. Applying the calculation rules on this example works as follows: All XOR sub-trees that are not matched by corresponding security artifacts can be ignored in the calculation; in our case these are nodes 3 and 8. In our case, all elements below the AND operator are matched, so the weights of node 2 and the matching XOR branch (node 4) are included in the calculations for numerator and denominator. Thus, the numerator is obtained by adding the weights of the matching nodes 1, 2, 4, 7, and the non-matching but NOT-inverted node 5, yielding a sum of 16. For the denominator,

Figure 3. Credibility example

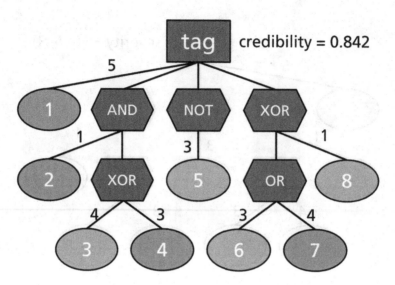

the weights of all nodes are added except for the non-matching XOR branches (node 3 and node 8), which are ignored, yielding a sum of 19. By dividing the numerator by the denominator, we finally obtain a credibility value of 0.842 for the tag placed by this tagging rule.

Of course, both severity and credibility assignments are only heuristics that guide the evaluator to the most promising security tags. The user can define a suitable threshold for filtering low-credibility security tags to improve the clarity in the graphical representation of the system under evaluation. We assume that a human is able to understand the dependencies and relations in the entire system much better than a machine does, and that the expert is in a better position to judge the true significance of the assigned tags for security, based on their credibility values.

Indicator Mappings

The knowledge base assigns each security tag to one or more indicators (refer to Figure 4). These assignments form the connection between abstract security goals (dictated by business needs) and the tagging rules (reflecting technical

system properties). Indicators help to structure the knowledge base by grouping security tags of similar meaning together. The idea is to group, for instance, programming language dependent tags and technology dependent tags to general tags, as in the »DES/AES encryption → encryption« example in Subsection »Tagging Rules«. This structure supports the security expert in finding the relevant security tags in the knowledge base.

Security Goals

Security goals form the highest level of abstraction in the knowledge base (Figure 4). We define six security goal trees that represent the six fundamental security objectives: confidentiality, integrity, availability, authentication, authorization, and accountability. The security goal trees are hierarchically decomposed into supporting indicators. The decomposition resembles the Security Goal Indicator Tree (SGIT) approach (Peine, Jawurek, & Mandel, 2008). We model security goals at the level of business logic, security functionality, security best practices, or simple security requirements as a tree structure that presents the

Figure 4. Excerpt of the knowledge base for »confidentiality«

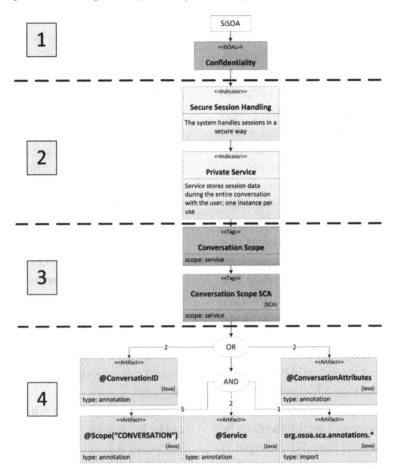

security knowledge in a way that is both reusable and understandable, even for non-experts.

Security goals and their subordinate indicators are defined in natural language and represent security knowledge that provides the basis for the SiSOA method. The security expert is encouraged to phrase the indicators in such a way that they can be manually ruled out during the Analysis phase—even by less experienced evaluators.

As new insights into SOA security aspects are gained—e.g., in the course of repeated SiSOA evaluations—the knowledge base can be adapted and extended to reflect these new facts. For example, after applying the SiSOA method, the user may notice that a security artifact is very

important for a specific security tag, but has only a low weight. Hence, he may adapt the artifact definition by adjusting the artifact's weight, thus improving the accuracy of the security tagging.

Figure 4 presents a simplified excerpt of the security goal »confidentiality«. The top-most layer 1 expresses the security goal. Layer 2 shows the related indicators. Security tagging rules follow at layer 3 with independent tags, which are further decomposed into programming language and technology dependent tags (language or technology are indicated in braces). Extractable security artifacts constitute the lowest level 4 of the hierarchy.

Identification

The Identification phase maps selected security artifacts in the extracted system model (comprising—among others—information about software artifacts and architecture of the SOA system) to security artifacts referenced in the knowledge base. To this end, it assigns tags to abstract system parts such as services, based on tagging rules from the knowledge base. A security tag is an attribute that can be assigned to an element of the system model. To know where to place this information, every security tag has a target parameter (e.g., service, class, trust zone). The tag indicates that the given security artifact affects the system security, and it specifies the type of influence. For example, a communication interface can be tagged as »SHA256-hashed« or »AES256-encrypted«, which positively affects security aspects such as integrity or confidentiality. But a service tagged with »Database Write Access« could be a security issue in data confidentiality and has therefore a negative influence. The non-existence of a security tag can also affect the system's security and can be interesting in the Analysis phase. For example, if all but one component has a security tag attached that is crucial for the overall security of the system, then the only untagged component is suspicious.

As tagging rules may have tags as subordinate parts, the tagging procedure has to be reiterated to aggregate existing security tags to new, derived security tags. The overall result of the Identification phase is the fully tagged system model, which provides the basis for the subsequent Analysis phase.

As indicated in Figure 5, identified system artifacts from the source code and from configuration files that are included in the system model can be mapped to their counterparts in the knowledge base. For example, after assessing the security rules in the tree, the tag »Conversation Scope SCA« can be assigned to the predefined application target »service«.

A security artifact can have multiple independent security tags assigned. For example, an artifact can be identified as having impact on both confidentiality and integrity of processed data. Similarly, the same security tag can be assigned to multiple system components (e.g., classes, services).

Tags can depend on programming languages and technologies, or they can denote technology-independent generic properties. In the subsequent analysis, the evaluator may query the model either for those elements tagged with one of the technology-specific leaf tags, or he can query for tags

Figure 5. Applying security tagging rules

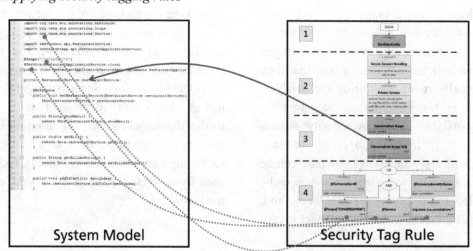

at a more abstract level referring to technology-independent concepts. For example, the evaluator may query for a specific »AES encrypted« tag to confirm that the required encryption standard has been deployed, or he can query for the generic »encrypted« tag to just verify that any kind of encryption is in place.

PROTOTYPICAL IMPLEMENTATION

This section describes our prototypical implementation of the SiSOA tool support. The prototype bases upon SAVE (Duszynski, Knodel, & Lindvall, 2009), a tool for the visualization and evaluation of software architectures. The prototype supports Apache Tuscany (The Apache Foundation, 2011) as an SCA-based SOA framework (OSOA, 2011), and the Java language.

We implemented two different architectural views showing the system under evaluation. The assigned security tags are displayed in these views.

The first view reflects the software system's code structure. It presents all packages and classes of the system, and relations between them (e.g., call, access, and import relations). This level of abstraction provides insights into relations between the different system classes. Specific class constellations unveil security characteristics.

The second view addresses the SOA aspect. It shows the service orchestration of the system under evaluation at a higher level of abstraction. This view is used for analyzing the security at the service level rather than the source code level. Note that software structure and service orchestration may differ from each other. For example, two different services can be based on the same implementation class. But the behavior of the service provided depends on specific configuration parameters. Hence, we will get two representations in the service view with different tag assignments (depending on the information from the configuration file), but only one representation in the system's class structure. The same implementation class

can have different impacts on the behavior and hence the security of the software system.

We are aware that our approach can cause a lot of false positive tags with low credibility. Having all these tags displayed in the diagrams would make the navigation in the diagrams confusing, complicating analysis. To mitigate this problem, we offer filters that help to navigate efficiently through the views.

There are filters for displaying, hiding, or coloring tags, depending on user-defined credibility or severity thresholds. Moreover, tags from the Identification phase can be filtered hierarchically by several mechanisms, such as checkboxes in tree structures reflecting the knowledge base hierarchy. Tags may also be filtered by relation types. Tag filtering is an important feature because the security expert can focus on individual tag groups addressing specific security objectives, for example, integrity only. The following gives a short overview of the currently implemented filters:

- **Tag Credibility Filter:** This filter allows the user to provide a threshold value between 0 and 1, which can be used to hide low-credibility tags in the architectural view.
- **Tag Severity Filter:** This filter is similar to the »Tag Credibility Filter« but applies to severity ratings.
- **Tag Type Filter:** This filter lists all tag types found in the Identification phase as checkable boxes. By selecting a checkbox, all components of the diagram that contain this tag type expand and present the assigned tag. In contrast, by deselecting the checkbox all affected components collapse. This filter is only available for the service view.
- **Tag Tree Type Filter:** This filter lists all tags, indicators, and security goals that have been found in the Identification phase as a tree structure according to the tag hierarchy of the knowledge base. When an

element of the tree is selected, the filter displays all components that contain a tag from the selected branch of the tree structure. In contrast, when an element is deselected, the corresponding tags are hidden.

- **Tag Color Filter:** This filter allows the user to specify different colors for tags with credibility and severity values within user-defined intervals. For example, the user can display all tags with credibility below 0.5 in green, between 0.5 and 0.75 in yellow, and above 0.75 in red.
- **Relation Filter:** All relation types of the view are listed as checkboxes (e.g., call relation, exception, etc.). When a check box is selected all relations of this type are hidden. In contrast, when a check box is deselected the relations are shown.

A transaction log shows the sequence of all filter applications. By pressing the reset button the log is erased and all applied filters are reverted.

Figure 6 shows a screenshot of our SiSOA prototype tool. The middle pane illustrates a Java package containing several classes in the structural view. The innermost class has four tags attached. The color filter has been used to highlight those tags with a high credibility. The left pane of our prototype contains the model browser, which allows the security expert to investigate the system model and attached tags. Under each security tag the found and missing artifacts are listed. Available filters are shown in the right pane.

EXAMPLE OF A SECURITY ANALYSIS

Assessing the security of the system means analyzing the tagged architectural views. A security expert has to select suitable security goals from the knowledge base that should be checked (e.g., confidentiality). Following the textual description of the assigned indicators for this security goal (provided by the knowledge base), the inspector is reminded what could be relevant for the analysis. Filter mechanisms support the analysis by hiding unrelated information on demand. For example,

Figure 6. Screenshot of our prototype tool showing the SiSOA view

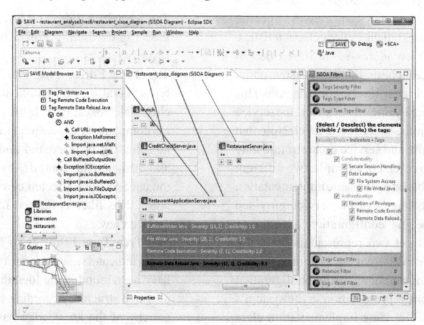

tags that are related to encryption algorithms are mostly irrelevant for the availability of the system, but they may be crucial for confidentiality.

Suppose that »confinement of sensitive data« is a business goal that needs to be evaluated. Then all classes that communicate out of a service scope (e.g., file writers) are potential information leaks. The indicator »Data Leakage« leads to appropriate security tags whose presence is evidence for such information leaks. The knowledge base supports finding such potential security issues in components, services, service configuration files, or source code snippets that can cause information disclosure. If »Data Leakage«-related tags are assigned, the security expert should have a closer look at the marked areas and check for potential problems. Conversely, the indicator »All service interfaces have to ensure tamper-proof communication« causes the security expert to check all service interfaces that have no integrity-related tags assigned. Hence, the security expert is guided to a potential security issue and has to inspect the respective source code. In this example, a missing assignment of the tag can give the key hint to a potential security vulnerability.

The behavior of a service regarding data handling across service requests is an architectural decision, reflected by the service's state. A service can be stateless. This means that every request is served by an independent instance of the service. Thus, the service does not store any data across requests. The opposite is a stateful service that maintains inter-request data. Stateful services can be differentiated in those services that create an individual instance for each client and those that provide one shared instance for all clients. In the latter case all clients can potentially access and modify the same data.

An adequate state model must be chosen judiciously to avoid information leakage. Having a complex SOA, the service-state related tags can help the security expert to uncover potential information flows in the system. For example, knowing that credit card data flows through stateful services should arouse the suspicion of the security expert. A service sharing credit card information across two requests is a potential security issue for information disclosure. By extracting the corresponding state-related attributes of the service architecture and by providing tagging rules that tag the service view accordingly, we can disclose such security issues and guide the assessment to vulnerable spots of the SOA system.

RELATED WORK

Our method combines different techniques to evaluate the security of a software system. It comprises static analysis and reverse engineering techniques for gathering security-related information at the level of SOA development and deployment artifacts, and knowledge aggregation for linking detailed system information to more abstract security properties, which are finally displayed in different views that support interactive security analysis at an architectural level.

Numerous works address static software analysis, some aiming at general quality defects and some specifically at potential security issues (Hovemeyer & Pugh, 2004; Larochelle & Evans, 2001; Livshits & Lam, 2005; Microsoft, 2011; Viega, Bloch, Kohno, & McGraw, 2000). Usually, analysis is restricted to source or byte code level, mostly disregarding the underlying design of the global system. The spectrum of available techniques reaches from simple local pattern matching (Viega, Bloch, Kohno, & McGraw, 2000) to sophisticated dataflow and control flow analysis (Livshits & Lam, 2005). However, advanced dataflow analysis suffers from considerable performance penalties, which constrains such approaches to small software components. Moreover, its automation is plagued by false positive and false negative results that require strong manual rectification effort. How to efficiently extend such local approaches to large and distributed software architectures is still an open problem. The SiSOA approach acknowledges that manual intervention by a human security expert will be indispensable for the foreseeable future.

The assessment of software architectures is a well-known best practice to verify that system quality requirements have been adequately addressed in design. A number of scenario-based assessment techniques have been proposed; see Dobrica and Niemelä (2002) for an overview. One of the most influential methods is SAAM (Kazman, Bass, Abowd, & Webb, 1994). The general approach is to select the relevant quality requirements, represent them by development, application, or maintenance scenarios, and evaluate the architecture against the chosen scenarios. However, current scenario-centric methods neither provide specific guidance for the assessment of security requirements, nor do they offer any substantial tool support. Moreover, scenario-based approaches strongly rely on human expertise. In contrast to SiSOA, few methods address the reuse of design knowledge and of insights gained during assessments.

Evaluating the specific quality attribute security at an architectural level is still in its infancy. Few tool-supported approaches exist that address security at levels more abstract than source code. Sohr and Berger (2010) describe an architecture-centric approach for static security analysis. Similar to SiSOA, they use a reverse engineering tool suite to extract structural information from source code. From the extracted system model, they recover relevant aspects of the software architecture, and derive different visual representations to guide manual assessment to potential trouble spots. Unlike SiSOA, their tool restricts fact extraction to source-code artifacts, and security views have to be defined individually for each system and evaluation scope. Systematic reuse of evaluation know-how is not addressed.

Another interesting idea is to combine static and dynamic system information. Karppinen, Lindvall, and Yonkwa (2008) describe an experimental study where they used architecture visualization to verify

that expected security functionality is actually in place in the implementation, and to identify hidden backdoors. To this end, they recovered the static architecture—mainly objects and call relations—from the source code and augmented it with dynamic information collected during system execution. By visualizing the augmented architecture they were able to detect security-related anomalies.

An intermediate approach is to analyze security at class or object level (Alshammari, Fidge, & Corney, 2009). However, such a local assessment still leaves a considerable conceptual gap because the security of small functional units is insufficient to ensure the security of the entire system.

Aggregating low-level information to higher-level quality attributes is a common concept for modeling security knowledge. Peine, Jawurek, and Mandel (2008) propose Security Goal Indicator Trees (SGITs) for mapping non-local security goals to positive, concrete system features that can be checked incrementally during an inspection. SGITs link security goals with a hierarchy of corresponding indicators that are structured as Boolean trees. They augment (in-)security indicators with information about recommended best practice to guide the security inspection process.

An alternative to the aggregation of security knowledge is decomposition. Attack Trees (Schneier, 1999) are a top-down approach for threat analysis that manually decomposes high-level attack goals (i.e., negated security goals) into more elementary low-level attacks. While the root nodes of an Attack Tree hierarchy are undesirable security conditions that compromise the system, SiSOA specifies desirable security goals that help to secure the system against attacks.

Byers and Shahmehri (2010) describe a unified modeling language that can represent the goal-driven SGIT model as well as the threat-driven Attack Tree model, providing an integrated view on security issues.

CONCLUSION AND FUTURE WORK

The SiSOA method demonstrates how security aspects can be analyzed at an architectural level by using reverse engineering techniques combined with a knowledge base, which is a key element in our approach. The knowledge base allows flexible refinement and adaptation of existing evaluation rules, and convenient addition of new security aspects to the analysis. It also enables reuse of security expertise gained during previous evaluations, even for non-experts. Moreover, its weighting scheme offers fine-tuning capabilities.

The SiSOA method is adaptable to specific needs and extensible for tackling new evaluation issues. However, the method is only as good as the security knowledge modeled in the knowledge base. Thus, the capability of our method depends mainly on the quality and the number of security tagging rules. The practical application of the approach will reveal potential improvements and refinements of rules in the knowledge base and especially of the weighting of corresponding artifacts. To gradually improve and maintain the overall quality of the knowledge base, a regular endorsement process must be established. Formal confirmation will ensure high quality and reliability of the stored knowledge.

Currently, we still lack practical experience beyond some small demonstrator scenarios such as those presented in this paper. Furthermore, our prototypical knowledge base only contains a limited set of exemplary rules that need to be complemented. For example, we assume that for analyzing the Java Authentication and Authorization Service (JAAS) we need one tagging rule for detecting the general structure of the service. However, to analyze custom modules, we will need one rule for each implementation variant (e.g., LDAP, X.509 certificates).

In the future, we plan to broaden the scope of our tool. Our approach and its tool support are not restricted to Java and SCA, but can be extended to handle other platforms as well. The extraction of system artifacts can easily be adapted to different SOA frameworks. Adaptation will include extending the knowledge base by rules for other programming language.

The SiSOA method still lacks systematic empirical evaluation. To gain better insights and to improve our methodology, we plan to apply the SiSOA method in an industrial setting. Evaluation experience will be used to further enhance the quality of our prototype and of the knowledge base. The effectiveness of the introduced metrics for filtering false-positive security tags needs further exploration.

Apart from the identification of potential security vulnerabilities, our approach may serve as a foundation for security metrics. The Analysis phase can be used to check all paths in the system for specific tag assignments. By performing this task, the SiSOA method can estimate, for example, the overall »confidentiality level« of the system. This potential requires further exploration.

ACKNOWLEDGMENT

This research was funded by the German Fraunhofer-Gesellschaft within the project »Zielgerichtete Sicherheitsbewertung von SOA-Anwendungen auf Architektur-Ebene (SiSOA)«, Grant No. 53-600113.

REFERENCES

Alshammari, B., Fidge, C., & Corney, D. (2009). Security metrics for object-oriented class designs. In *Proceedings of the 9th International Conference on Quality Software* (pp. 11-20). Washington, DC: IEEE Computer Society.

Antonino, P., Duszynski, S., Jung, C., & Rudolph, M. (2010). Indicator-based architecture-level security evaluation in a service-oriented environment. In *Proceedings of the 4th European Conference on Software Architecture: Companion Volume* (pp. 221-228). New York, NY: ACM.

Byers, D., & Shahmehri, N. (2010). Unified modeling of attacks, vulnerabilities and security activities. In *Proceedings of the ICSE Workshop on Software Engineering for Secure Systems* (pp. 36-42). New York, NY: ACM.

Chikofsky, E., & Cross, J. (1990). Reverse engineering and design recovery: A taxonomy. *IEEE Software*, 7(1), 13–17. doi:10.1109/52.43044

Davis, J. (2009). *Open source SOA* (1st ed.). Stamfort, CT: Manning.

Dobrica, L., & Niemelä, E. (2002). A survey on software architecture analysis methods. *IEEE Transactions on Software Engineering*, 28(7), 638–653. doi:10.1109/TSE.2002.1019479

Duszynski, S., Knodel, J., & Lindvall, M. (2009). SAVE: Software architecture visualization and evaluation. In *Proceedings of the European Conference on Software Maintenance and Reengineering* (pp. 323-324). Washington, DC: IEEE Computer Society.

Hovemeyer, D., & Pugh, W. (2004). Finding bugs is easy. In *Proceedings of the Companion to the 19th Annual ACM SIGPLAN Conference on Object-Oriented Programming Systems, Languages, and Applications* (pp. 132-136). New York, NY: ACM.

Karppinen, K., Lindvall, M., & Yonkwa, L. (2008). Detecting security vulnerabilities with software architecture analysis tools. In *Proceedings of the IEEE International Conference on Software Testing Verification and Validation Workshop* (pp. 262-268). Washington, DC: IEEE Computer Society.

Kazman, R., Bass, L., Abowd, G., & Webb, M. (1994). SAAM: A method for analyzing the properties of software architectures. In *Proceedings of the 16th International Conference on Software Engineering* (pp. 81-90). Washington, DC: IEEE Computer Society.

Larochelle, D., & Evans, D. (2001). Statically detecting likely buffer overflow vulnerabilities. In *Proceedings of the 10th Usenix Security Symposium* (p. 14). Berkeley, CA: USENIX.

Laws, S., Combellack, M., Feng, R., Mahbod, H., & Nash, S. (2011). *Tuscany SCA in action*. Stamfort, CT: Manning.

Livshits, V. B., & Lam, M. S. (2005). Finding security errors in java programs with static analysis. In *Proceedings of the 14th Usenix Security Symposium* (pp. 271-286). Berkeley, CA: USENIX.

Microsoft. (2011). *FxCop*. Retrieved September 6, 2011, from http://msdn.microsoft.com/en-us/library/bb429476.aspx

OASIS. (2010). *OASIS web services security specification*. Retrieved May 10, 2010, from http://www.oasis-open.org/specs/index.php#wssv1.0

OSOA. (2011). *Service component architecture (SCA)*. Retrieved September 6, 2011, from http://www.osoa.org/display/Main/Service+Component+Architecture+Home

Peine, H., Jawurek, M., & Mandel, S. (2008). Security goal indicator trees: A model of software features that supports efficient security inspection. In *Proceedings of the 11th High Assurance Systems Engineering Symposium* (pp. 9-18). Washington, DC: IEEE Computer Society.

Schneier, B. (1999). Attack trees. *Dr. Dobb's Journal*, 24(12), 21–29.

Sohr, K., & Berger, B. (2010). Idea: Towards architecture-centric security analysis of software. In F. Massacci, D. Wallach, & N. Zannone (Eds.), *Proceedings of the 2nd International Symposium on Engineering Secure Software and Systems* (LNCS 5965, pp. 70-78).

Steinberg, D., Budinsky, F., Paternostro, M., & Merks, E. (2008). *EMF: Eclipse modeling framework* (2nd ed.). Amsterdam, The Netherlands: Addison-Wesley.

The Apache Foundation. (2011). *Apache Tuscany.* Retrieved September 6, 2011, from http://tuscany. apache.org

Viega, J., Bloch, J. T., Kohno, Y., & McGraw, G. (2000). ITS4: A static vulnerability scanner for C and C++ code. In *Proceedings of the 16th Annual Computer Security Applications Conference* (pp. 257-267). Washington, DC: IEEE Computer Society.

This work was previously published in the International Journal of Secure Software Engineering, Volume 2, Issue 4, edited by Khaled M. Khan, pp. 19-33, copyright 2011 by IGI Publishing (an imprint of IGI Global).

Chapter 3
Eliciting Policy Requirements for Critical National Infrastructure Using the IRIS Framework

Shamal Faily
University of Oxford, UK

Ivan Fléchais
University of Oxford, UK

ABSTRACT

Despite existing work on dealing with security and usability concerns during the early stages of design, there has been little work on synthesising the contributions of these fields into processes for specifying and designing systems. Without a better understanding of how to deal with both concerns at an early stage, the design process risks disenfranchising stakeholders, and resulting systems may not be situated in their contexts of use. This paper presents the IRIS process framework, which guides technique selection when specifying usable and secure systems. The authors illustrate the framework by describing a case study where the process framework was used to derive missing requirements for an information security policy for a UK water company following reports of the Stuxnet worm. The authors conclude with three lessons informing future efforts to integrate Security, Usability, and Requirements Engineering techniques for secure system design.

1. INTRODUCTION

There is no longer any obvious reason why designing secure and usable systems should be so difficult, especially when guidance on applying Security and Usability Engineering best practice is no longer restricted to the scholarly literature. Several years ago, Nielsen claimed that cost was the principal reason why Usability Engineering techniques are not used in practice (Nielsen, 1994), but technology advances have reduced the financial costs of applying such techniques.

DOI: 10.4018/978-1-4666-2482-5.ch003

Similarly, practical techniques for identifying and mitigating security problems during system design are now available to developers in an easy to digest format (e.g., Schneier, 2000; Swiderski & Snyder, 2004).

Problems arise when considering how to use these approaches as part of an integrated process. Accepted wisdom in software engineering states that requirements analysis and specification activities should precede other stages in a project's lifecycle (Ghezzi et al., 2003). However, Information Security and HCI proponents argue that their techniques should instead come first. For example, ISO 13407 (ISO, 1999) states that activities focusing on the collection of empirical data about users and their activities should guide early design, but security design methods such as Braber et al. (2007) suggest that such stages should be devoted to high-level analysis of the system to be secured. Invariably, the decision of what concern to put first is delegated to the methodology followed by a designer. The designer has many approaches to choose from, some of which include treatment for security or usability concerns. To date, however, no approach treats both security and usability collectively, beyond treating them both as generic qualities contending with functionality.

The IRIS (Integrating Requirements and Information Security) framework was first introduced by the authors in Faily and Fléchais (2009) to explore the challenges of designing systems with both information security and HCI in mind. This framework encompassed three elements: a meta-model for usable secure requirements engineering (Faily & Fléchais, 2010), a user-centered design method (illustrated in Faily & Fléchais, 2010), and complementary tool-support (Faily & Fléchais, 2010). However, although the second element was described as a *method*, this is more aptly defined as a *methodology*. While a method describes a concrete procedure for getting something done, a methodology is a higher level construct motivating the need for choosing between different methods

(Iivari et al., 1998). Because the terms method and methodology are used interchangeably, the principles of information system methodologies have been encapsulated in several process *frameworks* that have, in recent years, emerged in Software, Security, and Usability Engineering. A framework can be defined as a set of milestones indicating when artifacts should be produced, as opposed to a *process* describing the steps to be carried out to produce the artifacts (Haley, 2007).

In this paper, we present the IRIS process framework, which is used for selecting techniques for specifying usable and secure systems. Building on the meta-model described in Faily and Fléchais (2010), we describe the different perspectives of IRIS, and how IRIS concepts and techniques are situated within these in Section 3. We propose a number of exemplar techniques for each perspective, and describe modifications, which are necessary to situate them within an IRIS process. In Section 4, we describe how the IRIS process framework was used to devise a user-centered approach for eliciting information security policy requirements for a UK water company. The management imperative for responding to the Stuxnet worm (Control Engineering UK, 2010) meant that policy decisions needed to be made where there was both a lack of time for data collection and restricted stakeholder availability. Finally, in Section 5, we describe some of the lessons learned carrying out this study, which, we believe, inform future approaches for secure system design.

2. RELATED WORK

Although frameworks exist for dealing with security and usability as quality requirements (e.g., Chung et al., 2004), we are unaware of existing frameworks dealing explicitly with both usability and security from a requirements perspective. There have, however, been processes and frameworks purporting to deal with each.

2.1. RESCUE

RESCUE (REquirements with SCenarios for a User-centered Environment) is a user-centered Requirements Engineering process (Maiden & Jones, 2004). Although not explicitly defined as a framework, the earlier phases of RESCUE afford leeway in technique application. RESCUE consists of the following four concurrent system engineering streams: Human Activity Modelling, i* system modelling (Yu, 1995), Use Case and Scenario Analysis (Cockburn, 2001), and Requirements Management. Human Activity Modelling involves analysing the way work is carried out, and partitioning the analysis of the problem domain into different aspects, such as the work domain, control task, and social organisation. When the system boundary has been agreed, i* models are used to map both the dependency network between actors, and the intentional description of activities, and the rationale relationships between actors and related resources, goals, and tasks. Use cases are then identified based on actor or system objectives, which are graphically represented in a use case model, and authored using a template based on style guidelines prescribed by Cockburn (2001). Requirements elicited as part of RESCUE are specified using a template based on the Volere Requirements shell (Robertson & Robertson, 2009) and managed using commercial requirements management tools.

RESCUE implicitly assumes that a secure and usable system will result by following its prescribed guidelines. Security and usability are both considered as non-functional requirements, and while the activity-centric nature of RESCUE means it is likely that the system's core functionality will be situated for its actors, the results of specifying security requirements may circumvent these activities. As it stands, security requirements may lead to use case changes, but it remains the task of the analyst to spot use cases, which be-

come unusable as a result of security constraints. Moreover, when problems are identified, the analyst needs to manually modify and maintain the traceability relations between i* models and downstream artifacts. RESCUE also fails to stipulate specific techniques for dealing with security concerns, making it an exercise for the analyst to select both the appropriate techniques and the points to apply them.

2.2. SQUARE

SQUARE (System QUAlity Requirements Engineering) (Mead et al., 2005) is a methodology which aims to build security into the early stages of a project lifecycle. It is applied within the context of a project by carrying out several steps. After agreeing a consistent set of security terms, project security goals are agreed in participatory workshops. With the aid of assistance of both domain and security experts, artifacts are then developed to support the definition of security requirements; these may include use cases and misuse cases (Sindre & Opdahl, 2005). After performing a risk assessment to identify and category the threats that need to be mitigated, security requirements elicitation techniques are selected and then applied. These elicited requirements are categorised as essential or non-essential, and of system, software, or architectural significance. A requirements prioritisation technique is then selected and applied with the aid of stakeholders. The final step involves selecting and applying a requirements inspection technique.

Although the selection of elicitation techniques is described as contextual, the selection of techniques for developing artifacts is not. Moreover, while several artifacts are recommended, no explicit guidance is afforded on how different techniques might contribute to each other besides reports of SQUARE applications.

3. THE IRIS FRAMEWORK

3.1. IRIS Perspectives

To provide guidance for eliciting concepts from the IRIS meta-model, the meta-model was divided into three intersecting groups: Usability, Requirements, and Security. This is illustrated in Figure 1. These groups are called *perspectives* because each views the specification process subjectively through a lens coloured by its related concepts. Each perspective also views the design process in a different way, and techniques situated within them share certain characteristics.

The Usability perspective views the design process as a means of understanding how a system can be situated in its contexts of use. Consequently, the techniques situated by this perspective

aim to model this understanding. The techniques associated with this perspective are often described as *user-centered*, but this is a misnomer. Instead, these techniques centre on one or more concepts within a context of use. Techniques within this perspective are also sensitive to human values. IRIS does not state what human *values* are conceptually, nor does it explicitly describe how these are portrayed from a stakeholder perspective. Instead, values are unpacked and elucidated by the usability techniques that elicit and analyse empirical data.

The Requirement perspective views the design process as a means of specifying the system being built. As such, the techniques situated by this perspective aim either to objectively specify the system being designed, or elicit models of how inter-related concepts situated in their contexts

Figure 1. IRIS perspective concepts

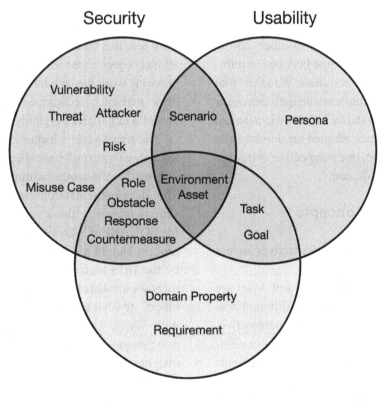

contribute to an objective specification. The techniques associated with this perspective can be described as *requirement-centered*. The ultimate ends of techniques situated in this perspective are prescriptive, objective, unambiguous, and bounded statements of system intent.

The Security perspective views the design process as a means of understanding how a system can be securely designed; specifically, how the design can make a system more secure. The techniques associated with this perspective can be described as *risk-centered*, because these aim either to understand what these are, or what design decisions are necessary to adequately respond to them. While what might be considered as *adequate* is subjective, it is, nonetheless, rational to the involved stakeholders. Consequently, techniques situated in this perspective not only discover what these risks are, but how they contribute to design in general.

The premise underpinning this framework is that the specification development process is hermeneutic rather than iterative. Nuseibeh alludes to this in his twin-peaks model (Nuseibeh, 2001), which talks about the dialogue between requirements and architectural activities. We assert that when specifying requirements, insights can occur at any time. While guidance is needed in a design process, the techniques adopted need to be agile enough to switch from one perspective to another should new insights dictate.

3.2. Converging Concepts

As Figure 1 illustrates, these perspectives are not mutually exclusive.

The concepts of Environment and Asset are shared by all perspectives, but for different reasons. In the Usability and Security perspective, these concepts are exploratory, while these reference or constraint concepts in the Requirements perspective.

Goals and tasks are conceptually shared between the Usability and Requirements perspectives; this is because user needs embodied by task descriptions in specific contexts eventually need to be reified by objective goals and requirements holding for all contexts of use. Similarly, roles, obstacles, responses, and countermeasures are conceptual interfaces between the Security and Requirements perspectives because they are used by techniques in both. Only scenarios are situated between the Security and Usability perspectives because, in both, these are used for exploring contexts of use rather than specifying elements within them.

3.3. Framework Techniques

We now consider techniques for eliciting the concepts from within these three perspectives. We have selected several candidate techniques, as summarised in Table 1. Because a *technique* is a particular way of carrying out a procedure or task, techniques can be construed as processes in their own right, albeit ones which require knowledge and experience in their use.

While this table does not purport to describe all techniques capable of eliciting IRIS concept, previous work has validated the effectiveness of these particular techniques when integrated as part of a larger process (Faily & Fléchais, 2010).

The framework is instantiated by devising an IRIS process: an ordered collection of techniques, informed by the context within which it is applied. This developmental context may be shaped by similar factors to those reported in Section 2.2 for SQUARE. Collectively, the techniques in a process should elicit all the concepts stipulated by the IRIS meta-model. There are no specific rules about what class of constraints should follow others, or what techniques can run concurrently with others. This is because the application of a technique from one perspective may lead to insights informing the analysis carried out using a technique in another. In general, however, the following principles apply:

Table 1. Techniques overview

Technique	Perspective	Input	Settings	Elicited Concepts	Output
Personas	• Usability	• Rich Picture	• Fieldwork • Analyst • Workshop	• Personas	• Persona specifications • empirical data
Activity Scenarios	• Usability	• Empirical data • Goals	• Workshop • Analyst	• Tasks • Scenarios • Usability Attributes	• Tasks
Grounded Theory	• Usability	• Empirical data	• Workshop • Analyst		• Qualitative models
Rich Pictures	• Requirements • Usability	• Empirical data	• Workshop • Analyst	• Roles • Environments	• Rich picture diagrams • Goals
KAOS	• Requirements • Security	• Empirical data • Goals	• Workshop • Analyst	• Goals • Obstacles • Domain Properties • Dependencies	• Goal Model
Volere	• Requirements	• Empirical data • Requirements	• Workshop • Analyst	• Requirements	• Requirements specification
AEGIS	• Security	• Empirical data	• Workshop • Analyst	• Assets • Security Attributes • Vulnerabilities • Attackers • Threats • Risks • Responses • Countermeasures	• Risk Analysis Model
Misuse Cases	• Security	• Risks	• Workshop	• Misuse Cases • Scenarios	• Risk Analysis Model • Task Model

- At the start of a process, one or more Requirements perspective techniques should be used to establish the scope of the system. Subsequent techniques assume that a context of design has been both agreed and specified.
- As the end product of a process is a specification, then a technique incorporating the validation of requirements is singularly or concurrently the last technique applied.

We describe these techniques in more detail in the following sections. For each technique, we present a brief overview of its key features, the rationale for using it, followed by interpretations and variations in its application as part of IRIS.

3.4. Grounded Theory

Grounded Theory is a qualitative data analysis technique for generating theory from observed real-world phenomena (Corbin & Strauss, 2008). These theories, and the sense-making activities associated with carrying them out, form the raw material that User-Centered Design artifacts can build upon. Although not traditionally construed as a design technique per se, it has been used for theory building in security and privacy research. For example, Fléchais (2005) used Grounded Theory to induce and refine a model of the factors affecting the design of secure systems, based on empirical data gathered from several different case studies.

Although we propose Grounded Theory be used for theory development in IRIS, induced theories are not developed for dissemination beyond the design team and system stakeholders. Instead, the sense-making associated with applying Grounded Theory is primarily used to support the elicitation and specification of other IRIS concepts.

3.5. Personas

Personas are archetypical specifications of indicative user behaviour. These were first introduced by Cooper (1999) to deal with programmer biases arising from the word *user*. These biases lead to programmers introducing assumptions causing users to bend and stretch to meet these needs; Cooper called this phenomenon *designing for the elastic user*. We chose personas as a user proxy for IRIS because of their grounded representations of users. Although personas are viewed as a narrative structured by different behavioural variable types, their authorship is the least time-consuming element of their construction. In IRIS, data is explicitly collected and analysed to identify clusters of behaviour. This data is collected from representative users or related stakeholders, ideally within contexts the system needs to be situated in.

Personas are fully developed (or at least as fully developed as possible) at an early stage using qualitative data analysis techniques; in Faily and Fléchais (2010), we demonstrated an example of such an approach. However, friction may arise when personas are introduced into a project environment when developers are unhappy about system features directly appealing to some aspect of a persona. To deal with this concern, recent work by the authors on *Persona Cases* demonstrated how, during an IRIS process, Grounded Theory models can be bridged with persona narratives using argumentation models (Faily & Fléchais, 2010). These models provide a means for validating personas inspecting the assumptions made during qualitative data analysis.

3.6. Activity Scenarios

Activity scenarios centre around activities performed by users, rather than on the users themselves. In Scenario-Based Usability Engineering (SBUE) (Rosson & Carroll, 2002), these are preceded by problem scenarios, which describe how hypothetical stakeholders tackle current practice; these scenarios may be based on empirical data or assumptions. Notable positive or negative consequences to stakeholders in problem scenarios are marked as *Claims*, which suggest possible design criteria rather than specific requirements. Activity scenarios are written to explore claims arising from problem scenarios. Claims may also be identified from activity scenarios, although these are used to describe the pros and cons of different approaches (Rosson & Carroll, 2008).

In IRIS, activity scenarios can be applied in individual and participatory settings, and used to explore the impact of possible design decisions. However, while the scenario component of activity scenarios and its contribution to the larger design process remains unchanged, IRIS is less generic about the role of stakeholders. Rather than treating users as hypothetical stakeholders, IRIS makes explicit assumptions about the use of personas, and the usability attributes of a persona (or personas) involvement with the scenario. Despite the implicit rationale links between activity scenario claims and requirements, personas and usability attributes act only in an exploratory role.

3.7. KAOS

The KAOS (Knowledge Acquisition in autOmated Specification) method (Dardenne et al., 1993) is a systematic approach for analysing, specifying, and structuring goals and requirements. KAOS defines a goal as a prescriptive statement of system intent; this is synonymous with the definition of goal in the IRIS meta-model, where a goal model represents an objective model of system requirements. This differs from agent-oriented goal modelling approaches such as i* (Yu, 1995) where goals describe an agent's intention; these may or may not be conducive to system objectives. The KAOS approach involves modelling goals from both a top-down and a bottom-up basis; goal models are annotated graphs of goals linked via AND/OR links. In addition to being refined to sub-goals, goals in KAOS may conflict with obstacles: conditions representing undesired behaviour and prevent an associated goal from being achieved (Lamsweerde & Letier, 2000). Like goals, obstacles can be modelled using an AND/OR refinement tree, where the root of the tree is an obstacle node associated with the goal it obstructs.

KAOS bridges between Usability and Security perspective techniques in three different ways. First, rather than operationalising goals by operations, we instead choose to operationalise goals using tasks. Although less precise, this modification affords the complementary use of goals and tasks for imparting the impact of goals on tasks, and vice versa in design sessions where non-technical stakeholders are present. Second, obstacles may obstruct goals, but we interpret these as both the accidental or intentional obstruction of goals. As

Faily and Fléchais (2010) indicates, these can be associated with threats or vulnerabilities. Third, we apply recent work (Lamsweerde, 2009), which describes how *concern links* can be associated between goals and classes; these can be used to model traceability links between goals and any assets they reference or constrain.

3.8. Rich Pictures

Rich pictures are a diagrammatic way of representing the main concepts associated with a problem, and the relationships between them. Rich pictures are not based on any particular syntax, although the meaning of the imagery drawn be they boxes or sketches, are meaningful to both the stakeholders and the situation being described. Although representing problems with pictures is timeless, rich pictures were first introduced by Checkland and Scholes (1990) in their Soft Systems Methodology.

Checkland and Scholes propose the use of rich pictures to help obtain a *Root Definition*: a succinct definition of a system under investigation or being built. Despite the close relationship between a rich picture and a root definition, this latter concept has not been incorporated into IRIS for two reasons. First, contributing artifacts from a rich picture used in IRIS are prescriptive high-level system goals, subject to refinement, rather than a joint descriptive and prescriptive statement about the system. Second, when a system is being scoped we are interested in *all* roles at play in a system, rather than differentiating between different classes of stakeholder. Understanding the politics associated with social classes may be useful from a Usability perspective, but not from a Requirements perspective unless these admit of requirements which need to be explicitly represented in a system specification. In such cases, the rationale behind these requirements also needs to be explicit, which, again, motivates the use of goals as an output from this stage of analysis rather than a root definition.

3.9. Volere Requirements Specification

Volere is a framework for Requirements Engineering encapsulating industry best practice for scoping, eliciting, specifying, and validating requirements (Robertson & Robertson, 2006). A characteristic element of Volere is its Requirements Specification template. This describes the format a specification document should take, and the elements of a single requirement. These elements are described as a *Requirements Shell* and include attributes such as a unique identifier, requirements type, description, rationale, priority, history, customer satisfaction, and fit criterion.

While the IRIS requirements specification template is largely based on that prescribed by Volere, attributes of an IRIS requirement do not include specific fields for history and customer satisfaction / dissatisfaction. In the case of the former, this is an attribute for tool-support, rather than something an analyst should have to manually maintain. In the case of satisfaction and dissatisfaction, it is arguably difficult to obtain reliable values for these attributes. The source of satisfaction or dissatisfaction may originate in early, contributory analysis, or may arise from a participant's subjective stake in the project. Although understanding the underpinnings of such value is useful, these are attributes best dealt with by Usability perspective techniques.

3.10. AEGIS

AEGIS (Appropriate and Effective Guidance for Information Security) (Fléchais et al., 2007) is a method for participative risk analysis. Under the guidance of a facilitator, and with the aid of one or more security experts, participants carry out an asset modelling exercise, identify risks from threats and vulnerabilities, select responses to these risks, and propose high-level security controls for risks requiring mitigation. Of the several approaches to dealing with the analysis and management of risks, which are typically frameworks like CORAS (Braber et al., 2007), AEGIS is a lightweight technique providing a simple, comprehensive, and straightforward structure for security analysis. For example, AEGIS prescribes the identification of vulnerabilities and threats, and the elicitation of requirements, but provides no explicit guidance on how these activities should be achieved. While this might be construed as a limitation, this is an advantage for IRIS as these activities can be carried out by complementary techniques.

When adopted in an IRIS process, focus groups are no longer a mandatory element of AEGIS. Although useful, participatory design activities can be time-consuming to participants, and the overall process of design may drag on if key participants are unavailable, or become compromised if participants are non-representative of users ultimately using the system. In lieu of multiple participants commenting on an asset model, insights are gleaned by interfacing AEGIS asset models with multiple techniques. For example, the asset-modelling phase in AEGIS may precede obstacle modelling in KAOS to identify vulnerabilities; these can be examined in more detail with other vulnerabilities and threats by AEGIS. Similarly, goal modelling to identify the requirements a countermeasure needs to satisfy may be injected as a stage between AEGIS risk response and countermeasure selection.

3.11. Misuse Cases

A misuse case is a sequence of actions, including variants that a system or other entity can perform, interacting with misusers of the entity, and causing harm to stakeholders if the sequence is allowed to complete (Sindre & Opdahl, 2005). Misuse cases extend the UML use case diagram notation by extending the actor node as a stick figure which is a black, as opposed to white, head, and adding additional relations between use cases and misuse cases, e.g., threaten and mitigate. Like use cases, and scenarios in general, misuse cases add context to risk analysis by modelling the attacker, and describing how an attacker can exploit or misuse the system. The simplest way of eliciting misuse cases is informed brainstorming, guided by a security expert asking questions about the system likely to have weaknesses; this activity mirrors the way attackers might think (Hope et al., 2004).

Although IRIS obtains the same value from misuse cases as the literature suggests, it reaches the final end using a different means. Rather than using them to elicit and explore threats, IRIS uses misuse cases to validate risks. For a risk to be considered valid, a misuse case needs to be authored commensurate to the risk's impact, which, in turn, is commensurate to the attributes of the exploited vulnerability, and the threat taking advantage of this. If a valid scenario cannot be written based on this analysis, then the underlying analysis needs to be re-visited. The IRIS meta-model is such that, with suitable tool-support, it should only be necessary for analysts to write a misuse case narrative because contributing information, such as the misuse case objective and attacker can be determined from existing risk analysis data.

4. CASE STUDY: A PLANT OPERATIONS SECURITY POLICY

Information security policies in Critical National Infrastructure (CNI) organisations need to be balanced. The growth in technologies such as distributed control systems and smart grids have meant that media reports about cyber-warfare and terrorism have heightened the security awareness of senior managers. However, the impact of such policies extends beyond the board rooms and offices where they are drafted. Poorly written policies that constrain the ability of staff to carry out their day-to-day work might compromise operations, leading to the introduction of vulnerabilities to get around them. These problems can be compounded by unforeseen events causing organisations to re-think their current stance on information security. When under pressure, the perception that security design is time consuming may lead policy decisions to be driven by fear rather than rationality. Because few people are fired for making policies too secure, as long as usability and security continue to be treated as qualities to be traded off against each other, policies will err on the side of constraint over freedom of action.

To evaluate the IRIS framework, we wished to understand how successful Usability and Requirements Engineering techniques might be for eliciting organisational Information Security requirements.

Because this evaluation would take place in a real-world context rather than a controlled environment, this case study was carried out as an *Action Research* intervention (Lewin, 1946). Action Research is an iterative research approach involving the planning of an intervention, carrying it out, analysing the results of the intervention, and reflecting on the lessons learned; these lessons contribute to the re-design of the social action, and the planning of a new intervention. Although primarily used in social science and educational studies research, Action Research has also been used to validate security design methods (e.g., Fléchais et al., 2007). The objective of the intervention was to elicit and specify missing requirements for an information security policy, as indicated in section Introduction. For reasons of confidentiality, this company will hereafter be known as ACME.

An earlier version of the IRIS framework demonstrated how Usability and Security Requirements Engineering techniques could be aligned in system design without considering Security and Usability as trade-off concerns (Faily & Fléchais, 2010). However, because this study took place over a period of several months, it is difficult to determine how useful these techniques might be when working to a tight deadline. In such situations, limited time is available for collecting empirical data and running focus groups or workshops.

The Action Research methodology used in this paper is that proposed by Baskerville (1999), who breaks an intervention into five distinct phases:

- **Diagnosis:** Identifying the influencing factors in the organisational context impacting the design of the intervention.
- **Actions Planned:** Devising the planned process to be adopted in order to meet the intervention's objectives.
- **Actions Taken:** Carrying out the planned steps taken as part of the intervention.
- **Evaluating:** Evaluating the outcome of the intervention.
- **Specifying Learning:** Stating the actions, which need to feed forward to future interventions or research.

For reasons of brevity, we will describe the actions planned and taken in Sections 4.3, 4.4, 4.5, and 4.6; the discussion in Section 5 constitute the results of the *Evaluating* and *Specifying Learning* phases for this intervention.

4.1. Influencing Factors

In July 2010, early reports of how the Stuxnet worm had infected several industrial plants around Europe began to appear. These reports shook up senior management at ACME for several reasons. First, a long held assumption that the obscurity of their SCADA (Supervisory Control and Data Acquisition) systems made them immune to security was dispelled; the virus explicitly targeted the same type of SCADA software used by ACME. Second, by combining knowledge of zero day threats with a realistic means of spreading the virus, i.e., via USB sticks, plant control software no longer seemed as isolated as it once was. Finally, although the motivation of the attacker was, at the time, unknown, the technical sophistication of the virus suggested that the virus was professionally developed to cause harm. While ACME didn't believe they were the virus' target, they were acutely aware that the impact of being infected was largely unknown. They did, however, agree that an effective means of mitigating the likelihood of being threatened was to devise a specific information security policy for those staff working in plant operations.

Although many of ACME's sites were unstaffed, the planned policy would cover staffed clean water plants and sewage works serving large urban areas. These plants were staffed by operators responsible for the running of the plant, and its treatment operations. Plant operators were acutely aware of the safety implications of clean and waste water treatment. If not properly treated, waste water effluent could have a significant impact on the ecosystem and the food chain. The clean water treatment processes are also critical enough that quality warnings are automatically forwarded to ACME chemists and quality assurance teams. Plant operators were also made aware of the security implications of deliberate attacks on the clean water infrastructure. Like other employees at ACME, information security communiques were regularly sent to all ACME staff, and police periodically visited clean water treatment plants due to the perceived risk of possible terrorist action. There was, however, a feeling held by the information security team that plant operators perceived the threats described in these communiques as irrelevant to their work.

The new security policy would need to cover both the existing infrastructure, and a new Enterprise SCADA system currently being rolled out to other parts of ACME. There were, however, two issues, which would need to be considered when designing policy requirements for this system. First, access to stakeholders working in this project was limited. The project relied on external contractors, several of whom were paid a substantial amount of money for their expertise. Their insight would be required for this intervention, but their time needed to be carefully managed. Second, several technical requirements had been stipulated by the Enterprise SCADA system manufacturer.

At the start of the intervention, it was unclear what impact these might have on the security policy, and ACME's ability to enforce it without compromising this new operating environment.

4.2. Approach Taken

Based on the influencing factors, we determined that the intervention needed to be completed in a timely manner; this would ensure that the initial analysis would be available to senior managers quickly. We also determined that stakeholders working at water treatment plants, from plant operators to managers, would need to be engaged in the process without underselling or overselling the importance of security and usability in policy decisions. Finally, design activities would need to be informed by the on-going design of the new Enterprise SCADA system, and access to resources working on the Enterprise SCADA project would need to be carefully managed.

To meet these criteria, we devised a user-centered process for eliciting policy requirements. This process was *user-centered* because of its early focus on the needs of the policy's users and tasks, and the grounding of these needs in empirical usage data. After agreeing the scope of the policy, a Fieldwork phase was undertaken; this involved holding in-situ interviews with users who would be affected by the policy at sites where the policy would be applied. This data was used to build a qualitative model of security perceptions held by plant operators. The results from this phase informed two further phases: Usability & Security Analysis, and Requirements & Risk Analysis.

Usability & Security Analysis entailed developing personas and, using scenarios, describing the typical activities they carried out. In parallel with this activity, KAOS goal trees were developed to model the policy requirements, and possible ways these requirements could be obstructed. These obstructions were modelled using KAOS obstacle trees. Where possible, obstacles were resolved at this stage using policy requirements. Risks were elicited on the basis of obstacles that

could not be resolved without being first discussed by stakeholders.

The Requirements & Risk Review phase involved creating misuse cases (Sindre & Opdahl, 2005) to describe the impact of the identified risks, and holding a focus group with key stakeholders to agree possible policy requirements for mitigating them.

As the UML diagram in Figure 2 suggests, several different models were generated as part of this process. The artifacts elicited during the analysis and review phases were managed using the CAIRIS (Computer Aided Integration of Requirements and Information Security) Requirements Management tool (Faily & Fléchais, 2010). CAIRIS builds upon the IRIS meta-model (Faily & Fléchais, 2010), which describes how the concepts underpinning these artifacts are linked. As a corollary, entering data about these artifacts into the tool automatically generates the different models according to the meta-model relationships.

Once the scope had been agreed, a little less than two weeks were set aside for carrying out the Fieldwork phase and supporting qualitative data analysis activities. Usability & Security Analysis took place over the following 3-week period before initial policy requirements were available for the Requirements & Risk Analysis review.

Further information about the process and how the different artifacts were generated are described in subsequent sections.

4.3. Agreeing Scope

Existing documentation about ACME information security policies was provided as an input to this process. On the basis of this input data, an initial rich picture diagram of the policy scope was developed. Due to time constraints, this was developed off-site and distributed to stakeholders via ACME's Information Security Manager. Although preparation for Fieldwork commenced during this stage, the scope of investigation was bounded only when the rich picture diagram was

Figure 2. Policy requirements elicitation process

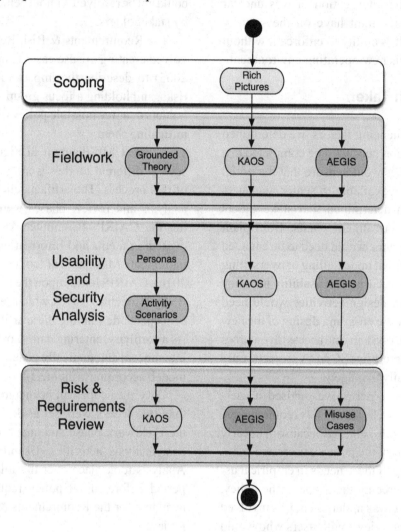

agreed with ACME. The feedback received from the ACME stakeholders involved word changes which seemed minor, but were semantically significant to ACME. For example, an association was drawn between one system in scope to another box named after the physical location of ACME's head office; ACME's telemetry group and their servers were located at this site. Although the association was valid, the box was renamed to Bunker to emphasise the data flow to the telemetry group rather than other groups located at the physical location; the name was commonly used to refer to the group because they were located in a bombproof building.

4.4. Fieldwork

The objective of the Fieldwork stage was to develop a qualitative model of plant operations security; this would be used to derive one or more personas representing plant operators for later design activities. We visited 4 different water-treatment works (2 clean water and 2 waste water) to hold in-situ qualitative interviews with plant operators and related stakeholders. Although these interviews were largely open-ended, high-level questions dealt with the nature of work undertaken, including what plant operators were responsible for, whom they worked with, and how they obtained help if necessary. Plant operators were also asked about important work items and activities, and the problems they often faced. Following the interviews, qualitative data analysis was carried out on the interview transcripts and, from this, a qualitative model of plant operator security perceptions was derived.

In addition to these fieldwork activities, goal modelling also commenced at this stage. The documents used to drive this activity included a draft security policy that ACME had prepared, an ACME information handling guidelines document, and ACME's organisational security policy. As the aim of the intervention was to elicit missing requirements from the first of these documents, this was the primary document used to elicit goals. For each policy recommendation in this document, a goal was defined. As they were elicited, a goal tree was induced based on statements, which relied on the satisfaction of other goals. Where supplemental documents were referenced, the referenced statements also formed the basis of goals.

In parallel with other activities, an asset model was progressively developed and, by the end of this stage, was mature enough to form the basis of analysing possible security issues. This asset model was based on the AEGIS Asset Model notation (Fléchais et al., 2007). The qualitative data analysis carried out indicated that the two prevalent contexts of interest to plant operations staff would be activities taking place during daylight hours (Day) and the hours of darkness (Night). With this in mind, assets and security values that stakeholders appeared to hold about them were modelled for each of these two contexts. Data about what constituted *Low*, *Medium*, and *High* value assets were based on ACME's own risk management documentation.

4.5. Usability and Security Analysis

4.5.1. Security Analysis

At this stage, the goal tree was analysed to find obvious vulnerabilities requiring further analysis. Although no obstacles were forthcoming, a number of goals suggested policy requirements needing to be present in order for them to be satisfied. One such requirement was *Authorised STCS network point data shall be available to authorised plant operators on the ACME portal*. This requirement arose from a goal stating that information about authorised network points should be available to authorised plant staff; this was necessary to allow plant staff to identify network points, which might be unauthorised.

Although no obstacles were obvious from the goal tree, examining the empirical data collected during the Fieldwork stage identified several vulnerabilities. Figure 3 provides an example of how these were integrated into the goal tree. During the site-visits, cabinets containing network infrastructure were found in publicly accessible areas of certain plants. Based on this, the *Exposed ICT Cabinets* obstacle was introduced; this obstructed pre-existing goals for securing the physical infrastructure. This particular obstacle was mitigated with the requirement *Key ICT equipment shall be stored in a restricted access computer room*. In the figure, this requirement is abbreviated with the label ICAB-1 because it references the ICT Cabinets asset (abbreviated as ICAB).

When all possible vulnerabilities were mitigated, a threat analysis step was carried out to identify possible attackers and the threats they might carry out. From the empirical data, two classes of attacker were identified. The first related to thieves attempting to break into plants to

Figure 3. Goal tree fragment associated with exposed ICT Cabinets vulnerability

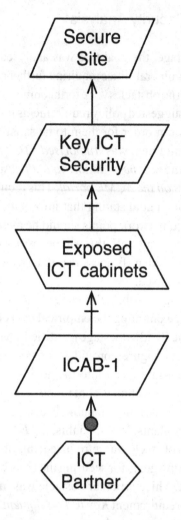

steal scrap metal or other equipment. Several plant operators expressed concern about these attackers because the damage to monitoring equipment they cause is inevitably greater than the value of the items stolen. Plant operators were also worried about their own personal safety should they be required to confront them out-of-hours. A *Kit Theft* threat was defined to model the impact of this attack.

The second class of attacker arose from a general indifference that plant operators and engineers held about information security threats. Even after describing the recent reports of Stuxnet,

participants interviewed were still unconvinced that "hackers" were as convincing a threat as the press and information security communiques would have them believe. Consequently, to portray an attacker that would be believable, a profile was developed based on a penetration tester that could, potentially, be commissioned by ACME; this attacker was grounded in a number of open-source intelligence resources and texts on penetration testing. Based on this attacker, several threats were identified, such as war-dialling modems, *foot-printing* to determine information about possible ACME network services, and enumeration of possible passwords using known defaults for software applications. Although several obstacles were elicited based on these threats, no mitigating requirements could be identified without further discussing the threats and their consequences with ACME stakeholders.

4.5.2. Usability Analysis

A plant operator persona (Rick) was derived from the qualitative model developed in section Fieldwork using the Persona Case technique introduced in Section 3.5.

Once the personas were ready, 3 scenarios were developed to describe how Rick would carry out his activities during the Day and Night contexts; these scenarios were modelled as tasks in CAIRIS, and textual narratives described how the task was carried out in each context. For example, the narrative associated with the *Resolve reservoir alarm* task during the Day context was as follows:

Rick looks at the SCADA monitor nearest to him and notices that the levels of the reservoir nearby are unusually high. When the level gets too high, the entire works need to be shutdown. In this situation, Rick knows exactly what to do. After stopping the alarm, Rick logs into the ICT PC next to the SCADA workstation, and clicks on the Xtraview icon. After logging into Xtraview, he finds the location of a pumping station 10 miles upstream on the map and connects to it. After a few moments, he masters the main pump before switching it off. Rick then returns the pump to its normal slave setting before shutting down Xtraview. The alarm periodically starts and stops again but, after about an hour, the reservoir level normalises again.

Although the above task was identical for both Day and Night contexts, there were a number of variations in other tasks. This was due to the necessity for on-call technicians to resolve problem that on-site staff could have fixed during working hours.

4.6. Requirements and Risk Analysis

The final stage involved running a focus group with ACME stakeholders and presenting the misuse cases encapsulating the unmitigated risks. These stakeholders were operational managers responsible for plant security and a representative ICT manager. Because only a limited amount of time was available, the presentation of the analysis was centred around a discussion of risks of most interest to ACME: a virus-infected SCADA workstation, and a site-break in. The misuse case associated with each risk was presented, discussed and, based on the outcome, mitigating strategies were proposed. For each discussed misuse case, a misuse case model was developed; as indicated at the beginning of the section, each model was generated automatically by CAIRIS.

For the first risk, a policy requirement was added to remove USB access to SCADA work-stations. Responsibility for the second risk was provisionally passed to ACME's facilities management department.

After updating the CAIRIS model based on these discussions, a revised specification document was re-issued to ACME. Because of the limited time available during the focus group, a more detailed review of the analysis took place at ACME's head-office several weeks later. In this one-to-one session with ACME's Information Security Manager, the goal model and elicited policy requirements were validated, and the risk analysis results were reviewed. The purpose of this session was to ensure that all goals and requirements were assigned a responsible role and responses were elicited for each risk.

On completion of the study, 106 separate policy goal statements had been elicited. The vast majority of these were associated with the Day context; this reflects the many day-to-day concerns that participants had with regards to security policy coverage. Similarly, the threats most evident from the empirical data were based on attacks expected to take place during daylight hours.

5. DISCUSSION

We believe the outcome of the intervention was a success for two reasons. First, despite the challenging time constraints, the study was completed comparatively quickly without compromising the quality of the artifacts created. As Section 4 reported, the study was largely completed in just over one month with ACME involvement limited to occasional email discussions, in-situ interview participation and a single focus group session to discuss key misuse cases. Second, all elicited policy requirements were accepted by ACME. Moreover, the design models created during the study were used to help with other security issues in ACME. For example, the Rick persona was subsequently used to inform design decisions about user account profiles. In the following sections, we describe three findings from this case study that, we believe, inform future efforts to harmonise Security, Usability, and Requirements Engineering techniques as part of secure system design.

5.1. Fieldwork is Security Sense-Making

Focusing on security design activities at the same time as Fieldwork activities heightened awareness of possible threats and vulnerabilities at an early stage. For example, on one site-visit, questioning the purpose of one particular PC led to the discovery that not only was it superfluous to plant operations, but the modem attached to it was vulnerable to war-dialling attacks. On another visit, a chance conversation about a car driving up to the plant's main gate on a CCTV screen led to the discovery that the plant had a second gate, and the access control system for this plant entrance was particularly weak. Based on these observations, we believe that fieldwork makes two important contributions to security design. First, de-familiarisation activities associated with in-situ interviews leads to identification of hitherto unseen affordances; these affordances are potentially exploitable by attackers. Second, opportunities for identifying and analysing vulnerabilities happen at any time and, quite often, such insights might have otherwise remained hidden.

5.2. Threats Without Up-Front Threat Analysis

Useful information about attackers and threats was collected without an upfront threat elicitation exercise. This is because threat analysis could be informed by the sense-making activities associated with other analysis. There are two reasons why this is an improvement over security design methods relying solely on anecdotal information from stakeholders or security experts to derive threats (e.g., Braber et al., 2007; Fléchais et al., 2007). First, threat elicitation is not exclusively contingent on participatory approaches, which rely on getting stakeholders together in a single location. Second, the task of eliciting attackers followed by threats is easier than trying to elicit

attacks in their own right. While the empirical data can point to possible attackers, further research is often necessary to determine what threats these attackers can give rise to and, as a result, which assets might be threatened.

5.3. Misuse Cases as Cases

Misuse cases were useful for spotting more general fallacies made when arguing against the feasibility of a risk. In particular, we noticed a tendency by stakeholders to undermine the impact of the threat or the severity of the vulnerability by focusing solely on the threat's likelihood and the asset directly under threat. During discussion of the *Site break-in* misuse case, some participants highlighted the limited number of staffed sites, coupled with the relatively high frequency of PC theft, as a reason why incorporating policy requirements to mitigate this risk might be infeasible. However, when it was highlighted that the PCs themselves were less important than the monitoring they facilitated, and that the quantity of staffed and unstaffed sites had little bearing on the impact of the risk, it was agreed to transfer responsibility of the risk rather than ignore it. When discussing the risk during the follow-up meeting with ACME's Information Security Manager, it was highlighted that transferring the risk in its entirety was inappropriate. Consequently, the policy goals related to securing physical sites were reviewed to determine which were the responsibilities of ACME's facilities management department, and which needed to be pro-actively managed by ACME's own security team.

6. CONCLUSION

In this paper, we have presented the IRIS process framework; this builds upon the IRIS meta-model by grouping concepts by Usability, Security, and Requirements perspectives. Based on these perspectives, the framework guides the construction of individual IRIS processes for eliciting secure system requirements using a number of exemplar techniques. To illustrate the framework, we have described a case study where the framework was used to devise a process for eliciting requirements for an information security policy for a CNI organisation. This paper has made three particular contributions towards improved harmonisation between usability, security, and software engineering.

First, we have successfully evaluated the efficacy of integrating selected usability, security, and Requirements Engineering techniques. Specifically, we have demonstrated that rather than adopting a single process model, judiciously selecting and applying appropriate design techniques for the organisational context can be economical in terms of manpower and time.

Second, we have motivated and presented the results of an Action Research intervention in a real-life context of contemporary interest; specifically, CNI following the initial outbreak of the Stuxnet worm.

Finally, we have illustrated how, by focusing on the up-front development of Usability, rather than Security, Engineering artifacts, we can re-use the sense-making activities and empirical data to elicit hitherto unseen vulnerabilities. From this, we can also glean insights about possible system attackers and threats.

ACKNOWLEDGMENT

The research described in this paper was funded by EPSRC CASE Studentship R07437/CN001. We are very grateful to Qinetiq Ltd for their sponsorship of this work.

REFERENCES

Baskerville, R. L. (1999). Investigating information systems with action research. *Communications of the Association for Information Systems, 2*(19), 1–32.

Checkland, P., & Scholes, J. (1990). *Soft systems methodology in action*. New York, NY: John Wiley & Sons.

Chung, L., Nixon, B. A., Yu, E., & Mylopoulos, J. (2000). *Non-functional requirements in software engineering*. Boston, MA: Kluwer Academic.

Cockburn, A. (2001). *Writing effective use cases*. Reading, MA: Addison-Wesley.

Control Engineering, U. K. (2010, 20 July). *'Stuxnet' Trojan Targets Siemens WinCC*. Retrieved from http://www.controlenguk.com/article.aspx?ArticleID=35267

Cooper, A. (1999). *The inmates are running the asylum: Why high tech products drive us crazy and how to restore the sanity* (2nd ed.). Upper Saddle River, NJ: Pearson Higher Education.

Corbin, J. M., & Strauss, A. L. (2008). *Basics of qualitative research: techniques and procedures for developing grounded theory*. Thousand Oaks, CA: Sage.

Dardenne, A., van Lamsweerde, A., & Fickas, S. (1993). Goal-directed requirements acquisition. *Science of Computer Programming, 20*(1-2), 3–50. doi:10.1016/0167-6423(93)90021-G

den Braber, F., Hogganvik, I., Lund, M. S., Stølen, K., & Vraalsen, F. (2007). Model-based security analysis in seven steps - A guided tour to the CORAS method. *BT Technology Journal, 25*(1), 101–117. doi:10.1007/s10550-007-0013-9

Faily, S., & Fléchais, I. (2009). Context-sensitive requirements and risk management with IRIS. In *Proceedings of the 17th IEEE International Requirements Engineering Conference* (pp. 379-380).

Faily, S., & Fléchais, I. (2010). A meta-model for usable secure requirements engineering. In *Proceedings of the 6th International Workshop on Software Engineering for Secure Systems* (pp. 126-135).

Faily, S., & Fléchais, I. (2010). Barry is not the weakest link: Eliciting secure system requirements with personas. In *Proceedings of the 24th British HCI Group Annual Conference on People and Computers: Play is a Serious Business* (pp. 113-120).

Faily, S., & Fléchais, I. (2010). The secret lives of assumptions: Developing and refining assumption personas for secure system design. In R. Bernhaupt, P. Forbrig, J. Gulliksen, & M. Lárusdóttir (Eds.), *Proceedings of the 3rd Conference on Human-Centered Software Engineering* (LNCS 6409, pp. 111-118).

Faily, S., & Fléchais, I. (2010). Towards tool-support for usable secure requirements engineering with CAIRIS. *International Journal of Secure Software Engineering*, *1*(3), 56–70. doi:10.4018/jsse.2010070104

Fléchais, I. (2005). *Designing secure and usable systems*. Unpublished doctoral dissertation, University College London, London, UK.

Fléchais, I., Mascolo, C., & Sasse, M. A. (2007). Integrating security and usability into the requirements and design process. *International Journal of Electronic Security and Digital Forensics*, *1*(1), 12–26. doi:10.1504/IJESDF.2007.013589

Ghezzi, C., Jazayeri, M., & Mandrioli, D. (2003). *Fundamentals of software engineering*. Upper Saddle River, NJ: Prentice Hall.

Haley, C. B. (2007). *Arguing security: A framework for analyzing security requirements*. Saarbrücken, Germany: VDM Verlag Dr Müller.

Hope, P., McGraw, G., & Anton, A. I. (2004). Misuse and abuse cases: getting past the positive. *IEEE Security & Privacy*, *2*(3), 90–92. doi:10.1109/MSP.2004.17

Iivari, J., Hirschheim, R., & Klein, H. K. (1998). A paradigmatic analysis contrasting information systems development approaches and methodologies. *Information Systems Research*, *9*(2), 164–193. doi:10.1287/isre.9.2.164

International Organization for Standardization (ISO). (1999). *ISO/IEC 13407: Human-centered design processes for interactive systems*. Geneva, Switzerland: ISO.

Lewin, K. (1946). Action research and minority problems. *The Journal of Social Issues*, *2*(4), 34–46. doi:10.1111/j.1540-4560.1946.tb02295.x

Maiden, N., & Jones, S. (2004). *The RESCUE requirements engineering process: An integrated user-centered requirements engineering process (Version 4.1)*. London, UK: City University.

Mead, N. R., Hough, E. D., & Steheny, T., II. (2005). *Security quality requirements engineering (SQUARE) methodology* (Tech. Rep. No. CMU/SEI-2005-TR-009). Pittsburgh, PA: Carnegie Mellon Software Engineering Institute.

Nuseibeh, B. (2001). Weaving together requirements and architectures. *Computer*, *34*(3), 115–117. doi:10.1109/2.910904

Robertson, J., & Robertson, S. (2009, January 14). *Volere requirements specification template*. Retrieved from http://www.volere.co.uk/template.htm

Robertson, S., & Robertson, J. (2006). *Mastering the requirements process*. Reading, MA: Addison-Wesley.

Rosson, M. B., & Carroll, J. M. (2002). *Usability engineering: scenario-based development of human-computer interaction*. New York, NY: Academic Press.

Rosson, M. B., & Carroll, J. M. (2008). Scenario-based design. In *The human-computer interaction handbook* (pp. 1041–1060). Mahwah, NJ: Lawrence Erlbaum.

Schneier, B. (2000). *Secrets & lies: Digital security in a networked world*. New York, NY: John Wiley & Sons.

Sindre, G., & Opdahl, A. L. (2005). Eliciting security requirements with misuse cases. *Requirements Engineering, 10*(1), 34–44. doi:10.1007/s00766-004-0194-4

Swiderski, F., & Snyder, W. (2004). *Threat modeling*. Sebastopol, CA: Microsoft Press.

van Lamsweerde, A. (2009). *Requirements engineering: from system goals to UML models to software specifications*. New York, NY: John Wiley & Sons.

van Lamsweerde, A., & Letier, E. (2000). Handling obstacles in goal-oriented requirements engineering. *IEEE Transactions on Software Engineering, 26*(10), 978–1005. doi:10.1109/32.879820

Yu, E. (1995). *Modeling strategic relationships for process reengineering*. Unpublished doctoral dissertation, University of Toronto, Toronto, ON, Canada.

This work was previously published in the International Journal of Secure Software Engineering, Volume 2, Issue 4, edited by Khaled M. Khan, pp. 1-18, copyright 2011 by IGI Publishing (an imprint of IGI Global).

Chapter 4
Organizational Patterns for Security and Dependability:
From Design to Application

Yudis Asnar
University of Trento, Italy

Fabio Massacci
University of Trento, Italy

Ayda Saidane
University of Trento, Italy

Carlo Riccucci
Engineering Ingegneria Informatica S.p.A, Italy

Massimo Felici
Deep Blue, Italy

Alessandra Tedeschi
Deep Blue, Italy

Paul El-Khoury
SAP Research, France

Keqin Li
SAP Research, France

Magali Séguran
SAP Research, France

Nicola Zannone
Eindhoven University of Technology, The Netherlands

ABSTRACT

Designing secure and dependable IT systems requires a deep analysis of organizational as well as social aspects of the environment where the system will operate. Domain experts and analysts often face security and dependability (S&D) issues they have already encountered before. These concerns require the design of S&D patterns to facilitate designers when developing IT systems. This article presents the experience in designing S&D organizational patterns, which was gained in the course of an industry lead EU project. The authors use an agent-goal-oriented modeling framework (i.e., the SI* framework) to analyze organizational settings jointly with technical functionalities. This framework can assist domain experts and analysts in designing S&D patterns from their experience, validating them by proof-of-concept implementations, and applying them to increase the security level of the system.

DOI: 10.4018/978-1-4666-2482-5.ch004

INTRODUCTION

Security and Dependability (S&D) are critical aspects in the development of IT systems (Anderson, 2001). The usual approach towards the inclusion of S&D concerns within a system is to identify security requirements after system design. Unfortunately, this makes the process inefficient and error-prone, mainly because security mechanisms have to be fitted into a pre-existing design which may not be able to accommodate them.

The literature in requirements engineering has highlighted the importance of analyzing S&D aspects since the early phases of the software development process (Giorgini et al., 2005a; Liu et al., 2003). It is also well accepted that S&D cannot be considered as purely technical issues but should be analyzed together with the organizational environment (Anderson, 1993). In this direction, goal-oriented approaches (Dardenne et al., 1993; Bresciani et al., 2004) have gained momentum in the community showing their relevance to model and analyze security issues within the organizational setting. This has spurred the definition of several goal-oriented frameworks for security requirements engineering (e.g., Giorgini et al., 2005a; Elahi et al., 2007). Requirements analysis, thus, is an iterative process where domain experts and analysts have to collaborate to elicit and analyze S&D requirements, besides the functional requirements of socio-technical systems. Often these security needs are common or "similar" to problems that security experts have seen before, and consequently the solution can be "similar" as well. The idea of using S&D patterns to provide solution to security requirements stems from this simple observation above. Patterns have been adopted into software engineering as a method for object-based reuse (Gamma et al., 1994) and security patterns (Yoder et al., 1997; Schumacher, 2003) have been proposed to capture and structure collective experience in the S&D domains and make this know-how available and exploitable for application designers. This transfer

of knowledge is intended to improve the quality of the developed systems from an S&D point of view. However, most S&D patterns presents in the literature are technical patterns. Here we focus on organizational patterns where we consider the overall interactions between human and software components and the relative dependencies.

This article presents the process for capturing, validating, and applying S&D organizational patterns. Our proposed patterns have been used in widely different industrial contexts: Air Traffic Management (ATM) and e-Health Smart Items. In our work, we have adopted the *SI** modeling framework (Massacci et al., 2008), an agent, goal-oriented framework that extends the *i** framework (Yu, 1997) with the concepts of ownership, trust, delegation, and event for capturing and analyzing security and trust requirements of socio-technical systems (Giorgini et al., 2005a), designing access control policies (Massacci et al., 2008), and risk analysis (Asnar et al., 2008). In this article, we show how the *SI** framework has been used by industries for the capturing of S&D organizational patterns and their validation by proof-of-concept implementation. We also discuss how patterns can be applied to a system so that it has a sufficient level of security.

The article is organized as follows. Next, we introduce S&D organizational-patterns, their elicitation process using the *SI** modeling language (§2) and the formal frameworks underlying *SI** for pattern validation (§3). We present an excerpt of our library of S&D organizational patterns (§4) and describe how these patterns can be used in real systems (§5). Finally, we discuss related work and conclude with lessons learned from the case studies (§6).

Designing S&D Organizational Patterns

At the organizational level, a system can be seen as a set of interacting actors (e.g., humans, organizations, software agents), each of them is in charge of a set of goals that must be accomplished. An S&D pattern at organizational level must therefore capture how these actors and the relationships among them can be evolved in order to meet an S&D requirement. Along the line suggested in our previous work (Busnel et al., 2008; Campagna et al., 2009), we define S&D patterns as triples of the form *<Context; Requirement; Solution>* where:

- **Context:** Defines the context and the conditions of applicability of the pattern;
- **Requirement:** Encodes the needs of a system to enhance its S&D level;
- **Solution:** Specifies how the requirement is achieved.

An organizational solution corresponds to a list of modifications applied to an initial system where the S&D requirements are not fulfilled; and that results to a different system where they are fulfilled. These modifications aim to revise the structure of the organization (when it is possible) or the procedures and policies governing the system. Organizational solutions can be various and can be implemented, for instance, by adding software or hardware components, by requiring a contract signed by two actors to solve a lack of trust, or throughout a new distribution of efforts among the actors involved in the system.

In order to explain how such patterns are constructed we will use the ATM scenario as a running example.

Case Study 1: ATM is the dynamic and integrated management of air traffic flow to minimize delays and congestion while guaranteeing safety and efficiency of operation in the airspace. In particular we focus on Air Traffic Controllers (ATCOs) who are in charge of issuing instructions to flight crews in order to maintain separation among aircraft. The airspace is statically organized into adjacent volumes, called sectors, and airways. Each sector has a predefined capacity (i.e., the

maximum number of flights that can be safely managed) and is operated by a team of two ATCOs, consisting of an Executive Controller (EC) and a Planning Controller (PC), working together as a team and sharing the responsibility for safe and efficient operations within the sector (Serenity Consortium, 2008).

The process for the design of S&D organizational patterns (Table 1) starts with the elicitation of system requirements. Initially, analysts together with domain-experts identify the stakeholders relevant to the system and categorize them into three different types of actors: role, agent, and group. Afterwards, stakeholders' goals are also identified and refined using goal analysis (i.e., refinement, contribution, and means-end analysis). Afterward, the objectives, entitlements, and capabilities of each actor are identified.

Notice that the design process does not explicitly separate the S&D features (e.g., entitlements, and risk factors) from functional features (e.g., functional objectives and system obstructions). They are dealt with in the same step. In traditional Software Engineering, analysts model functional requirements and afterward elicit and analyze S&D requirements. This approach is fragile because it could happen that S&D requirements conflict with functional requirements (Example 1), are not effective (Example 2), or even that functional requirements themselves are the source of risks (Example 3).

Example 1: The ATM system must provide necessary data easily for performing any Air Traffic Control (ATC) related activities. As S&D requirement, ATCOs should be authenticated each time they want to use any service provided by an ATM system (i.e., including gathering any data: flight plan, weather, runway, map, etc.).

Table 1. Design of S&D organizational patterns

Step	Description
A Elicit requirements	
A.1 Identify stakeholders	Identify the actors involved in the system along their goals
A.2 Identify strategic rationale	Analyze the objectives, entitlements, and capabilities of actors
A.3 Identify trust relationship	Analyze actors' expectation concerning the behavior of other actors
A.4 Identify dependencies	Identify execution dependencies and permission delegations between actors
A.5 Identify risk factors	Identify uncertain events that may obstruct the system and define the acceptable risk level
B Analyze elicited requirements	Analyze the model whether it has fulfilled S&D requirements and risks are below the acceptable level
C Refine requirements	Improve the model such that it fulfill S&D requirements
D Abstract the context and solution	Generalize identified context and solution, for easy reuse
E Validate the pattern	Verify whether the pattern actually satisfies S&D requirements using the GR or the ST Solver

In practice, the authentication requirement hinders the easiness of ATCOs in obtaining necessary data. Analysts must manage potential conflicts through trade-off decisions that best meet their requirements. For instance, analysts can employ authentication mechanisms only for critical activities of the ATM system (e.g., controlling aircraft) and not for non-critical activities (e.g., gathering weather data).

Example 2: Flight plans should be kept confidential by employing some encryption techniques. Unfortunately, this security measure will not be effective because each flight plan is printed in a flight strip to ease ATCOs' work. Therefore, analysts should elicit other ways to maintain the confidentiality of flight plans.

A functional requirement can also be the source of a vulnerability that might compromise the security and dependability of the system.

Example 3: The ATM system is required to be connected with Internet to provide arrival and departure time in the real time, but it is too risky because it allows hacker attacks from the Internet.

Working with S&D and functional requirements at the same time avoid these problems.

To support the steps in Table 1 we need to have a language that is more precise than natural language and more amenable to verification. In this work, we have adapted the *SI** modeling framework (Asnar et al., 2008; Massacci et al., 2008), an extension of the *i** framework (Yu, 1997) with concepts specific to security and dependability. The *SI** framework borrows from *i** the concepts of actor, goal, task, resource, and introduces the concepts of objective, entitlement, capability, delegation, trust, and event for modeling and analyzing S&D risks and requirements. We present them in Table 2 along with their graphical notation.

Interested readers are referred to Asnar et al. (2008) and Massacci et al. (2008) for a comprehensive description of the *SI** framework.

Example 4: In the ATM scenario, workers have to cope with complex activities where tight

Table 2. SI* Concepts and relationships

	Agent	an active entity with concrete manifestation
	Role	abstract characterization of the behavior of an active entity
	Goal	strategic interest of an actor
	Resource	physical or informational entity
	Request	denote the objectives of actors
	Own	denote entitlements of actors
	Provide	denote capabilities of actors
	Execution Dependency	transfer of objectives (or permissions) from the depender to the dependee
	Trust of Execution	trustor's expectation about the ability and dependability of the trustee
	Decomposition	combines AND and OR refinements of a root goal into subgoals, modeling a finer goal structure
	Contribution	identify goals and tasks that contribute positively or negatively in the fulfillment of the goal
	Means-end	identify goals, tasks, and resources that provide means for achieving a goal

coordination among them is crucial. In particular, where the failure of one subgoal has a negative impact to another subgoal and compromises the correct functioning of the whole activity. Paula (PC) and Luke (EC) are part of Sector SU-Team which is responsible to achieve "managing air traffic" in Sector SU, and each of the team members is in charge to achieve part of the aircraft management duties.

The identifications of stakeholders are easy in this example (A.1 and A.2) and the process proceeds with the identification of interdependencies between stakeholders. The *SI** framework employs two types of dependencies (Table 2): an actor (*depender*) can depend on another actor (*dependee*) for the fulfillment of a goal, or an actor (delegator) can delegate the permission to achieve a goal to another actor (*delegatee*). By depending for the fulfillment of a goal, the *depender* becomes vulnerable. The *depender* can fail to fulfill her goal because the *delegatee* does not fulfill the assigned responsibilities. Similarly, a delegator takes risks because the *delegatee* can misuse the granted permission. Indeed, the dependability of a system does not only depend on the reliability of a machine, but also depends on the interdependency among agents in the system.

This is captured by dependencies/delegations to *untrusted* actors. When the delegator grants permission to the *delegatee*, it does not imply that the delegator trusts the *delegatee*. Sometimes, the delegator should grant permission for accessing a resource to someone who he does not trust. This situation emerges when an actor must delegate the fulfillment of a goal or give permission in which it does not have any power to choose another agent (e.g., defined by regulations) or it does not have any other option (e.g., no trusted *delegatees*).

Moreover, analysts need to identify uncertain events that might obstruct the fulfillment of a goal. These uncertain events can have negative or positive impact to the goal; risk is an uncertain event with negative impact, while opportunity is the one with positive impact. To mitigate a risk, one can employ a treatment (depicted as a task) that reduces the likelihood of the event or alleviates the negative impact of the event.

Example 5: A planner (i.e., Paula) sometime is exposed to an event of "immediate traffic increase" that hampers the achievement of the goal "plan flights". Some measures (e.g., partial air space delegation, air traffic limitation policy, assist traffic planning) can be used to mitigate the risks introduced by the event, but analysts must analyze carefully the side-effects of those measures.

Figure 1 shows the *SI** model resulting from this discussion in the concrete case of Example 4.

Figure 1. Initial organizational structure within ATC Team

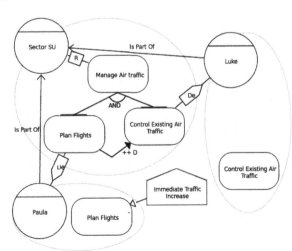

Once requirements have been captured and modeled, domain experts and analysts should verify if the designed system satisfy S&D requirements. This can be done, for instance, using the formal frameworks behind the *SI** framework. The analysis may end up with the identification of some problems (e.g., events) that can obstruct the fulfillment of the S&D requirements.

Example 6: In Figure 1, the goal "plan flights" is threaten by the event of "immediate traffic increase" which is defined as unavailability of the flight plan. The occurrence of the event obstructs the achievement of "plan flights" which later can increase the (D)enial evidence for the achievement of "control existing air traffic".

Domain experts need to revise the requirements and provide solutions that increase the security level of the system. A possible solution is depicted in Figure 2. It consists in adding mitigation "assist traffic planning" performed by a team mate (Luke), such that the risk is less severe.

To generate an S&D pattern the context analyzed in Examples 4 and its solution should be abstracted from the contingent situation. This

abstraction is the key step in the definition of S&D patterns. An abstraction of the solution is depicted in Figure 3. The resulting pattern consists of application pre-conditions (i.e., the context), the requirements to be fulfilled, and the solution.

Security and Dependability Analysis

The aim of *SI** analysis (Figure 4) is to formally verify whether S&D patterns fulfill the S&D requirements for which they have been designed. Essentially, this analysis is founded on two basic formal frameworks: Secure Tropos (Giorgini et al., 2005b) that verifies security properties (e.g., availability, authorization) and Tropos Goal-Risk (Asnar et al., 2007) that assesses the level of risk. In previous works, we have presented the formal definition of *SI** models. This analysis can be performed using the *SI** Tool (http://sesa.dit. unitn.it/sistar_tool/). The *SI** Tool assists analysts in representing an S&D pattern in terms of *SI** diagrams, and then transforms those graphical models into formal specifications and verifies their compliance with S&D requirements.

Figure 2. Revised organizational structure within ATC Team

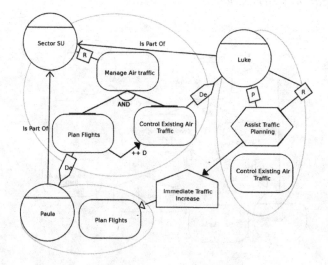

Figure 3. Collaboration in small group for a risky activity

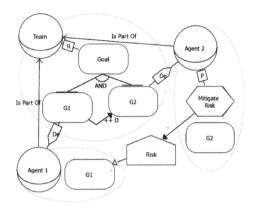

Logical Assessment of S&D Properties (ST Solver)

According this approach (Giorgini et al., 2005b) the semantics of *SI** concepts are defined using the *Answer Set Programming* (ASP) paradigm. The ASP paradigm is a variant of *Datalog* with negation as failure. This paradigm supports specifications expressed in terms of facts and Horn clauses, which are evaluated using the stable model semantics. A fact consists of a relation symbol, called predicate, together with an appropriate number of well-formed arguments. We distinguish two types of predicates: extensional and intentional.

A predicate is extensional if it does not appear on the left-hand side of any clause. Extensional predicates represent primitive concepts in *SI**. All other predicates are called intentional, and they are used for requirements verification. The *SI**

Tool supports the translation of Secure Tropos diagrams into ASP specifications.

Example 8: Figure 5 shows the list of facts corresponding to the context diagram of a collaboration in small group pattern given in Figure 3.

To validate S&D patterns, the framework supports formal analysis of rules and constraints (i.e., rules where the head is empty). Rules (or axioms) are used to complete specifications in order to derive the information needed for pattern validation. For instance, designers need to identify who is in charge of achieving goals, performing tasks, and delivering resources. To this intent, Secure Tropos uses the following axiom (Giorgini et al., 2005b):

Figure 4. SI* analysis process

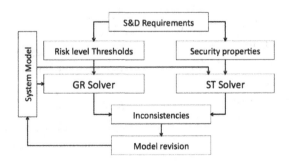

Figure 5. Extensional description in ASP

```
role(team).
role(role_1).
role(role_2).
is_part_of(role_1,team).
is_part_of(role_2,team).
goal(goal).
goal(g1).
goal(g2).
event(event).
task(mitigate_risk).
```

```
and_decomposition2(goal,g1,g2).
pos_contribution(g1,g2).
neg_contribution(event,g1).
neg_contribution(mitigate_risk,event).
request(team,goal).
provide(role_2,mitigate_risk).
dependency(team,role_1,g1).
dependency(team,role_2,g2).
```

(Ax1) aim(A,S) ← request(A,S)

(Ax2) aim(A,S1) ← aim(A,S) ∧ and decomposition(S,S1,S2)

(Ax3) aim(A,S2) ← aim(A,S) ∧ and decomposition(S,S1,S2)

(Ax4) aim(A,S) ← aim(B,S) ∧ dependency(B,A,S)

Ax1 states that an actor aims to achieve a goal, perform a task or deliver a resource if this is one of his objectives. *Ax2* and *Ax3* propagate objectives through AND decomposition, and *Ax4* through dependency.

Example 9: Applying such axioms to our example (Figure 3), one can infer that the Team aims to achieve goal Goal because of Ax1, and G1 and *G2* because of Ax2 and Ax3. The reasoning system also infers that *role1* aims to achieve *G1* and *role2* aims to achieve *G2* because of Ax4.

The complete specification can be used by designers to verify if the model complies with desirable security properties (Table 3). The framework supports domain experts and analysts through the use of constraints (Gelfond et al., 1991). Constraints are formulations of conditions which must not be true in the model. If all constraints are not simultaneously satisfied, weaknesses or vulnerabilities may occur in the actual pattern solution.

Example 10: Analysts need to verify the availability of goal G for an actor team in the model of Figure 3. To verify the compliance of the model with Pro2 in Table 3, Secure Tropos uses the following constraint:

(Pro2) ← request(A,B,S) ∧ not can satisfy(A,S)

The analysis reveals the presence of weaknesses in model: the requester cannot satisfy G because he depends for the achievement of the (sub)goals on actors that do not have the capabilities to achieve the assigned duties.

Inconsistencies of properties might be due to either unspecified requirements or conflicting requirements. Thus, detecting and solving inconsistencies helps analysts to detect implicit and unspecified requirements, understand system vulnerabilities, and identify and evaluate solutions for mitigate vulnerabilities. Failing to resolve such inconsistencies can erode the acceptance of S&D patterns by application designers.

Quantitative Risk Estimates (GR-Solver)

To reason about risk in a *SI** model we follow the techniques from Asnar et al. (2008). Essentially, we identify two types of evidence for each construct (being it goal or resource): satisfaction (SAT) and denial (DEN) evidence. SAT quantifies the value of satisfaction evidence of particular constructs - goals to be fulfilled, tasks to be executed, resources to be furnished, and events occurrences. Con-

Table 3. Security properties

Availability	
Pro1	Actors delegate the execution of their (direct or indirect) objectives only to actors that they trust.
Pro2	Requesters can satisfy their objectives; that is, they have assigned their objectives to actors that have the capabilities to achieve them.
Pro3	Requesters are confident their objectives will be satisfied; that is, they have assigned their objectives to actors that have the capabilities to achieve them and are trusted.
Authorization	
Pro4	Actors delegate permissions on their (direct or indirect) entitlements only to actors they trust.
Pro5	Owners are confident that their entitlements are not misused; that is, permission on their entitlements is assigned only to actors they trust.
Pro6	Actors, who delegate permissions to achieve a goal, execute a task, or furnish a resource, have the right to do so.
Availability & Authorization	
Pro7	Requesters can achieve their objectives; that is, they have assigned their objectives to actors that have both the permissions and capabilities to achieve them.
Pro8	Requesters are confident to achieve their objectives; that is, they have assigned their objectives to actors that have both the permissions and capabilities to achieve them and are trusted.
Pro9	Providers have the permissions necessary to accomplish assigned duties.
Privacy	
Pro10	Permission has been granted to actors who actually need it to perform their duties.

versely, DEN represents the evidence that the goal will be denied. These two attributes are quantified into three range qualitative values: full, partial, and none. Notice the concept of evidence differs from the notion of probability. In the probability theory, if the probability of E is 0:34 then we may assume the probability of E does not occur as 0:66 (i.e., $P(:A) = 1 \neg P(A)$). However, the evidence of denial cannot be derived for the satisfaction one. Somehow, they appear as two independent variables as proposed in the Dempster-Shafer theory of evidence (Dempster, 2008).

The evidence -SAT and DEN- must be provided for each input-nodes and leaf-events such as events or basic objectives. Then forward reasoning propagates those inputs all over the *SI** model. Finally, the evidence of the top-goals (i.e., goal

Goal in Figure 3) is calculated. By knowing the final evidence of top-goals, one may conclude whether the risk level (i.e., the level of denial evidence) of top-goals is acceptable or not. If not, then mitigation objectives need to be introduced (i.e., reduce likelihood or severity) as depicted in the solution in Figure 3.

As mentioned in Table 1, the model of the system is finally analyzed to ensure whether S&D requirements are fulfilled and calculate the risk level of the model. On the base of the results, analysts refine the model (the strategic rationale, dependency, or trust relations) such that all the S&D requirements hold and introduce a set of treatments (i.e., tasks) so that the risk levels are acceptable. In Example 5, we want to ensure the availability and the reliability of aircraft management in *Sector SU*. The analysis reveals that the failure of one subgoal has a bad impact to the satisfaction of another subgoal. If *Paula* fails to perform her responsibility to plan incoming traffic, then *Luke* will have difficulties to manage current traffic.

Example 11: We want to ensure the safe operation of the team. The aircraft management in Sector SU must always be executed correctly (availability and reliability), even if one of the team members is temporarily absent.

The analysis demonstrates that the system fails if one of the agents is unavailable or faulty.

Organizational Patterns Library

In this section, we provide the natural language description of the organizational patterns extracted from the different case studies. The proposed patterns have been formalized and validated using the *SI** framework and detailed information can be found in Serenity Consortium (2009). The validation aimed at verifying that the new organizational structure of the system fulfils the S&D requirements identified earlier. As explained before, the context and the solutions are specified by means of *SI** models. However, in this section we show only few *SI** models because of space constraints.

We tried to cover a wide spectrum of security management issues: legal patterns (14), privacy patterns (4), security patterns (11), dependability patterns (15), and a number of integration schemes (5) for combining different kinds of patterns.

As we have used the ATM case study as a running example, we show first some dependability organizational patterns are applicable to different application domains that we can immediately recognize in the Examples that we have just illustrated.

DP2 – Collaboration in Small Groups

- **Context:** This pattern deals with any situation in which it is essential to cope with complex activities where tight coordination among workers is crucial. The success of an agent (e.g., Agent 1) carrying its task is not only the interest of the agent itself, but also his (or her) team mate (e.g., Agent 2). If the Agent 1 fails to satisfy the goal G1 then the goal G2 is also disrupted. This condition may lead also to the denial of the Goal of the group.
- **Requirements:** Reliability on Goal of the Group and Reliability on G1.
- **Solution:** To prevent the goal G1 from failure, Mitigate Risk should be introduced to mitigate the Risk affecting the satisfaction of G1. Consequently, the goal G1 will not affect G2. In this setting, Agent 2 has capability to perform Mitigate Risk therefore it is its responsibility to perform it. Applying this pattern also means choosing the group size and its composition in terms of members' capabilities, expertise, and knowledge.

The solution of this pattern is shown in Figure 3. Instead Figure 6 describes the context and the solution for another dependability pattern that we have informally discussed.

DP1 – Redundancy for Reliability

- **Context:** The Agent requests the execution of one critical Goal to the Service Provider. The Service Provider is trusted to deliver Goal but the Agent would like to be sure of the results reported by the Goal. The SI* model in Figure 6(a) depicts the context.
- **Requirements:** The Agent shall have enough information to be able to rely

Figure 6. Redundancy for reliability

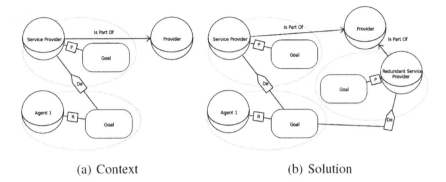

(a) Context   (b) Solution

on the Service Provider s reported Goal information.

- **Solution:** The Agent shall request the same Goal from a redundant Service Provider and result shall be validated between the two reported Goals. The **SI*** model in Figure 6(b) depicts the solution.

DP5 – Assistance Through Experience

- **Context:** This pattern is concerned with effects of prescribed career trajectory amongst tightly coupled groups of workers in safety critical, control room settings. The agents Supervisors have thoroughgoing knowledge and experience of positions below their present standing and therefore, how these different 'sub-roles' work to compose the overall activity. As a result a Supervisor has the ability to monitor, supervise, assess and explain to his sub-roles, as well as being able to fluidly assist and take over the sub-roles of other agents as required.
- **Requirements:** Provide extra dependability trough personnel recruiting and career trajectory.
- **Solution:** Be sure that composing work teams the personnel with higher roles and responsibilities have knowledge and experience of the activities that feed into their

work. This pattern provides checking and redundancy:

1. Workers in higher roles are experts in the roles below them.
2. Workers in higher roles have an overall view of the system.
3. Workers in higher roles can supervise the roles below them.

Workers in higher roles can carry out the duties of those in roles below if and as required.

In terms of security patterns, we have tried to see how far we could get in terms of coverage. In Figure 7, we show the coverage in red of our S&D Patterns on ISO 27001 security management standard concepts in order to show the generality and coverage of security management notions by the considered patterns. Of course such coverage is not exhaustive as there can be significantly more patterns covering a single aspect of ISO 27001.

In the following, we present some sample of those security organizational patterns.

SP1 – Proof of Fulfillment for Ensuring Non-Repudiation

- **Context:** To accomplish its daily tasks an organization exploits its social infrastructure by decomposing each task into subtasks that are then distributed/delegated

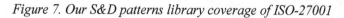

Figure 7. Our S&D patterns library coverage of ISO-27001

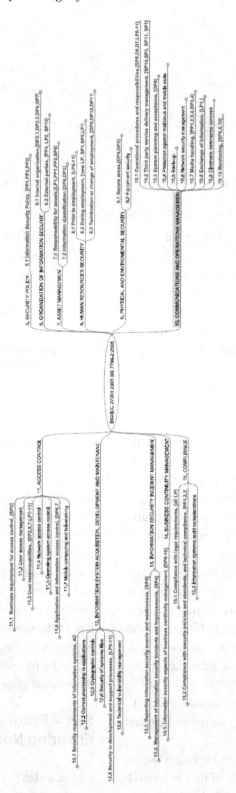

among groups of actors having pre-defined relations. The Delegator requests the achievement of a commitment and delegates its execution to the Executor, but the former has no warranties that the latter takes the responsibility of achieving the commitment.

- **Requirements:** The Delegator shall have evidence that the Executor cannot repudiate his commitment.
- **Solution:** The Delegator refines the commitment into two sub-parts. The first part is used to check the evidence about responsibilities taken by the Executor and the second represents the actual desire of fulfilling the commitment.

To achieve the commitment, the Delegator delegates the execution of the commitment to the Executor together with a request for a proof of commitment. Once received, this proof ensures the Delegator that the Executor has taken the responsibility of the commitment.

SP2 – Artefact Generation as an Audit Trail

- **Context:** This pattern concerns with any situation in which there is the need to share information, keep track of modification and promoting non-repudiation. Agent 1 and Agent 2 share Resource 1. Both Agent 1 and Agent 2 can read, modify and update data stored on Resource 1. This allows Agent 1 and Agent 2 to share information between and to keep track of the history of modifications on Resource 1.
- **Requirements:** It is necessary to enhance accountability by promoting non-repudiation and recording work and traceability of modifications. Additionally, the recorded data need to be stored securely, i.e., secured against unauthorized access and modifications, but this is not part of this pattern.

- **Solution:** Guarantee the possibility to retain details of individual work, allow attachments, comments, on the shared resource. It shows what has been changed, by whom, and why, maintaining a record always available for the workers. The resource is enhanced with an annotation system.

Patterns Usage

At runtime, the patterns library is used for ensuring that the fulfillment of the S&D requirements will be maintained whatever happen in the system and its environment (Serenity Consortium, 2008). In fact, the generic S&D solutions are implemented as executable components that are invoke-able by the applications through their known interface. The system reacts to context change by selecting the appropriate patterns to be deployed. At organizational level, we define different categories of implementations depending on the organizational infrastructure used by an organization to perform its business activities.

In this section, we show the deployment of the previously presented patterns in the context of the different scenarios.

eHealth Smart Items Based scenario

In this section we show how our S&D patterns have been deployed in the eHealth scenario.

Case Study 2: The objective of remote healthcare systems is to remotely monitor the patient health status and provide the necessary assistance. To reach this objective, healthcare systems should support the interaction and collaboration between doctors, pharmacists, patients, social workers and emergency medical teams especially during emergency situations.

Patient's health condition can be monitored through various wearable medical sensors worn as a washable smart T-shirts. All these sensors form the Body Sensor Network (BSN). The measured data are collected and pre-processed by a personal mobile hub such as a Personal Digital Assistant (PDA). Similarly, the patient's house is equipped with a sensor network and a local server, which centrally processes the sensor data, for monitoring the activity of the patient and the environmental setting. The information collected by the BSN and smart home are sent to the Monitoring and Emergency Response Centre (MERC), the organization responsible for the maintenance and storage of patient's medical data, such as the Electronic Health Record (EHR). The MERC processes such data to have a constant snapshot of the patient's health status and promptly initiates proper healthcare procedures when a potential emergency alert is identified. The logical architecture of the prototype is represented in Figure 8.

The smart items prototype aims at providing reliable monitoring capabilities and appropriate facilities to react in case of emergency. These activities are refined into: (1) enhancing situation awareness; (2) support decision making; (3) monitoring actions; (4) giving alerts and requests for urgent actions; (5) improving coordination and cooperation among the different actors. All these activities are tightly connected with the

usage of the S&D patterns listed above, as reported in Table 4.

The pattern DP1 (Redundancy for reliability) is applied to the Smart Items case study in several points. In the deployment process we followed the guidelines offered. The redundant service provider has to be installed and activated. Results of the redundant service provider has to some extends be homogeneous to the initial service provider's results. In such cases the mean is calculated and provided back to agent 1. If not then, in addition to the mean returned to agent1, a warming is also reported. Hereafter, we particularly highlight at the implementation level how we applied these guidelines. For example, in the Smart House, we had only one sensor reporting the status (open/closed) of the fridge's door. As the case for several other sensors, we installed a complementary sensor that plays the redundant service provider role. The first detects if the fridge is open and the second detects if somebody is in front of the bridge. Since we want to ensure reliability of the open action of the fridge, we applied the reliability pattern. Thus we used the second sensor as the redundant one function that checks the following: when sensor 1 reports that the fridge s door is open then sensor 2 has to detect that somebody is near the fridge (both sensors return Booleans values so the checking is trivial).

Moreover, the pattern SP1 (Proof of Fulfillment for Ensuring Non-Repudiation) is also applied in

Figure 8. Logical architecture of the smart items scenario

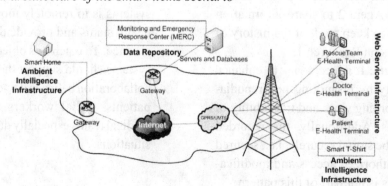

Table 4. Matching prototype functionalities to S&D patterns

Feature	DP1	SP1
Situation Awareness	X	X
Decision Support	X	-
Action Monitoring	X	X
Request for Action	-	X
Coordination	-	X

this prototype by using these provided guidelines: The executor has to sign and encrypt a message showing the fulfillment of the assigned work. This message is sent back to the benefiter as a proof of fulfillment. We learnt this best practice from this pattern and we applied it in several location of our prototype. An example of the implementation is applied to the JSP page used by Bob for sending the alert request. An alert is highly critical for the life of the patient. The WS alert WS (invoked by this JSP page) initiates the emergency process in the MERC s workflow. For auditing reasons, the alert WS should be able to proof the fulfillment of its expected actions.

The application of this pattern is by adding a notification operation to the operations supported by the alert WS. This notification is sent by the alert WS to the JSP to acknowledge the initiation of processing of the alert request. This notification signs the alert message identifier by the alert WS (the signature encompasses the name and

emergency level of the patient to eliminate some XML types of attacks) and then send it back to the JSP page, that is (required to be) stored as an xml document and that is shown as a notification at the JSP page. Part of the monitoring for this pattern is to verify whether resource holding the proof of commitment has been tampered. Basically, if the resource is not the same as the message sent by the alert WS, then it has been tampered (by checking the hashing).

A live demo of the system including the deployment of patterns is also illustrated in a video (Asnar et al., 2009).

Air Traffic Management Scenario

The Air Traffic Management (ATM) Scenario distilled robust solutions based on complex socio-technical organizations in order to provide a dependable assistance service to flights. In particular, the ATM Scenario concerns a case of Re-sectorisation (Figure 9) and Partial Airspace Delegation resulted from an unplanned increase of air traffic exceeding the sector capacity in an Italian Area Control Centre (ACC). The unusual and unexpected increase of traffic is due to two contemporary events: a World Convention in Germany and an ATCO's strike in progress in the France ACCs, at West of Italian ACCs.

Peculiarities of the ATM Scenario are: (1) the stress on organizational and management aspects

Figure 9. Re-Sectorisation of airspace

(a) Sectors in an Airspace (b) Airspace before re-sectorization (c) Airspace after re-sectorization

of S&D; (2) the focus on safety, dependability and resilience, more than on security. The S&D Patterns drawn from the analysis of the ATM scenario, and described in the previous section, explicitly state the roles that are supposed to be played by human operators. A runtime framework has been developed (ATM Coordination Tool-ATC) to deal with S&D solutions comprising human elements in order to improve the coordination among ATCOs. ATC aims to improve safety and efficiency of ATM by helping ATCOs in their daily work and by performing the following activities: (1) enhancing situation awareness; (2) support decision making; (3) monitoring actions; (4) giving alerts and requests for urgent actions; (5) improving coordination and cooperation among ATCOs. All these activities are tightly connected with the usage of the S&D patterns listed, as reported in Table 5.

The S&D patterns are used for: (1) enabling proactive functionalities for managing S&D properties provided by ACT; (2) ensuring the usage of already developed and fully validated S&D solutions. Thus ACT supports controllers' activities described above by implementing the following functionalities:

- **(F1) Reminder:** ACT reminds the controllers the Internal Permanent Instructions and any other information related to the daily situation;
- **(F2) Communicator:** ACT supports communication between controllers, i.e., discovery of active communication channels, delivery of messages, etc.;

- **(F3) Recorder:** the ACT records the commands issued by controllers in case of multiple possibilities and records all the controller inputs and actions in case of deviation from the existing rules (for statistical, reporting and auditing purposes);
- **(F4) Advisor:** the ACT supports controllers in establishing alternative action plans in order to deal with specific situations. Also the ATM daily activities enhanced by ACT and the four ACT s main functionalities are connected, as shown in Table 6.

We will report some practical examples about the usage of organizational patterns in the ATM Scenario, with respect to the relevant activities identified above and the specific ACT functionalities that support and improve them.

Situation Awareness: In ATM, the situation awareness of ATCOs is already widely implemented through a rich activity context full of technology, e.g., by means of electronic strip bay, radar display, weather forecast display. Notwithstanding ACT improves existing technologies, by using in particular two patterns: Multiple Representations of Information and Public Artefact. The ACT GUI and the Reminder and Communicator functionalities are designed on the basis of these patterns.

Example 12: ACT User Interface is different for the different roles (Executive, Planner or Supervisor) by highlighting different information in a different manner.

Table 5. Matching S&D patterns to prototype functionalities

Feature	SP4	DP1	DP2	DP3	DP4	DP5	DP6	DP7	DP8	DP9	DP10
Situation Awareness	-	-	X	X	X	X	X	X	X	X	X
Decision Support	-	-	-	X	X	X	-	-	-	X	X
Action Monitoring	X	X	-	-	X	-	-	X	-	-	-
Request for Action	-	X	X	-	-	-	X	-	-	-	-
Coordination	X	-	-	-	-	-	-	X	-	X	X

Table 6. Matching prototype features to controllers activities

Feature	F1	F2	F3	F4
Situation Awareness	X	X	-	X
Decision Support	X	-	-	X
Action Monitoring	-	-	X	-
Request for Action	-	X	-	X
Coordination	X	-	-	-

Example 13: ACT let communicate different actors and permits to share common information.

Monitoring Action: One can envision ACT as a watchful tool during critical performances or unexpected solutions. By using the RECORDER Functionality, ATCOs can monitor and record actions and decisions taken in risky situations in order to report them to the qualified authority. Related patterns are: Artifact as an Audit Trail and Evolution of Procedures.

Example 14: Some months later a similar situation is presented to another control team in a different ACC. The Supervisor checks in the System if there is a further procedure to manage safely the high traffic and the System propose the Delegation of Airspace already adopted, recorded by the tool and sent to the competent authority for becoming a new procedure.

Request for Action: ACT is a proactive tool able to promptly request for urgent and pressing activities to be performed by means of the REMINDER and ADVISOR functionalities. Patterns involved are, in particular: Public Artefact and Multiple Representations of Information.

Example 15: The PLC Paula notices on the ACT display that notwithstanding the re–sectori-

sation there is still a report for an increase of traffic exceeding the capacity of Sector SU 1.

Coordination (Cooperation Support): ACT, by its Communicator Functionality, can be used as a non intrusive dialogue tool, enhancing communication activity among ATCOs that permits to notify news or requests, ask for help and assistance, exchange information, interactively share and modify documents. Patterns involved are: Collaboration in Small Groups, Public Artefact (both in Example 12), Assistance trough Experience (Example 13).

Example 16: Robert and Mary (the Supervisors of the 2 ACCs) consider the possibility to perform a vertical re-sectorisation of Sector SU 1 extending the upper limit of Sector N from FL 280 to unlimited.

Example 17. The PLC Paula notifies the expected increase of traffic to the SUP Robert, by communicating the amount of expected traffic. Paula points out the situation to Robert asking for a solution.

In this section we showed how S&D organizational patterns account for ATM organizational and procedural aspects, thus enabling the definition and implementation of software functionalities that support the ATM activity and enhance the safety and the overall resilience of the System (Di Giacomo et al., 2008).

RELATED WORKS AND CONCLUSION

Many works have been proposed for modeling and evaluating dependable mission critical systems (SQUALE Consortium, 1999; Stamatelatos et al., 2002; Van Lamsweerde et al., 2003). The most appropriate type of model framework depends on the complexity of system behavior and the S&D requirements to be taken into account.

State-space based models include Markov models and high level approaches which have an underlying Markov model. These models provide great expressiveness for dependability specifications and have been extensively applied to model the dependability and to analyze the hardware software reliability (Zhang et al., 2005). This class of models includes queuing networks and Generalized Stochastic Petri Nets (Betous-Almeida et al., 2002; Fota et al., 1998), which have been the most commonly used. Recently, many frameworks based on UML (Gabor et al., 2000) have been proposed. Generally, they propose to embed Petri Nets for describing the system properties and validating the solutions.

In this article, we have presented how to capture the knowledge of S&D experts using the *SI** framework, how to elicit organizational S&D patterns and how to deploy them into different scenarios. We present in this section the concluding remarks expressed by the prototype developers who used the S&D patterns to build real systems. The usage of the organizational patterns varies according to the infrastructure deployed by the organization.

The smart items scenario is composed of a combination of three publicly available infrastructures namely WIFI, GSM, and GPRS communication networks. This results in a hybrid communication architecture that meets the high reliability needs strongly required by our e-health case study. Patients' e-health remote assistance is accomplished by means of a set of workflows properly defined in, stored, and maintained by the MERC. The MERC comprises of hybrid infrastructure made

four types of infrastructures, namely, SOA web services, human resource, Data Protection Directive (Directive 95/46/EC) and the sensors and actuators in the Smart House.

In the ATM scenario, we have investigated how S&D patterns can inform at runtime the reaction to threats or attacks. In particular, we are concerned about how, during the unfolding of unexampled threats or attacks, S&D patterns could enable an ad-hoc reaction. In this context, S&D patterns provide models for reaction processes because: (1) patterns represent the portion of the reaction process that is relevant to S&D features; (2) reaction processes adjust their behavior in order to reflect changes into S&D patterns;(3) S&D patterns specify what parts of the processes can be automatically interpreted and those parts that are left to interpretation to users. The prototype relies on the runtime framework (Serenity Consortium, 2008a), which manages the matching between a reaction plan, its execution and the S&D patterns. The actors participating in the reaction process exploits, directly via the run-time framework console or indirectly via the interface or logic of the application, the knowledge formalized by S&D patterns.

REFERENCES

Anderson, R. (1993). Why cryptosystems fail. In *Proceedings of the 1st ACM Conference on Computer and Communications Security* (pp. 215-227).

Anderson, R. (2001). *Security engineering: A guide to building dependable distributed systems*. New York, NY: John Wiley & Sons.

Asnar, Y., Bonato, R., Giorgini, P., Massacci, F., Meduri, V., Riccucci, C., & Saidane, A. (2007). Secure and dependable patterns in organizations: An empirical approach. In *Proceedings of the IEEE International Conference on Requirements Engineering* (pp. 287-292).

Asnar, Y., Dalpiaz, F., Massacci, F., Nguyen, V. H., & Saidane, A. (2009). *Security and dependability engineering for ambient assisted living: A report on the research results by UniTN*. Retrieved from http://www.disi.unitn.it/~massacci/Download/SERENITY-MPEG.mpg

Asnar, Y., Moretti, R., Sebastianis, M., & Zannone, N. (2008). Risk as dependability metrics for the evaluation of business solutions: A model-driven approach. In *Proceedings of the 3rd International Workshop on Dependability Aspects on Data Warehousing and Mining Applications* (pp. 1240-1248).

Betous-Almeida, C., & Kanoun, K. (2002). Stepwise construction and refinement of dependability models. In *Proceedings of the Conference on Dependable Systems and Networks* (pp. 515-524).

Bresciani, P., Giorgini, P., Giunchiglia, F., Mylopoulos, J., & Perini, A. (2004). TROPOS: An agent-oriented software development methodology. *Journal of Autonomous Agents and Multi-agent Systems, 8*(3), 203–236. doi:10.1023/B:AGNT.0000018806.20944.ef

Busnel, P., El Khoury, P., Li, K., Saidane, A., & Zannone, N. (2008). S&D pattern deployment at organizational level: A prototype for remote healthcare system. *Electronic Notes in Theoretical Science, 244*, 27–39. doi:10.1016/j.entcs.2009.07.036

Compagna, L., Khoury, P. E., Krausová, A., Massacci, F., & Zannone, N. (2009). How to integrate legal requirements into a requirements engineering methodology for the development of security and privacy patterns. *Artificial Intelligence and Law, 17*(1), 1–30. doi:10.1007/s10506-008-9067-3

Dardenne, A., van Lamsweerde, A., & Fickas, S. (1993). Goal-directed requirements acquisition. *Science of Computer Programming, 20*, 3–50. doi:10.1016/0167-6423(93)90021-G

Dempster, A. (2008). The dempster-shafer calculus for statisticians. *International Journal of Approximate Reasoning, 48*(2), 365–377. doi:10.1016/j.ijar.2007.03.004

Di Giacomo, V., Felici, M., Meduri, V., Presenza, D., Riccucci, C., & Tedeschi, A. (2008). Using security and dependability patterns for reaction processes. In *Proceedings of the 19th International Conference on Database and Expert Systems* (pp. 315-319).

Elahi, G., & Yu, E. (2007). A goal oriented approach for modeling and analyzing security trade-offs. In C. Parent, K.-D. Schewe, V. C. Storey, & B. Thalheim (Eds.), *Proceedings of the 26th International Conference on Conceptual Modeling* (LNCS 4801, pp. 375-390).

Fota, N., Kaaniche, M., & Kanoun, K. (1998). Dependability evaluation of an air traffic control computing system. In *Proceedings of the 3rd IEEE International Symposium on Computer Performance and Dependability* (pp. 206-215).

Gabor, H., & Istvin, M. (2000). Quantitative analysis of dependability critical systems based on UML statechart models. In *Proceedings of the 5th IEEE International Symposium on High Assurance Systems Engineering* (pp. 83-92).

Gamma, E., Helm, R., Johnson, R., & Glissades, J. (1994). *Design patterns: Elements of reusable object-oriented software*. Reading, MA: Addison-Wesley.

Giorgini, P., Massacci, F., Mylopoulos, J., & Zannone, N. (2005a). Modeling security requirements through ownership, permission and delegation. *International Journal of Information Security, 5*(4), 257–274. doi:10.1007/s10207-006-0005-7

Giorgini, P., Massacci, F., & Zannone, N. (2005b). Security and trust requirements engineering. In A. Aldini, R. Gorrieri, & F. Martinelli (Eds.), *Proceedings of the Tutorial Lectures on Foundations of Security Analysis and Design III* (LNCS 3655, pp. 237-272).

Kolmogorov, A. N. (1956). *Foundations of the theory of probability* (2nd ed.). Providence, RI: Chelsea Publishing.

Liu, L., Yu, E. S. K., & Mylopoulos, J. (2003). Security and privacy requirements analysis within a social setting. In *Proceedings of the IEEE International Conference on Requirements Engineering* (pp. 151-161).

Massacci, F., & Zannone, N. (2008). A model-driven approach for the specification and analysis of access control policies. In R. Meersman & Z. Tari (Eds.), *Proceedings of the Confederated International Conferences of On the Movie to Meaningful Internet Systems* (LNCS 5332, pp. 1087-1103).

Schumacher, M. (2003). *Security engineering with patterns: Origins, theoretical models, and new applications*. Berlin, Germany: Springer-Verlag.

Serenity Consortium. (2008a). *A7.d4.2 - Scenario S&D solutions*. Retrieved from http://www.serenity-project.org

Serenity Consortium. (2008b). *A6.D3.2 - Specification of serenity architecture*. Retrieved from http://www.serenity-project.org

Serenity Consortium. (2009). *The final set of S&D patterns at organizational level*. Retrieved from http://www.serenity-project.org

SQUALE Consortium. (1999). *SQUALE: Security, safety and quality evaluation for dependable systems*. Retrieved from http://spiderman-2.laas.fr/TSF/cabernet/squale/

Stamatelatos, M., Vesely, W., Dugan, J., Fragola, J., Minarick, J., & Railsback, J. (2002). *Fault tree handbook with aerospace applications*. Retrieved from http://www.hq.nasa.gov/office/codeq/doctree/fthb.pdf

Van Lamsweerde, A., Brohez, S., Landtsheer, R. D., & Janssens, D. (2003). From system goals to intruder anti-goals: Attack generation and resolution for security requirements engineering. In *Proceedings of the International Conference on High Assurance Systems Engineering*.

Yoder, J., & Barcalow, J. (1997). Architectural patterns for enabling application security. In *Proceedings of the Conference on Pattern Languages of Programs*.

Zhang, Z., Shen, H., Defago, X., & Sang, Y. (2005). A brief comparative study on analytical models of computer system dependability and security. In *Proceedings of the 6th International Conference on Parallel and Distributed Computing Applications and Technologies* (pp. 493-497).

This work was previously published in the International Journal of Secure Software Engineering, Volume 2, Issue 3, edited by Khaled M. Khan, pp. 1-22, copyright 2011 by IGI Publishing (an imprint of IGI Global).

Chapter 5
Not Ready for Prime Time:
A Survey on Security in Model Driven Development

Jostein Jensen
Norwegian University of Science and Technology, Norway

Martin Gilje Jaatun
SINTEF, Norway

ABSTRACT

Model Driven Development (MDD) is by many considered a promising approach for software development. This article reports the results of a systematic survey to identify the state-of-the-art within the topic of security in model driven development, with a special focus on finding empirical studies. The authors provide an introduction to the major secure MDD initiatives, but the survey shows that there is a lack of empirical work on the topic. The authors conclude that better standardization initiatives and more empirical research in the field is necessary before it can be considered mature.

1. INTRODUCTION

Model Driven Development (MDD) has been considered a promising approach to software development since its introduction about a decade ago. The Object Management Group (OMG, 2010) is the most prominent standardization body within the MDD domain, and has developed a framework for model driven development called Model Driven Architecture (MDA). MDA is a framework for developing applications and writing specifications, where improved portability, platform independence and cross-platform interoperability are among keywords used by OMG to describe the benefits of using this framework.

Kleppe et al. (2003) present the MDA development lifecycle. The basis for development is platform independent models (PIM), which

DOI: 10.4018/978-1-4666-2482-5.ch005

specify functionality and behavior. These models are abstracted away from the technology that will be used to realize the system. PIMs can then be transformed into platform specific models (PSM), adding technology specific details to the PIM. PSM again can then be transformed into code. Kleppe and colleagues also mention a third model type used during the requirements and analysis phase of development, called computational independent model (CIM).

Figure 1 shows the MDA software development lifecycle as it is depicted by Kleppe et al. (2003). The ovals to the left represent generic software development phases, while the squares to the right represent artifacts produced in an MDA context. Artifacts developed during the requirements phase and used for analysis are often referred to as Computational Independent Models (CIM). Platform independent models (PIM) are abstract representations of the system to be built, and independent of any implementation technology. PIMs are transformed, preferably automatically using tool support, to Platform Specific Models. These are specific to the technology that will be used to realize future systems. Continuing the MDA lifecycle, PSMs are transformed into

code. Since PSMs are close to the technology, this transformation is by some considered to be straightforward (Kleppe et al., 2003).

Note that real life seldom has a perfect match for theoretical frameworks such as the MDA lifecycle presented in Figure 1. Thus, in concrete examples one will not always find that all the models such as CIM, PIM and PSM are actually used in practice, and in such cases one must modify the map to fit the terrain.

PIMs form the basis for low-level system designs and as such constitute an important part of a system's documentation (while still providing important abstractions). The layering between platform independent models, platform specific models and code are the key to solve problems related to portability, platform independence and interoperability. Developers are mainly supposed to work with the platform independent models, and since these are platform and technology neutral it should be a relatively simple task to transform them into different platforms and technology solutions.

In traditional software development, security aspects are often considered late in the development lifecycle, if they are considered at all (Wyk & McGraw, 2005). However, the cost of eliminating

Figure 1. MDA Software development lifecycle

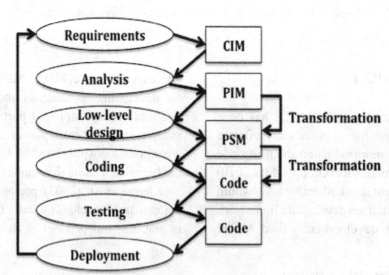

security flaws increases by magnitudes the later they are discovered and fixed (Boehm & Basili, 2001). A good recommendation has therefore been to include security aspects from the very start of software projects (Tøndel, Jaatun, & Meland, 2008). The Microsoft Security Development Lifecycle (Howard & Lipner, 2006) and McGraw's touchpoints (McGraw, 2006) illustrate how security activities can be included in every phase of a software project.

With its focus on high-quality design in early development phases through detailed PIM modeling, MDD/MDA should be a well suited development framework to include security aspects in design models from the very start of a project. Consistent and sound security solutions throughout the entire application could be the result.

The remainder of this article is organized as follows: In Section 2 we present our research questions, followed by a description of our research method in Section 3. We present our results in Section 4, and discuss our findings in Section 5. Section 6 concludes the article.

2. RESEARCH QUESTIONS

This article reports results related to a systematic survey that was carried out in order to learn how scientific communities deal with security in model driven development. The study aims to answer the following research questions:

RQ1: What are the major scientific initiatives describing automatic code generation from design models within the context of security in MDD?

RQ2: What empirical studies exist on the topic "security within MDD/MDA"?

RQ3: What are the strengths of the evidence showing that security aspects successfully can be modeled as an inherent property and transformed to more secure code?

3. METHOD

A systematic literature review approach (Kitchenham, 2004) is used as research method leading to the results presented in this article. This method requires rigor with respect to planning, conducting, and reporting the review. The aim of this systematic survey was to identify scientific literature that could provide answers to our research questions listed in the previous section.

3.1. Identification of Research

The starting point for the survey is a research protocol where the research questions and the search strategy are defined. To support the paper selection process, the protocol also specifies inclusion and exclusion criteria. A rigorous and comprehensive search is key to identify all the relevant scientific literature. Both sources for scientific literature and search phrases were specified prior to the search. We used four online databases for scientific literature to search for studies:

- IEEE Xplore (http://ieeexplore.ieee.org/)
- ACM Digital Library (http://portal.acm.org/dl.cfm)
- ISI Web of Knowledge (http://apps.isiknowledge.com)
- Compendex (http://www.engineeringvillage2.org/)

According to experiences made by Dybå et al. (2007), this should be sufficient to find relevant literature within the information systems field. The use of other databases will lead to duplicate findings, and as such, lead to extra work. For each of these databases we used the following search phrase and keywords:

1. "Model driven development"
2. "Model driven architecture"
3. MDD
4. MDA
5. Security

These were combined as follows: (1 OR 2 OR 3 OR 4) AND 5.

The searches were performed March 12, 2010, meaning that scientific literature indexed up until then are included within this study. The search resulted in a total of 2844 titles that needed to be evaluated based on title, abstract and content. We performed a follow-up search in June 2011, which yielded an initial result of 27 titles (these are treated separately).

3.2. Selection of Primary Studies

All references and abstracts were imported to the reference tool EndNote. The next step was to exclude papers based on titles. All titles that clearly did not treat the wanted topics were filtered out. After this process a total of 366 studies remained. The following task was to read through the abstracts of these papers and evaluate whether they were relevant or not. For both these steps the following exclusion criteria were used:

- Exclude everything that is clearly not related to model driven software development.

Our research interest is on use of models to generate code. Some studies e.g., present research where MDD principles are used to generate firewall rules. Such studies were excluded.

- Exclude everything that clearly not concerns both model driven development and security research.

122 papers remained after reading the abstracts, and these papers were all read to make a final evaluation whether they should be part of our primary studies or not. This evaluation resulted in 56 remaining papers. A last exclusion criterion was used for the purpose of this article in order to answer RQ1:

- Exclude studies by authors and research groups who have published 3 or fewer papers on the topic.

There is a chance that this exclusion criterion can give a somewhat inaccurate view of the current state, as some important initiatives conceivably could be treated and enhanced by a large number of research groups, but where each individual group has not published more than 3 papers. For the purpose of this article, it is however considered sufficient to give a rough idea about the current state. With this last exclusion criterion the number of papers to include as primary studies in this report was limited to 30.

3.3. Quality Assessment, Classification and Synthesis

RQ2 and RQ3 can only be answered with a scientific validity if empirical studies following a rigorous research protocol on the topic are found. However, within the topic of model driven development and security, this study shows that no empirical studies seem to exist. Within this article we therefore give a short introduction to the included papers considered for answering RQ1. Studies are grouped based on the originating research groups. A qualitative reflection about how MDD and security is covered in existing research works is given at the end of this article.

4. RESULTS

Our survey identified 5 research approaches which will be described in the following.

4.1. Model Driven Security

One of the earliest initiatives for including security in model driven architecture came from Basin et al. (2003). Their solution, called Model Driven Security (MDS), is a specialization of the

MDA approach. Security models are integrated with what Basin et al. call UML process models, and the combined models are transformed into executable systems with integrated security infrastructures. The focus of their work is to include access control constraints based on role based access control (RBAC) in design models. They describe a security metamodel for expressing RBAC properties in UML, and this UML extension is called SecureUML (see Figure 2, adapted from Basin et al., 2006). Basin et al. (2006) give a more detailed description of the Model Driven Security approach, while Clavel et al. (2008) build on this work to gain practical experience with the approach. See also Section 5.1 for more discussion on MDS.

4.2. SECTET

Alam et al. (2004) describe an approach to specify role-based access control policies for web services using the Object Constraint Language (OCL). OCL was initially a language extension of UML and is used to ensure a platform independent specification of access control policies. This work is used and extended by Breu et al. (2005) who show how security can be built into web service-based systems supporting inter-organizational workflows. To model inter-organizational workflows they specify three model levels: global workflow model, local workflow model and interface model. The global workflow models show an abstract view of interactions between autonomous organizations, the local workflow models show intraorganizational workflows within each organization, and the interface models present the services offered by each component in the system. OCL is used together with the interface models to describe access control constraints for operations/services provided by a web service. The same team builds on these concepts in a later publication (Hafner, Breu, Breu, & Nowak, 2005) where the focus is to integrate security into the global workflow model. They use OCL-like expressions to assign security qualities such as confidentiality and integrity to data sent between actors.

The research team behind the above mentioned reports (Alam et al., 2004; Breu et al., 2005; Hafner et al., 2005) has built on these results and come up with a model driven security framework called SECTET. Three software engineering paradigms are combined in this framework (Hafner & Breu, 2009): Model Driven Architecture as methodical concept, Service Oriented Architecture as architectural paradigm, and web services as technical standard. The three model levels described above is kept, and the OCL security policy definitions are refined into an OCL-based language they call SECTET-PL. Alam et al. (2006) present the SECTET framework with a focus on integrating

Figure 2. SecureUML metamodel

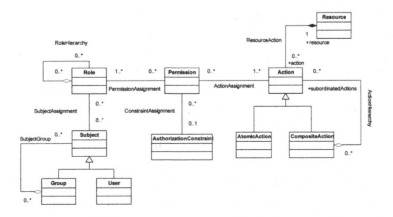

access control policies in the interface models. They give a detailed description on how they specify dynamic access control constraints using SECTET-PL, and how these policy rules are combined with UML models at the interface level. In Alam, Hafner, Breu, and Unterthiner (2007) SECTET-PL is used to describe how delegation rights in service-oriented architectures can be implemented, and in Alam, Breu, and Hafner (2007) and Alam, Seifert, and Xinwen (2007) SECTET is presented in a trust management perspective.

While the early reports (Alam et al., 2004; Breu et al., 2005; Hafner et al., 2005) only were at the idea phase (Alam et al., 2006) describes the whole tool chain to carry out model-to-model transformation and model-to-code transformation. They define UML meta-models for their concepts to formalize the modeling process sufficiently to allow tool-supported transformations, and Hafner et al. (2006) focus on using the OMG transformation specification Meta Object Facility Query/View/Transformation (MOF-QVT: http://www.omg.org/spec/QVT/1.1/Beta2/) to formalize transformation rules.

Fernandez-Medina et al. (2009) describe the SECTET-framework to be one of the most complete frameworks to integrate security engineering with Model Driven Architecture.

4.3. Secure Development of Data Warehouses

Data warehouses (DW) are repositories where enterprises electronically can store data from their various business systems (http://searchsqlserver.techtarget.com/definition/data-warehouse). This is done to facilitate reporting and analysis of the data. Often data is "… extracted from multiple heterogeneous, autonomous, and distributed sources of information" (Soler, Trujillo, Fernandez-Medina, & Piattini, 2007b). Single data elements in the repository can be sensitive, but also the total amount of business information collected soon becomes business sensitive. Soler et al. (2007b) therefore argue that security engineering must be

included from the earliest phases of development of such systems. Soler and his colleagues (Soler et al., 2007b; Soler, Trujillo, Fernandez-Medina, & Piattini, 2007c; Soler, TruJillo, Fernandez-Medina, & Piattini, 2007a) argue that MDA is a well suited development framework to create DW solutions, but with the disadvantage that the MDA framework does not include mechanisms to sufficiently express security requirements (it may be argued that such mechanisms were never intended to be a part of MDA), and as such perform a transformation from PIM to PSM. In their work based on the UML modeling language they show how they use UML profiles and model a security enriched PIM meta-model for the DW domain. In their framework, they also provide a set of QVT transformation rules so that PIMs can be transformed and mapped to concepts in a security enriched PSM meta-model that they also have defined. In addition to the security concepts defined in the two meta-models, dynamic security rules, such as audit and authorization rules can be added to the model using the OCL language. While Soler et al. focused on PIM to PSM transformations, Blanco et al. (Blanco, de Guzman, Fernandez-Medina, Trujillo, & Piattini, 2008; Blanco, Fernandez-Medina, Trujillo, & Piattini, 2008) build on this work and demonstrate with a prototype that it is feasible to go all the way in the MDA lifecycle, from secure PIMs to secure PSM to code with security properties, in order to build secure data warehouses. Soler et al. (2009) supplement this work.

The framework for development of secure data warehouses is further extended in Soler et al. (2008) and Trujillo, Soler, Fernández-Medina, and Piattini (2009b). In these works the authors build on the i* modeling language, which is designed to support modeling of business requirements. i* concepts are converted to a UML profile to fit the DW MDA approach, and some extensions are made to the original i* concepts to be able to sufficiently express security requirements in the DW domain. This new i* UML-profile supports elicitation of requirements at the business level, and is considered as being a CIM. Guidelines for transforming the business security requirements models to PIM are given to align the approach with MDA.

Blanco et al. (2009) present an approach for modernizing existing DWs by means of the above mentioned techniques for secure DW development. By going backwards in a reverse engineering style, they claim that code for existing DWs, presumably with insufficient security, can be analyzed and converted to a PSM. This PSM is again transformed into a PIM, and finally a CIM. Now, the CIM can be analyzed from a business perspective. Security requirements can be added, and then the new secure DW approach can be followed to get a more secure DW with the same functionality as it had before modernization.

To bring the secure DW MDA approach closer to completion, Trujillo et al. (2009a) define an engineering process to support the framework shown in Figure 3 (adapted from Trujillo et al., 2009a). This paper defines the process that starts with i*-based CIM models, which are transformed into secure PIMs, PSMs and code through transformation T1 to T3. It shows that security can be included from the very beginning of a project by using an MDA approach.

4.4. Security in Business Process Models

Rodriguez et al. (2006a, 2006b) present initial ideas on how UML 2.0 activity diagrams, which are used to model business processes, can be enriched to include security properties. The authors claim that the advantage of including security in the business process modeling stage is that this important aspect then can be included from the very beginning of a software development project, and that a business analyst's considerations about security can be captured. They define a UML profile consistent with OMG MOF, similar to the ideas of Hafner et al. (2006). A graphical notation to represent security requirements is added to the activity diagram notation. In Rodriguez, Fernandez-Medina, and Piattini (2007) the same authors suggest how the business process models, which they consider to be CIMs, can be transformed into use case models, which they consider to be PIMs. The transformation process is based on OMGs QVT specification, checklists and refinement rules. The feasibility of the approach is demonstrated through a prototype tool (Rodriguez, Fernandez-Medina, & Piattini, 2008). Use case models are often the starting point in software development projects where they are used to capture functional requirements. With this work, functional security requirements can be visually illustrated from the start in these models.

4.5. Secure Smart Card Application Development

Moebius et al. (2009a, 2009b) and Moebius, Stenzel, and Reif (2009) use a model driven approach, which they call secureMDD, to develop security critical applications for smart cards. Their illustrating case is the development of an application that can be used for payment. From the PIMs they design, a transformation to three new

Figure 3. Framework for designing secure data warehouses

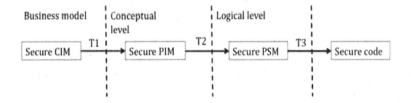

model types is made: to card PSM, to terminal PSM and to a formal PSM. The two first model types define the functionality on, and interaction between the payment card and the terminal in which the card is used. The latter is a formal security specification of their models that can be analyzed to determine the correctness with respect to security of their models.

Moebius and her colleagues emphasize the importance of both modeling static and dynamic aspects of the application. UML is the preferred modeling language in their approach.

The secureMDD approach is introduced in Moebius, Stenzel et al. (2009b), and the approach to go from PIM to PSM to code is specified in more detail in Moebius, Stenzel et al. (2009a). Class diagrams are used to model an application's static view, while sequence and activity diagrams are used for modeling of dynamic aspects. The transformation from PIMs to formal specifications is shown in Moebius, Stenzel, and Reif (2009).

4.6. Recent Contributions

We repeated the search procedure in June 2011, in order to determine if studies published after the acceptance of our SecSE paper (Jensen & Jaatun, 2011) were likely to affect our results. The initial search yielded an additional 27 papers, but on closer examination, none of the papers provided significantly new information. However, we find it prudent to mention two survey articles published in 2011. The first is published by the group responsible for the Model Driven Security concept (Basin, Clavel, & Egea, 2011), and is primarily a stock-taking of their own work over the last decade.

The second survey is an independent contribution (Kasal, Heurix, & Neubauer, 2011) which in one way is complementary to our own, in that none of the approaches they discuss satisfy the "executability" criterion (see Table 1 in their paper). In our opinion, their survey is less focused than our own, since they cover both UMLsec

(Jürjens, 2005), aspect-oriented approaches and formal security protocol analysis tools. It is thus not surprising that they conclude that none of the approaches have general applicability, and different approaches may be most suitable depending on the case at hand.

5. DISCUSSION

The premise of MDD/MDA is that developers will use model-based tools to develop general software. This premise was challenged during the audience discussion after the presentation of our SecSE paper (Jensen & Jaatun, 2011), and opinions were voiced to the effect that MDD will only be used for software deemed to be particularly critical with respect to safety or security. Several members of the audience expressed doubts to whether MDD/MDA will ever find its way to the mainstream developer community.

5.1. What Can We Learn from the Literature?

The existing papers on the topic can be categorized as lessons learned or experience reports, where approaches are demonstrated primarily by implementing prototypes. They provide little evidence to prove that the final code is more secure or better than what it would have been if another development approach had been used. The contribution that comes closest to being an empirical study is the paper written by Clavel et al. (2008). They provide an experience report where the Model Driven Security (MDS) approach defined by Basin et al. (Section 4.1) has been tested in an industrial setting. Their feedback on the approach is quite optimistic, and with respect to MDS their major findings are

- "The security design models integrate security models with system design models, remaining at the same time technology independent, reusable, and evolvable."

- "The security design models are understandable by those familiar with the UML-notation"
- The security-enhanced models were "expressive enough to model the access control policy defined in the original requirements document" provided by their clients.

This seems promising, but there are still several challenges that should be addressed in the coming years. Some of the promises of MDD/MDA are that the approach will ensure portability, platform independence and cross-platform interoperability. However, the studies included in this article all explain different approaches for including security into the modeling languages and the processes they use. Since it is recognized that security modeling is not part of any standardization initiatives for MDD, e.g., MDA, researchers define their own extensions to existing modeling languages to model the security aspects they need for their projects. An example of this is the use of OCL, which is the standardized UML constraint language used as starting point for specifying dynamic security aspects in the two most complete MDA frameworks: SECTET and secure DW. Both research teams found limitations with respect to modeling security constraints in the OCL language. Consequently, they started adapting it. In the SECTET framework, the SECTET-PL was the resulting constraint language used, and in the DW design they extended a DW UML profile in order to better integrate concepts from the OCL expressions into their models. In general, standardization initiatives exist with the purpose of encouraging the development of interoperable systems, so when standards are adapted and extended in different ways by different research teams it can be questioned whether final systems really will be interoperable and portable and so on.

McDermott (2005) argues that one topic not sufficiently covered within security modeling, is

related to modeling of security protocols. Moebius and her colleagues treat this in their approach for secure smart card application development. However, they do not follow a standardized MDD approach such as the MDA framework. At the same time it can be questioned whether the descriptions of their approach is sufficient to reconstruct their transformations from PIMs expressing protocol information to PSMs and then code. Thus, McDermott's point still seems to be valid.

A key ingredient in MDD is the transformation rules guiding conversion from PIM to PSM to code. Based on the papers included in this study, the transformation rule development seems like a complex task, which requires a lot of expertise both with respect to the used development approach and technology platforms. This raises questions whether the team of security experts responsible for analyzing security needs and requirements, also need to be experts on the modeling approach. If a transformation rule is flawed in a sense that it does not correctly transform a security requirement/model to code, then the whole system's security can be compromised. Security experts should therefore also be able to evaluate the quality of transformation rules in all parts of the transformation chain to successfully benefit from the promises of security in MDD. Unfortunately, the situation seems to be that development teams and security teams often are separated, and that the real security experts usually do not themselves develop software (Wyk & McGraw, 2005). This situation must be changed if high-quality secure code is going to be produced in an MDD context with automated code generation.

There is one important topic related to security that has not been discussed in the papers identified in this study; the possibility to model input validation constraints. Data sent to interfaces should be validated before they are accepted. Both the length and type of data must be checked in order to avoid security vulnerabilities related to injection attacks. To date, these types of vulnerabilities are the most prevalent security flaws in existing web applications (OWASP, 2011). It should be possible to include modeling of input validation constraints in order to eliminate injection attack threats from the start of software development, similar to modeling of access control constraints.

5.2. Excluded Studies

There have been significant initiatives on topics related to this study that have been excluded due to RQ1 and the exclusion criteria used for the purpose of selecting primary studies. A notable example is UMLsec, an extension of UML supporting secure systems development (Jürjens, 2005). Security requirements such as confidentiality, integrity and authenticity can be modeled in UML diagrams through the extension mechanisms stereotypes and tags. Modeling with UMLsec and analysis of industrial systems using this approach is even tested in industrial projects (Best, Jurjens, & Nuseibeh, 2007; Jürjens, Schreck, & Bartmann, 2008; Lloyd & Jürjens, 2009). However, even though UMLsec is an important contribution to security engineering research in general and in the core of security in model driven development, papers on this topic were excluded due to our focus on automatic code generation.

Another topic not dealt with in this study is aspect oriented modeling. In aspect oriented modeling crosscutting concerns for an application, or aspects, are treated separately. Each aspect is then modeled and, by tool support, woven together into the final product. Examples of what an aspect might be include security, mobility and availability. Aspect oriented modeling papers were excluded since security was not treated specifically, but as one of several aspects. Still, we recognize that this approach may be worth looking into in future studies.

In the past there have been attempts to identify empirical research on the wide topic of model driven development. The systematic survey performed by Haug (2007) returned a total of 21 papers, but this was only 2.2% of the studies from the initial search; none with special focus on security. There were, however, limitations in this study with respect to sources used to find relevant literature; only selected journals and conference proceedings were searched. One of the key objectives of the review presented in this article was to identify empirical studies on the topic of security in MDD, which is a narrow field compared to what Haug presented. A search strategy with a wider scope with respect to publication databases was used in hope of finding relevant literature despite the findings by Haug. However, the observations made in our study (including the studies that are not presented in this article) indicate that such empirical studies do not exist for the topic of security in Model Driven Development.

5.3. Further Work

From the discussion above, the following paths for future research are identified:

- Empirical research should be performed to determine whether security successfully can be included properly in MDD/MDA to build more secure systems.
- Modeling of security should be included as a standardization activity in the MDD frameworks, such as MDA.
- More research should be performed related to how security protocols can be modeled and transformed to final systems.
- Research should be performed to find an approach for modeling of input validation constraints.

Additionally, a follow up of what is presented within this article seems natural. Here we have presented an introduction to the major initiatives within the field of security in MDD. Future work must cover a deeper analysis, which includes evaluating the maturity of the presented approaches, to see if they are ready to be applied within an industrial setting. It is also worth studying the main differences and commonalities of each approach to determine to what extent their elements can be combined or reconciled. Finally, it is worth looking into a refinement of the research protocol, maybe widen the scope of the research questions and exclusion criteria, so that initiatives such as UMLsec and Aspect Oriented Modeling will be covered.

A more fundamental challenge, however, resides in the area of measuring code security, i.e., comparing two pieces of code to determine which is most "secure". Current approaches are limited to counting the accumulated number of discovered bugs/flaws in a software product (CVE, 2011), or (reverse) modeling a given implementation and comparing it to an "ideal" model (Best et al., 2007; Jürjens et al., 2008; Lloyd & Jürjens, 2009) the latter approach assumes that the "ideal" model always will produce more secure code, but unless you can measure the security property, there is no way to know for sure. It is not clear whether this problem is solvable, and we are not aware that anyone is currently working on it. The authors of UMLsec state that "Automated theorem provers and model checkers automatically establish whether the security requirements hold" (Jürjens et al., 2008), but this is no panacea if the security requirements themselves are flawed (or missing).

In order to minimize potential bias in this study, the inclusion and exclusion criteria in the research protocol have been followed stringently. Yet, it is recognized that this is not the optimal situation. The consequences of this threat to validity would, however, have been more severe in a study where empirical evidence would have been subject to quantitative meta-analysis. This article reports the state-of-the art merely, and provides a qualitative reflection on this.

6. CONCLUSION

In this article we have presented state-of-the art within security research in model driven development and identified the most comprehensive works. The study shows that there is a need for more empirical studies on the topic, and we believe that standardization is key to achieve the objectives of MDD/MDA, which are increased portability and interoperability.

REFERENCES

Alam, M., Breu, R., & Breu, M. (2004). Model driven security for web services (MDS4WS). In *Proceedings of the 8th International Multitopic Conference* (pp. 498-505).

Alam, M., Breu, R., & Hafner, M. (2007). Model-driven security engineering for trust management in SECTET. *Journal of Software*, *2*(1). doi:10.4304/jsw.2.1.47-59

Alam, M., Hafner, M., & Breu, R. (2006). Constraint based role based access control (CRBAC) for restricted administrative delegation constraints in the SECTET. In *Proceedings of the International Conference on Privacy, Security, and Trust: Bridge the Gap between PST Technologies and Business Services*, Markham, ON, Canada.

Alam, M., Hafner, M., Breu, R., & Unterthiner, S. (2007). A framework for modelling restricted delegation of rights in the SECTET. *Computer Systems Science and Engineering*, *22*, 289–305.

Alam, M., Seifert, J. P., & Xinwen, Z. (2007). A model-driven framework for trusted computing based systems. In *Proceedings of the 11th IEEE International Enterprise Distributed Object Computing Conference* (pp. 75-75).

Basin, D., Clavel, M., & Egea, M. (2011). A decade of model-driven security. In *Proceedings of the 16th ACM Symposium on Access Control Models and Technologies.*

Basin, D., Doser, J., & Lodderstedt, T. (2003, June 2-3). Model driven security for process-oriented systems. In *Proceedings of the 8th ACM Symposium on Access Control Models and Technologies*, Villa Gallia, Como, Italy.

Basin, D., Doser, J., & Lodderstedt, T. (2006). Model driven security: From UML models to access control infrastructures. *ACM Transactions on Software Engineering and Methodology, 15*(1), 39–91. doi:10.1145/1125808.1125810

Best, B., Jurjens, J., & Nuseibeh, B. (2007). Model-based security engineering of distributed information systems using UMLsec. In *Proceedings of the 29th International Conference on Software Engineering.*

Blanco, C., de Guzman, I. G. R., Fernandez-Medina, E., Trujillo, J., & Piattini, M. (2008). Automatic generation of secure multidimensional code for data warehouses: An MDA approach. In R. Meersman & Z. Tari (Eds.), *Proceedings of the International Conference of On the Move to Meaningful Internet Systems* (LNCS 5332, pp. 1052-1068).

Blanco, C., Fernandez-Medina, E., Trujillo, J., & Piattini, M. (2008, March 4-7). Implementing multidimensional security into OLAP tools. In *Proceedings of the 3rd International Conference on Availability, Security, and Reliability*, Barcelona, Spain.

Blanco, C., Pérez-Castillo, R., Hernández, A., Fernández-Medina, E., & Trujillo, J. (2009). Towards a modernization process for secure data warehouses. In T. B. Pedersen, M. K. Mohania, & A. M. Tjoa (Eds.), *Proceedings of the 11ᵗʰ International Conference on Data Warehousing and Knowledge Discovery*, Linz, Austria (LNCS 5691, pp. 24-35).

Boehm, B., & Basili, V. R. (2001). Software defect reduction top 10 list. *IEEE Computer, 34*, 135–137.

Breu, R., Hafner, M., Weber, B., & Novak, A. (2005, March 2-4). Model driven security for inter-organizational workflows in e-government. In M. Böhlen, J. Gamper, W. Polasek, & M. A. Wimmer (Eds.), *Proceedings of the International Conference on E-Government: Towards Electronic Democracy*, Bolzano, Italy (LNCS 3416, pp. 122-133).

Clavel, M., Silva, V., Braga, C., & Egea, M. (2008). Model-driven security in practice: An industrial experience. In *Proceedings of the 4th European Conference on Model Driven Architecture: Foundations and Applications* (pp. 326-337).

CVE. (2011). *Common vulnerabilities and exposures (CVE)*. Retrieved from http://cve.mitre.org/

Dybå, T., Dingsøyr, T., & Hanssen, G. K. (2007). Applying systematic reviews to diverse study types: An experience report. In *Proceedings of the 1st International Symposium on Empirical Software Engineering and Measurement* (pp. 225-234).

Fernandez-Medina, E., Jurjens, J., Trujillo, J., & Jajodia, S. (2009). Model-driven development for secure information systems. *Information and Software Technology, 51*, 809–814. doi:10.1016/j.infsof.2008.05.010

Hafner, M., Alam, M., & Breu, R. (2006, October 1-6). Towards a MOF/QVT-based domain architecture for model driven security. In O. Nierstrasz, J. Whittle, D. Harel, & G. Reggio (Eds.), *Proceedings of the 9th International Conference on Model Driven Engineering Languages and Systems*, Genova, Italy (LNCS 4199, pp. 275-290).

Hafner, M., Breu, M., Breu, R., & Nowak, A. (2005). Modelling inter-organizational workflow security in a peer-to-peer environment. In *Proceedings of the IEEE International Conference on Web Services.*

Hafner, M., & Breu, R. (2009). *Security engineering for service-oriented architectures.* Berlin, Germany: Springer-Verlag.

Haug, T. H. (2007). *A systematic review of empirical research on model-driven development with UML.* Unpublished master's thesis, University of Oslo, Oslo, Norway.

Howard, M., & Lipner, S. (2006). *The security development lifecycle.* Sebastopol, CA: Microsoft Press.

Jensen, J., & Jaatun, M. G. (2011). Security in model driven development: A survey. In *Proceedings of the 5th International Workshop on Secure Software Engineering.*

Jürjens, J. (2005). *Secure systems development with UML.* New York, NY: Springer.

Jürjens, J., Schreck, J., & Bartmann, P. (2008). Model-based security analysis for mobile communications. In *Proceedings of the 30th International Conference on Software Engineering.*

Kasal, K., Heurix, J., & Neubauer, T. (2011, January 4-7). Model-driven development meets security: An evaluation of current approaches. In *Proceedings of the 44th Hawaii International Conference on Systems Science.*

Kitchenham, B. (2004). *Procedures for performing systematic reviews.* Staffordshire, UK: Keele University.

Kleppe, A. G., Warmer, J., & Bast, W. (2003). *MDA explained: The model driven architecture: Practice and promise.* Reading, MA: Addison-Wesley.

Lloyd, J., & Jürjens, J. (2009). Security analysis of a biometric authentication system using UMLsec and JML. In *Proceedings of the 12th International Conference on Model Driven Engineering Languages and Systems.*

McDermott, J. (2005). *Visual security protocol modeling.* Paper presented at the New Security Paradigms Workshop.

McGraw, G. (2006). *Software security: Building security.* Reading, MA: Addison-Wesley.

Moebius, N., Stenzel, K., Grandy, H., & Reif, W. (2009a). Model-driven code generation for secure smart card applications. In *Proceedings of the Australian Software Engineering Conference.*

Moebius, N., Stenzel, K., Grandy, H., & Reif, W. (2009b). SecureMDD: A model-driven development method for secure smart card applications. In *Proceedings of the International Conference on Availability, Reliability and Security.*

Moebius, N., Stenzel, K., & Reif, W. (2009). Generating formal specifications for security-critical applications - A model-driven approach. In *Proceedings of the ICSE Workshop on Software Engineering for Secure Systems* (pp. 68-74).

OMG. (2010). *Executive overview - Model driven architecture.* Retrieved September, 2011, from http://www.omg.org/mda/executive_overview.htm

OWASP. (2011). *Category: OWASP top ten project.* Retrieved from http://www.owasp.org/index.php/Category:OWASP_Top_Ten_Project

Rodriguez, A., Fernandez-Medina, E., & Piattini, M. (2006). Security requirement with a UML 2.0 profile. In *Proceedings of the 1st International Conference on Availability, Reliability and Security.*

Rodriguez, A., Fernandez-Medina, E., & Piattini, M. (2006). Towards a UML 2.0 extension for the modeling of security requirements in business processes. In S. Fischer-Hübner, S. Furnell, & C. Lambrinoudakis (Eds.), *Proceedings of the 3rd International Conference on Trust and Privacy in Digital Business* (LNCS 4083, pp. 51-61).

Rodriguez, A., Fernandez-Medina, E., & Piattini, M. (2007). Towards CIM to PIM transformation: From secure business processes defined in BPMN to use-cases. In G. Alonso, P. Dadam, & M. Rosemann (Eds.), *Proceedings of the 5th International Conference on Business Process Management* (LNCS 4714, pp. 408-415).

Rodriguez, A., Fernandez-Medina, E., & Piattini, M. (2008). CIM to PIM transformation: A reality. In *Proceedings of the IFIP TC 8 WG 8.9 International Conference on Research and Practical Issues of Enterprise Information Systems II* (Vol. 255, pp. 1239-1249).

Soler, E. TruJillo, J., Fernandez-Medina, E., & Piattini, M. (2007a). Application of QVT for the development of secure data warehouses: A case study. In *Proceedings of the 2nd International Conference on Availability, Reliability and Security* (pp. 829-836).

Soler, E., Stefanov, V., Mazon, J.-N., Trujillo, J., Fernandez-Madina, E., & Piattini, M. (2008). Towards comprehensive requirement analysis for data warehouses: Considering security requirements. In *Proceedings of the 3rd International Conference on Availability, Reliability and Security* (pp. 104-111).

Soler, E., Trujillo, J., Blanco, C., & Fernandez-Medina, E. (2009). Designing secure data warehouses by using MDA and QVT. *Journal of Universal Computer Science, 15*(8), 1607–1641.

Soler, E., Trujillo, J., Fernandez-Medina, E., & Piattini, M. (2007b). A framework for the development of secure data warehouses based on MDA and QVT. In *Proceedings of the 2nd International Conference on Availability, Reliability and Security* (pp. 294-300).

Soler, E., Trujillo, J., Fernandez-Medina, E., & Piattini, M. (2007c). A set of QVT relations to transform PIM to PSM in the design of secure data warehouses. In *Proceedings of the 2nd International Conference on Availability, Reliability and Security* (pp. 644-654).

Tøndel, I. A., Jaatun, M. G., & Meland, P. H. (2008). Security requirements for the rest of us: A survey. *IEEE Software, 25*(1), 20–27. doi:10.1109/MS.2008.19

Trujillo, J., Soler, E., Fernández-Medina, E., & Piattini, M. (2009a). An engineering process for developing secure data warehouses. *Information and Software Technology, 51*, 1033–1051. doi:10.1016/j.infsof.2008.12.003

Trujillo, J., Soler, E., Fernández-Medina, E., & Piattini, M. (2009b). A UML 2.0 profile to define security requirements for data warehouses. *Computer Standards & Interfaces, 31*(5), 969–983. doi:10.1016/j.csi.2008.09.040

Wyk, K. R. v., & McGraw, G. (2005). Bridging the gap between software development and information security. *IEEE Security and Privacy, 3*, 75–79. doi:10.1109/MSP.2005.118

This work was previously published in the International Journal of Secure Software Engineering, Volume 2, Issue 4, edited by Khaled M. Khan, pp. 49-61, copyright 2011 by IGI Publishing (an imprint of IGI Global).

Chapter 6

Security Gaps in Databases:
A Comparison of Alternative Software Products for Web Applications Support

Afonso Araújo Neto
University of Coimbra, Portugal

Marco Vieira
University of Coimbra, Portugal

ABSTRACT

When deploying database-centric web applications, administrators should pay special attention to database security requirements. Acknowledging this, Database Management Systems (DBMS) implement several security mechanisms that help Database Administrators (DBAs) making their installations secure. However, different software products offer different sets of mechanisms, making the task of selecting the adequate package for a given installation quite hard. This paper proposes a methodology for detecting database security gaps. This methodology is based on a comprehensive list of security mechanisms (derived from widely accepted security best practices), which was used to perform a gap analysis of the security features of seven software packages composed by widely used products, including four DBMS engines and two Operating Systems (OS). The goal is to understand how much each software package helps developers and administrators to actually accomplish the security tasks that are expected from them. Results show that while there is a common set of security mechanisms that is implemented by most packages, there is another set of security tasks that have no support at all in any of the packages.

INTRODUCTION

This paper studies the security features offered by different software packages in the context of database-centric web applications, focusing particularly on the mechanisms provided by Operating Systems (OS) and Database Management Systems (DBMS), the two main software elements that can be found in any database server. The study focuses in seven largely used software packages, composed of four different DBMS engines (Oracle 10g, SQL Server 2005, PostgreSQL 8, and MySQL

DOI: 10.4018/978-1-4666-2482-5.ch006

Community Edition 5) and two different operating systems (Windows XP and Red Hat Enterprise Linux 5). The main goal of the work is to understand how much support these products provide for fulfilling well-known security best practices that administrators are expected to follow. Even though there are not the latest versions, these products are representative of the state of the art technology currently available for provisioning database installations and are frequently used to support the deployment of business critical web applications.

The study consists of comparing the characteristics of the software packages against a comprehensive list of security concerns, which should be taken into account when deploying a database-centric web application. This list was created based on an extensive field research where we were able to identify the most important security practices for database systems. In our methodology, each security best practice was mapped onto a desirable system state - called a *System State Goal* - that represents the state of the system when the practice is being correctly applied. That system goal was used to extrapolate and identify the functionalities and mechanisms needed to implement the practice. The final list of security mechanism was used to build a gap analysis table that maps the security features actually provided by the software packages assessed with the mechanisms that are needed to fulfill the security best practices initially identified.

This work is motivated by the central role played by databases in the security of today's web applications. In fact, it is well known that security aspects must be an everyday concern of a system administrator, in particular of Database Administrators (DBA). When installing a database server to support a web application, the DBA must consider several complex requirements, including performance, recovery time and security, following a defense-in-depth approach (Howard & Leblanc, 2002). These requirements have strong implications in the hardware and software to be used in the database infrastructure. The problem of performance and recovery in databases has been largely studied in the past (Vieira & Madeira, 2002; Kanoun & Spainhower, 2008; TPC, 2011). However, assessing and comparing the security features provided by software packages is still an open issue.

Web application security (and, in particular, database security) arises from the need to protect from unauthorized attempts to access private data and loss or corruption of critical data due to malicious actions (Bertino et al., 1995; Castano et al., 1994, Pernul & Luef, 1992; Schell & Heckman, 1987). Other concerns include protecting against malicious interferences that may cause undue delays in accessing or using data, or even denial of service.

The problem is that different software products offer different sets of security mechanisms that target diverse security concerns. This, adding to the fact that several software systems are needed to install a database server (the minimum set is composed by an OS and a DBMS), makes it very difficult to map what is nowadays supported by software with the actual database administrators security needs. Our study shows that different software packages for databases allow implementing different security concerns and that there are security concerns for which few (or none) software products provide easy to use mechanisms. Furthermore, there is a small set of security mechanisms that is available in all the packages considered.

Several security evaluation methods have been proposed in the past (Cachin et al., 2000; Commission of the European Communities, 1993; Common Criteria, 1999; Department of Defense, 1985; Sandia National Laboratories, 2011; Vieira & Madeira, 2005). However, to the best of our knowledge, none of the existing methods provide a comprehensive comparison of widely used software products for database installations, or even a methodology to fairly achieve one. Furthermore, practical experience shows that these methods are very complex and hardly could be used by systems administrators that are not security experts (Baumhardt, 2006; Jackson, 2007).

In Vieira and Madeira (2005) the authors propose an approach to classify the security mechanisms of database systems. In this approach the DBMS is classified using a set of security classes. However, the list of mechanisms presented in the paper is limited as it is based on the actual mechanisms already implemented in most DBMS engines. Additionally, the set of software products considered was very small (only Oracle 9i and PostgreSQL 7.3 DBMS were considered) and the influence of the operating systems were disregarded. In our study, we devise the mechanisms from security best practices without considering what is or is not implemented in modern DBMS engines, thus having a much more relevant and detailed list of security mechanisms that could be available in a system.

In Araújo Neto and Vieira (2008, 2009), the authors propose an assessment tool to evaluate the security of DBMS configurations. The tool is composed by a set of recommendations and a set of tests to verify the correct implementation of those recommendations in a given installation. The work presented in Araújo Neto and Vieira (2009) focuses on the assessment of the final configuration of a database engine (i.e., the mechanisms and parameters implemented in a concrete installation) and is not concerned with the actual capabilities provided (or not) by the engines.

The structure of the paper is as follows. The next section presents the software products analyzed. After, we describe the procedure we followed to identify the list of security mechanisms and to compare that list with what is provided by the different software packages. The following section discusses our findings in detail. The last section concludes the paper.

SOFTWARE PRODUCTS ANALYZED

In a typical database installation, the core element is the relational database management system (DBMS). However, from a security perspective, a vulnerability in the underlying operating system (OS) has a high probability of being exploited and allowing an attack to the database (in spite of the DBMS used). This way, the OS and the DBMS are two key software systems that must be carefully selected before deploying a database installation with security needs. Moreover, several DBMS implementations take advantage of the security mechanisms present in the underlying operating system, so the security of both components is actually tied. Obviously, additional components can be used to improve security (e.g., firewall, antivirus). In the scope of this work we consider that a basic software package for a database installation includes an OS and a DBMS. Although installing additional software components to complement this basic set is a common approach, this approach adds complexity, increases cost, introduces performance overhead and boosts maintenance effort.

In this context, we focused our study in a representative set of database solutions that can be found in many real web application installations. In fact, the seven packages considered (summarized in Table 1) represent a very large percentage of the database installations found in the field. From the DBMS perspective, we selected two commercial DBMS engines, Oracle 10g (Oracle Corporation, 2011b) and Microsoft SQL Server 2005 (Microsoft Corporation, 2011a), and two open sources, PostgreSQL 8 (PostgreSQL Global Development Group, 2011) and MySQL Community Edition 5 (Oracle Corporation, 2011a). Oracle and SQL Server are two of the most widely used commercial DBMS, and these particular

Table 1. Software packages analyzed

DBMS Engine	Operating system	Package #
SQL Server 2005	Windows XP	1
Oracle 10g	Red Hat Enterprise Linux 5	2
	Windows XP	3
PostgreSQL 8	Red Hat Enterprise Linux 5	4
	Windows XP	5
MySQL Community Edition 5	Red Hat Enterprise Linux 5	6
	Windows XP	7

versions account for a representative number of installations. PostgreSQL and MySQL account for the majority of DBMS installations that use open source software, and are very popular alternatives to commercial software.

From the operating system perspective, we used the same rationale, therefore choosing Microsoft Windows XP (Microsoft Corporation, 2011b) and Red Hat Enterprise Linux 5 (Red Hat, 2011). Both operating systems are widely representative choices to support the DBMS mentioned above, but we are aware that several other alternatives would be interesting as well (e.g., Suse Linux and Microsoft Windows Server 2003, among many others). Excluding Microsoft SQL Server 2005, that is only available over Windows platforms, the other three DBMS could be installed on top of both operating systems.

ANALYSIS PROCEDURE

To make a worthwhile comparison, we need a comprehensive list of the security concerns in the databases domain that can be used to identify the security mechanisms necessary to solve those concerns. The security features included in a given software package can then be compared with this list of mechanisms, allowing us to find existing security gaps and understanding how each

package helps the execution of practical security tasks. This way, the main steps of our study were the following:

1. *Definition of security best practices* based on an extensive field research to identify the most important security practices for database systems.
2. *Identification of security mechanisms* needed to implement the best practices defined before.
3. *Analysis of the software packages* by mapping the provided features with the security mechanisms identified in Step 2.

Security Best Practices Definition

A list of security best practices for database installations was built by conducting an extensive field research to identify the important security recommendations. In fact, we found an enormous quantity of security recommendations for databases in the form of books, web pages, white papers, expert knowledge, etc. The two main sources of information for our study were the Center for Internet Security (CIS) (Center for Internet Security, 2008) and the USA Department of Defense (DoD) (Defense Information Systems Agency, 2007). The first one, CIS, has created a series of security configuration documents for several commercial and open source DBMS, namely: MySQL, SQLServer 2000/2005, and Oracle 8i/9i/10g. These documents focus on the practical aspects of the configuration of each DBMS and state the concrete values each configuration option should have in order to enhance overall security of real installations. The second source, DoD, developed the Database Security Technical Implementation Guide (Defense Information Systems Agency, 2007) for the use within the USA Department of Defense. This document contains a series of mandatory or recommended requisites that the DoD employees must follow when installing a database to be used in the department.

In the analysis of the CIS documents, we identified the security property being targeted and analyzed the value and/or procedure recommended. This allowed us to determine the more general best practice being addressed by each recommended setting. Additionally, several complementary best practices were found in the DoD document (which is written in a generic form and is supposedly applicable to any database engine), but the overlap of recommendations between the CIS documents and the DoD document was significant.

Our first analysis of the sources resulted in a list with a mix of very clear statements (e.g., "always do backups"), very narrow suggestions about a particular software (e.g., "after installing the software XYZ, delete the file XPTO.exe"), and very specific configuration values (e.g., "set the server timeout to 60 seconds"), all of them aimed at helping improving the security of the DBMS. This first list contained more than 500 security recommendations. Each recommendation was then analyzed, filtered, and grouped into general security best practices, as shown in Table 2. To accomplish this, we used the knowledge of a group of security experts, which methodically discussed the advantages, disadvantages, expected effects and the general security consequences of each of the suggestions of the list.

There are four key aspects that should be emphasized about the procedure carried out by this group:

- **Conflicting Recommendations:** As we collected information from different sources, we found some contradictory approaches to tackle the same security problem. Expert judgment and more field research was used to determine which approach was the correct one, or if one of them was more widely accepted than the other.
- **Recommendations Associated with the Same Single Best Practice:** This happened not only because different sources mention similar things, but also because a lot of specific suggestions are related to the application of one practice in several different instances. For example "delete the application file X" and "disable the access to the functionality Y" are recommendations that can both be related to unneeded application extensions that should be removed to prevent attackers from exploiting them to gain privileges that they should not have.
- **Recommendations Associated With More than One Best Practice**: For example, a common recommendation for Oracle DBMS configuration is that the "tkprof" utility, used to access trace data, should either be removed from the system (which can be associated to a best practice stated as "deny access to extended unneeded functionalities") or have its permissions reviewed in order to be available only to authorized people (related to a best practice such as "set permissions to authorized users"). In these cases, field experience and expert judgment were used to determine if both were equally relevant or if there was a prevalent one.
- **Practices Representing Special Cases of More General Others:** The problem here was to decide when a specialization of a particular best practice is relevant enough to spawn a new one. Past experience on security tradeoffs was used to evaluate and decide when such separation is important.

The final set is summarized in Tables 2 and 3 (descriptions are abbreviated due to space reasons) and includes 64 configuration best practices.

Security Mechanisms Identification

The list of security recommendations for database installations was used to extrapolate the mechanisms necessary to fulfill those recommendations. However, this process is complex and required

Table 2. DBMS configuration security best practices devised from the analysis of the CIS documents

#	SECURITY BEST PRACTICE (CIS)	Recommendations			
		M	O8	O10	S
ENVIRONMENT					
1	Use a dedicated machine for the database	1	1	1	28
2	Avoid machines which also run critical network services (naming, authentication, etc)	1	1	1	1
3	Use Firewalls: on the machine and on the network	1	3	3	1
4	Prevent physical access to the DBMS machine by unauthorized people				1
5	Remove from network stack all unauthorized protocols		1	1	1
6	Create a specific user to run the DBMS daemons	1	1	1	
7	Restrict DBMS user access to everything he doesn't need	1	4	4	3
8	Prevent direct login on the DBMS user account	2	1	3	3
INSTALLATION SETUP					
9	Create a partition for log information	2	1	1	1
10	Only the DBMS user should read/write in the log partition	1			
11	Create a partition for DB data	1	1	1	2
12	Only the DBMS user should read/write in the data partition	1			
13	Separate the DBMS software from the OS files	1	2	2	2
	Remove/Avoid default elements:				
14	»»»Remove example databases	1			1
15	»»»Change/remove user names/passwords	1	4	4	2
16	»»»Change remote identification names (SID, etc...)		3	1	
17	»»»Change TCP/UDP Ports		1	1	1
18	»»»Do not use default SSL certificates	1			
19	Separate production and development servers		1	1	
20	No developer should have access to production server		5	5	
21	Use different network segments for production and development servers		1	1	1
	Verify all the installed DBMS application files:				
22	»»»Check and set the owner of the files	1	2	3	
23	»»»Set read/running permissions to authorized users	4	18	22	14
OPERATIONAL PROCEDURES					
24	Keep the DBMS software updated	3		1	1
25	Make regular backups	1			4
26	Test the backups	1		1	
SYSTEM LEVEL CONFIGURATION					
27	Avoid random ports assignment for client connections		1	1	
28	Enforce communication encryption with strong algorithms	1	1	11	3
29	Use server side certificate if possible	1		1	
30	Use IPs instead of host names to configure access permissions (prevents DNS spoofing)		1	1	
31	Enforce strong user level authentication	2	6	8	4
32	Prevent idle connection hijacking		2	2	

continued on following page

Table 2. Continued

33	Ensure no remote parameters are used in authentication	1	2	1	
34	Avoid host based authentication		1	1	
35	Enforce strong password policies	1	2		2
36	Apply excessive failed logins lock		1	1	
37	Apply password lifetime control		1	1	
38	Deny regular password reuse (force periodic change)		2	2	
39	Use strong encryption in password storage	3			
40	Enforce comprehensive logging	1	2	1	
41	Verify that the log data cannot be lost (replication is used)		2	2	1
42	Audit sensitive information		14	19	25
43	Verify that the audit data cannot be lost (replication is used)		1		1
	Ensure no "side-channel" information leak (don't create/restrict access):				
44	»»»From configuration files		2	1	
45	»»»From system variables	1			
46	»»»From core_dump/trace files		8	8	1
47	»»»From backups of data and configuration files		1	1	4
	Avoid interaction between the DBMS users and the OS:				
48	»»»Deny any read/write on file system from DBMS used	2	3	2	
49	»»»Deny any network operation (sending email, opening sockets, etc...)		4	3	
50	»»»Deny access to not needed extended libraries and functionalities	1	11	11	54
51	»»»Deny access to any OS information and commands	2			
APPLICATION LEVEL CONFIGURATION AND USAGE					
52	Remove user rights over system tables	1	23	25	1
53	Remove user quotas over system areas		3	1	
54	Implement least privilege policy in rights assignments		9	10	6
55	Avoid ANY and ALL expressions in rights assignments	1	3	3	
56	Do not delegate rights assignments	1	3	3	3
57	No user should have rights to change system properties or configurations	3	4	4	2
58	Grant privileges to roles/groups instead of users		1	1	3
59	Do not maintain the DB creation SQL files in the DB server		1		
Total number of recomendations		**48**	**166**	**183**	**177**

M: MySQL; O8: Oracle 8i and 9i; O10: Oracle 10g; S: SQLServer 2000/2005

several steps of careful analysis. We started by analyzing the 64 security recommendations, where each recommendation was classified in terms of the type of support needed for its implementation, namely:

- **Hardware Support:** Recommendations that require either specific hardware components or a specific physical setup for the underlying hardware;
- **Network Support:** Recommendations that require the network to have some specific setup or characteristic;

Table 3. Complementary DoD best practices

#	Complementary Best Practices (DoD)	Group
1A	Monitor the DBMS application and configuration files for modifications	Operational Procedures
2A	Do not use self signed certificates	System Level Config.
3A	Protect/encrypt application code	Appl. L. Config./Usage
4A	Audit application code changes	Appl. L. Config./Usage
5A	Employ stored procedures and views instead of direct table access	Appl. L. Config./Usage

- **Plain Policies:** General guidelines that do not require any mechanism in particular, and are just behaviors that should be enforced;
- **OS Support:** Recommendations that require some features of the operating system;
- **DBMS Support:** Recommendation that requires some specific DBMS features;
- **Third Party Support:** Recommendations that require complementary software not usually found in a basic database software package (DBMS and OS).

Table 4 presents the number of best practices that were classified in each class. Note that, some practices could be classified in more than one class, which explains why the second column of the table adds to more than 64 practices. This first classification allowed us to focus on the practices that required at least some support for software components (a total of 51 out of 64 security practices).

The next step consisted of restating the practices in a way that allows clearly identifying the security mechanisms needed to support them. The best practices were stated as actions that should

be conducted on the system to enhance security. However, these actions may contain several factors that may be implicit when they are defined, such as: what are administrators' responsibilities, what actions require software support, and what the environment dependent elements are. This way, instead of trying to identify security mechanisms directly from the best practices, we decided to use two intermediary steps that helped in exposing implicit factors. Obviously, these steps could have been bypassed, but we believe that by performing them explicitly we were able to achieve more effective results.

In the first step we restated each of the best practices as a *System State Goal* representing the state of the system in a point in time when the practice is being correctly applied. For instance, one of the best practices related to the operating system is stated as follows: "Remove from the network stack all unused/unauthorized protocols". A potential system state goal for this best practice is: "The OS network stack has no unused/unauthorized protocol active". Notice that, although obvious in some cases, this rewriting step moves the focus from the action to the consequences of the action. This is extremely important to disclose the fundamental effects that are expected when applying a best practice. Additionally, as several practices can actually be applied in several software components at the same time (e.g., password related practices must be applied at both OS and DBMS levels), this rephrasing forced this distinc-

Table 4. Classification of databases security best practices in regard to their requisites

Requirements	N. of Practices
Network Requisites	2
Hardware Requisites	4
Plain Policies (no requirement)	10
OS Support	28
DBMS Support	38
Third-Party Support	2

tion to be made clear, allowing us to identify the practices for which more than one System State Goal should be defined (i.e., one for each of the components of the software package).

When analyzing the Systems State Goals it became possible to start distinguishing the effects of the practices that are exclusively administrators' tasks (e.g., defining what are unauthorized protocols) and the ones that can be automated, and therefore can be supported by security mechanisms. From a high level perspective, any security practice is a policy that requires an action from the administrator (in the sense that he can always choose to not implement it), and can typically be automated to a certain point. For instance, the administrator may manually check if the users' passwords are strong enough, but the software may also perform this check automatically and do not allow users to even choose weak passwords in the first place. Obviously, maintaining the System State Goal in the first case (manual verification) is much more difficult than in the second case (when automation is present). In fact, it is widely accepted that the least work the administrator has to do to enforce security policies, the better is his productivity and higher are the chances that these policies are correctly implemented. Thus, to identify the mechanisms needed to support a security practice, we needed to look for all the tasks that can be automated in a way that allows achieving the result described as the System State Goal.

In the second step, we rewrote again the System State Goals, but this time in terms of *Mechanisms Goals*. This additional step was used to define more precisely what are the steps needed to accomplish the System State Goal in terms of the software at hand (DBMS or OS). In fact, the Mechanisms Goals can be seen as the functions that make the steps towards the accomplishment of the System State Goal as simple as possible (i.e., the complexity of the steps is hidden behind automation). Continuing the previous example, the Mechanisms Goals for the "*the OS network stack has no unused/unauthorized protocol active*" System State Goal

can be described as two simple steps: "*Identify active protocols*" and "*disable unauthorized/unused protocols*". Note that, defining what the unauthorized/unused protocols are is environment dependent and can only be done by the system administrator. However, identifying the active ones and allowing them to be easily removed are software features that can help accomplishing the System State Goal.

The identification of the security mechanisms based on the Mechanisms Goals was then quite straightforward. An important issue is that, in some cases, more than one mechanism may be required for the state goal to be accomplished. In other cases, different mechanisms may be used to accomplish the same goal, possibly with different amount of automation. Alternative ways for performing the same tasks are useful to suit different administrators, environments and requisites. Table 5 presents a few examples of the mapping of security best practices into System State Goal and Mechanisms Goals.

By following this process we have identified the 112 security mechanisms, which are presented in Tables 7, 8 and 9. The first column of each table describes the mechanisms that a target software component (second column) is expected to facilitate. The mechanisms should be read as "*The software provides automated support for…*". Note that these mechanisms are not tied to any specific product and are described in a broad way to allow a posterior assessment of their existence in the considered software packages.

Software Packages Gap Analysis

With the list of mechanisms defined, analyzing the software packages was a straightforward process that consisted of verifying which of 112 security mechanisms are provided by each package. In practice, we checked whether each security mechanism is present on the software package being analyzed which resulted in a "gap" list of mechanisms that are not available in each pack-

Table 5. Examples of the mapping between security best practices, system state goals and mechanisms goals

Security Best Practice	Component	System State Goals	Mechanisms Goals
Remove from the network stack all unauthorized protocols	OS	The OS network stack has no unused/unauthorized protocol active.	Identify active protocols and disable unauthorized/unused ones.
Change default passwords	OS	No OS userid password is the default.	Prevent the installation of default passwords in the OS or allow identification and removal of default passwords.
	DBMS	No DBMS userid password is the default.	Prevent the installation of default passwords in the DBMS or allow identification and removal of default passwords .
Do not delegate privileges assignments	DBMS	Privileges a user have should not be delegated.	Prevent users from delegating their privileges or identify the use of privilege delegation operations.
Keep the software updated	OS	No patches provided by the OS vendor are unapplied.	Not allow an available OS patch to remain unapplied.
	DBMS	No patches provided by the DBMS vendor are unapplied.	Not allow an available DBMS patch to remain unapplied.
Restrict database OS userid access to everything it does not need	OS	The database OS userid has access only to DBMS software.	Set privileges to the dedicated DBMS userid to access only DBMS software.
		The database OS userid has access only to designated peripherals.	Set privileges to the dedicated DBMS userid to access only the defined peripherals.
Prevent idle connection hijacking	DBMS	Remote connections drop when unused for some period of time.	Set connections to timeout after a period of inactivity.
Change/remove default userids	OS	The OS has no default userid operational.	Prevent the existence of default userids in the OS (during or after the installation).
	DBMS	The DBMS has no default userid operational.	Prevent the existence of default userids in the DBMS (during or after the installation).
Make regular backups of the data	DBMS	There is an up-to-date copy of the DBMS data in a safe storage.	Make updated copies of all DBMS data.
Avoid ANY and ALL expressions in privileges assignments	DBMS	No user has privileges assigned from ANY and ALL expressions.	Prevent or warn the use of ANY and ALL expressions on privileges assignments.
Ensure no "side-channel" information leak through configuration files	OS	Configuration files do not contain sensitive information.	Avoid the inclusion of sensitive information in configuration files.

age. This list allowed us to conduct the analysis presented in the next section. It is important to note that, to guarantee the correctness of the results, the assessment was conducted in cooperation with two database experts.

It is important to emphasize that our results are not supposed to be used alone to decide what is the best software package for a database installation. Several other factors must also be considered (e.g., cost, performance, availability, and familiarity). Nevertheless, although there are tools to help

evaluating several of these factors, security is one that has largely been ignored.

We believe that the outcomes of this study will be extremely helpful for databases administrators in their task of selecting the software package that best fits their needs. Although the analysis includes only seven packages, the software products considered are quite representative of the current state-of-the-art software for database installations. Additionally, database administrators can easily apply the analysis procedure to additional software packages. By highlighting the security weaknesses of software for databases, this work also points out research needs and may serve as motivation for researchers to identify future research work.

LESSONS LEARNED: PRODUCTS COMPARISON AND DISCUSSION

This section presents and discusses the results of our study. We start with an overall analysis of the set of mechanisms and then move to the analysis of the mechanisms present in all packages, the mechanisms not available in any package, and, finally, the mechanisms available in only some packages.

Overall Analysis of the Mechanisms and Packages

The first observation is on the number of mechanisms related to each of the two software components being studied (i.e., the OS and the DBMS). As presented in Figure 1, more than a third of the 112 mechanisms identified are expected to be provided by the OS. This suggests that, despite the database engine being used, security is strongly tied to the capabilities of the underlying platform. Even more important is the fact that, for several DBMS, the

provision of some security mechanisms is highly dependent on the operating system being used (e.g., some authentication features of PostgreSQL are only natively provided if the operating system has the Pluggable Authentication Module (PAM) installed, which is, for instance, available on Red Hat Enterprise Linux 5, but not on Windows XP). It is then clear that, from a security point of view, the two software systems must be selected simultaneously.

The next important global observation is the general availability of the 112 mechanisms in the analyzed packages. Figure 2 presents the percentages of mechanisms available in all packages, mechanisms available in none of the packages, and mechanisms available in at least one package. As shown, little more than half of the devised mechanisms are supported by all the packages analyzed, which is much lower than what one would expect. Worse than that is the fact that 21% of the mechanisms are not provided by any of the packages analyzed. This suggests that many security best practices cannot be easily implemented (or additional software has to be acquired for their implementation) due to the inexistence of support in the DBMS and/or OS.

Figure 3 breaks down the number of mechanisms supported by combinations of packages. Interestingly, a very high number of mechanisms

Figure 1. Mechanisms by component of the analyzed packages

Mechanism Type

OS, 42, 37%

DBMS, 70, 63%

Figure 2. Mechanisms by component of the analyzed packages

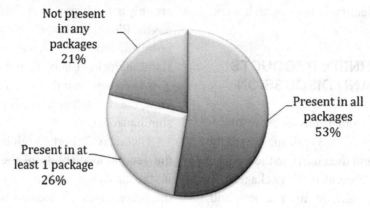

Availability of the 112 Mechanisms

Not present in any packages 21%

Present in all packages 53%

Present in at least 1 package 26%

appear on a minority of the packages (e.g., 20 mechanisms appear on three or less packages). This suggests that these mechanisms, although provided by some packages, do not seem to be universally considered a requirement for databases.

Another interesting observation is related to the total number of mechanisms provided by each software package. Table 6 presents the overall results. The column MP stands for the number of mechanisms provided by the package (and the last column is the percentage within the total 112 mechanisms). Although package number 1 clearly presents the biggest number of mechanisms, the actual number of mechanisms available in the seven packages does not vary considerably.

This suggests that vendors follow some common trends when deciding what mechanisms should be made available in their products. Note, however, that a higher number of mechanisms do not imply more security as the importance of the different mechanisms may vary. Additionally, it may be the case that important features are missing in the package that provides the higher number of mechanisms. What it does mean is that having more mechanisms facilitates the implementation of a higher number of practices, and therefore requires the adoption of fewer third party solutions (which may imply less time and money spent in security).

Figure 3. Number of mechanisms available across packages

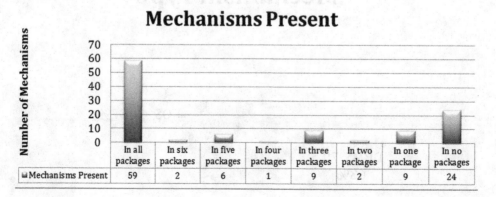

Mechanisms Present

	In all packages	In six packages	In five packages	In four packages	In three packages	In two packages	In one package	In no packages
Mechanisms Present	59	2	6	1	9	2	9	24

Table 6. Overall results of the evaluation of the 7 different software packages

DBMS Engine	Operating system	Package N.	MP	%
SQL Server 2005	Windows XP	1	79	71%
Oracle 10g	Red Hat Enterprise Linux 5	2	74	66%
	Windows XP	3	73	65%
PostgreSQL 8	Red Hat Enterprise Linux 5	4	73	65%
	Windows XP	5	68	61%
MySQL Community Edition 5	Red Hat Enterprise Linux 5	6	66	59%
	Windows XP	7	66	59%

Mechanisms Available in All Packages

Table 7 presents the 59 mechanisms that are provided by all the packages. The first observation is that there are 28 DBMS mechanisms and 31 OS mechanisms in this group. This observation, together with the total number of mechanisms initially identified for DBMS (70 mechanisms) and OS (42 mechanisms), shows that the operating systems analyzed implement a higher percentage of the expected security mechanisms than the databases suggesting that operating systems vendors are more concerned about helping the users in hardening their systems than the DBMS vendors on helping DBAs to harden their databases. On one hand, the operating system is in fact a more fundamental layer of software than the DBMS (which is more of a targeted use) and may be used in a variety of distinct scenarios (requiring more security awareness). On the other hand, this does not justify more concern with security. In fact, although operating systems may also host critical end users information, DBMS are actually designed to do so. Therefore, security of both layers of software is equally important.

Another key remark is that most common settings and configuration mechanisms are present in this group. Password settings, privilege settings, some installations choices and the definition of some general operational parameters are allowed by all packages, which confirm that these mechanisms are accepted as universal requirements for databases. Very few informational mechanisms, however, can be found in this group. For example, the easy verification of the current working state and configuration of the system is NOT a universal concern of DBMS and OS developers.

Mechanisms Not Available in Any Packages

Table 8 shows the mechanisms that could not be found in any of the packages. A very important observation is that the vast majority of the mechanisms in this group are specified by the actions of *Identifying (8)*, *Testing (4)*, *Warning (4)* and *Blocking (3)*.

Identifying mechanisms are expected to easily provide general information about the system state and configuration. Not having these mechanisms forces the administrator to guess if a given setting is active or not, to create miraculous queries over poorly documented system tables, to analyze gigantic and cryptic configuration text files or to read enormous manuals to find the information. Obviously, to help DBAs improving security, gathering this kind of information should be as simple and intuitive as possible.

Testing mechanisms are mechanisms designed to verify either if some important operation was carried out successfully or if it will be carried out successfully when attempted (e.g., data backups and software updates, respectively). Testing is

Table 7. List of mechanisms available in all packages

Security Mechanism (*The package offers support for...*)	ComponentTarget
Disabling access to extended stored procedures and functions	DB
Config. the system to always encrypt a remote connection to the DBMS	DB
Encrypting the connection of developer applications	DB
Removing system privileges of DBMS userids	DB
Restricting read/write privileges of a partition to a specific userid	OS
Automated installation of OS pending patches	OS
Configuring the DBMS to store credential information using a reliable encryption scheme	DB
Configuring the OS to store credential information using a reliable encryption scheme	OS
Defining all DBMS passwords during the installation phase	DB
Defining all OS passwords during the installation phase	OS
Relying the OS on an outside specialized authentication mechanism	OS
Warning OS users, in a password change operation, that their new passwords are weak and cannot be accepted	OS
A DBMS authentication procedure that requests only credential information to the remote users	DB
An OS authentication procedure that requests only credential information to the remote users	OS
Configuring the DBMS so only administrators have access to log information	DB
Denying login into the OS from a credential with more than a specified number of failed authentication attempts	OS
Forcing the OS users to change their passwords when they're older than a specified time frame	OS
Identifying systems privileges of DBMS userids	DB
Setting read/write/execution privileges over files	OS
Setting that a userid cannot login	OS
Setting who can change configuration files	OS
Setting who can change environment variables	OS
Using custom defined SSL certificates for encrypted connections	DB
Changing OS userids already in use	OS
Changing passwords of DBMS userids already in use	DB
Changing passwords of OS userids already in use	OS
Creating an OS userid with limited privileges	OS
Creating file systems partitions	OS
Identifying users with privileges over systems tables	DB
Making a backup copy of the database	DB
Storing the backup in a custom storage place	DB
Using a privilege limited userid to successfully load a DBMS process.	OS
Warning the administrator that there are OS vendor patches remaining to be applied	OS
Allowing the DBA to not use ANY and ALL expressions	DB
Allowing to explicitly state that a particular privilege cannot be delegated	DB
Changing listening TCP/UDP ports	DB
Changing remote identification information already in use. (e.g., SID)	DB
Configuring the system to always establish connections through the same TCP/UDP ports.	DB

continued on following page

Table 7. Continued

Security Mechanism (*The package offers support for...*)	ComponentTarget
Defining all remote identification information during the installation phase	DB
Disabling the generation of core_dump files	OS
Disabling the generation of trace files	DB
Preventing specifying sensitive information in configuration files. (e.g., not require specifying password in configuration files, etc.)	OS
Preventing the general use of sensitive information in systems variables	OS
Setting and discarding a complex password for a userid	OS
Setting the owner of files	OS
Specifying important events which occur in the OS that should generate a finger print	OS
Specifying privileges in a database level	DB
Specifying privileges in a table level	DB
Warning OS users that their passwords are older than a specified time frame	OS
Writing procedures that generate a trace for data changes	DB
Creating stored procedures	DB
Creating views	DB
Disabling a network protocol	OS
Identifying active protocols in the network stack	OS
Removing a database	DB
Selecting a different partition for OS log information	OS
Selecting a different partition than the main OS partition for DBMS log information	DB
Selecting a different partition than the main OS partition for the data files	DB
Setting/unsetting read/write/execute privileges over files	OS

crucial to guarantee the system availability (either in the moment or in the future), but it is simply disregarded by developers of both operating systems and databases.

Warning mechanisms provide security related notifications. As these warnings may be a hindrance when the system is known to be working as expected, it should be possible to turn them off. However, when turned on the report information about important operations that should not occur normally. Providing such mechanisms is simply not considered in any of the packages analyzed (e.g., warning about outdated backups or about the modification of configuration parameters).

Blocking mechanisms are configuration options that result in some operations not being allowed. In this case, the blocking mechanisms

that were not found in any package are related to privilege delegation. We believe that these mechanisms (although optional) are important because they allow the DBAs to better track how privileges are distributed within the database. For instance, whenever a particular user is the owner of some entity, he can decide who can access his entity and how. In critical security scenarios, however, the DBA may want to control this kind of delegation even about entities not owned by him, and this cannot be done in any of the DBMS analyzed unless the DBA owns all objects.

Most of these mechanisms are security specific and are not related to any major functional aspects of databases. As they simply do not provide any obvious functional advantage to clients that are not security experts, it seems that they are not con-

Table 8. List of mechanisms not available in none of the packages

Security Mechanism (*The package offers support for...*)	ComponentTarget
Defining all OS userids during the installation phase	OS
Removing all privileges of users over all systems tables.	DB
Configuring the OS so only admins. have access to log information	OS
Identifying DBMS userids with default passwords	DB
Identifying default DBMS userids	DB
Identifying default OS userids	OS
Identifying OS userids with default passwords	OS
Testing the installation of DBMS new patches	DB
Testing the installation of OS new patches	OS
Warning the administrator that the last OS backup is not up-to-date anymore	OS
Blocking non-DBAs from delegating their privileges	DB
Blocking privileges not inherited from groups/roles	DB
Blocking the usage of ANY and ALL expressions in privileges granting	DB
Encrypting backups with a reliable encryption algorithm	OS
Identifying available functions that interact with the operating system	DB
Warning the administrator if any important configuration or file was modified	OS
Identifying available extended functions in general	DB
Identifying available functions that can be used to perform network operations	DB
Identifying available functions that can be used to read/write in the file system	DB
Identifying example databases	DB
Testing if a recently created backup correctly restores the database data to its corresponding state	DB
Testing if a recently created backup correctly restores the system to its corresponding state	OS
Warning administrators of ANY and ALL expressions used in privileges assignments	DB
Warning admin of users with the power of delegating their privileges	DB

sidered to add a significant *Return of Investment* value to the software. However, the importance of security in databases nowadays should be enough for vendors to consider this kind of features from a perspective of not losing credibility in the future.

Mechanisms Available in Some Packages

This group includes the mechanisms that exist in at least one package, but not in all of them (see Table 9). We can divide this group in two subgroups: the mechanisms that are *present in most of the packages* (four or more packages,

corresponding to a total of 9 mechanisms) and the ones that are *present in just a few packages* (three or less packages, corresponding to a total of 20 mechanisms). These two subgroups seem to arise from two distinct situations.

Most mechanisms of the group *present in most packages* appear to be widely considered as important. In most cases, they are not present in some packages for very clear reasons, namely: specific platform migration decisions and feature inheritance from old versions. In other cases, vendors opted by excluding some mechanisms, but openly admit the lack of support (e.g., inexistence of groups/roles in packages 6 and 7). Note that,

Table 9. List of mechanisms available in some of the packages (X means that the mechanism is available in the corresponding package)

Security Mechanism (*The package offers support for...*)	ComponentTarget	Package 1	Package 2	Package 3	Package 4	Package 5	Package 6	Package 7
Automated installation of DBMS pending patches	DB	X						
Defining all DBMS userids in the installation phase	DB	X						
Relying the DBMS on an outside specialized authentication mechanism	DB	X	X	X	X	X		
Warning DBMS users, in a password change operation, that their new passwords are weak and cannot be accepted	DB				X			
An authentication procedure for remote clients that identify individual end users instead of individual applications	DB	X						
Configuring the system to drop idle connections after a specific period of inactivity	DB		X	X	X	X	X	X
Configuring the system to require that remote clients have the correct server certificate installed	DB	X			X	X	X	X
Denying login into the DBMS from a credential with more than a specified number of failed authentication attempts	DB				X			
Forcing the DBMS users to change their passwords when they're older than a specified time frame	DB				X			
Specifying privileges in a row/ value level	DB		X	X				
Changing DBMS userids already in use	DB	X			X	X	X	X
Making a backup copy of the OS which can be used to restore the environment to its current state	OS	X		X		X		X
Using a privilege limited userid to successfully install the DBMS.	OS		X		X		X	
Warning the admin that the last data backup is not up-to-date anymore	DB	X						
Warning the administrator that there are DBMS vendor patches remaining to be applied	DB	X						
Auditing a variety of important DBMS events	DB	X	X	X				

continued on following page

Table 9. Continued

Security Mechanism (*The package offers support for...*)	ComponentTarget	Package 1	Package 2	Package 3	Package 4	Package 5	Package 6	Package 7
Auditing data changes	DB	X	X	X				
Config. the DBMS so only DBAs have access to audited information	DB	X	X	X				
Configuring the system to always establish connections through the same TCP/UDP ports during the installation phase.	DB	X			X	X	X	X
Defining listening TCP/UDP ports during the installation phase	DB		X	X	X	X		X
Preventing the installation of a database example during installation	DB		X	X	X	X	X	X
Removing quotas over systems areas	DB	X	X	X				
Setting privileges to groups or roles	DB	X	X	X	X	X		
Specifying important events which occur in the DBMS that should generate a finger print	DB	X	X	X				
Specifying privileges in a column level	DB	X						
Warning DBMS users that their passwords are older than a specified time frame	DB				X			
Identifying users with quotas over systems areas	DB	X	X	X				
Selecting a different partition than the main OS partition for auditing info	DB	X	X	X				
Setting/unsetting access privileges over peripherals	OS		X		X		X	

knowing if a particular mechanism is important for a particular environment should influence the decision of what is the best package for it.

The mechanisms of the group *present in just a few packages*, on the other hand, do not seem to be considered universally important. Take, for instance, setting privileges at row level, only available in packages 2 and 3. It seems that it is not seen as a required feature, as this kind of privilege filter is usually carried out by the client applications themselves. However, it might happen that client applications do not use this feature exactly because it is not usually available, and not the other way around. Using directly a DBMS feature is often more reliable than implementing them at a different layer. Therefore, providing these mechanisms allow the users to develop systems that are less error prone than when having to design specific tailored solutions.

In order to understand if there is any pattern behind the distribution of mechanisms provided only by some packages, we explicitly analyzed the number of common mechanisms in each possible combination between the seven packages. This analysis is presented in Table 10. When looking to the mechanisms from this point of view, it stands out the fact that Packages 1, 2 and 3 provide uniquely 7 mechanisms, and Package 1 provides uniquely 6 mechanisms. On the first case, most of these mechanisms are related to auditing, which is only provided by the commercial DBMS analyzed (Oracle and SQLServer). Open source databases do not usually provide these mechanisms. In the second case, SQL Server database stands out by providing a few features that no other DBMS provides (e.g., some types of backup warnings, more installation options, column level privilege settings and a few automatic updates facilities). This helps confirming the fact that this DBMS has most security mechanisms implemented out-of-the-box, as was detected in our overall analysis (shown previously in Table 6).

In summary, all the security mechanisms identified in this work should be seen as important, even when they are not usually used by most ap-

plications. In the light of the current situation, where the set of mechanisms implemented by each available package is defined by factors not necessarily having to do with requirements of the end users, the analysis presented in this paper seems to be very useful in helping clarifying and deciding which package would be the best choice for a particular target environment.

CONCLUSION AND FUTURE WORK

In this paper we presented an experimental study on the security features of seven widely used software packages for database installations, frequently used for the deployment of business-critical web applications. We evaluated each package in terms of what are the security mechanisms that are provided by the package from the perspective of what are the real necessities of the administrators. The study resulted in two main outcomes: an overall comparative analysis of the number of mechanisms available in each package and a set of standard security mechanisms that can be used as a gap analysis tool that allows the comparison of distinct packages in terms of the presence (or not) of security mechanisms.

Results show that there is a common set of security mechanism that is implemented by most DBMS while several important mechanisms have no support at all on the packages analyzed. The reasons for this are open for debate, but we can conjecture that it has to do with a tradition of copying what has already being proposed in the field and has proven to work, without rethinking the whole features from scratch. When these systems are comprehensively analyzed then the missing features become highlighted. We believe that the analysis we done in this work is of utmost importance for database administrators and could be of great interest for vendors to improve the security characteristics of future software products and packages.

Table 10. Mechanisms available only in specific sets of packages

Set of packages	Number of mechanisms provided uniquely by this set
Packages 2,3,4,5,6,7	2
Packages 1,2,3,4,5	2
Packages 1,4,5,6,7	3
Packages 2,3,4,5,7	1
Packages 1,3,5,7	1
Packages 2,4,6	2
Packages 1,2,3	7
Packages 1,4	1
Packages 2,3	1
Package 1	6
Package 4	3

Future work includes the extension of this study to other system elements needed to deploy a web application (e.g., web servers, application servers, authentication servers). Also, we intend to define a standard benchmark that helps administrators on selecting the best package taking into account the security needs of their software installations.

REFERENCES

Araújo Neto, A., & Vieira, M. (2008). Towards assessing the security of DBMS configurations. In *Proceedings of the International Conference on Dependable Systems and Networks* (pp. 90-95).

Araújo Neto, A., Vieira, M., & Madeira, H. (2009). An appraisal to assess the security of database configurations. In *Proceedings of the 2nd International Conference on Dependability* (pp. 73-80).

Baumhardt, F. (2006). *Common criteria - It security certification, or shiny sales sticker? (IN) Security architecture.* Retrieved from http://blogs. technet.com/fred/archive/2006/03/02/421014. aspx

Bertino, E., Jajodia, S., & Samarati, P. (1995). Database security: Research and practice. *Information Systems Journal, 20*(7).

Cachin, C., Camenisch, J., Dacier, M., Deswarte, Y., Dobson, J., Horne, D., et al. (2000). *Reference model and use cases* (Tech. Rep. No. IST-1999-11583). Retrieved from http://spiderman-2.laas. fr/TSF/cabernet/maftia/deliverables/D1.pdf

Castano, S., Fugini, M. G., Martella, G., & Samarati, P. (1994). *Database security*. Reading, MA: Addison-Wesley.

Center for Internet Security. (2008). *CIS benchmarks/scoring tools*. Retrieved from http://www. cisecurity.org

Commission of the European Communities. (1993). *Information technology security evaluation manual (ITSEM)*. Brussels, Belgium: Author.

Common Criteria. (1999). *Common criteria for information technology security evaluation: User guide*. Retrieved from http://www.commoncriteriaportal.org/files/ccfiles/CCPART2V3.1R2.pdf

Defense Information Systems Agency. (2007). *Database - Security technical implementation guide, version 8, release 1*. Washington, DC: Author.

Department of Defense. (1985). *Trusted computer system evaluation criteria*. Washington, DC: Author.

Howard, M., & Leblanc, D. E. (2002). *Writing secure code* (2nd ed.). Sebastopol, CA: Microsoft Press.

Jackson, W. (2007). *Under attack: Common Criteria has loads of critics, but is it getting a bum rap?* Retrieved from http://www.gcn.com/ print/26_21/44857-1.html

Kanoun, K., & Spainhower, L. (2008). *Dependability benchmarking for computer systems*. Los Alamitos, CA: Wiley-IEEE Computer Society Press. doi:10.1002/9780470370506

Microsoft Corporation. (2011a). *Microsoft SQL server 2005*. Retrieved from http://www.microsoft.com/sqlserver/en/us/default.aspx

Microsoft Corporation. (2011b). *Microsoft Windows XP*. Retrieved from http://windows.microsoft.com/en-US/windows/products/windows-xp

Oracle Corporation. (2011a). *MySQL community edition 5*. Retrieved from http://www.oracle.com/ technetwork/database/express-edition/overview/ index.html

Oracle Corporation. (2011b). *Oracle 10g express edition*. Retrieved from http://www.oracle.com/ technetwork/database/express-edition/overview/ index.html

Pernul, G., & Luef, G. (1992). Bibliography on database security. *SIGMOD Record, 21*(1). doi:10.1145/130868.130884

PostgreSQL Global Development Group. (2011). *PostgreSQL 8*. Retrieved from http://www.postgresql.org

Red Hat. (2011). *Enterprise Linux 5*. Retrieved from http://www.redhat.com/rhel/

Sandia National Laboratories. (2011). *The information design assurance red team*. Retrieved from http://www.idart.sandia.gov/

Schell, R., & Heckman, M. (1987). Views for multilevel database security. *IEEE Transactions on Software Engineering, 13*(2).

Vieira, M., & Madeira, H. (2002). Recovery and performance balance of a COTS DBMS in the presence of operator faults. In *Proceedings of the International Conference on Dependable Systems and Networks* (pp. 615-624).

Vieira, M., & Madeira, H. (2005). Towards a security benchmark for database management systems. In *Proceedings of the International Conference on Dependable Systems and Networks*, Yokohama, Japan (pp. 592-601).

This work was previously published in the International Journal of Secure Software Engineering, Volume 2, Issue 3, edited by Khaled M. Khan, pp. 42-62, copyright 2011 by IGI Publishing (an imprint of IGI Global).

Section 2
Formal Techniques and Tools

Chapter 7
Using Executable Slicing to Improve Rogue Software Detection Algorithms

Jan Durand
Louisiana Tech University, USA

Nicholas Kraft
University of Alabama, USA

Juan Flores
Louisiana Tech University, USA

Randy Smith
University of Alabama, USA

Travis Atkison
Louisiana Tech University, USA

ABSTRACT

This paper describes a research effort to use executable slicing as a pre-processing aid to improve the prediction performance of rogue software detection. The prediction technique used here is an information retrieval classifier known as cosine similarity that can be used to detect previously unknown, known or variances of known rogue software by applying the feature extraction technique of randomized projection. This paper provides direction in answering the question of is it possible to only use portions or subsets, known as slices, of an application to make a prediction on whether or not the software contents are rogue. This research extracts sections or slices from potentially rogue applications and uses these slices instead of the entire application to make a prediction. Results show promise when applying randomized projections to cosine similarity for the predictions, with as much as a 4% increase in prediction performance and a five-fold decrease in processing time when compared to using the entire application.

1. INTRODUCTION

With today's market globalization of software development and the proliferation of malicious attackers, it is becoming almost impossible to have any trust in the software that is loaded onto our systems. Rogue applications, or applications in which code has been added, modified or removed with the intent of causing harm or subverting a system's intended function (McGraw & Morrisett, 2000), are becoming more and more prevalent. To combat these infiltrations, consumers, as well

DOI: 10.4018/978-1-4666-2482-5.ch007

as corporations, are turning to anti-virus software products, which contain virus detection engines. Though very good at what they do, virus detection engines rely on a database of signatures to detect known rogue applications. Signature based systems inherently limit the detection of new and previously unknown types of rogue attacks. To that end there have been several research attempts to overcome these limitations. In one of these attempts (Atkison, 2009) we have shown the value of using randomized projection algorithms in detecting malicious applications.

The purpose of this paper is to provide methods and techniques to overcome the limitations inherent in the signature-based systems mentioned above. Through this research effort, we will provide a methodology for detecting rouge applications by enhancing the random projection, dimensionality reduction concept by using executable slicing. Executable slicing is a strategic method of compartmentalizing applications, and is used as a pre-processor to the algorithm. It will be shown that by adding this pre-processing step a significant gain in accuracy as well as in precision and recall can be achieved.

The following section provides a background description of previous methods that involve static analysis, information retrieval and randomized projection. In Section 3, the experimental design of this work is discussed including software and data used. In Section 4, results achieved are described. Finally, in Section 5 the conclusion and future directions are presented.

2. BACKGROUND

Developing effective potential solutions to the malicious software detection problem is an important direction in host security research. There have been few research papers, (Kang, Poosankam, & Yin, 2007; Perdisci, Lanzi, & Lee, 2008) are good examples, that pose the option of executable slicing while looking at malicious detection. Though

their focus is directed toward packed executables, the focus of this paper is to show that statically analyzing sections or slices of an executable will improve prediction rates of non-packed, stand-alone executables. It is important to understand the methods and techniques that are used for these predictions. Since the randomized projection technique in this solution is used in conjunction with an information retrieval prediction algorithm we will include a small background on information retrieval as well as static analysis.

2.1. Static Analysis

Static analysis, sometimes referred to as static program analysis or static code analysis, is the examination of the source or object code of an application in order to identify patterns that indicate potential design errors and/or security threats (Food and Drug Administration [FDA], 2010). This analysis approach eliminates the need to execute an application in order to determine its behavior, contrary to its counter-part dynamic analysis, thus avoiding the potential compromise of the host system.

Static analysis has proven to be a very useful tool in detecting undesirable or vulnerable code in applications. There have been several research efforts such as (Bergeron, et al., 2001; Bergeron, Debbabi, Erhioui, & Ktari, 1999; Christodorescu & Jha, 2003; FDA, 2010; Jovanovic, Kruegel, & Kirda, 2006) that have incorporated the use of static analysis to detect malicious code in executable files.

Christodorescu et al. (2003) presented a static analysis framework for identifying malicious code patterns in executables and implemented SAFE, a static analyzer for executables. In their research, they show that SAFE is resilient to common obfuscation transformations on malicious code while three popular anti-virus scanners were susceptible to these attacks (Christodorescu & Jha, 2003).

Bergeron et al. (1999, 2001) present a three-step approach for detecting malicious code in applications, which they claim is capable of detecting unknown malicious code. This approach consists of generating an intermediate representation, analyzing control and data flows to capture security-oriented program behavior, and performing static verification of critical behaviors against security policies (Bergeron, et al., 2001).

Jovanovic et al. (2006) tackle the problem of vulnerable Web applications using static code analysis. They make use of a number of static analysis techniques including flow-sensitive, interprocedural and context-sensitive data flow analysis to locate vulnerable points in an application and then improve the accuracy of the search results via alias and literal analysis (Jovanovic, et al., 2006). This framework was then implemented as Pixy, an open-source Java tool which targets taint-style vulnerabilities such as SQL injection attacks and cross-site scripting (Jovanovic, et al., 2006).

The research proposed in this paper makes use of static analysis techniques such as executable slicing in conjunction with information retrieval techniques and randomized projection in order to detect malicious applications.

2.2. Information Retrieval

Information retrieval traditionally is the part of computer science, which from a collection of written documents studies the retrieval of information (not data) (Baeza-Yates & Ribeiro-Neto, 1999). These retrieved documents' aim is to satisfy an information need (Baeza-Yates & Ribeiro-Neto, 1999). The process can be thought of as combing through a set of documents, called the corpus, to find a certain piece of information that has a relationship to a given entity, called the query. That piece of information can either be an entire document, set of documents or a subset of a document. Within the information retrieval community several methods exist for finding these pieces of relevant information. These methods include vector space models, latent semantic indexing models

and statistical confidence models as well as others. The first approach to represent a document as a set of terms were vector space models (Liu, et al., 2004). As their name implies vector space models represent their data as a vector with each dimension being defined as a term which may or may not have a weight associated with it (Salton, Wong, & Yang, 1975). One of the most common vector space models is cosine similarity. Cosine similarity determines the similarity between two data vectors by measuring the angular distance between them. The property of cosine is that it is 1.0 for identical vectors and 0.0 for orthogonal vectors (Singhal, 2001) The following is the formula used in our work for computing cosine similarity.

$$Cosine\ Similarity\ (Q, D) = \frac{\sum_i w_{Q,i} w_{D,i}}{\sqrt{\sum_i w_{Q,i}^2} \sqrt{\sum_i w_{D,i}^2}}$$

(2.1)

This formula computes the similarity between a query Q and a document D. It does so by summing the individual components of the two entities represented in the formula as w. The individual components for this research are defined as n-grams. An n-gram is any substring of length n (Baeza-Yates & Ribeiro-Neto, 1999), that can also be described as a feature. A feature in this context is an extracted piece of information that in part describes the item from which it was extracted. Here the gram (which will be the composite of the substring) is a byte in hexadecimal form extracted from a binary executable in the corpus. For example, the string '03 A4 EC 17' represents 4 bytes in hexadecimal form and '03A4' is an n-gram of length 2 of that string. Therefore, w_{Qi} is the weight of the ith n-gram in the query and w_{Di} is the weight of the ith n-gram in the document.

There have been other efforts (Abou-Assaleh, Cercone, Keselj, & Sweidan, 2004a, 2004b; Henchiri & Japkowicz, 2006; Kephart et al., 1995; Marceau, 2000; Reddy & Pujari, 2006) to use the information retrieval concept of *n*-grams as features. Henchiri et al. (2006) and Abou-Assaleh et al. (2004a, 2004b) both use the Common N-Gram (CNG) analysis method, which uses the most frequent *n*-grams to represent a class, to detect rogue applications. Henchiri further limits the number of features by imposing a "hierarchical feature selection process" (Henchiri & Japkowicz, 2006). Marceau (2000) puts an interesting twist on the problem of using *n*-grams as features by having "multiple-length" grams instead of the traditional single *n*-length gram. Marceau does this by first creating and then compacting a suffix tree, a structure that allows fast string operations be provides suffixes of given strings, to a Directed Acyclic Graph (DAG). Reddy et al. (2006) develop their own unique *n*-gram feature selection measure called, 'class-wise document frequency.'

2.3. Randomized Projection

Rogue application detection, following the genre of information retrieval, suffers from the problem that the data, once processed, is encoded in extremely high dimensions. This high-dimensional data limits the kind and amount of analysis that can be performed. One method for dealing with the reduction of this type of high-dimensional data is known as feature extraction. Feature extraction transforms, either linearly or non-linearly, the original feature set into a reduced set that retains the most important predictive information. Examples of this type include principle component analysis, singular value decomposition and randomized projection.

In randomized projection, using a random matrix whose columns have unit lengths the original high-dimensional data is projected onto a lower-dimensional subspace (Bingham & Mannila, 2001). This type of projection attempts to retain the maximum amount of information embedded in the original feature set while substantially reducing the number of features required. This feature reduction will allow for greater

amounts of analysis to be performed. The core concept has been developed out of the Johnson-Lindenstrauss lemma (Johnson & Lindenstrauss, 1984) which states that any set of *n* points in a Euclidean space can be mapped to R^t where t = $O(\log n / \varepsilon^2)$ with distortion $\leq 1 + \varepsilon$ in the distances. Such a mapping may be found in random polynomial time. A proof of this lemma can be found in Dasgupta and Gupta (1999).

There have been some efforts (Bingham & Mannila, 2001; Mannila & Seppänen, 2001; Papadimitriou, Raghavan, Tamaki, & Vempala, 2000) that look at using randomized projection techniques for dimensionality reduction. Randomized projection refers to projecting a set of points from a high-dimensional space to a randomly chosen low-dimensional subspace (Vempala, 2004). Minnila et al. (2001) use random projection techniques to map sequences of events and find similarities between them. Their specific application is in the telecommunication field looking at how to better handle network alarms. Their goal is to show the analyst past circumstances that resemble the current one (Mannila & Seppänen, 2001) so that a more informed decision about the current situation can be made. Though their proposed solution is not perfect, it does show the promise of using randomized projections in a similarity based application.

Bingham and Mannila (2001) apply randomized projections to an image and text retrieval problem. In comparison to this research problem, their dimensions are not as large, 2500 for images and 5000 for text but the results are still significant. The purpose of their work was to show that compared to other more traditional dimensionality reduction techniques, such as principle component analysis or singular value decomposition, randomized projections offered a greater detail of accuracy. The authors were also able to show that there was a significant computation saving by using randomized projections over other feature extraction techniques, such as principle component analysis.

In another text retrieval application, Kaski (1998) successfully applied randomized projections in his text retrieval application that used WEBSOM, a graphical self-organizing map. Again Kaski turned to randomized projection as a method to overcome the computation expense that made other dimensionality reduction techniques infeasible when handling high-dimensional data sets. After incorporating randomized projection into their tool the authors gained an additional 5% increase in classification and topic separation over previous methods used (Kaski, 1998).

The following efforts (Kurimo, 1999; Lin & Gunopulos, 2003; Papadimitriou et al., 2000) use randomized projection in conjunction with latent semantic indexing. Papadimitriou et al. (2000), looking at another information retrieval technique, show positive results in using randomized projections as a pre-processor to the computationally expensive Latent Semantic Indexing. By simply applying randomized projection to their data before computing the Latent Semantic Indexing, their asymptotic running time for the overall system improved from $O(mnc)$ to $O(m(\log^2 n + c \log n))$, where m and n are the matrix size, c is the average number of terms per document (Papadimitriou et al., 2000).

3. EXPERIMENT

For the experiments presented in this paper, a rogue application detection tool suite was developed. All of the experiments were run on commodity hardware running the Fedora Linux operating system. It is very significant that we were able to complete all of these experiments on commodity hardware. It shows that large, specialized machines are not needed to perform rogue application detection and that this work can be broadly applied across almost any level of architecture that researchers/developers may have and still gain the significantly

positive results that were obtained and discussed below. In addition, this software and the methods that it supports can easily take advantage of commodity cluster hardware for substantial gains in performance.

3.1. Similarity Software

The rogue application detection tool suite created for this experiment provides functionality to input Windows formatted binary executables and then creates an m-dimensional data space that contains vectors representing those applications. It can create these vectors from the entire application or slices (sections) of the application. The sections used in these experiments were the data and code sections. In these experiments, m is the number of total possible n-grams that can be extracted from the ingested applications, one dimension for each possible n-gram. The information stored in each of the dimensions can take on one of several possible values: the absolute total number of occurrences of the particular n-gram in the application, the normalized value of the total number of occurrences of the particular n-gram in the application, or finally a 1 if the application contained the particular n-gram or a 0 if it did not. Once the m-dimensional vectors have been created, the randomized projection matrix algorithm is then applied. In the method of randomized projection via matrix multiplication, the original m-dimensional data, let's say a $d \times m$ matrix D, is projected to a k-dimensional ($k \ll m$) subspace through the origin, using a random $m \times k$ matrix R whose columns have unit lengths (Bingham & Mannila, 2001). Selecting vectors that are normally distributed random variables with a mean of 1 and a standard deviation of 0, populates the random matrix. After the original feature matrix is multiplied by the random matrix, the resulting $d \times k$ matrix is a low-dimensional embedding of the original high-dimensional features. The cosine similarity algorithm is then applied to the query application's vector and the corpus applications' vectors. The cosine similarity algorithm followed is the same as shown in Equation (2.1). A special feature of this software is that it has the ability to shift the *n*-gram window not only by the more traditional byte offsets but also by bit offsets. This allows for a more fine grain tuning of the vector values, e.g., if the malicious attacker performs bit shifting on the rogue applications. It also provides for more accurate similarity result calculations.

3.2. Data Set

The data set that was compiled together for the experiments described in this section consisted of 1544 Windows formatted binary executable files. None of the files in the data set were larger than 950KB. Of these files 303 were extracted from a fresh installation of the Windows XP operating system. Another 406 were extracted from a fresh installation of Windows Vista operating system. Both of these sets were obtained by installing the respective operating system in a virtual environment on a commodity PC. These virtual environments were not connected to the Internet and therefore provided a safe location. This ensured that it would allow for application extraction without the worry of rogue infiltration during the gathering phase of the research effort. This process provided a total of 709 files that were in the data set and that were considered benign. The remaining 835 files for the data set were rogue, Trojan horse applications that were downloaded from various websites on the Internet including http://www.trojanfrance.com and http://vx.netlux.org.

3.3. Procedure

This section describes the overall flow of this experiment. The feature set (*n*-grams) was extracted from the corpus. The size of the *n*-grams was varied from a 3-byte, 5-byte and a 7-byte window. The randomized projection method described above in section 3.1 was applied to the original high-dimensional data set to produce three separate new low-dimensional embeddings, which contained 500, 1000 and 1500 features each. The cosine similarity algorithm was then applied between each vector in these reduced dimensional data sets over a range of cosine similarity threshold values, ranging from 0 to 1.0 in 0.05 increments, to produce prediction values. These prediction values were then used to classify each document vector as either malicious or benign. The results obtained from these experiments are presented below.

4. RESULTS

To determine if executable slicing can be a useful pre-processing tool, multiple instantiations of the data set were created. The first instantiation involved using the entire or whole application itself. This instantiation of the data is the one that is used by all of the researchers that are mentioned in the literature survey described in section 2. The remaining three were created through extracting and combining well-known defined sections from the whole application. The second and third instantiations were created by extracting the code and data sections from each application using the PE Explorer tool from Heaventools Software (2009). To confirm the accuracy of this tool several of the applications in the data set were hand dissected, comparing these to the results provided by PE Explorer and the tool proved to be very accurate. To create the fourth instantiation of the data set, the data and code sections were combined together via a string append operation. These additional instantiations were done to determine if extracted sections of each application could prove more fruitful in detection than just using the entire application. The thought process behind creating these multiple instantiations was as follows. Since all of the applications in the data set were valid Windows format executables, there would have to be an inherent similarity in all of them. This comes from both structure and header contents that may hamper attempts to produce valid and viable rogue application detection. By extracting the data and code sections, this inherent similarity was removed and allowed the detection methods to concentrate on the true differences in the applications. It must be noted that with the combined data and code data set instantiation a potentially 'false' set of features is created at the point of fusion. For example, consider the union of byte sequences '0F 1C A2' and '45 B0 12'. Extracting *n*-grams of length 3 from the resulting sequence '0F 1C A2 45 B0 12', where 1 gram is 2 contiguous characters, the *n*-grams '1CA245' and 'A245B0', are produced at the junction 'A2 45'. This set of *n*-grams is considered 'false' since its members do not exist in the individual strings. However, the cardinality of this set is extremely small, at most 6 for these experiments, when compared to the entire set of features that are extracted and therefore will not hamper any detection capabilities of the tool suite.

4.1. Validation

As with any new method, technique or technology that is introduced, a system for determining its accuracy or validity must also be presented. Validation is a key component to providing feasible confidence that any new method is effective at reaching a viable solution, in this case a viable solution to the rogue application detection problem. Validation is not only comparing the results to what the expected result should be, but it is also comparing the results of our techniques and methodologies to other published methods.

For this research, the authors are comparing multiple data slices to determine their usefulness in the prediction process. To that end several performance values were used to measure and compare the performance of the experiments conducted in this research effort. These values include true positive rate (TPR), false positive rate (FPR), accuracy and precision. TPR, Equa-

tion4.1 below, also known as recall, is defined as the proportion of relevant applications that are retrieved, calculated by the ratio of the number of relevant retrieved applications to the total number of relevant applications that are in the data set (Salton & Buckley, 1988). In other words TPR is the ratio of actual positive instances that were correctly identified. FPR, Equation4.2, is the ratio of negative instances that were incorrectly identified. Accuracy, Equation4.3, is the ratio of the number of positive instances, either true positive or false positive, that were correct. Precision, Equation4.4, is defined as the proportion of retrieved applications that are relevant, calculated by the ratio of the number of relevant retrieved applications to the total number of retrieved applications (Salton & Buckley, 1988), or the ratio of predicted true positive instances that were identified correctly. All of these values are derived from information provided from the truth table. A truth table, also known as a confusion matrix, provides the actual and predicted classifications from the predictor. The following are the mathematical definitions of the performance formulas as well as the truth table (Table 1) where, *a* (true positive) is the number of rogue applications in the data set that were classified as rogue applications, *b* (false positive) is the number of benign applications in the data set that were classified as rogue applications, *c* (false negative) is the number of rogue applications in the data set that were classified as benign applications, and *d* (true negative) is the number of benign applications in the data set that were classified as benign applications (Schultz, Eskin, Zadok, & Stolfo, 2001). Below are the formulas for the four performance calculations that were used in this research effort for validation of the predicted results.

$$TPR = \frac{a}{a + c} \qquad (4.1)$$

Table 1. Definition of Truth Table

		Actual	
		Positive	Negative
Predicted	Positive	a	b
	Negative	c	d

$$FPR = \frac{b}{b+d} \qquad (4.2)$$

$$Accuracy = \frac{a+d}{a+b+c+d} \qquad (4.3)$$

$$Precision = \frac{a}{a+b} \qquad (4.4)$$

Using these calculated performance values this work can be validated and show that the proposed executable slicing method performed "better" than not using executable slicing. Better is defined in terms of absolute comparison of the validation methods presented above.

4.2. Instantiation Performance

As discussed above the pre-processing of the data set produced four data slices: whole, data, code and a combination of data and code. It is important to note that the results presented in this paper are just samples of the entire breadth of experiments that were performed on this data set.

Figures 1 and 2 depict a 3-gram experiment where the dimensionality was reduced to 500 from a range of ~500,000 to ~7,000,000, and a 4-gram experiment where the dimensionality was reduced to 1500 from a range of ~650,000 to ~13,000,000, respectively. The upper left quadrant contains the validation accuracy calculation results for the range of cosine similarity threshold values. By cosine similarity threshold value, we mean that two documents with a cosine similarity below this cut-off point are considered dissimilar. The

lower left quadrant contains the TPR calculation while the lower right contains the calculations for precision. For each of the quadrants in the figure we are looking for the highest peak. For example in the upper left quadrant the highest peak would equate to the highest accuracy value for the range of threshold values. The upper right quadrant is defined as the FPR, for this value the lower value is the better result.

Beginning with the accuracy values (upper left quadrant) it can be seen that a 4% increase in total accuracy can be reached by using the slicing method (data – green line, code – blue line, combination – purple line) when compared to not using the slicing method (whole – red line). This value can be seen in Figure 1 when comparing the whole set (95%) to either the code or combination of code and data sets (both at 99%), each with threshold values of 0.25. Continuing to use those threshold values we can turn our attention to the TPR rate where the executable slicing provides a 2% increase. The precision is approximately the same but there is a 5% decrease in overall FPR. Similar results are seen as well in Figure 2.

This important result of the extracted instantiations outperforming the whole application can be seen throughout the experiment. This is a positive and significant step in that this type of slicing of applications to make a rogue application detection determination has not been published before at this level. By extracting these sections from an application, the data search space becomes much smaller and therefore allows for a faster detection time and a more accurate detection because of the ability to include more applications in the detection corpus. The slicing process adds a very minimal time to the preprocessing stage. Through the entire set of experiments the prediction processing time was decreased by as much five-fold, excluding the feature extraction phase.

When the results are examined from a data set instantiation viewpoint holding the remaining variables of *n*-gram size and dimensionality reduction

Figure 1. 3-gram, 500-features

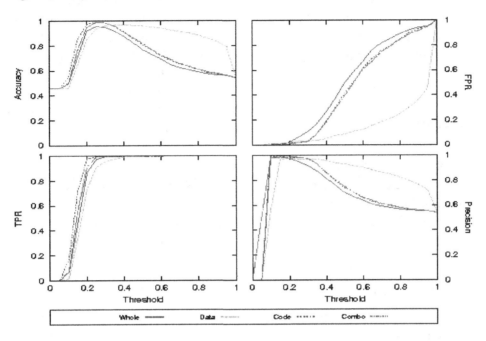

size constant, it is clear that using the extracted data set instantiations provided a considerable increase in accuracy when compared to using the entire or whole application. It can be further derived that the code instantiation provides better results than the data instantiation. Even better results can be

Figure 2. 4-gram, 1500-features

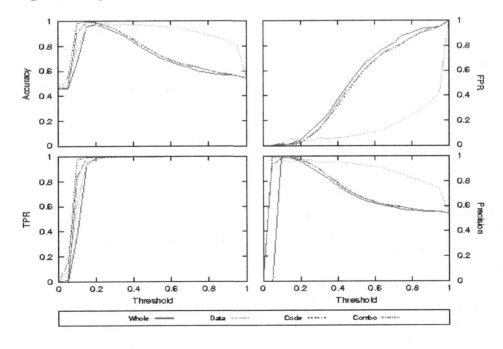

obtained by the combination of the data and code instantiations. However, with a minimal loss in overall prediction performance, about 1%, one could use just the code instantiation and gain in time performance.

5. CONCLUSION

The results support the idea that a better malicious software classifier can be created by applying an executable slicing technique as a pre-processing step to the technique of randomized projection. It has been shown through direct comparison that adding the executable slicing step generates results that have a higher accuracy value as well as better precision and recall values when compared to the randomized projection without using the executable slicing, pre-processing step.

There is no claim that this is a complete solution but rather a tool designed to fit into the security administrator's toolbox as a data point or first pass to help reduce the number of applications needing review. This potential reduction in the number of applications to sort through can provide an administrator or analyst with valuable time savings by not having to analyze applications that clearly do not contain rogue software. With more and more applications not being developed "in-house," this is a positive result for those responsible for providing secure solutions.

Future efforts for this research are to expand it with the addition of prediction algorithms from the data mining realm, for example decision trees. Also the author plans to investigate additional dimensionality reduction methods and techniques in order to further expand and enhance the analysis capability. It would be very interesting to determine if similar gains can be seen using executable slicing on other techniques. It is worth noting that this approach may be able to detect the slight variances in different instances of a polymorphic virus; however, this still needs to be tested. While detecting viruses which use self-encryption is out of the scope of this effort, it would be a notable path for future research. Additional research is also planned for determining the threshold values for the similarity algorithm. As seen in the results above, determining the key factors in choosing an optimal threshold value is crucial to gaining high confidence and to the success rate of the algorithm.

ACKNOWLEDGMENTS

This material is based upon work supported by the U.S. Air Force, Air Force Research Laboratory under Award No. FA9550-10-1-0289. The authors would also like to thank Mr. Richard Libby, from Intel for equipment donation and Dr. Box Leangsuksun for high performance computing services.

REFERENCES

Abou-Assaleh, T., Cercone, N., Keselj, V., & Sweidan, R. (2004a). Detection of new malicious code using n-grams signatures. In *Proceedings of the 2nd Annual Conference on Privacy, Security and Trust*, New Brunswick, Canada (pp. 193-196).

Abou-Assaleh, T., Cercone, N., Keselj, V., & Sweidan, R. (2004b). N-gram-based detection of new malicious code. In *Proceedings of the 28th Annual International Computer Software and Applications Conference* (pp. 41-42).

Atkison, T. (2009). Applying randomized projection to aid prediction algorithms in detecting high-dimensional rogue applications. In *Proceedings of the 47th ACM Southeast Conference*, Clemson, SC (p. 23).

Baeza-Yates, R., & Ribeiro-Neto, B. (1999). *Modern information retrieval*. Harlow, UK: Addison-Wesley.

Bergeron, J., Debbabi, M., Desharnais, J., Erhioui, M. M., Lavoie, Y., Tawbi, N., et al. (2001). Static detection of malicious code in executable programs. In *Proceedings of the Symposium on Requirements Engineering for Information Security* (pp. 184-189).

Bergeron, J., Debbabi, M., Erhioui, M. M., & Ktari, B. (1999). Static analysis of binary code to isolate malicious behaviors. In *Proceedings of the IEEE 8th International Workshop on Enabling Technologies: Infrastructure for Collaborative Enterprises* (pp. 184-189).

Bingham, E., & Mannila, H. (2001). Random projection in dimensionality reduction: Applications to image and text data. In *Proceedings of the 7th ACM SIGKDD International Conference on Knowledge Discovery and Data Mining* (pp. 245-250).

Christodorescu, M., & Jha, S. (2003). Static analysis of executables to detect malicious patterns. In *Proceedings of the 12th Conference on USENIX Security Symposium* (p. 12).

Dasgupta, S., & Gupta, A. (1999). *An elementary proof of the Johnson-Lindenstrauss Lemma*. Berkley, CA: International Computer Science Institute.

Food and Drug Administration. (2010). *Infusion pump software safety research at FDA*. Retrieved from http://www.fda.gov/MedicalDevices/ProductsandMedicalProcedures/GeneralHospitalDevicesandSupplies/InfusionPumps/ucm202511.htm

Haventools Software. (2009). *Heaventools: PE Explorer*. Retrieved from http://www.heaventools.net

Henchiri, O., & Japkowicz, N. (2006). A feature selection and evaluation scheme for computer virus detection. In *Proceedings of the 6th International Conference on Data Mining* (pp. 891-895).

Johnson, W. B., & Lindenstrauss, J. (1984). Extensions of Lipschitz mappings into a Hilbert space. *Contemporary Mathematics, 26*, 189–206.

Jovanovic, N., Kruegel, C., & Kirda, E. (2006). Pixy: A static analysis tool for extracting web application vulnerabilities. In *Proceedings of the IEEE Symposium on Security and Privacy* (pp. 258-263).

Kang, M. G., Poosankam, P., & Yin, H. (2007). Renovo: A hidden code extractor for packed executables. In *Proceedings of the ACM Workshop on Recurring Malcode*.

Kaski, S. (1998). Dimensionality reduction by random mapping: Fast similarity computation for clustering. In *Proceedings of the IEEE World Congress International Joint Conference on Neural Networks and Computational Intelligence* (pp. 413-418).

Kephart, J. O., Sorkin, G. B., Arnold, W. C., Chess, D. M., Tesauro, G. J., & White, S. R. (1995). Biologically inspired defenses against computer viruses. In *Proceedings of the 14th International Joint Conference on Artificial Intelligence*, San Francisco, CA (pp. 985-996).

Kurimo, M. (1999). Indexing audio documents by using latent semantic analysis and SOM. *Kohonen Maps*, 363-374.

Lin, J., & Gunopulos, D. (2003, May). Dimensionality reduction by random projection and latent semantic indexing. In *Proceedings of the Text Mining Workshop at the 3rd SIAM International Conference on Data Mining*.

Liu, N., Zhang, B., Yan, J., Yang, Q., Yan, S., Chen, Z., et al. (2004). Learning similarity measures in non-orthogonal space. In *Proceedings of the Thirteenth ACM International Conference on Information and Knowledge Management* (pp. 334-341).

Mannila, H., & Seppänen, J. K. (2001). Finding similar situations in sequences of events. In *Proceedings of the 1st SIAM International Conference on Data Mining.*

Marceau, C. (2000). Characterizing the behavior of a program using multiple-length n-grams. In *Proceedings of the Workshop on New Security Paradigms* (pp. 101-110).

McGraw, G., & Morrisett, G. (2000). Attacking malicious code: A report to the Infosec Research Council. *IEEE Software, 17*(5), 33–41. doi:10.1109/52.877857

Papadimitriou, C. H., Raghavan, P., Tamaki, H., & Vempala, S. (2000). Latent semantic indexing: A probabilistic analysis. *Journal of Computer and System Sciences, 61*(2), 217–235. doi:10.1006/jcss.2000.1711

Perdisci, R., Lanzi, A., & Lee, W. (2008). Classification of packed executables for accurate computer virus detection. *Pattern Recognition Letters, 29*(14), 1941–1946. doi:10.1016/j.patrec.2008.06.016

Reddy, D. K. S., & Pujari, A. K. (2006). N-gram analysis for computer virus detection. *Journal in Computer Virology, 2*(3), 231–239. doi:10.1007/s11416-006-0027-8

Salton, G., & Buckley, C. (1988). Term-weighting approaches in automatic text retrieval. *Information Processing and Management: an International Journal, 24*(5), 513–523. doi:10.1016/0306-4573(88)90021-0

Salton, G., Wong, A., & Yang, C. S. (1975). A vector space model for automatic indexing. *Communications of the ACM, 18*(11), 613–620. doi:10.1145/361219.361220

Schultz, M., Eskin, E., Zadok, E., & Stolfo, S. (2001). Data mining methods for detection of new malicious executables. In *Proceedings of the IEEE Symposium on Security and Privacy* (pp. 38-49).

Singhal, A. (2001). Modern information retrieval: A brief overview. *A Quarterly Bulletin of the Computer Society of the IEEE Technical Committee on Data Engineering, 24*(4), 35–43.

Vempala, S. S. (2004). *The random projection method.* Providence, RI: American Mathematical Society.

This work was previously published in the International Journal of Secure Software Engineering, Volume 2, Issue 2, edited by Khaled M. Khan, pp. 53-64, copyright 2011 by IGI Publishing (an imprint of IGI Global).

Chapter 8
EII Secure Information System Using Modal Logic Technique

Yun Bai
University of Western Sydney, Australia

Khaled M. Khan
Qatar University, Qatar

ABSTRACT

In this paper, the authors propose a formal logic technique to protect information systems. As the widespread use of computer systems grows, the security of the information stored in such systems has become more important. As a security mechanism, authorization or access control ensures that all accesses to the system resources occur exclusively according to the access polices and rules specified by the system security agent. Authorization specification has been widely studied and a variety of approaches have been investigated. The authors propose a formal language with modal logic to specify the system security policies. The authors also provide the reasoning in response to system access requests, especially in situations where the security agent's knowledge base is incomplete. The semantics of this language is provided by translating it into epistemic logic program in which knowledge related modal operators are employed to represent agents' knowledge in reasoning. The authors demonstrate how this approach handles the situation where the security agent's knowledge on access decision is incomplete. The proposed mechanism effectively prevents unauthorized and malicious access to information systems.

1. INTRODUCTION

As the widespread use of computer systems, the security of the information stored in such systems has become more and more important. When measuring computer system performance, the system

security is just as important as its efficiency, speed and cost. There are several mechanisms to provide computer system security. Typical ones are authentication and authorization. The authentication service only allows legitimate users access the system, while the authorization service controls

DOI: 10.4018/978-1-4666-2482-5.ch008

the legitimate users only performing legitimate operations on the system resource. Authorization is to ensure that all accesses to the system resources occur exclusively according to the access polices and rules specified by the security agent of the information system. In this paper, we investigate the authorization or access control mechanism. Authorizations or access control has been widely studied (Atluri et al., 2002; Chomicki et al., 2000; Fernandez et al., 1995; Zhou et al., 2008) and a variety of authorization specification approaches such as access matrix (Dacier et al., 1994; Denning, 1976), role-based access control (Crampton et al., 2008), access control in database systems (Bertino et al., 1996; Meadow, 1991), authorization delegation (Murray et al., 2008), procedural and logical specifications (Bai et al., 2003; Bertino et al., 2003) have been investigated. Since logic based approaches provide a powerful expressiveness (Fagin et al., 1995; Das, 1992; Fernandez et al., 1989) as well as flexibility for capturing a variety of system security requirements, increasing work has been focusing on this aspect. Jajodia et al. (2001) proposed a logic language for expressing authorizations. They used predicates and rules to specify the authorizations; their work mainly emphasizes the representation and evaluation of authorizations. The work of Bertino et al. (2000) describes an authorization mechanism based on a logic formalism. It mainly investigates the access control rules and their derivations. In their recent work (Bertino et al., 2003), a formal approach based on C-Datalog language is presented for reasoning about access control models. Damiani et al. (2002) presented a language for specification of access control by exploiting the characteristics of XML to define and enforce access control directly on the structure and content of the document. They provided a flexible security mechanism for protecting XML documents. Murata et al. (2003) proposed a static analysis for XML access control. Given an access control policy and an access query, they use a static analysis to decide if to grant or deny such

an access request. In this way, run-time evaluation is only needed when the static analysis is unable to decide. This pre-execution analysis improves the performance of the system response to a query.

However, there were some limitations so far in these approaches. These approaches made access decision based on the security domain the agent know, and the domain is complete. When the security agent does not have complete, specific information about the security domain, how to reason and answer access queries under such a scenario? For instance, if the agent knows that Alice can access the classified file if Alice is a manager. At the moment, it is believed that Alice is a manager. Is Alice allowed to access the file?

Another example, the agent currently does not know clearly who can access the classified file between Alice and Bob, but knows only one of them can. This can be specified by a disjunctive logic program (Baral, 2003) as follows:

$$AliceCanAccessFile \lor BobCanAccessFile \leftarrow,$$

$$AliceCanAccessFile \leftarrow not\ BobCanAccessFile,$$

$$BobCanAccessFile \leftarrow not\ AliceCanAccessFile.$$

If a query asks if Alice can read the classified file, the agent will not be able to make the decision, because this program has two different answer sets: *AliceCanAccessFile*} and {*BobCanAccessFile*}. In fact, under many circumstances, using disjunctive logic programming to specify security policies is not sufficient to precisely handle incomplete information.

In this paper, we propose a knowledge based formal languages $\mathcal{L}^k$ to specify authorization domain with incomplete information in secure computer systems. We introduce modal logic to specify and reason about a security domain then translate the domain into an epistemic logic program. We show that our approach has an expressive power to describe a variety of complex security scenarios.

In our presentation, we assume the existence of a single, local system security officer or security agent administering the authorizations. This assumption enables us to concentrate on a single administering agent system and hence avoids the problem of coordination among multi agents. Access control in a multi-security system or administered by multi-security agents is out of the scope of this paper.

The rest of the paper is organized as follows. Section 2 describes language $\mathcal{L}^k$ by outlining its syntax and gives some authorization policy examples specified by the language. Section 3 explains the semantics of language $\mathcal{L}^k$. We start by introducing a general overview of epistemic logic program, then map the domain description specified by $\mathcal{L}^k$ into the logic program, and we give some examples to show the process and the domain description and its corresponding logic program. In section 4, we present a case study to demonstrate the reasoning of our system. Section 5 outlines the implementation issue. Section 6 concludes the paper with some remarks.

2. THE SYNTAX OF THE LANGUAGE $\mathcal{L}^k$

In this section we define the basic syntax of a high level language $\mathcal{L}^k$ which includes a modal operator K for representing a security agent's knowledge about the system security policies.

Language $\mathcal{L}^k$ includes the following disjoint sorts for *subject, group-subject, access-right, group-access-right, object, group-object* and together with predicate symbols *holds*, $\in$, $\subseteq$ and logic connectives $\wedge$ and $\neg$ and a modal operator K.

The details of these six disjoint sorts and the other logic symbols are defined as follows:

1. Sort *subject*: with subject constants $S, S_1, S_2, \cdots$, and subject variables $s, s_1, s_2, \cdots$.

2. Sort *group-subject*: with group subject constants $G, G_1, G_2, \cdots$, and group subject variables $g, g_1, g_2, \cdots$.

3. Sort *access-right*: with access right constants $A, A_1, A_2, \cdots$, and access right variables $a, a_1, a_2, \cdots$.

4. Sort *group-access-right*: with group access right constants $GA, GA_1, GA_2, \cdots$, and group access right variables $ga, ga_1, ga_2, \cdots$.

5. Sort *object*: with object constants $O, O_1, O_2, \cdots$, and object variables $o, o_1, o_2, \cdots$.

6. Sort *group-object*: with group object constants $GO, GO_1, GO_2, \cdots$, and group object variables $go, go_1, go_2, \cdots$.

7. A modal operator K to represent the agent believes to be true.

8. A ternary predicate symbol *holds* which takes arguments as *subject* or *group-subject*, *access-right* or *group-access-right* and *object* or *group-object* respectively.

9. A binary predicate symbol $\in$ which takes arguments as *subject* and *group-subject* or *access-right* and *group-access-right* or *object* and *group-object* respectively.

10. A binary predicate symbol whose both arguments are *group-subjects, group-access-rgiths* or *group-objects*.

We also introduce a model operator K to represent what an agent *knows* to be true. We use *Khold(Sue,Read,File)* to represent that "it's believed that Sue can read File".

In $\mathcal{L}^k$, a subject S has *read* right to an object *FILE* is represented as *holds(S,read,FILE)*. It defines an atomic formula of the language. The modal operator K represents what an agent *knows* to be true. We use *Khold(Sue,Read,File)* to represent that "it's believed that Sue can read File".

we define a *fact f* to be an atomic formula or its negation. A *ground fact* is a fact without variable occurrence. We view $\neg\neg f$ as *f*. A *fact expression* ϕ of $\mathcal{L}^k$ is defined as follows: (1) each fact ϕ is a fact expression; (2) if ϕ and ψ are fact expressions, then $\phi \wedge \psi$ and $\phi \vee \psi$ are also fact expressions. A *ground fact expression* is a fact expression without variable occurrence. A ground fact expression is called a *ground instance* of a fact expression if this ground fact expression is obtained from the fact expression by replacing each of its variable occurrence with the same sort constant. A fact expression ϕ is called *conjunctive* (or *disjunctive*) if it is of the form $\phi_1 \wedge \cdots \wedge \phi_n$ (or $\phi_1 \vee \cdots \vee \phi_n$ respectively), where each φ_i is a fact.

Now we are ready to formally define the propositions in $\mathcal{L}^k$. An *initial proposition* in $\mathcal{L}^k$ is defined as

$$\textbf{initially } \phi \tag{1}$$

where ϕ is either a conjunctive or disjunctive fact expression. That is, ϕ is of the form $\phi_1 \wedge \cdots \wedge \phi_n$ or $\phi_1 \vee \cdots \vee \phi_n$, where each ϕ_i is a fact.

An *objective proposition* is an expression of the form

$$\phi \textbf{ if } \psi \textbf{ with absence } \gamma \tag{2}$$

where ϕ is either a conjunctive or disjunctive fact expression, ψ and γ are two conjunctive fact expressions.

A *subjective proposition* is an expression of the form

$$\phi \textbf{ if } \psi \textbf{ with absence } \gamma \textbf{ knowing } \beta, \tag{3}$$

or

$$\phi \textbf{ if } \psi \textbf{ with absence } \gamma \textbf{ not knowing } \beta, \tag{4}$$

where ϕ is a conjunctive or disjunctive fact expression, and ψ, γ and β are conjunctive fact expressions.

A proposition is called a *ground proposition* if it does not contain variables. A *policy domain description D* in $\mathcal{L}^k$ is a finite set of initial propositions, objective propositions and subjective propositions.

In the following, we describe a few complex security scenarios using language $\mathcal{L}^k$, and demonstrate that $\mathcal{L}^k$ is an expressive language to represent incomplete information, default information, and agents' knowledge in relation to various access control situations.

Example 1: *The example mentioned in the introduction can be represented by a domain description:*

```
initially holds(Alice, Access, File) ∨
holds(Bob,Access,File),
holds(Alice,Access,File) if
¬holds(Bob, Access, File),
holds(Bob,Access,File) if
¬holds(Alice, Access, File)
```

Here the initial fact holds(Alice,Access,File) $\vee holds(Bob, Access, File)$ *represents an incomplete information about Alice and Bob's access right to the file.*

Example 2: *Consider a domain description D consists of the following propositions:*

```
initially holds(S,Own,O),
holds(S,Write,O) if holds(S,Own,O)
with absence ¬holds(S,Write,O),
¬holds(S,Own,O)) if ¬holds(S,Read,O).
```

This domain description expresses the following policies: initially subject S owns object O. If there is no evidence that S cannot write on O is absent from the domain, then S has write right on O, and S will no longer owns O if somehow S cannot read O anymore. Here **with absence** *represents a default information. As long as there is no clear information indicating* $\neg holds(S, Write, O)$ *, it would be assumed that S can write O.*

Example 3: *Let us look at another example. A policy says that if a subject group G can read file F, then a member* S_1 *of G will be assumed to be able to read F as well if we don't know that* S_1 *cannot read F. This can be specified by the following propositions:*

initially $holds(G, Read, F)$,
initially $S_1 \in G$,
$holds(S_1, Read, F)$ **if**
$holds(G, Read, F)$, $S_1 \in G$,
not knowing $\neg holds(S_1, Read, F)$

This example represents a policy involving agent (subject)'s knowledge for making decision. As we will show next, the semantics of knowledge in $\mathcal{L}^k$ *will be defined based on epistemic logic programming.*

3. SEMANTICS OF THE LANGUAGE $\mathcal{L}^k$

Given a domain description D, we will translate it into an epistemic logic program $\Pi(D)$, then the semantics of D will be defined based on the *world view semantics* of program $\Pi(D)$.

In the following, we first introduce epistemic logic programs, and then define the semantics of $\mathcal{L}^k$.

3.1. Overview of the Epistemic Logic Programs

Epistemic logic programs are an extension of disjunctive extended logic programs. They are used to overcome the difficulties faced in reasoning about incomplete information. In this section, we present a general overview on epistemic logic programs. Gelfond extended the syntax and semantics of disjunctive logic programs to allow the correct representation of incomplete information in the presence of multiple extensions (Gelfond, 1994). In epistemic logic programs, the language of (disjunctive) extended logic programs is expanded with two modal operators K and M. M. KF is read as "F is known to be true" and MF is read as "F may be believed to be true". In this paper, we only consider the modal operator K in the security domain application. We consider propositional epistemic logic programs where rules containing variables are viewed as the set of all ground rules by replacing these variables with all constants occurring in the language. The semantics for epistemic logic programs is defined by the pair $(\mathcal{A}, W)$, where $\mathcal{A}$ is a collection of sets of ground literals which is also simply called is a collection of *belief sets*, and W is a set in $\mathcal{A}$ called the agent's *working set of beliefs*. The truth of a formula F in $(\mathcal{A}, W)$ is denoted by $(\mathcal{A}, W) \vDash F$ and the falsity is denoted by $(\mathcal{A}, W) =| F$. They are defined as follows.

$(\mathcal{A}, W) \vDash p$ iff $p \in W$ where p is a propositional atom.

$(\mathcal{A}, W) \vDash KF$ iff $(\mathcal{A}, W_i) \vDash F$ for all $W_i \in \mathcal{A}$.

$(\mathcal{A}, W) \vDash MF$ iff $(\mathcal{A}, W_i) \vDash F$ for some $W_i \in \mathcal{A}$.

$(\mathcal{A}, W) \vDash F \wedge G$ iff $(\mathcal{A}, W) \vDash F$ and $(\mathcal{A}, W) \vDash G$.

$(\mathcal{A},W) \vDash F \ or \ G$ iff $(\mathcal{A},W) \vDash \neg(\neg F \wedge \neg G)$.

$(\mathcal{A},W) \vDash \neg F$ iff $(\mathcal{A},W) =| F$.

$(\mathcal{A},W) =| F$ iff $\neg F \in W$ where F is a ground atom.

$(\mathcal{A},W) =| KF$ iff $\qquad$ 1.

$(\mathcal{A},W) =| MF$ iff $(\mathcal{A},W) \not\vDash MF$.

$(\mathcal{A},W) =| F \wedge G$ iff $(\mathcal{A},W) =| F$ or $(\mathcal{A},W) =| G$.

$(\mathcal{A},W) =| F \ or \ G$ iff $(\mathcal{A},W) =| F$ and

$(\mathcal{A},W) =| G$.

It is worth mentioning that since belief set W allows both positive and negative propositional atoms, in Gelfond's semantics, $(\mathcal{A},W) =| \varphi$ is not equivalent to $(\mathcal{A},W) \not\vDash \varphi$ in general. For instance, $(\{\{a,b\}\},\{a,b\}) \not\vDash c$, but we do not have $(\{\{a,b\}\},\{a,b\}) =| c$ (i.e. $(\{\{a,b\}\},\{a,b\}) \vDash \neg c$. Consequently, here K and M are *not* dual modal operators here[2]. Consider $\mathcal{A} = \{\{a,b\},\{a,b,\neg c\}\}$. Clearly we have $\mathcal{A} \vDash \neg K \neg c$. But having $\mathcal{A} \vDash Mc$ seems to be wrong.

If a formula G is of the form KF, $\neg KF$, MF or $\neg MF$ (where F is a propositional formula), then its truth value in $(\mathcal{A},W)$ will not depend on W. In this case we call G a *subjective formula*. If F is a propositional literal, then we call KF, $\neg KF$, MF, and $\neg MF$ *subjective literals*. On the other hand, if G does not contain K or M, then its truth value in $(\mathcal{A},W)$ will only depend on W and we call G an *objective formula* or objective literal if G is a propositional literal. In the case that G is subjective, we simply write $\mathcal{A} \vDash G$ instead of $(\mathcal{A},W) \vDash G$, and $W \vDash G$ instead of $(\mathcal{A},W) \vDash G$ in the case that G is objective. In general, we simply write $A \vDash G$ if for each $W \in A$, we have $(\mathcal{A},W) \vDash G$ each $\mathcal{A}$

An *epistemic logic program* Π is a finite set of rules of the form:

$$F \leftarrow G_1, \cdots, G_m, not \, G_{m+1}, \cdots, not \, G_n. \qquad (5)$$

In (5), $m,n \geq 0$, F is of the form F_1 or ... or F_k $(k \geq 1)$ and $F_1, \cdots, F_k$ are objective literals, $G_1, \cdots, G_m$ are objective or subjective literals, and $G_{m+1}, \cdots, G_n$ are objective literals. For an epistemic logic program $\mathcal{P}$, its semantics is given by its *world view* which is defined in the following steps:

Step 1: Let Π be an epistemic logic program not containing modal operators K and M and negation as failure *not*. A set W of ground literals is called a *belief set of* Π iff W is a minimal set of satisfying conditions:

1. For each rule $F \leftarrow G_1, \cdots, G_m$ from Π such that $W \vDash G_1 \wedge \cdots \wedge G_m$ we have $W \vDash F$; and

2. If W contains a pair of complementary literals then $W=Lit$, i.e. W is an inconsistent belief set[3].

Step 2: Let Π be an epistemic logic program not containing modal operators K and M and W be a set of ground literals in language Π. By Π_W we denote the result of

1. Removing from Π all the rules containing formulas of the form *not G* such that $W \vDash G$ and

2. Removing from the rules in Π all other occurrences of formulas of the form *notG*.

Step 3: Finally, let Π be an arbitrary epistemic logic program and $\mathcal{A}$ a collection of sets of ground literals in its language. By $\Pi_{\mathcal{A}}$ we denote the epistemic logic program obtained from Π by

1. Removing from Π all rules containing formulas of the form G such that G is subjective and $\mathcal{A} \not\models G$, and

2. Removing from rules in Π all other occurrences of subjective formulas.

Now we define that a collection $\mathcal{A}$ of sets of ground literals is a *world view* of Π if $\mathcal{A}$ is the collection of all belief sets of $\Pi_{\mathcal{A}}$.

Example 4. *Consider a simple epistemic logic program Π consisting of the following rules:*

$a \vee b \leftarrow \neg Mc$,

$d \leftarrow Ka$,

$e \leftarrow b, not\, e$.

Let $\mathcal{A} = \{\{a,d\}\}$, then from the above definition, we have its belief sets $\Pi_{\mathcal{A}}$:

$a \vee b \leftarrow$,

$d \leftarrow$,

$e \leftarrow b, not\, \neg e$.

Then it is easy to see that $\{a,d\}$ is the only answer set of $\Pi_{\mathcal{A}}$. So $\mathcal{A}$ is a world view of Π. It can be also verify that $\mathcal{A}$ is the unique world view of Π.

3.2. From a Domain Description to an Epistemic Logic Program

In this subsection, we define the semantics of $\mathcal{L}^k$ based on the world view semantics of epistemic logic programs. Let D be a given domain description of $\mathcal{L}^k$, i.e. D is a finite set of propositions as illustrated in section 2.1. We specify an epistemic logic program Π(D) translated from D as follows:

For an initial policy proposition (1): **initially** ϕ, if ϕ is a conjunctive fact expression $\phi_1 \wedge \cdots \wedge \phi_n$, then it is translated to a set of rules[4]:

$\phi_1 \leftarrow$,

$\cdots$,

$\phi_n \leftarrow$,

if ϕ is a disjunctive fact expression $\phi_1 \vee \cdots \vee \phi_n$, then it is translated to *one* rule:

$\phi_1 \vee \cdots \vee \phi_n \leftarrow$,

For each objective access proposition (2): ϕ **if** ψ **with absence** γ, here $\psi = \psi_1 \wedge \cdots \wedge \psi_k$ and $\gamma = \gamma_1 \wedge \cdots \wedge \gamma_l$, if ϕ is a conjunctive fact expression $\phi_1 \wedge \cdots \wedge \phi_n$, then it is translated to a set of rules:

$\phi_1 \leftarrow \psi_1, \cdots, \psi_k, not\, \gamma_1, \cdots, not\, \gamma_l$,

$\cdots$,

$\phi_n \leftarrow \psi_1, \cdots, \psi_k, not\, \gamma_1, \cdots, not\, \gamma_l$,

if ϕ is a conjunctive fact expression $\phi_1 \vee \cdots \vee \phi_n$, then it is translated to *one* rule:

$\phi_1 \vee \cdots \vee \phi_n \leftarrow \psi_1, \cdots, \psi_k,$
$not\, \gamma_1, \cdots, not\, \gamma_l$,

For each subjective access proposition (3): ϕ **if** ψ **with absence** γ **knowing** β, where $\psi = \psi_1 \wedge \cdots \wedge \psi_k$, $\gamma = \gamma_1 \wedge \cdots \wedge \gamma_l$, and $\beta = \beta_1 \wedge \cdots \wedge \beta_r$, if ϕ is a conjunctive fact expression $\phi_1 \wedge \cdots \wedge \phi_n$, then translate it to a set of rules:

$$\phi_1 \leftarrow \psi_1, \cdots, \psi_k,$$
$$K\beta_1, \cdots, K\beta_r, not\,\gamma_1, \cdots, not\,\beta_r,$$

$$\cdots,$$

$$\phi_n \leftarrow \psi_1, \cdots, \psi_k,$$
$$K\beta_1, \cdots, K\beta_r, not\,\gamma_1, \cdots, not\,\beta_r,$$

if ϕ is a disjunctive fact expression $\phi_1 \vee \cdots \vee \phi_n$, then translate it to *one* rule:

$$\phi_1 \vee \cdots \vee \phi_n \leftarrow \psi_1, \cdots, \psi_k,$$
$$K\beta_1, \cdots, K\beta_r, not\,\gamma_1, \cdots, not\,\beta_r,$$

For each subjective access proposition (4): ϕ **if** ψ **with absence** γ **not knowing** β, where $\psi = \psi_1 \wedge \cdots \wedge \psi_k$, $\gamma = \gamma_1 \wedge \cdots \wedge \gamma_l$, and $\beta = \beta_1 \wedge \cdots \wedge \beta_r$, if ϕ is a conjunctive fact expression $\phi_1 \wedge \cdots \wedge \phi_n$, then translate it to a set of rules:

$$\phi_1 \leftarrow \psi_1, \cdots, \psi_k,$$
$$\neg K\beta_1, \cdots, \neg K\beta_r, not\,\gamma_1, \cdots,$$
$$not\,\beta_r,$$

$$\cdots,$$

$$\phi_n \leftarrow \psi_1, \cdots, \psi_k,$$
$$\neg K\beta_1, \cdots, \neg K\beta_r, not\,\gamma_1, \cdots,$$
$$not\,\beta_r,$$

if ϕ is a disjunctive fact expression $\phi_1 \vee \cdots \vee \phi_n$, then translate it to *one* rule:

$$\phi_1 \vee \cdots \vee \phi_n \leftarrow \psi_1, \cdots, \psi_k,$$
$$\neg K\beta_1, \cdots, \neg K\beta_r, not\,\gamma_1, \cdots, not\,\beta_r,$$

Now we specify $\Pi(D)$ to be the collection of all rules translated from D by the above procedure. It is noted that $\Pi(D)$ is an epistemic logic program without modal operator M.

Since positions in D may contain variables, program $\Pi(D)$ may also contain variables. In this case, a ground epistemic logic program generated from $\Pi(D)$ by replacing each variable with all possible corresponding sort constants occurring in $\Pi(D)$. Without much confusion, we may still use notion $D(\Pi)$ to denote this corresponding ground program.

Definition 1: *Let D be a domain description of $\mathcal{L}^k$, $\Pi(D)$ the epistemic logic program translated from D as described above, and f a ground fact. We say that D entails f, denoted as $D \vDash f$, if $\Pi(D)$ has a world view, and for each world view $\mathcal{A}$ of $\Pi(D)$, $\mathcal{A} \vDash f$.*

Example 5: *Consider Example 3 presented in section 2. According to the above procedure, we can translate the domain description D as the following program $\Pi(D)$:*

$$holds(G, Read, F) \leftarrow,$$

$$S_1 \in G \leftarrow,$$

$$holds(S_1, Read, F) \leftarrow holds(G, Read, F),$$

$$S_1 \in G, \neg K \neg holds(S_1, Read, F).$$

Now suppose we need to answer a query whether S_1 can read file F, i.e. whether $D \vDash holds(S_1, Read, F)$. It is not difficult to see that program $\Pi(D)$ has a unique world view

$\mathcal{A} =$

$\{\{holds(G, Read, F), S_1 \in G, holds(S_1, Read, F)\}\}$,

and $\mathcal{A} \vDash holds(S_1, Read, F)$. So we conclude that $D \vDash holds(S_1, Read, F)$.

4. THE APPLICATION: A CASE STUDY

In this section, we demonstrate a case study from which we show that this approach can overcome some difficulties in the reasoning about access control when incomplete information is involved.

We consider a typical hospital scenario that doctor assistants take responsibility to manage patients' files and access relevant files and data from other department. In order to ensure the confidentiality of all patients' medical records, a number of authorization policies must be implemented in all departments in a hospital.

Suppose that Hobson is a cardiologist in a hospital. He is planning a by-pass surgery for his patient John. To carry out the surgery, he needs to fully review John's all recent medical records beforehand. Alice and Sue are the personal assistants to Hobson. Each of them can access doctor Hobson's all patients' records, while Sue also takes responsibility to request patients' medical records from other departments in the hospital.

By using our language $\mathcal{L}^k$, we first formalize the general authorization policies across the hospital as follows:

$holds(x, Read, All\_heart\_records)$ **if knowing**

$\qquad\qquad\qquad assistant(x, Hobson),$

$\qquad\qquad\qquad\qquad\qquad\qquad\qquad (6)$

$holds(x, Read, y\_heart\_record)$ **if**

$holds(x, Read, All\_heart\_records)$

$\qquad\qquad\qquad \wedge\, patient(y, Hobson),$

$\qquad\qquad\qquad\qquad\qquad\qquad\qquad (7)$

$holds(Hobson, Read, y)$ **if** $holds(x, Read, y) \wedge$

$\qquad\qquad\qquad assistant(x, Hobson),$

$\qquad\qquad\qquad\qquad\qquad\qquad\qquad (8)$

$sendRequest(Sue, Read, y)$ **if**

$request(Hobson, y)$ **with absence** $\qquad (9)$

$\qquad \neg sendRequest(Sue, Read, y),$

$sendRequest(Alice, Read, y)$ **if** $request(Hobson, y)$

$\qquad\qquad$ **with absence** $sendRequest(Sue, Read, y).$

$\qquad\qquad\qquad\qquad\qquad\qquad\qquad (10)$

$waitingApproval(x, Read, y)$ **if**

$sendRequest(x, Read, y) \wedge \qquad\qquad (11)$

not knowing $approved(x, Read, y),$

$approved(x, Read, y)$ **if**

$sendRequest(x, Read, y) \wedge \qquad\qquad (12)$

$assistant(x, d) \wedge specialist(d),$

$holds(x, Read, y)$ **if** $approved(x, Read, y).$

$\qquad\qquad\qquad\qquad\qquad\qquad\qquad (13)$

Let us take a closer look at these rules. Basically, rules (6) and (7) say that if it is known that x is a personal assistant of Doctor Hobson, then x can access (read) Doctor's all patients' heart records, and if someone is already permitted to read all patients' heart records, and y is a patient of Doctor, then this person can also read y's heart record. Note that rule (7) plays a role of inheritance for access control. Also, rule (8) implies the fact that once Doctor Hobson's assistant x obtains the access read for some patient record from other department, then Doctor Hobson should have the access right on this record obviously.

Rule (9) indicates that if Doctor Hobson has a request of accessing patient y's record from other departments, then *usually* Sue should send this request for approval. Note that this rule is defeasible due to **with absence**. For instance, if Sue is on leave, then $\neg sendRequest(Sue, Read, y)$ will be presented and hence this rule will not be initiated any more. Rule (10) describes the case that Alice will do Sue's duty when she is not available. On the other hand, rule (11) means that once a request is sent out, it is on the waiting status if no approval from that department is explicitly informed. Rule (12) states that the corresponding department will approve the request sent by *x* about *y*'s record if *x* is a personal assistant of some doctor *d* who is a registered specialist of the hospital. Finally, rule (13) is quite straightforward that if *x* receives the approval of the department that holds patient record, *x* can then access *y*'s record in that department.

Now suppose we have the following facts:

initially *assistant(Alice,Hobson),*   (14)

initially *assistant(Sue,Hobson),*   (15)

initially *patient(John,Hobson),*   (16)

initially *specialist(Hobson),*   (17)

initially *request(Hobson, John_generalHealth_ record),*   (18)

initially $\neg sendRequest(Sue, Read,$ *John_generalHealth_record),*   (19)

we would like to know how the access right "Read" for patient John's general health record can be obtained by Doctor Hobson. Let *D* be the domain description consisting of propositions (6) - (19). Then applying our translation procedure described in section 3.2, we can obtain the following epistemic logic program $\Pi(D)$:

$$holds(x, Read, All\_heart\_records) \leftarrow$$
$$Kassistant(x, Hobson),$$

$$holds(x, Read, y\_heart\_record) \leftarrow$$
$$holds(x, Read, All\_heart\_records),$$

$$patient(y, Hobson)$$

$$holds(Hobson, Read, y) \leftarrow$$
$$holds(x, Read, y), assistant(x, Hobson),$$

$$sendRequest(Sue, Read, y) \leftarrow$$
$$request(Hobson, y),$$
$$not \neg sendRequest(Sue, Read, y),$$

$$sendRequest(Alice, Read, y) \leftarrow$$
$$request(Hobson, y), n$$
$$not\, sendRequest(Sue, Read, y),$$

$$waitingApproval(x, Read, y) \leftarrow$$
$$sendRequest(x, Read, y),$$
$$\neg Kapproved(x, Read, y),$$

$$approved(x, Read, y) \leftarrow$$
$$sendRequest(x, Read, y), assistant(x, d),$$
$$specialist(d),$$

$$holds(x, Read, y) \leftarrow approved(x, Read, y),$$

$$assistant(Alice, Hobson) \leftarrow,$$

$$assistant(Sue, Hobson) \leftarrow,$$

$$patient(John, Hobson) \leftarrow,$$

$$specialist(Hobson, H) \leftarrow,$$

$$request(Hobson, John\_generalHealth\_record) \leftarrow,$$

$\neg sendRequest(Sue, Read,$

$John\_generalHealth\_record) \leftarrow .$

It is easy to see that $\Pi(D)$ has a unique world view *A,* presented in Box 1:

From *A* we can finally derive that the following results:

$D \vDash sendRequest(Alice, Read,$
$\qquad John\_generalHealth\_record),$

$D \vDash approved(Alice, Read,$
$\qquad John\_generalHealth\_record),$

$D \vDash holds(Alice, Read,$
$\qquad John\_generalHealth\_record),$

$D \vDash holds(Hobson, Read,$
$\qquad John\_generalHealth\_record).$

5. THE IMPLEMENTATION

A system for epistemic logic programming has been implemented. In this section we briefly outline the implementation of our epistemic logic programming system and explain how the proposed formal language $\mathcal{L}^k$ in this paper is fulfilled by the system.

The system implemented is called World Views Solver, simply denoted as Wviews. The essential function of Wviews is to compute one or all world views (models) of an input epistemic logic program. To compute the world views of an epistemic logic program Π, Wviews first *guess* a collection $\mathcal{A}$ of sets of propositional literals as a potential candidate world world, then performs a reduction to transform Π into a traditional disjunctive logic program (DLP) Π^A, finally by calling the disjunctive logic program solver dlv to compute all answer sets of Π^A. If the collection of all answer sets of Π^A is exactly the same as $\mathcal{A}$, then $\mathcal{A}$ is a world view of Π. Otherwise, another computation will be needed.

The Wviews system consists of the following functions: parser, grounding, computer model, reduction, world view generator. The security domain which is represented by $\mathcal{L}^k$ inputs to the system, it goes through general syntax and other error checking, correct programs then are grounded, these variable free programs are then reduced according to the world view semantics, from candidate epistemic valuation, the epistemic programs are then reduced to disjunctive form and then are passed to dlv for solving, then the

Box 1.

```
{{(assistant(Alice,Hobson), assistant(Sue,Hobson),
patient(John, Hobson),specialist(Hobson),
request(Hobson,John_generalHealth_record),
¬sendRequest (Sue,Read,John_generalHealth_record)
sendRequest(Alice,Read,John_generalHealth_record),
holds(Alice,Read,All_heart_records)
holds(Sue,Read,All_heart_records),
holds(Alice,Read,John_heart_records)
holds(Sue,Read,John_heart_records),
approved(Alice,Read,John_generalHealth_record)
holds(Alice,Read,John_generalHealth_records)}}
```

valid world view are generated. Then it's ready to answer any access query to the system.

In summary, by using system Wviews, we can easily implement our policy language $\mathcal{L}^k$ in the following way: taking the domain description D as the input, which is a finite set of $\mathcal{L}^k$ propositions (see section 2), we implement a transformation procedure as illustrated in section 3, to translate D into an epistemic logic program $\Pi(D)$, then by calling system Wviews, we will be able to compute one or all world views (models) of $\Pi(D)$.

6. CONCLUSION

In this paper, we proposed a formal language L^k to specify security polices by an authorization domain with incomplete information. Different from previous policy specification languages, our formal language L^k has knowledge as its key feature to deal with incomplete domains. We specified the semantics of such knowledge oriented authorization specification language based on the well known world view semantics of epistemic logic programs. Epistemic logic programs are an extension of disjunctive extended logic programs. They are used to overcome the difficulties faced in reasoning about incomplete information. They are effective in representing security agent's epistemic reasoning based on the agent's knowledge. The examples showed demonstrated that this approach has a rich expressive power to describe a variety of complex security requirements. Related semantic and computational properties of epistemic logic programs have been studied in (Zhang, 2007), which will help us to fully using the expressive power of epistemic logic programming for representing and reasoning about knowledge based authorization policies. This is our current research focus. The inclusion of the modal operator M will be considered in our future work.

ACKNOWLEDGMENT

This publication was supported by a grant from the Qatar National Research Fund under its NPRP Grant No. 09-079-1-013.

REFERENCES

Atluri, V., & Gal, A. (2002). An authorization model for temporal and derived data: Securing information protals. *ACM Transactions on Information and System Security*, 5(1), 62–94. doi:10.1145/504909.504912

Bai, Y., & Varadharajan, V. (2003). On transformation of authorization policies. *Data & Knowledge Engineering*, 45(3), 333–357. doi:10.1016/S0169-023X(02)00194-5

Baral, C. (2003). *Knowledge representation, reasoning, and declarative problem solving*. Cambridge, MA: MIT Press. doi:10.1017/CBO9780511543357

Bertino, E., Buccafurri, F., Ferrari, E., & Rullo, P. (2000). A logic-based approach for enforcing access control. *Computers & Security*, 8(2), 109–140.

Bertino, E., Catania, B., Ferrari, E., & Perlasca, P. (2003). A logical framework for reasoning about access control models. *ACM Transactions on Information and System Security*, 6(1), 71–127. doi:10.1145/605434.605437

Bertino, E., Jajodia, S., & Samarati, P. (1996). Supporting multiple access control policies in database systems. In *Proceedings of the IEEE Symposium on Research in Security and Privacy* (pp. 94-107).

Chomicki, J., Lobo, J., & Naqvi, S. (2000). A logical programming approach to conflict resolution in policy management. In *Proceedings of the International Conference on Principles of Knowledge Representation and Reasoning* (pp. 121-132).

Crampton, J., & Khambhammettu, H. (2008). Delegation in role-based access control. *International Journal of Information Security, 7*, 123–136. doi:10.1007/s10207-007-0044-8

Dacier, M., & Deswarte, Y. (1994). Privilege graph: An extension to the typed access matrix model. In *Proceedings of the European Symposium on Research in Computer Security* (pp. 319-334).

Damiani, E., Vimercati, S., Paraboschi, S., & Samarati, P. (2002). A fine grained access control system for XML documents. *ACM Transactions on Information and System Security*, 160–202.

Das, S. K. (1992). *Deductive databases and logic programming*. Reading, MA: Addison-Wesley.

Denning, D. E. (1976). A lattice model of secure information flow. *Communications of the ACM, 19*, 236–243. doi:10.1145/360051.360056

Fagin, R., Halpern, J. Y., Moses, Y., & Vardi, M. Y. (1995). *Reasoning about knowledge*. Cambridge, MA: MIT Press.

Fernandez, E. B., France, R. B., & Wei, D. (1995). A formal specification of an authorization model for object-oriented databases. *Database Security, IX: Status and Prospects*, 95-109.

Fernandez, E. B., Gudes, E., & Song, H. (1995). A security model for object-oriented databases. In *Proceedings of the IEEE Symposium on Research in Security and Privacy* (pp. 110-115).

Gelfond, M. (1994). Logic programming and reasoning with incomplete information. *Annals of Mathematics and Artificial Intelligence, 12*, 98–116. doi:10.1007/BF01530762

Jajodia, S., Samarati, P., Sapino, M. L., & Subrahmanian, V. S. (2001). Flexible support for multiple access control policies. *ACM Transactions on Database Systems, 29*(2), 214–260. doi:10.1145/383891.383894

Meadows, C. (1991). Policies for dynamic upgrading. *Database Security, IV: Status and Prospects*, 241-250.

Murata, M., Tozawa, A., & Kudo, M. (2003). XML access control using static analysis. In *Proceedings of the ACM Conference on Computer and Communications Security* (pp. 73-84).

Murray, T., & Grove, D. (2008). Non-delegatable authorities in capability systems. *Journal of Computer Security, 16*, 743–759.

Zhang, Y. (2007). Epistemic reasoning in logic programs. In *Proceedings of the 20th International Joint Conference on Artificial Intelligence* (pp. 647-652).

Zhou, J., & Alves-Foss, J. (2008). Security policy refinement and enforcement for the design of multi-level secure systems. *Journal of Computer Security, 16*, 107–131.

ENDNOTES

[1] We denote $(\mathcal{A}, W)/\vDash \varphi$ iff $(\mathcal{A}, W) \vDash \varphi$ does not hold.

[2] *K* and *M* are called *dual* if $\neg K \neg \varphi$ is logically equivalent to $M\varphi$.

[3] Note that in our context, a belief set is simply a set of ground literals. Here a belief set of a program is a belief set that satisfies the conditions (1) and (2).

[4] Note that each φ_i is an atom or a negation of an atom.

This work was previously published in the International Journal of Secure Software Engineering, Volume 2, Issue 2, edited by Khaled M. Khan, pp. 65-76 copyright 2011 by IGI Publishing (an imprint of IGI Global).

Chapter 9

A Formal Language for XML Authorisations Based on Answer Set Programming and Temporal Interval Logic Constraints

Sean Policarpio
University of Western Sydney, Australia

Yan Zhang
University of Western Sydney, Australia

ABSTRACT

The Extensible Markup Language is susceptible to security breaches because it does not incorporate methods to protect the information it encodes. This work focuses on the development of a formal language that can provide role-based access control to information stored in XML formatted documents. This language has the capacity to reason whether access to an XML document should be allowed. The language, $A^{xml(T)}$, allows for the specification of authorisations on XML documents and distinguishes itself from other research with the inclusion of temporal interval reasoning and the XPath query language.

INTRODUCTION

The Extensible Markup Language (XML) (WWW Consortium, 2008) has steadily become a common encoding format for software applications. It is a popular and reliable formatting structure for the storage, presentation, and communication of data

over the Internet. Many applications use XML to encode important, and in many cases, private information. Because XML does not have an inherent security model as part of its specification there is a necessity for methods in which access to XML documents can be controlled (WWW Consortium, 2008).

In this paper, we present the development of a formal language that will provide access control

DOI: 10.4018/978-1-4666-2482-5.ch009

to XML documents. $A^{xml(T)}$ is used to define a security policy base capable of specifying all the access rights that subjects in the scope of an XML environment should have or be denied.

The formal language has particular aspects that differ from most other implementations. First, it incorporates the XML query language, XPath, into it for the purpose of defining which documents (or elements within a document) we would like to restrict access to (WWW Consortium, 1999). An XPath is a string representation of traversing through an XML document to return an element within the document. For example, the following is an XPath that follows the tree-like structure of a document to return the element author:

```
/library/books/book/author
```

XPath also includes other interesting features. These include, but are not limited to, XPath predicates and wildcards which allow for broader and much more expressive XPath queries (WWW Consortium, 1999). As opposed to static XPath's which are only meant to return specific nodes within XML documents, we can use these features to write dynamic paths that can represent zero to many elements within the database of documents.

Secondly, the formal language uses the Role-based Access Control model (Ferraiolo et al., 1995) as a basis for the structure of authorisations to subjects. This primarily means rather than applying authorisations directly to subjects, we create roles that can have one or more specified authorisations. This gives us better control over which subjects have what authorisations and is the foremost reason this model is chosen over others (i.e., Discretionary and Mandatory Access Control models; Ferraiolo et al., 1995). Consequently, it also allows us to easily incorporate the principles of separation of duty and conflict resolution directly into the language (Ferraiolo et al., 1995).

Finally, we incorporate temporal interval logic reasoning into the formal language. Temporal intervals are representative of specific sections of quantitative time. Temporal interval logic is the study of relating these various points and sections

of time with each other. We use temporal intervals in our formal language for the purpose of specifying when authorisations to XML documents should be applied. We also use temporal logic to reason upon relationships that authorisations could have with each other with respect to time.

Temporal logic is a well studied field and many models or methods have been proposed in the last decades. For our purposes, we choose to use Allen's Temporal Interval Relationship algebra (Allen, 1984). Allen's temporal relationships cover all possible ways in which intervals can relate to one another (such as before, meets, equal, etc.) and are incorporated into the syntax of our formal language. However, it should be noted that what makes Allen's temporal interval logic differ from others, and what makes it appealing for our work, is that it forgoes relating intervals with specific quantities of time. Simply, Allen's logic relates intervals without the need to specify or know exactly when an interval takes place. This is possible due to the fact that when a temporal interval takes place is implied by its relationship(s) with all other intervals. Therefore, for an interval to exist and be relevant, it only need have at least one of Allen's relationships with at least one other interval.

The semantics of our formal language is provided through its translation into a logic program. Answer Set Programming (ASP) is a relatively new form of programming in the field of knowledge representation and reasoning. It is a form of declarative programming for search problems involving non-monotonic reasoning and is based on Gelfond's and Lifschitz's (1988) stable model semantics of logic programming (Gelfond & Lifschitz, 1988; Baral, 2003; Lifschitz, 2008).

ASP is used to represent known information which can be reasoned upon to produce further knowledge or answers based on the validity of said information. This is possible because the initial information can be non-deterministically written with variableness so that different outputs can be computed from it. Simply, we can describe a scenario with an understanding that various conclusions or answer sets are achievable within it. We can then query under what conditions those conclusions can be met.

Access control specific to XML documents is an issue still sought out in the field of computer security. There have been different approaches to the problem. One of those approaches involves the principle of the fine-grained access control model (Damiani et al., 2002). This model takes an XML document and designates access rights on each element. Implementations of rule propagation, positive and negative authorisations, and conflict resolution exist in the model. Through their algorithm, a source XML document can be processed by removing all objects of negative authorisation and returning a document with only elements that are allowed to be viewed (Damiani et al., 2002). In most cases, this is the general framework for XML access control. However, we believe that an approach that closely resembles the role-based access control model is preferred.

In Bertino et al. (2000) and Bertino et al. (2004), they discussed their own implementation of an access control system for XML documents. Their work does follow the role-based access control model to a certain extent (we did not see methods for role propagation or separation of duty). Subjects are granted authorisation through credentials and objects are specified through XPath's. The implementation includes features such as the propagation of policy rules and conflict resolution. Bertino et al. (1998) include in their formalisation temporal constraints based on their previous work in (Bertino et al., 1998). However, their approach seems restricted in terms of handling XPath expressions in authorisation reasoning.

Besides Bertino et al. (1998) only a small group of other researchers have produced research utilizing logic programming for XML policy base descriptions (Anutariva et al., 2003; Gabillion, 2005). To the best of our knowledge, a logic based formal language for XML authorizations has not yet been developed with the inclusion of temporal constraints, the complete role based access control model, and non-monotonic reasoning capabilities of answer set programming.

The aim of this paper is to introduce the application and expressive power of our formal language of authorisation for XML documents. The rest of the paper is organised as follows. The following section presents the formal syntax of our language $A^{xml(T)}$, illustrates its expressive power through various XML access control scenarios, and defines queries on XML policy bases. Next, we describe the semantics of language $A^{xml(T)}$ based on its translation into a logic program under answer set semantics. Following this, a case study is presented to show the application of $A^{xml(T)}$ in XML authorisation specification and reasoning. Finally, we briefly introduces an experimental software implementation of $A^{xml(T)}$ before concluding the paper with some remarks.

Formal Language $A^{xml(T)}$

Our language, $A^{xml(T)}$, consists of a finite set of predicate statements. These statements are used to create various rules in a security policy base. We present the syntax of our language in Backus-Naur Form (Figure 1) with a definition of each element.

A rule is a conditional statement that allows the policy writer to specify a predicate statement to be validated based on the truth of other predicates. Rules include non-monotonic reasoning derived through the absence of predicates. Our language also includes deny-rule statements which are for specifying conditional states that should never be allowed.

The head-statement from a rule consists of the predicate statements that will be validated true if the rules conditions are true as well. The head-statement itself can either be one of five statements; a relationship-statement, grant-statement, query-statement, auth-statement, or role-statement.

The body-statement(s) of a rule are the conditions that are reasoned upon to validate the head-statement. These are also made up of the same five statements used in the head-statement.

A relationship-statement confirms that some relationship between two objects in the security policy base are true. These relationships are represented by those predicate symbols found under the relationship-atom. There are a few relationship-atoms available that can be used in relationship-statements. Relationships for example could be hierarchical (below), mutually exclusive (separate), or be based on Allen's Temporal Interval relationships (during, starts, meets, etc.) (Allen, 1984).

The role-statement creates an access control role. The role-atom used in the statement includes a role-name, a sign which represents either positive or negative access to the object in question, an xpath-statement to identify an XML object, and finally the privilege that can be performed on the object.

An xpath-statement in $A^{xml(T)}$ is a formal representation of an XPath expression. These expressions include the primary features of the syntax of XPath, such as single node queries, tree-like structured queries, wildcard queries, and predicate filters on nodes and attributes (WWW Consortium, 1999) (Figure 1).

Grant-statements serve the purpose of assigning an access control role to a subject (a person requiring authorisation). This statement also includes a temporal argument to specify when the roles authorisation should be applied.

A query-statement is used when a query for subject authorisation is made. It represents the policy writers attempt to discover if a particular subject can perform the authorisation rights of a role at a specific temporal-interval.

Auth-statements specify that a subject who has been previously granted a role now has authori-

Figure 1. BNF for $A^{zml(T)}$

```
          <rule> ::= <head-statement> [ if [ <body-statements> ] ] [ with absence
                     <body-statements> ] ]
     <deny-rule> ::= admin will deny [ if [ <body-statements> ] ] [ with absence
                     <body-statements> ] ]
<head-statement> ::= <relationship-statement> | <grant-statement> |
                     <query-statement> | <auth-statement> |
                     <role-statement>
<body-statements> ::= <body-statement> | <body-statement>, <body-statements>
 <body-statement> ::= <relationship-statement> | <grant-statement> |
                     <query-statement> | <auth-statement> |
                     <role-statement>
<relationship-statement> ::= admin says <relationship-atom>
    <grant-statement> ::= admin grants <role-name> to <subject> during
                     <temporal-interval>
<relationship-atom> ::= below( <role-name>, <role-name> ) |
                     separate( <role-name>, <role-name> ) |
                     during( <temporal-interval>, <temporal-interval> ) |
                     starts( <temporal-interval>, <temporal-interval> ) |
                     finishes( <temporal-interval>, <temporal-interval> ) |
                     before( <temporal-interval>, <temporal-interval> ) |
                     overlap( <temporal-interval>, <temporal-interval> ) |
                     meets( <temporal-interval>, <temporal-interval> ) |
                     equal( <temporal-interval>, <temporal-interval> )
        <subject> ::= <subject-constant> | <subject-variable>
      <role-name> ::= <role-name-constant> | <role-name-variable>
<temporal-interval> ::= <temporal-interval-constant> | <temporal-interval-variable>
 <auth-statement> ::= admin says that <subject> can use the <role-atom>
                     during <temporal-interval>
<query-statement> ::= admin asks does <subject> have <privilege> rights to <xpath-statement>
                     during <temporal-interval>
 <role-statement> ::= admin creates <role-atom>
      <role-atom> ::= role( <role-name>, <sign>, <xpath-statement>, <privilege> )
           <sign> ::= + | -
 <xpath-statement> ::= in <document-name>, return <xpath-expressions>
  <document-name> ::= <document-name-constant> | <document-name-variable>
<xpath-expressions> ::= <xpath-node> | <xpath-node>, <xpath-expressions>
     <xpath-node> ::= [ / ] <node-name> [<xpath-predicate>] /
      <node-name> ::= <node-name-constant> | <node-name-variable> | * | //
 <xpath-predicate> ::= <child-node-name> <predicate-relationship> <variable-value> |
                     <attribute-name> <predicate-relationship> <variable-value>
 <child-node-name> ::= <child-node-name-constant> | <child-node-name-variable>
 <attribute-name> ::= <attribute-name-constant> | <attribute-name-variable>
<predicate-relationship> ::= < | > | =
      <privilege> ::= read | write
```

sation to access an object. We create rules in the policy base that will validate these statements by checking if a subject has positive authorisation to a role and that there are no conflicting rules. If these are true, then an auth-statement is created.

A Policy Base, which defines all the rights which subjects have over XML documents, is made up of rule statements and other facts about the access controlled environment. Rules, which can be written with variable arguments, are reasoned upon to determine when a subject is allowed to access a particular XML document (specified with an XPath expression). Facts are additional information such as <relationship-statements> that define role or temporal interval relations or <grant-statements> which specify that a subject be granted membership to a role. Facts aid in the reasoning of rules. We define a policy base as follows:

Definition 1: A policy base DA consists of finite facts and rules defining the access control rights that subjects have over XML objects in a database. Subjects, roles, XML objects, temporal intervals and all the relationships that exist between them exist within a domain and can be represented in DA using the formal language $A^{xml(T)}$.

Expression Examples in $A^{xml(T)}$

In this section, we demonstrate utilising our formal language to express some common relationships and rules for a security policy base. In all cases, the $A^{xml(T)}$ expressions have a similar natural language meaning.

Creating a Temporal Interval Relationship

The policy base writer can specify that the interval morning tea is before afternoon tea and that the interval play time meets nap time, as presented in Box 1.

XML Elements and Attributes

Using the xpath-statement, an arbitrary element named cleaning log with the child element cleaning area from the document "database.xml" can be represented like this (presented in Box 2).

The policy writer can also specify more in the XPath by using predicates or wildcards. This xpath-statement uses a wildcard (*) to specify a single step between the elements cleaning information and cleaning log. The policy writer also uses a predicate expression to filter cleaning area's that have the attribute type equal to office, as demonstrated in Box 3.

Role Creation, Role Relationships, and Granting Authorisations

The policy writer can create the janitor role, as presented in Box 4. This role is allowed to read the element specified in our XPath from the previous example.

The policy writer can specify relationship statements between roles. They can state that the role staff is below the role manager, or in other words, is a child role, and that they also be mutually exclusive by specifying that they be separate.

Box 1.

```
admin says before(morning tea, afternoon tea).
admin says meets(play time, nap time).
```

Box 2.

```
in database.xml, return cleaning log/cleaning area
```

```
admin says below(staff, manager).
admin says separate(staff, manager).
```

The policy writer can add a subject to a role's membership, as presented in Box 5. For example, they can add the subject Tyler to the role janitor. He will be able to access this role only during the afternoon temporal interval.

Here, the policy writer creates a complex rule stating that if any subject is a member of the role janitor during any time, then they should also be a member of the role window washers during the same interval. The interval must also finish at the same time as maintenance time. They add the condition that the subject also not be a member of the electrician role, as demonstrated in Box 6.

The deny-rule is useful for specifying rules where the validity of the body-statements are not desired. A deny-rule can be written to indicate that Patrick should never be a member of the role janitor during any interval, as presented in Box 7.

Query Statements

The policy writer can query if a subject has the privilege to access an XML node(s) at a specific time. For example, they can check if Joel can read /a/b/c during morning, as presented in Box 8.

We have demonstrated some of the general expressiveness of $A^{xml(T)}$. However, we have purposely only shown how to specify XML ob-

Box 3.

```
in database.xml, return /janitor logs/
cleaning information/*/cleaning log/cleaning area(@type="office")
```

Box 4.

```
admin creates role(janitor, +, in database.xml, return /janitor logs/
cleaning information/*/cleaning log/cleaning area(@type="office"), read).
```

Box 5.

```
admin grants janitor to tyler during afternoon.
```

Box 6.

```
admin grants window washer to SubX during TimeY
if admin grants janitor to SubX during TimeY,
admin says finishes(TimeY, maintenance time),
with absence admin grants electrician to SubX during TimeZ.
```

Box 7.

```
admin will deny if admin grants janitor to patrick during TimeY.
```

jects, roles, and subject membership to those roles. We have not explained how we know if or when a subject is allowed to perform the privileges given for a role. To do this, we must reason upon the policy base with a variety of rules. We discuss these rules in the next section.

Producing Authorisations with the XML Policy Base

With a security policy base DA written in $A^{xml(T)}$, it is possible to find which subjects have authorisations to what objects based on the roles they have been granted membership to. To do this, we reason upon statements that have been written in the policy base. The subject authorisations are found with a rule we refer to as the authorisation rule, as presented in Box 9.

This rule is written to pertain to all grant-statements. It ensures that a role be positively authorised for use by a subject only if it does not conflict with a possible negative role with the same privileges and temporal interval (conflict

resolution) (Ferraiolo et al., 1995). If this rule produces an auth-statement, that is the indication that the subject in question does in fact have authorisation based on those specified in the role-statement.

Other defined rules like this applying to many aspects of our formal language must also be reasoned upon before authorisation is given to a subject. We refer to these as language rules within $A^{xml(T)}$. They are discussed in more depth in the formal semantics of our language and are defined in two groups:

- Role-based Access Control Rules are included to ensure that features of the model are present (i.e., separation of duty, conflict resolution, role propagation) and that authorisations are generated when querying the policy base (i.e., the authorisation rule).
- Temporal Interval Relationship Reasoning Rules allow for defined temporal intervals to adhere to the relationships defined in Allen's work (Allen, 1984).

Box 8.

```
admin asks does joel have read rights to in example.xml, return /a/b/c during
morning.
```

Box 9.

```
admin says that SUBJECT can use role(ROLE-NAME, +, XPATH, PRIVILEGE) during
INTERVAL
if admin grants ROLE-NAME to SUBJECT during INTERVAL,
admin creates role(ROLE-NAME, +, XPATH, PRIVILEGE),
with absence role(ROLE-NAME, -, XPATH, PRIVILEGE).
```

By using $A^{xml(T)}$ to define a security policy base, we now have a determinable way to reason who has authorisation to what XML objects based on facts about subject privileges. However, to produce these authorisations and to also prove that our policy base written in $A^{xml(T)}$ is satisfiable, we need a method to compute a result. To do this, we provide the semantics of our language in the form of an answer set program.

Semantics

We chose Answer Set Programming as the basis for our semantics because it provides the reasoning capabilities to compute the authorisations defined using our formal language. If properly translated, we can use an ASP solver (such as *smodels*) to find which authorisations will be validated true (Niemela et al., 2000).

What we want to produce is an answer set that will have the same results as those produced from our formal language $A^{xml(T)}$. We first present the alphabet of our ASP based language A^{LP} and then its formal semantics.

The Language Alphabet A^{LP}

Entities

Subjects, temporal intervals, role names, role properties, XPath's, and XPath properties make up the types of entities allowed in the language. These can either be constant or variable entities,

distinguished by a lowercase or uppercase first letter respectively.

Function Symbols

- *role(role-name, sign, isXPath(), priv)*, where role-name is the name of this role, sign is a + or − depending on if the role is allowing or disallowing a privilege, isXPath is an XPath predicate representing an element(s) from an XML document, and priv is the privilege that can be performed on the object (i.e., read or write).

- *node(name, id, level, doc)*, represents a node in an XML document, where name is the name of that node (element), id is a distinct key in the document, level represents its hierarchical placement, and doc the document it originates from. We label each node with an ID and level for the purpose of distinguishing individual nodes. The reasoning behind this is based on various methods to do with query rewriting. This concept is presently beyond the scope of our work, however, we do direct you to their purposes in (Fan et al., 2004; di Vimercati et al., 2005; Almendros-Jimenez et al., 2008).

- *xpred(axis, query)*, represents an XPath predicate, where axis is the location of the node to apply the predicate query on.

Predicate Symbols

The first set of symbols are used for representing relationships between roles and temporal intervals. Their definitions are taken directly from $A^{xml(T)}$.

```
below(role-name2, role-name1)
separate(role-name2, role-name1)
during(tempint2, tempint1)
starts(tempint2, tempint1)
finishes(tempint2, tempint1)
before(tempint2, tempint1)
overlap(tempint2, tempint1)
meets(tempint2, tempint1)
equal(tempint2, tempint1)
```

This next set of symbols, presented in Box 10, is used for defining and querying authorisations in the policy base and are also similar to their $A^{xml(T)}$ equivalents.

A new predicate symbol is introduced in A^{LP} for conflict resolution reasoning on subject authorizations, as presented in Box 11.

This states that at least one negative grant for a subject exists.

And finally, four predicates are also introduced for providing relationships between XML nodes, as demonstrated in Box 12.

Formal Definitions

We define the semantics of our formal language by translating $A^{xml(T)}$ into an answer set program. We refer to this translation as Trans. A policy base, DA, is a finite set of rules and/or deny-rules, ψ, written in $A^{xml(T)}$ as specified in Figure 1. The generic rules, or language rules, for the same

policy base, DA, are a finite set of statements, α, written in $A^{xml(T)}$.

α contains statements to provide:

- Conflict resolution,
- Separation of duty,
- Role propagation,
- Temporal interval relationship reasoning, and
- Authorisation reasoning

Definition 2: Let DA be a policy base. We define Trans(DA) to be a logic program translated from DA as follows:

1. for each rule or deny-rule, ψ, in DA, Trans(ψ) is in Trans(DA)
2. for each statement α in DA, Trans(α) is in Trans(DA)

A translated rule or deny-rule, Trans(ψ), has the same form as those defined in Gelfond et al's Stable Model Semantics and answer set programming (Baral, 2003; Gelfond & Lifschitz, 1988). A translated rule has the following form:

```
Trans(head-statement)ₖ ←
Trans(body-statement)ₖ₊₁, ...,
Trans(body-statement)ₘ,
not Trans(body-statements)ₘ₊₁, ...,
not Trans(body-statements)ₙ .
```

A translated deny-rule has the same form except for the dismissal of the head-statement.

The conflict resolution rules in α are located in the authorisation rule. In Trans(α), conflict resolution rules are transformed into a new rule that checks if a subject has at least one negative

Box 10.

```
grant(subject, role-name, tempint)
query(subject, isXPath(), priv, tempint)
auth(subject, isXPath(), priv, tempint)
```

Box 11.

```
exist_neg(subject, xpath(), priv, tempint)
```

grant for a role. We use this to reason if a conflict with a positive grant is possible. In A^{LP}, exist neg was introduced for this purpose. The translated rule is as follows in Box 13.

Separation of duty in α is translated with a simple deny rule, presented in Box 14.

Role propagation in α is also translated similarly in Trans(α) with two generic rules. The original rules were (1.) to do with transitivity between roles and (2.) for propagation of role properties. Their translation is as follows (Box 15):

1. Below(R1, R3) ← below(R1, R2), below(R2, R3).
2. Role(R1, Si, isXPath(node(N, I, L, D), xpred(A, Q)), P) ←

α contains numerous rules that pertain to temporal interval relationship reasoning. Again,

Box 12.

```
isXPath(node(), xpred()), represents an XPath, consisting of a node() and
xpred().
isNode(node()), indicates that the node() function exists.
isParent(node2 (), node1 ()), means node2 is the parent or is hierarchically
above node1, where both are node functions.
isLinked(node2 (), node1 ()), means node2 can be reached directly (is descend-
ed) from node1, where both are node functions.
isAttr(attr name, node()), means attr_name is an XML attribute of the node
function.
```

Box 13.

```
exist_neg(S, isXPath(node(N, I, L, D), xpred(A, Q)), P, T) ←
grant(S, R, T),
role(R, -, isXPath(node(N, I, L, D),
xpred(A, Q)), P).
```

Box 14.

```
← grant(S, R1, T1), grant(S, R2, T2), separate(R2, R1).
```

Box 15.

```
below(R1, R2), role(R2, Si, isXPath(node(N, I, L, D), xpred(A, Q)), P).
```

many of these rules are transformed from $A^{xml(T)}$ to A^{LP} trivially. We show some of these rules from Trans(α) in Box 16.

Classical Negated Temporal Interval Rules:

As part of our semantics, we have also included classical negation in some aspects of the language. We use it in temporal interval reasoning for finding inconsistencies in the relationships defined in the policy base. For example, it is understood that if the predicate during(A, B) is true, then before(A, B) can not exist. The following rules are included to find this and any similar violations. We use the ¬ symbol to indicate classical negation of predicates.

```
¬before(T2 .T1) ← during(T2, T1).
¬overlap(T2 .T1) ← during(T2, T1).
¬meets(T2 .T1) ← during(T2, T1).
¬equal(T2 .T1) ← during(T2, T1).
¬during(T2 .T1) ← before(T2, T1).
¬overlap(T2 .T1) ← before(T2, T1).
¬equal(T2 .T1) ← before(T2, T1).
¬during(T2 .T1) ← overlap(T2, T1).
¬before(T2 .T1) ← overlap(T2, T1).
¬meets(T2 .T1) ← overlap(T2, T1).
¬equal(T2 .T1) ← overlap(T2, T1).
¬during(T2 .T1) ← meets(T2, T1).
¬overlap(T2 .T1) ← meets(T2, T1).
¬equal(T2 .T1) ← meets(T2, T1).
¬during(T2 .T1) ← equal(T2, T1).
¬before(T2 .T1) ← equal(T2, T1).
```

Box 16. Temporal Interval Containment Rule

```
grant(S, R, T2) ←
grant(S, R, T1), during(T2, T1).
Implicit Temporal Interval Relationships:
during(T2, T1) ← starts(T2, T1).
during(T2, T1) ← finishes(T2, T1).
before(T2, T1) ← meets(T2, T1).
Temporal Interval Transitive Relationships:
before(T1 .T3) ← before(T1, T2), before(T2, T3).
during(T1 .T3) ← during(T1, T2), during(T2, T3).
starts(T1 .T3) ← starts(T1, T2), starts(T2, T3).
finishes(T1 .T3) ← finishes(T1, T2), finishes(T2, T3).
equal(T1 .T3) ← equal(T1, T2), equal(T2, T3).
Temporal Interval Bounded Rule:
during(T4, T1) ←
starts(T2, T1), finishes(T3, T1),
before(T2, T4), before(T4, T3).
```

```
¬overlap(T2 .T1) ← equal(T2, T1).
¬meets(T2 .T1) ← equal(T2, T1).
```

We did not define rules for starts and finishes as they will have been already implicitly included under the predicate during. We can use a deny-rule to ensure that these rules are enforced. The general rule would be like this:

```
← ¬during(T2 .T1), during(T2, T1).
```

A deny-rule similar to this would be written for each temporal relationship predicate.

The Temporal Interval Equality Rule:

This rule simply ensures that any relationships for an interval that is equal to another will be repeated. For example, the rule would be written like the following for the predicate symbol during, and just like the classical negated rules, one would be written for every predicate in A^{LP}, as presented in Box 17.

Finally, the authorisation rule (Section 2.3) in $A^{xml(T)}$ is translated in Trans(α) as follows in Box 18.

A query on DA, φ, written in $A^{xml(T)}$ is a query statement, as specified in Figure 1, and its translation, Trans(φ), is a query predicate from A^{LP}.

Definition 3: Let φ be a query on a policy base DA written in $A^{xml(T)}$. We define Trans(φ) as the translation of the query statement from $A^{xml(T)}$ to A^{LP}.

An answer from a query φ is denoted as π and has the form of an authorisation statement, speci-

fied in Figure 1, while its translation, Trans(π), is an auth predicate from A^{LP}.

Definition 4: Let π be the answer from a query φ on policy base DA written in $A^{xml(T)}$. We define Trans(π) as the translation of the authorisation statement from $A^{xml(T)}$ to A^{LP}.

We define the relationship between our formal language and its translation into the semantics of answer set programming.

Definition 5: Let DA be a policy base, φ a query on it, and π the answer from that query. We say DA entails π, or DA $|= \pi$, iff for every answer set, S, of the logic program Trans(DA) with the query Trans(φ), Trans(π) is in S.

```
DA |= π iff Trans(DA) |= Trans(π)
```

A Case Study

We will demonstrate the creation of a security policy for a scenario requiring access control to XML documents.

Scenario Description

A hospital requires the implementation of an access control model to protect sensitive information it stores in a number of XML documents (see Figure 2). We will discuss roles created for four particular subjects at the hospital.

Box 17.

```
during(T3, T2) ← equal(T1, T2), during(T3, T1).
```

Box 18.

```
auth(S, isXPath(node(N, I, L, D), xpred(A, Q)), P, T) ←
grant(S, R, T),
role(R, +, isXPath(node(N, I, L, D), xpred(A, Q)), P),
not exist neg(S, isXPath(node(N, I, L, D), xpred(A, Q)), P, T).
```

Hospital Roles

An administration role in the hospital will have access to read two nodes named board_minutes and financial_info from a document named board_db. Roles that are below the administration role will also inherit this rule. For example, a role named board_member will inherit these privileges. However, we will also include within the board_member role the privilege to write to the document.

The role admin_doctor will inherit its initial authorisations from board_member. Admin_doctor will be able to write to the board_minutes section of the board_db document. however, we will not allow them to write to the financial_info document.

In our policy base, we will allow the admin_doctor role to read and write to a few other documents. They will have access to read a staff_contact_info document and both read and write to the patient_db and doctor_db documents.

Finally, to demonstrate separation of duty, we will make the admin_doctor role mutually exclusive with the administration and board_member roles. The following is these roles and rules written in A$^{xml(T)}$, presented in Box 19.

Our first subject, Paul, will be granted membership to the administration role. Next, John will be a board_member and receive the same privileges as Paul in addition with being able to write to the board_db XML document. Both subjects will be granted their roles during the interval Wednesday.

Figure 2. Hospital roles/XML database

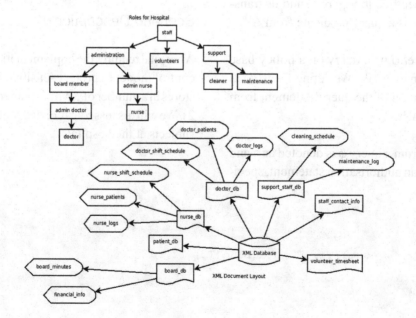

Box 19.

```
admin creates role(administration, +, in board_db, return /, read).
admin says below(board_member, administration).
admin creates role(board_member, +, in board_db, return /, write).
admin says below(admin_doctor, board_member).
admin says separate(admin_doctor, board_member).
admin says separate(admin_doctor, administration).
admin creates role(admin_doctor, -, in board_db, return /financial_info,
write).
admin creates role(admin_doctor, +, in staff_contact_info, return /, read).
admin creates role(admin_doctor, +, in patient_db, return /, read).
admin creates role(admin_doctor, +, in patient_db, return /, write).
admin creates role(admin_doctor, +, in doctor_db, return /, read).
admin creates role(admin_doctor, +, in doctor_db, return /, write).
```

Lucy and Rita will both be members of the admin_doctor role. Lucy will utilise the privileges of the admin_doctor role for a single specific interval while Rita must be active in that same role at an interval directly following Lucy's. We will grant Lucy the admin_doctor role during Monday.

The XML access control rules in which these subjects must abide to in the hospital are as follows. First, we will state relationships for some intervals like so, demonstrated in Box 20.

With these statements, the intervals Monday, Tuesday, Wednesday and midWeekMeeting will be created. We can then make rules to specify during what temporal intervals our subjects should be granted membership to their roles, as demonstrated in Box 21.

The last rule states that Rita be granted the role admin_doctor during a variable interval that must proceed Lucy's membership of the same role.

Logic Program Translation

With a completed policy base, we can translate all of the $A^{xml(T)}$ rules into an A^{LP} answer set program. For our case study, we will demonstrate the translation of some of the policies for our subjects.

Role Translations

From the defined roles, we will show the translation of some of the $A^{xml(T)}$ rules. This is the translation of the administration roles only privilege; the ability to read the board_db XML document, presented in Box 22.

The XPath in this rule represents the root node of the board_db document, which is at the top-level (0) of the document and has the ID 00.

This next role was originally written in $A^{xml(T)}$ to specify that the admin_doctor not be allowed to write to the financial_info node in the board_db

Box 20.

```
admin says meets(monday, tuesday).
admin says meets(tuesday, wednesday).
admin says starts(midWeekMeeting, wednesday).
```

Box 21.

```
admin grants administration to paul during wednesday.
admin grants board_member to john during wednesday.
admin grants admin_doctor to lucy during monday.
admin grants admin_doctor to rita during INT_J
if admin grants admin_doctor to lucy during INT_I,
admin says meets(INT_I, INT_J).
```

Box 22.

```
role(administration, +, isXPath(node(/, 00, 0, board_db), xpred(self, `''')),
read).
```

document. In A^{LP} it is written as presented in Box 23.

The XPath in this rule represents the financial_info node, with any ID (variable), at level (1) of the board_db document. The following translated rules are for the hierarchical relationships of the roles and for the separation of duty for the admin_doctor role (presented in Box 24.)

The above below statements will in turn generate the following language rules for role propagation where it will be reasoned that admin_doctor is below administration due to transitive hierarchy and that the authorisation rights for

those propagated roles should also be inherited (Box 25).

The separate predicates would generate deny-rule statements, however, due to space, we will just show the general rules with variables. In the real policy base, the variables representing the subjects and temporal intervals would be replaced with all those that exist. In our case, we are only concerned with the rules that pertain to subjects who may be members of admin_doctor and are attempting to join either board_member or administration or conversely, as presented in Box 26.

Box 23.

```
role(admin_doctor, -, isXPath(node(/financial_info, ID, 1, board_db),
xpred(self, `''')), write).
```

Box 24.

```
below(board_member, administration).
below(admin_doctor, board_member).
separate(admin_doctor, board_member).
separate(admin_doctor, administration).
```

Box 25.

```
below(admin_doctor, administration) ←
below(admin_doctor, board_member), below(board_member, administration).
role(board_member, +, isXPath(node(/, 00, 0, board_db), xpred(self, '''')),
read) ←
below(board_member, administration), role(administration, +,
isXPath(node(/, 0a, 0, board db),
xpred(self, '''')), read).
role(admin_doctor, +, isXPath(node(/, 00, 0, board_db), xpred(self, '''')),
write) ←
below(admin_doctor, board_member), role(board_member, +,
isXPath(node(/, 0a, 0, board_db),
xpred(self, '''')), write).
role(admin_doctor, +, isXPath(node(/, 00, 0, board_db), xpred(self, '''')),
read) ←
below(admin_doctor, administration), role(administration, +,
isXPath(node(/, 0a, 0, board_db),
xpred(self, '''')), read).
```

Grant and Temporal Interval Relationship Translations

We will now translate the rules granting subjects membership to roles and the temporal intervals we are using in the example. In A^{LP}, they are straightforwardly translated as presented in Box 27.

Implied Rules

Because of the language rules of $A^{xml(T)}$ and A^{LP}, rules created in the policy base that agree with them may produce other implied rules as well.

In this section, we will explain some of those implied rules, presented in Box 28.

The first rule is generated because of the implicit temporal interval relationships we incorporate into the formal language. Briefly, if an interval starts or finishes another interval, then it is contained within it and a during relationship is implied. This relationship is seen with our intervals midWeekMeeting and Wednesday.

The second and third rules, which demonstrate the temporal interval containment rule, use the new knowledge of midWeekMeeting's containment within Wednesday to produce implied grant statements for Paul and John.

Box 26.

```
← grant(S, admin_doctor, T1), grant(S, board member, T2),
separate(admin_doctor, board_member).
...
← grant(S, admin_doctor, T1), grant(S, administration, T2),
separate(admin_doctor, administration).
...
```

Box 27.

```
meets(monday, tuesday).
meets(tuesday, wednesday).
starts(midWeekMeeting, wednesday).
grant(paul, administration, wednesday).
grant(john, board_member, wednesday).
grant(lucy, admin_doctor, monday).
grant(rita, admin_doctor, INT J)←
grant(lucy, admin_doctor, INT I), meets(INT I, INT J).
```

Box 28.

```
during(midWeekMeeting, wednesday) ← starts(midWeekMeeting, wednesday).
grant(paul, administration, midWeekMeeting) ←
grant(paul, administration, wednesday), during(midWeekMeeting, wednesday).
grant(john, board_member, midWeekMeeting) ←
grant(john, board_member, wednesday), during(midWeekMeeting, wednesday).
```

Experimenting with the A^{LP} program

We now present some examples of experimenting with the authorisations and rules of our A^{LP} policy base. The following queries and actions will be attempted:

1. Can Lucy write to the financial information XML node of the database on Monday?
2. Can Rita read the doctor database XML node of the database on Tuesday?
3. Can John read a node from the board database during the interval midWeekMeeting.
4. Can Paul read a node from the patient database node on Wednesday if we grant him membership to the admin_doctor role?

We will explain the outcomes along with the A^{xml(T)} and A^{LP} statements made for each.

In query 1., we use the following A^{xml(T)} query to determine if Lucy can perform the action she is requesting, demonstrated in Box 29.

It is translated into its logic program equivalent like so, demonstrated in Box 30.

When the A^{LP} policy base is reasoned upon, the authorisation rule would determine that Lucy can in fact not do this action. This is because the admin_doctor role, which she is a member of, has a specific rule denying her this right. When the policy base is reasoned, an exist neg predicate would be validated true for her. This would then in turn invalidate the authorisation rule hence denying her the auth predicate required to access the XML node. The following, presented in Box

Box 29.

```
admin asks does lucy have write rights to in board_db, return /financial_info
during monday.
```

Box 30.

```
query(lucy, isXPath(node(/financial_info, 01, 1, board_db), xpred(self, '''')),
write, monday).
```

31, is the A^{LP} fragment highlighting the exist_neg predicate.

To reiterate its meaning, because a role statement disallowing admin doctors from writing to the financial info node exists and a grant for this role exists for Lucy on monday, an exist neg will be generated.

In query 2., the following $A^{xml(T)}$ and A^{LP} queries are written for Rita, as presented in Box 32.

It is translated into its logic program equivalent like so, demonstrated in Box 33.

In this case, in our original policy base we did not write that Rita have membership to the admin doctor on any specific temporal intervals (her membership would imply the privilege to read the database). We did however write a rule that specified she be granted the role during a temporal interval that directly followed one where Lucy was a member of the role. Upon reasoning the policy base, that rule would generate a grant statement for Rita like so:

```
grant(rita, admin_doctor, tuesday)←
grant(lucy, admin_doctor, monday),
meets(monday, tuesday).
```

Note the replacement of the variable temporal intervals with ones that would conclude with Rita being a member of the admin_doctor role. This rule would consequently produce an auth predicate for Rita since no other rules in the policy base would conflict with it. For the purpose of completion, here is the authorisation rule for Rita presented in Box 34.

Our query matches an auth predicate found in the reasoned policy base. Therefore, we use this knowledge to determine that although it was not directly specified, Rita can in fact read the doctor db on tuesday.

Box 31.

```
exist_neg(lucy, isXPath(node(/financial_info, 01, 1, board_db), xpred(self,
''''), write, monday) ←
grant(lucy, admin_doctor, monday),
role(admin_doctor, -, isXPath(node(/financial_info, 01, 1, board db),
xpred(self, ''''')), write).
```

Box 32.

```
admin asks does rita have read rights to in doctor_db, return / during tues-
day.
```

Box 33.

```
query(rita, isXPath(node(/, 00, 0, doctor_db), xpred(self, ''')), read, tues-
day).
```

Query 3. has a similar result to query 2. Although it is not directly specified in the policy base, it will be determined that John can read the board db XML document during the interval midWeekMeeting. The queries are as follows, presented in Box 35.

It is translated into its logic program equivalent like so, demonstrated in Box 36.

We already showed in the previous section that because of the language rules of our formal language some implied rules are generated when the policy base is reasoned. We wrote that John should be a member of the board member role during Wednesday. This query is however concerned with the interval midWeekMeeting. Fortunately, that interval starts Wednesday. In our language, we specified that the relationship starts implies the relationship during as well. This implication therefore produces a during predicate for the two intervals. Our policy base is further

reasoned upon to determine that the following circumstances suffice for the temporal interval containment rule to produce a grant statement for John giving him membership to board member during midWeekMeeting as well as Wednesday.

Therefore, with the implied grant statement present and the absence of any conflicting rules, the authorisation rule would produce an auth predicate allowing John to read the node similar to the one for query 2.

Finally, in query 4, the principle of separation of duty is demonstrated. We actually can dispense with the query in this example because the action of attempting to grant Paul membership to the role admin doctor will produce a fault in our policy base therefore making the query pointless.

Originally, we granted Paul membership to the role administration. However, we also stated that this role be separate from the admin doctor role. We already discussed the generation of deny-rules

Box 34.

```
auth(rita, isXPath(node(/, 00, 0, doctor db), xpred(self, ''')), read, tues-
day) ←
grant(rita, admin doctor, tuesday),
role(admin doctor, +, isXPath(node(/, 00, 0, doctor db), xpred(self, ''')),
read),
not exist neg(rita, isXPath(node(/, 00, 0, doctor db), xpred(self, ''')),
read, tuesday).
```

Box 35.

```
admin asks does john have read rights to in board_ db, return / during mid-
WeekMeeting.
```

Box 36.

```
query(john, isXPath(node(/, 00, 0, board_db), xpred(self, '''')), read, mid-
WeekMeeting).
```

for separation of duty in the previous section. In this case, if we attempted to include the statement the following deny-rules body would validate as true and therefore invalidate the whole policy base, demonstrated in Box 37.

As soon as the violating grant statement is present, the policy base is considered incorrect and any queries followed ignored until the violation is corrected.

This case study has demonstrated a minor amount of the expressive power of $A^{xml(T)}$ and A^{LP}. We were able to show some simple examples of access control using the language rules and principles incorporated into it. However, we only just touched upon areas of the language such as the temporal interval reasoning rules and role propagation. In any case, a general understanding of the formal language should have been gained.

Consideration for Implementation

Presently, we have an initial implementation to test the true expressiveness, capability, and limitations of $A^{xml(T)}$ (Policarpio & Zhang, 2010). This implementation is only an experimental prototype, so we intentionally limited its development so that it was strictly capable of only doing the following primary functions:

- $A^{xml(T)}$ policy base management (adding, editing, deletion of rules)
- Translation of the $A^{xml(T)}$ policy base into an A^{LP} logic program
- Computation of authorisations
- Querying of the computed authorisations to discover what privileges a subject has during some interval

Eventually, this prototype will be able to be extended so that it provides a full fledged access controlled XML environment, however, at this point we were currently only focused on examining $A^{xml(T)}$'s feasibility as an access control model and not as real world application. Our plan was to have the prototype perform and produce the same actions and results we presented in our case study.

The high-level structure of the prototype application is shown in Figure 3. We designed a management module called pb mgr (policy base manager) that contains a majority of the functionality mentioned. For ease of use, we incorporated a web-based user interface to execute the module. Besides the functionality already mentioned, note the presence of an ASP solver and XML Documents database in Figure 3. The Answer Set Program solver represents the tools we use to ground the variables in the translated policy base and also compute a stable model from

Box 37.

```
grant(paul, admin doctor, wednesday).
← grant(paul, admin doctor, wednesday), grant(paul, administration, wednes-
day),
separate(admin doctor, administration).
```

Figure 3. System structure

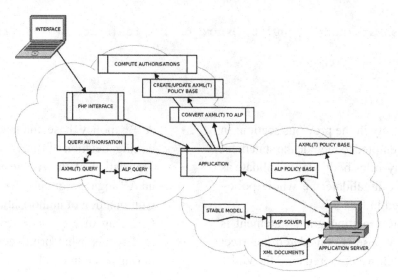

it. For the sake of simplicity, and because this is only an experimental implementation, we stored the XML documents in a local directory rather than a sophisticated XML storage system.

The policy base manager (pb_mgr) is written in the Python scripting language while the web interface was written in PHP. We setup a local Linux server with the Apache HTTP Server Project (httpd 2.2.15), PHP (5.3.2), and Python (2.6.5).

We tested the prototype with various policy base scenarios, similar to the one shown in our case study, to ensure that everything was working properly. Expectedly, $A^{xml(T)}$ performed well in terms of the basic features and principles we incorporated into its formalisation and semantic translation. We did encounter various implementation difficulties. However, for an in-depth explanation of the prototype, its design, and the solutions to those difficulties, please refer to our future implementation paper.

CONCLUSION

In this paper, we presented a formal language of authorisation for XML documents. We demonstrated its expressive power to provide role-based access control with temporal constraints. We provided a semantic definition through the translation of the high level language into an answer set program. We presented a case study that defined some security policies in $A^{xml(T)}$, translated them into an A^{LP} logic program, and then computed the output from some queries and actions performed on it. Finally, we briefly discussed our initial experiment with an $A^{xml(T)}$ software implementation.

In our continued research, we are looking into the concept of query containment. It may have been noticed, but the examples used in this paper do not fully consider the fact that further authorisations may also be implied when the results of an XPath query are contained within another XPath used in an auth statement. We briefly touched upon this idea with the temporal interval containment rule. In either case, if it can be determined that containment is present, then authorisations should be understood or generated for the contained results.

Query containment is useful because it allows us to bypass the reasoning required for contained queries. If we can determine (1) the containment of queries and (2) the validity of the container query then a considerable amount of work can be eliminated by deducing that (3) the contained queries are also valid.

We plan to present a newly updated formal language that will incorporate this idea as a feature.

REFERENCES

Allen, J. F. (1984). Towards a general theory of action and time. *Artificial Intelligence*, *23*(2), 123–154. doi:10.1016/0004-3702(84)90008-0

Almendros-Jimenez, J. M., & Becerra-Teron, A., & Enciso-ba Nos, F. J. (2008). Querying xml documents in logic programming*. *Theory and Practice of Logic Programming*, *8*(3), 323–361. doi:10.1017/S1471068407003183

Anutariya, C., Chatvichienchai, S., Iwaihara, M., Wuwongse, V., & Kambayashi, Y. (2003). A rule-based xml access control model. In *RuleML* (pp. 35-48).

Apache Software Foundation. (2010). *The apache. http server project*. Retrieved from http://httpd. apache.org/

Baral, C. (2003). *Knowledge Representation, Reasoning and Declarative Problem Solving*. Cambridge, UK: Cambridge University Press. doi:10.1017/CBO9780511543357

Bertino, E., Bettini, C., Ferrari, E., & Samarati, P. (1998). An access control model supporting periodicity constraints and temporal reasoning. *ACM Transactions on Database Systems*, *23*(3), 231–285. doi:10.1145/293910.293151

Bertino, E., Braun, M., Castano, S., Ferrari, E., & Mesiti, M. (2000). Author-x: A java-based system for xml data protection. In *Proceedings of the IFIP Workshop on Database Security* (pp. 15-26).

Bertino, E., Carminati, B., & Ferrari, E. (2004). Access control for xml documents and data. *Information Security Technical Report*, *9*(3), 19–34. doi:10.1016/S1363-4127(04)00029-9

Consortium, W. W. W. (1999). *Xml path language (xpath) version 1.0*. Retrieved from http://www. w3.org/TR/xpath

Consortium, W. W. W. (2008). *Extensible markup language (xml) 1.0* (5th ed.). Retrieved from http:// www.w3.org/TR/REC-xml/

Damiani, E., di Vimercati, S. D. C., Paraboschi, S., & Sama-rati, P. (2002). A fine-grained access control system for xml documents. *ACM Transactions on Information and System Security*, *5*(2), 169–202. doi:10.1145/505586.505590

di Vimercati, S. D. C., Marrara, S., & Samarati, P. (2005). An access control model for querying xml data. In *Proceedings of the 2005 workshop on Secure web services (SWS '05)* (pp. 36-42). New York: ACM.

Fan, W., Chan, C., & Garofalakis, M. (2004). Secure xml querying with security views. In *Proceedings of the 2004 ACM SIGMOD international conference on Management Data (SIGMOD 2004)*. New York: ACM Press.

Ferraiolo, D. F., Cugini, J. A., & Kuhn, D. R. (1995). Role-based access control (rbac): Features and motivations. In *Proceedings of the 11th Annual Computer Security Applications*.

Gabillon, A. (2005). *A formal access control model for xml databases* (LNCS 3674, pp. 86-103). New York: Springer.

Gelfond, M., & Lifschitz, V. (1988). The stable model semantics for logic programming. In R. A. Kowalski & K. Bowen (Eds.), *Proceedings of the Fifth International Conference on Logic Programming* (pp. 1070-1080). Cambridge, MA. The MIT Press.

Lifschitz, V. (2008). What is answer set programming? In *Proceedings of the 23rd national conference on Artificial intelligence (AAAI'08)* (p. 1594). Cambridge, MA: MIT.

Niemela, I., Simons, P., & Syrjanen, T. (2000). Smodels: a system for answer set programming. In *Proceedings of the 8th International Workshop on Non-Monotonic Reasoning*.

Policarpio, S., & Zhang, Y. (2010). *An implementation of $A^{xml(T)}$: A formal language of authorisation for xml documents*.

Python Software Foundation. (2010). *Python programming language*. Retrieved from http://www.python.org/

The, P. H. P. Group. (2010). *Php: Hypertext preprocessor*. Retrieved from http://www.php.net/

This work was previously published in the International Journal of Secure Software Engineering, Volume 2, Issue 1, edited by Khaled M. Khan, pp. 22-39, copyright 2011 by IGI Publishing (an imprint of IGI Global).

Chapter 10
Building Secure Software Using XP

Walid Al-Ahmad
King Saud University, Saudi Arabia

ABSTRACT

Security is an important and challenging aspect that needs to be considered at an early stage during software development. Traditional software development methodologies do not deal with security issues and so there is no structured guidance for security design and development; security is usually an afterthought activity. This paper discusses the integration of XP with security activities based on the CLASP (Comprehensive Lightweight Application Security Process) methodology. This integration will help developers using XP develop secure software by applying security measures in all phases and activities, thereby minimizing the security vulnerabilities exploited by attackers.

INTRODUCTION

Software attacks are possible because software systems contain vulnerabilities in architecture, design, and implementation. According to the Computer Emergency Response Team (CERT), the number of vulnerabilities continues to increase. The total number of vulnerabilities cataloged in the year 2004 was 3,780 while in 2006 the approximate number was 8,064, which indicates an increase of 113% (CERT, 2011). According to another source (NVD, 2011), the National Vulnerability Database, the number of vulnerabilities reported in 2006 was 6,608 while in 2009 the number was 7,171.

Security is not a feature that can just be added on to a software system. This is the reason why more and more organizations are making software security a priority. Due to the increasing frequency and sophistication of malicious attacks against software systems, mainstream software devel-

DOI: 10.4018/978-1-4666-2482-5.ch010

opment methodologies must include security as one of the main objectives. Security should be integrated into all activities of a software development methodology. A number of researchers have recently recognized the need for security to be integrated into the Software Development Lifecycle (SDLC) (Aderemi & Seok-Won, 2010; DHS, 2011; Ge et al., 2006; Jones & Rastogi, 2004; Nicolaysen et al., 2010). The importance of building secure software has also been recognized by many international standardization and governments agencies such as ISO 27001 (International Organization for Standardization, 2005), NIST (Kissel et al., 2008), the Department of Homeland Security (DHS, 2011), among others.

Agile processes are of increasing interest in software development, most significantly in web applications. IT projects may fail due to many reasons. One of the root causes for IT projects failure is related to requirements. Software projects developed by programmers who start programming without detailed understanding of requirements (including security requirements) and design can create chaos and cause the failure of the project. eXtreme Programming (XP) is an agile and flexible software development methodology that has smaller iterations and accepts changing requirements (XP, 2011). It is the most documented and widely used agile software development methodology. As is the case with all agile software development methodologies, XP does not provide support for security in a systematic way. A study carried out by Nicolaysen et al. (2010), focusing on how information security is addressed in an agile context, has indicated that most agile software development organizations do not use any particular methodology to achieve security goals. According to the study, security issues must be addressed adequately during an agile software development process. The reasons for neglecting security issues in software development efforts are well-explained in Jones and Rastogo (2004).

The main objective of this research work is to fill in this gap by integrating security into XP in a systematic way while preserving its agility. The contribution of this research work is not the development of a new method or process that addresses security concerns. Rather, the research investigates the XP development method and the structured and comprehensive CLASP security method in order to integrate them to address the development of secure software.

CLASP provides a structured way to concentrate on security issues throughout the software development lifecycle (SDLC) (Viega, 2005). It has been developed by the Open Web Application Security Project (OWASP) which is a non-for-profit organization focused on improving security of applications (http://www.owasp.org/). CLASP is process-oriented and can fit into traditional models such as the waterfall as well as iterative such as IBM Rational Unified Process (RUP) and XP. In fact, a CLASP plug-in has already been implemented to add security to the IBM RUP software development framework (IBM, 2011).

This paper discusses the integration of CLASP security methodology into the well-known XP agile software development methodology. This will help developers build more secure software using the XP method. Our approach to extend XP with security uses the XP practices to complement them with CLASP security activities.

This paper is structured as follows: First, the basics of XP are briefly described with a focus on XP key practices that will be targets for integration with security activities. Next, the article describes the best practices of the CLASP methodology that form the cornerstones of the integration process. Further, the reasons why CLASP has been used to fully integrate security into the XP methodology are explained. The approach to integrate CLASP into XP is then presented and discussed. Finally, the article presents some conclusions and provides glimpses of future work.

EXTREME PROGRAMMING (XP)

Extreme Programming (XP) is one of the most widely used agile software development methodologies. Agile methodologies are those capable of adapting to changing requirements unlike the traditional methodologies such as the Waterfall model where requirements have to be fully understood before development (XP, 2011). XP deals well with changing requirements through an iterative lifecycle with shorter cycles. XP has four main activities in its lifecycle: coding, testing, listening and designing (Paulk, 2001). Each of these activities involves programmers, customers, mangers, as equal partners. It focuses on customer satisfaction by allowing customers to work hand-in-hand with developers in requirement identification, testing the program and adding to the system according to the new requirements. The team works collaboratively and organizes itself around the problem to solve it in the most efficient way (XP, 2011).

The core of XP has four key values which are: Communication – team members communicate with each other and with the customer daily and face to face; Feedback – working software is delivered to the customer after each iteration and changes are done according to his feedback; Simplicity – do only as much as needed to keep the system simple; Courage – be frank about the project progress and estimates. XP has twelve defining practices which are:

- **Testing:** XP recommends developing test cases for each feature and making sure that the code will pass these cases before another feature is implemented.
- **Pair Programming:** Developers work in teams of two to minimize errors and increase quality. One developer may write the code while the other writes test cases or does other tasks. However, XP recommends dynamic pairing and role switching which in general results in better code.

- **Coding Standards:** Coding must be done upon agreed standards to keep it consistent and easy for the entire team. XP team should choose a set of standards and adopt it within the project.
- **Simple Design:** Design should be easy to implement and extend. XP does not recommend putting a design for the whole project especially because user requirements are changing; therefore, it suggests designing user stories and adding to their functionality as needed.
- **On-Site Customer:** Keep the customer involved in the development and testing process as part of the team which in turn will ensure his satisfaction. This activity will also give the participating customer the most knowledge about the system and facilitate the knowledge transfer from XP team to the customer.
- **Planning Game:** XP has three different plans. The top-level plan is the Release Plan which manages the scope and date of the next release. First the customer writes user stories or what the system is supposed to do ranks them according to business values, and negotiates the scope and date of the next release with developers based on resources and business values. The second level is the Iteration Plan where each release is decomposed into a number of iterations (e.g., each iteration takes 1 to 3 weeks usually) and the duration can be modified later on. The lowest level is the Daily Plan which describes the daily activities of development.
- **Collective Ownership of Code:** All developers are involved in the development and testing process. No one owns a specific part of the code, everyone in the team owns it all. This will increase knowledge sharing and cross-training across the team members.

- **Small Releases:** Demonstrated releases to the customer frequently to get his feedback and do the necessary amendments. These releases are easier to plan, implement and adjust.

- **Continuous Integration:** Integration is a continuous task that is done every few hours or daily. Each programmer integrates his code and runs the required tests on the integration machine before starting a new task. This will facilitate managing the integration process with less effort and time.

- **Constant Refactoring:** Make sure that redundancy and unused functionality is removed. XP recommends refactoring the code after each iteration.

- **Common Metaphor:** Understand the system's overall functionality and guide the development process accordingly as a shared story.

- **The 40-Hour Week:** XP does not encourage developers to work for more than 40 hours a week. Overtime indicates a problem in project planning and estimation.

CLASP METHDOLOGY

CLASP has a number of activities and best practices that can be integrated into any software development methodology to improve security. It has thirty activities and seven best practices that help developers integrate security into the development process. Through these best practices and activities CLASP provides a structured guidance for developers to build more secure software. Next, the CLASP best practices are described in more detail.

CLASP includes seven best practices (Viega, 2005; OWASP, 2011). For each best practice, the CLASP activities and the roles responsible for their implementation are given.

- **BP1 - Institute Awareness Programs:** As security is considered an after-thought for many developers who may miss many important security concepts; it is essential to educate everyone involved in the project. These awareness programs should be held regularly to ensure that the staff keeps up with up-to-date techniques. Project managers should institute accountability for security issues and motivate the team to consider security as a factor as important as schedule and quality. Moreover, project managers may appoint a security officer who is a person with good knowledge in security and may act as an internal auditor. Another way to increase team's commitment to security is to reward employees following security guidelines consistently or who find risks within the project. The CLASP activities *Institute security awareness program* and *Research and assess security solutions* emphasizes the importance of educating and the development team on security.

- **BP2 - Perform Application Assessments:** The role responsible for the implementation of this best practice is the Test Analyst. It emphasizes the practice of "Defense-in-Depth" where tests should be carried out to find flaws in design, specification or implementation. These tests should span through all the development lifecycle phases. CLASP recommends the following:
  - *Identify Security Tests for Individual Requirements:* Each requirement specified should have security relevance that will be tested.
  - *Identify Resource-Driven Security Tests:* Building tests to check how resources are accessed with special attention to unauthorized access and users who try to gain privileged access.
  - *Identify Other Relevant Security Tests:* Determine other tests that are

appropriate to the system using test checklists. These tests may show a gap in requirements specification and should be reported back to the requirement specifier.

○ *Implement Test Plan*: Some tests may require writing test scripts or acquiring some tools.

○ *Execute Security Tests*: Perform the tests as specified in the test plan.

○ *Perform Security Analysis of System Requirements and Design* (Threat Modeling): This role is for Security Auditor who is responsible for the following:

- **Understand the System:** Read all the documentation relevant to the project. Any unclear or inconsistent points should be discussed with the requirement specifier before the beginning of analysis.

- **Determine and Evaluate Security Relevant Assumptions:** Any system will be built based on assumptions of attackers' behavior and the operational environment, therefore the security auditor should specify the operational environment, system resources and how users can access them, data flow diagram, and misuse cases.

- **Review Non-Security Requirements:** To check if these requirements have any security implications and whether they were addressed in a proper way within security requirements. Moreover, security auditors should assess the completeness of security requirements.

- **Identify Threats On Assets/ Capabilities:** The goal is to identify threats that apply to the system and examine the controls adopted against them. The auditor should see the system from the viewpoint of attackers and think if I were the attacker how would I break this system? Any answer to this question is a threat.

- **Determine Level Of Risk:** CLASP provides threat trees to model decision making process for an attacker. Microsoft DREAD methodology may also be used for threat modeling. DREAD is an acronym for Damage (how bad would the attack be), Reproducibility (how easy it is to reproduce the attack), Exploitability (how much work is needed to exploit the system), Affected users (how many people will be affected), and Discoverability (how easy it would be for an attacker to discover a problem and use it for an attack). Effectiveness of current controls and cost of implementing other controls should be estimated.

- **Identify Compensating Controls**: For each risk with an inadequate control, ways of improvement associated with cost and effectiveness should be identified.

- **Evaluate Findings:** The auditor should report his findings and suggest recommendations. The project manager should review the findings and make sure that they are correctly assessed, and then choose the right action.

- **BP3 - Capture Security Requirements:** make sure that security requirements are considered as important as other functional requirements. CLASP recommends the following:
  - *Identify and Detail Misuse Cases*: This role is for the requirement specifier. Misuse cases are the same as use cases but the actor is attempting to abuse the system in some way. It includes a brainstorming activity which could be done based on previous knowledge of common threats, or based on the list of system resources and how their services (authentication, confidentiality, access control, integrity, and availability) will be affected, or based on a set of existing use cases (how attackers may use these use cases in a malicious way). Defense mechanisms should also be identified.
  - *Document Security-Relevant Requirements*: This role is for the requirement specifier as well. All requirements should be SMART+ requirements (e.g., Specific, Measurable, Appropriate, Reasonable, and Traceable) (Viega, 2005). Customers are unable to specify security requirements but they may specify the preferable way of authentication, confidentiality for network traffic and long term storage and some privacy concerns.
  - *Identify Attack Surface*: This role is for the designer. System entry points are identified such as open ports, points where system files are touched, methods that can be called externally while the system is running. The designer should document these entry points with a detailed description and a unique identifier for each. For each entry point, identify all the roles that could access it and resources that could be accessed through it.

- **BP4 - Implement Secure Development Practices:** this best practice includes other activities and roles that spans from designer to implementer to others. CLASP recommends the following:
  - *Annotate Class Designs with Security Properties*: This role is for the designer in which each data element in the system should have a security policy for it that is defined by the system requirements and design, either explicitly or implicitly. Methods that access data should also be annotated to identify operations performed.
  - *Apply Security Principles to Design*: This role is also for the designer. It emphasizes hardening the system design with security principles.
  - *Implement and Elaborate Resource Policies and Security Technologies*: This role is for the implementer. It includes identifying any other ambiguous security specifications necessary for building the system and discussing them with the designer.
  - *Implement Interface Contracts*: This role is also for the implementer. It emphasizes semantic input validation to identify reliability issues. Many implementers ignore interfaces in the development process but CLASP strongly recommends keeping those checks to prevent incidental or intentional misuse.
  - *Integrate Security Analysis into Source Management Process*: This role is for the integrator. There are two broad ways for analysis, either dynamic analysis tools which require running the program for checking the maximum effectiveness, or static

analysis tools which analyses the program without running it. Dynamic analysis tools are better for manual quality assurance process. Results of this analysis will be reported to the developer or security auditor and will also be stored to be used in future analysis.

○ *Perform Code Signing*: This role is for the integrator to provide stakeholders with a way to validate the origin of the software through a trusted third party such as Verisign. Signing is performed on a unit that contains all parts of an application.

- **BP5 - Build Vulnerability Remediation Procedures:** This role is for the designer. It ensures that identified security risks are taken into consideration. When a security issue is identified, further investigation should be done to find the possible causes of an exploit, the worst case scenario and all consequences. A remediation should be determined, implemented and validated within the whole system to make sure that it does not affect other parts. Project managers should also manage security issue disclosure process which includes communicating with the clients and with security researchers.

- **BP6 - Define and Monitor Metrics:** This role is for the project manager. Metrics are useful in measuring what you need to manage. CLASP provides worksheet-based metrics as simple questionnaires that help in assessing systems. Questions are divided into "critical", "important" and "useful". They are useful in assessing the overall security posture of a system but could be difficult in acquiring more details. Another important metrics is the attack surface metrics which indicates the number of entry points for an attack such as the number of inputs to the program or

system. Risk associated with each entry point should be evaluated and assigned to a value. Even with a weighted average, there is no threshold at which an attack surface should be considered unacceptable. In all cases, the attack surface should be kept down to the minimum feasible size, which will vary based on other requirements. Therefore, it may not be useful within all organizations. Coding guideline adherence measurement may be used as a metrics. Other lexical scanning tools such as RATS may also be preferable. The way this metrics data should be used goes hand-in-hand with choosing metrics. It should also be identified how often metrics are collected and examined.

- **BP7 - Publish Operational Security Guidelines:** This role is for the implementer. Security does not end after the deployment of the system. CLASP recommends building operational security guide which provides the stakeholders with documentation on the operational security measures on how to secure the system. The following should be documented:

○ Pre-install configuration requirements which specifies the environmental requirements to be satisfied before the system is installed.

○ The application activity: document any security-relevant use of resources such as network ports, files and system files.

○ Security architecture should also be documented such as security protocols, authentication mechanisms and other policies and functions.

○ Security configuration mechanisms: explain how these mechanisms work and what the default and recommended settings are.

○ Significant risks and known compensating controls: known security risks that may be found should be documented along with the mitigating controls.

It is important to mention here that CLASP provides a number of artifacts that support building and documenting security in a system. This makes CLASP a powerful methodology to inject security into software development activities. These artifacts are as follows:

- **Security Resources:** It provides a comprehensive glossary of concepts, principles and standards, besides a lexicon of vulnerabilities that could happen in source code and their causes to help developers write the code in a more secure way.
- **Root-Cause Database:** Provides information about problems, their causes, how to detect, avoid and handle them. This information is supported with code examples and guidelines for writing secure code.
- **Code Inspection Worksheets:** To make the process repeatable throughout the code modules. These work sheets guide the auditor in performing code inspection making use of the root-cause database to find vulnerabilities and their causes.
- CLASP also provides a number of additional artifacts such as a detailed list of common security requirements that could be adopted for the system besides sample business rules and constraints. A guide for architectural security assessment is available called threat model containing detailed checklist of security checks.

CLASP SECURITY ACTIVITIES

CLASP has thirty activities that can be integrated in a software development process. Each CLASP activity is divided into discrete process components and linked to one or more specific project

roles. In this way, CLASP provides guidance to project participants such as project managers, security auditors, developers, architects, testers, and others, which is easily adaptable to their way of working. This results in incremental improvements to security that are easily achievable, repeatable, and measurable. Table 1 lists the thirty CLASP activities and their related project roles. These activities are used to implement the CLASP best practices, in addition to the use of all tools and techniques, and other resources that support CLASP.

WHY CLASP

Integrating software security best practices into the software development lifecycle (SDLC) is central in software security. There are several approaches to integrating security best practices into SDLC; the most popular are CLASP (OWASP, 2011; Secure Software, 2005), SDL (Howard & Lipner, 2006), TouchPoints (McGraw, 2006), and Fortify (http://www.fortify.com). While CLASP, TouchPoints, and Fortify introduce seven best practices, SDL has sixteen best practices. McGraw states that by limiting the best practices to seven, it is hoped that they can be easily adopted while still making a huge impact on software security (McGraw, 2006). Therefore, the SDL best practices have been reduced to seven to better compare it with the other methodologies (Table 2). The original best practices of SDL are:

- Perform core security training;
- Security Requirements;
- Quality Gates/Bug Bars;
- Security and privacy risk assessment;
- Design Requirements;
- Attack surface reduction;
- Threat modeling;
- Use approved tools;
- Deprecate unsafe functions;
- Static analysis;

Table 1. CLASP security activities and project roles

No.	CLASP Activity	Project Role
1	Institute security awareness program	Program Manager
2	Monitor security metrics	Program Manager
3	Manage certification process	Program Manager
4	Specify operational environment	Requirement Specifier
5	Identify global security policy	Requirement Specifier
6	Identify user roles and requirements	Requirement Specifier
7	Detail misuse cases	Requirement Specifier
8	Perform security analysis of requirements	Security Auditor
9	Document security design assumptions	Software Architect
10	Specify resource-based security properties	Software Architect
11	Apply security principles to design	Designer
12	Research and assess security solutions	Designer
13	Build information labeling scheme	Designer
14	Design user interface (UI) for security functionality	UI Designer
15	Annotate class designs with security properties	Designer
16	Perform security functionality usability testing	UI Designer
17	Manage system security authorization agreement	Security Auditor
18	Specify database security configuration	Database Designer
19	Perform security analysis of system design	Security Auditor
20	Integrate security analysis into build process	Integrator
21	Implement and elaborate resource policies	Implementer
22	Implement interface contracts	Implementer
23	Perform software security fault injection testing	Implementer
24	Address reported security issues	Implementer
25	Perform source-level security review	Security Auditor
26	Identify and implement security tests	Test Analyst
27	Verify security attributes of resources	Tester
28	Perform code signing	Integrator
29	Build operational security guide	Implementer
30	Manage security issue disclosure process	Project Manager

- Dynamic program analysis;
- Fuzz testing;
- Threat model and attack surface review;
- Incident response plan;
- Final security review;
- Release/Archive.

The reduction of SDL best practices to seven core ones does not really affect the overall outcome. For example, Dynamic analysis is performed during testing through the use of automatic test cases. Also the Deprecate unsafe functions can be viewed as an activity to implement the Perform core security training.

Table 2. Security best practices in different approaches

TouchPoints	CLASP	Fortify	SDL
Code review	BP1- Institute awareness programs	Educate	Perform core security training
Architectural risk analysis	BP2- Perform application assessments	Specify the risk and threats to the software	Security Requirements
Abuse cases	BP3- Capture security requirements	Review the code	Threat model and attack surface review
Security requirements	BP4- Implement secure development practices	Test and verify the code	Security and privacy risk assessment
Penetration testing	BP5- Build vulnerability remediation procedures	Build a gate code	Threat modeling
Risk-based security testing	BP6- Define and monitor metrics	Measure	Static/ dynamic analysis
Security operations	BP7- Publish operational security guidelines	Quick evaluation and plan	Fuzz testing

In fact, there is not much conceptual difference between SDL, the Touchpoints, and CLASP. There is nothing where these processes fundamentally disagree. They each cover the bases of what an organization should be doing, with some just give different orderings to the activities, and talk about the sub-steps in different ways (Shiva et al., 2008). This also applies to Fortify when compared with the other approaches. The security best practices discussed in Yasar et al. (2008) and Safecode (2011) include the practices in Table 2. Therefore, the practices mentioned in Table 2 can be considered as the commonly accepted set of best practices for secure software development.

CLASP defines the activities and roles responsible for implementing its best practices, making it easier for adoption. Moreover, CLASP

is defined as a set of independent activities that have to be integrated in the development process and its operating environment. The choice of the activities to be executed and the order of execution are left open for the sake of flexibility (Grégoire et al., 2007).

CLASP includes instructions, guidance, and checklists, for activities that comprise its structured process. CLASP describes the application of the activity (e.g., when and how it should be performed), the level of risk associated with omitting the activity, and the estimated cost for implementing the activity. All these factors form the basis for the cost/benefit analysis of applying CLASP to a specific application development effort, and a rationale for adopting the methodology.

The following summarizes the main reasons why CLASP was selected to add security to XP:

- It adds security to XP while maintaining the agility characteristics of XP due to its flexibility.
- The CLASP security best practices are the commonly accepted security practices.
- The comprehensiveness of CLASP in terms of its activities, resources, guiding principles, etc.

INTEGRATING CLASP INTO XP

After describing the CLASP best practices and why it is a good candidate for extending XP with security, the new approach to integrate CLASP into the XP activities is discussed next. In fact, CLASP is designed to allow easy integration of its security-related activities into existing application development activities.

To be effective, best practices of software application security must have a reliable process to guide a development team in creating and deploying a software application that is as resistant as possible to security vulnerabilities. Within a software development project, the CLASP Best

Practices are the basis of all security-related software development activities — whether planning, designing or implementing — including the use of all tools and techniques that support CLASP (OWASP, 2011; Secure Software, 2005).

As explained earlier, the ways in which the different security approaches differ tend to be more along the lines of ordering the activities, what to include in, or what to leave out at a specific development phase. To equip agile methodologies with security features, it is acceptable to use these experienced and proposed activities for secure software development. On the other hand, integrating some heavy weight activities with agile processes may lead to a process that cannot be named agile and possibly will be unacceptable for project's team (Keramati & Mirian-Hosseinabadi, 2008); the process-oriented nature of CLASP may introduce extra overheads to the development activities. However, the fact that CLASP activities are not mandatory and can be selected when needed alleviates this problem in the context of agile development. Also, it is known that project goals may conflict with each other and the project manager should strike a balance between all these competing goals. If security is a major concern in a project, then developers should design for security and accept the impact on other goals and practices.

Table 3 shows the XP activities and the corresponding CLASP best practices that should be integrated with them to build security in the software. One or more best practice may be added to the XP activity to implement security. Table 3 also shows the CLASP activities that can be used to implement the CLASP best practices. As explained above, several CLASP activities are responsible for the implementation of a best practice. The choice of the activities is left for the development team and the security needs of the project. CLASP provides an Implementation Guide to lessen the burden on a project manager and his development team by giving guidance to help assess the appropriateness of CLASP

activities. For example, some activities are only applicable when building applications that will use a back-end database. Other activities are not appropriate for maintaining legacy software that wasn't designed with security in mind (OWASP, 2011; Secure Software, 2005).

As an example, let's look at how the XP Planning Game core activity can be integrated with CLASP activities. According to Table 3, this XP activity is integrated with CLASP BP3 best practice, namely Capture security requirements. Table 4 shows the CLASP activities that can be used to implement this best practice, their corresponding purposes, and a brief discussion on how XP may implement them. Notice that Table 4 can be easily extended with the remaining XP practices and their corresponding CLASP activities following the explanations provided for the Planning Game activity.

The software industry is making great efforts at improving software security by applying security best practices such as the ones described earlier in this article. Software systems which have implemented best practices are already seeing a dramatic improvement in software security. These are practices that should be considered, tailored and adopted by any software methodology. CLASP addresses the commonly accepted best practices by providing developers with a roadmap to implementing them.

RELATED WORK

The integration of security engineering methods with agile software development methods has been advocated by Ge et al. (2006). The authors present an approach to integrate agile processes and risk assessment for building web applications. There have been some efforts to add security to XP. One approach to add security to XP is described in Sinn (2008). It complements the XP practices with some security activities that are not necessarily based on a specific security methodology

Table 3. Integrating CLASP into XP

XP Activity	CLASP Best Practices	CLASP Activities
Planning game	BP3 - Capture security requirements	4, 5, 6, 7, 8
Small Releases	BP4 – Implement secure development practices	9, 10, 11, 14, 15, 20, 21, 22, 28
Common metaphor	BP4 - Implement secure development practices BP6 - Define and monitor metrics	9, 10, 11, 14, 15, 20, 21, 22, 28 2
Simple Design	BP3 - Capture security requirements (task - Identify attack surface) BP4 - Implement secure development practices (tasks- Annotate class designs with security properties; Apply security principles to design) BP5 - Build vulnerability remediation procedures	4, 5, 6, 7, 8 9, 10, 11, 14, 15, 20, 21, 22, 28 24, 30
Testing	BP2 - Perform application assessments	12, 16, 17, 19, 23, 25, 26, 27
Refactoring	BP2 - Perform application assessments BP4 – Implement secure development practices	12, 16, 17, 19, 23, 25, 26, 27 9, 10, 11, 14, 15, 20, 21, 22, 28
Pair Programming	BP1 - Institute awareness programs which in fact spans through all the activities. BP4 - Implement secure development practices BP7 - Publish operational security guidelines	1 9, 10, 11, 14, 15, 20, 21, 22, 28 3, 13, 18, 29
Collective Ownership	A developer can find a bug, improve design, and add functionality, so all the CLASP best practices would match in this activity from an XP perspective.	
Continuous Integration	BP2 - Perform application assessments BP4 - Implement secure development practices (tasks: Integrate security analysis into source management process; Perform code signing)	12, 16, 17, 19, 23, 25, 26, 27 9, 10, 11, 14, 15, 20, 21, 22, 28
40-hour week	no addition from CLASP	
On-site Customer	The customer will be involved in all the best practices (requirements, testing, etc.)	
Coding Standards	BP4 – Implement secure development practices	9, 10, 11, 14, 15, 20, 21, 22, 28

such as CLASP or SDL as in our approach. The approach follows the recommendations of adding "just enough security". The authors in Boström et al. (2006) propose extending XP with security requirements engineering activities. Basically they propose security activities like threat modeling and abuse cases. They do recognize that their extension will also affect other XP activities such as implementation and testing. For example they suggest using vulnerability testing and static analysis. The authors emphasize that the usefulness of an extension would however also be reduced if it did not incorporate essential security engineering activities. They add that the correct extension will depend on the situation of an actual project (Boström et al., 2006). The integrated framework for developing secure software (Alkussayer & Allen, 2010) is based on the combination of secure development best practices, mainly advocated by CLASP, SDL, TouchPoints, and security patterns. In Beznosov (2003), a proposal is provided to apply XP practices to security engineering projects to achieve "good enough security". Nicolaysen et al. (2010) suggested two extensions to add security to the agile Scrum method. However, these extensions do not address all the common best practices for developing secure software

Table 4. Implementing XP planning game activity using CLASP activities

CLASP Activity	CLASP Activity Purpose	XP Implementation
Specify operational environment	Document assumptions and requirements about the operating environment, so that the impact on security can be assessed.	The customer and the development team will work together to: - specify host-level and network-level operational environment. - build a global project security policy. - identify capabilities that should be mediated via an access control mechanism. - map system roles to capabilities - identify attacker profiles. - identify threats on assets/ capabilities. They can use security user stories to express security-related issues, which then can be ranked and prioritized to be implemented in the different releases and iterations. The daily status meeting should also address security issues that arise during development. The XP team may use the CLASP artifacts and resources to implement the security activities.
Identify global security policy	Provide default baseline product security business requirements.	
Identify user roles and requirements	- Provide a structured foundation for understanding the security requirements of a system. - Define system roles and the capabilities/resources that the role can access.	
Detail misuse cases	Communicate potential risks to stakeholder.	
Perform security analysis of requirements	- Assess likely system risks in a timely and cost-effective manner by analyzing the requirements and design. - Identify high-level system threats that are documented neither in requirements nor in supplemental documentation. - Identify inadequate or improper security requirements. - Assess the security impact of non-security requirements.	

In the approach outlined in this paper, security activities defined by CLASP are applied to the XP practices to achieve security assurance to software built using XP. The author strongly believes that a comprehensive and a structured method is required to address security in XP during the project lifecycle and that CLASP best practices and activities addresses all security issues adequately.

Since CLASP is a lightweight process that can be modified to fit any software methodology, it is believed that this integration will not be at the expense of the agility characteristics of XP. The proposed integration will be implemented in a real-world XP project as a future work to validate its applicability.

CONCLUSION

Building security into an SDLC is of paramount importance in keeping an organization protected from threats, regardless of using a traditional, web-based, agile, or any other approach to software development. This paper discussed how to integrate security into XP which is one of the most popular agile methodologies. The integration follows the guidelines of CLASP security methodology, which provides a structured lightweight methodology for addressing security issues during development. The integration is based on interweaving the XP core practices with CLASP security best practices.

REFERENCES

Aderemi, A., & Seok-Won, L. (2010). Assimilating and optimizing software assurance in the SDLC: A framework and step-wise approach. *International Journal of Secure Software Engineering, 1*(4).

Alkussayer, A., & Allen, W. (2010). The ISDF framework: Towards secure software development. *Journal of Information Processing Systems, 6*(1). doi:10.3745/JIPS.2010.6.1.091

Beznosov, K. (2003). Extreme security engineering: On employing XP practices to achieve 'good enough security' without defining it. In *Proceedings of the First ACM Workshop on Business Driven Security Engineering*, Fairfax, VA.

Boström, G., Wäyrynen, J., & Bodén, M. (2006). Extending XP practices to support security requirements engineering. In *Proceedings of the ACM International Workshop on Software Engineering for Secure Systems* (pp. 11-18).

Computer Emergency Response Team. (2011). *CERT statistics.* Retrieved from http://www.cert.org/stats/

DHS. (2011). *Security in the software lifecycle.* Retrieved from http://home.himolde.no/~molka/lo205/booknotes-06/Security-Software-Lifecycle2006.pdf

eXtreme Programming. (2011). *A gentle introduction.* Retrieved from http://www.extremeprogramming.org/

Ge, X., Paige, R. F., Polack, F. A. C., Chivers, H., & Brooke, P. J. (2006). Agile development of secure web applications. In *Proceedings of the 6th International Conference on Web Engineering* (pp. 305-312).

Grégoire, J., Buyens, K., De Win, B., Scandariato, R., & Joosen, W. (2007). On the secure software development process: CLASP and SDL compared. In *Proceedings of the Third International Workshop on Software Engineering for Secure Systems* (p. 1).

Howard, M., & Lipner, S. (2006). *The security development lifecycle: SDL: A process for developing demonstrably more secure software.* Sebastopol, CA: Microsoft Press.

IBM. (2011). *Rational software.* Retrieved from http://www-01.ibm.com/software/rational/

International Organization for Standardization. (2005). *ISO 27001: Information technology—Security techniques—Information security management systems—Requirements.* Retrieved from http://www.iso27001security.com/html/27001.html

Jones, R., & Rastogi, A. (2004). Secure coding: Building security into the software development life cycle. *Information Systems Security, 13*(5).

Keramati, H., & Mirian-Hosseinabadi, S. H. (2008). Integrating software development security activities with agile methodologies. In *Proceedings of the IEEE/ACS International Conference on Computer Systems and Applications* (pp. 749-754).

Kissel, R., Stine, K., Scholl, M., Rossman, H., Fahlsing, J., & Gulick, J. (2008). *Security considerations in the system development life cycle.* Gaithersburg, MD: NIST.

McGraw, G. (2006). *Software security: Building security in.* Reading, MA: Addison-Wesley.

National Vulnerability Database. (2011). *Statistics.* Retrieved from http://web.nvd.nist.gov/view/vuln/statistics

Nicolaysen, T., Sassoon, R., Line, M., & Jaatun, M. (2010). Agile software development: The straight and narrow path to secure software? *International Journal of Secure Software Engineering, 1*(3). doi:10.4018/jsse.2010070105

Paulk, M. (2001). Extreme programming from a CMM perspective. *IEEE Software, 18*(6). doi:10.1109/52.965798

Safecode. (2011). *Software assurance: An overview of current industry best practices.* Retrieved from http://www.safecode.org

Secure Software. (2005). *The CLASP application security process.* Retrieved from http://www.ida.liu.se/~TDDC90/papers/clasp_external.pdf

Shiva, S., Stoian, T. R., Satharla, R. R., Ba, E. A., & Hollahan, T. P. (2008). Towards an augmented secure software development lifecycle. In *Proceedings of the Computer Security Conference.*

Sinn, R. (2008). *Software security technologies: A programmatic approach*. Australia: Thomson.

Viega, J. (2005). Building security requirements with CLASP. In *Proceedings of the Workshop on Software Engineering for Secure Systems*.

Yasar, A. U. H., Preuveneers, D., Berbers, Y., & Bhatti, G. (2008). Best practices for software security: An overview. In *Proceedings of the IEEE International Multitopic Conference* (pp. 169-173).

This work was previously published in the International Journal of Secure Software Engineering, Volume 2, Issue 3, edited by Khaled M. Khan, pp. 63-76, copyright 2011 by IGI Publishing (an imprint of IGI Global).

Section 3
Standard Security Functions

Chapter 11
Analysis of ANSI RBAC Support in EJB

Wesam Darwish
The University of British Columbia, Canada

Konstantin Beznosov
The University of British Columbia, Canada

ABSTRACT

This paper analyzes access control mechanisms of the Enterprise Java Beans (EJB) architecture and defines a configuration of the EJB protection system in a more precise and less ambiguous language than the EJB 3.0 standard. Using this configuration, the authors suggest an algorithm that formally specifies the semantics of authorization decisions in EJB. The level of support is analyzed for the American National Standard Institute's (ANSI) specification of Role-Based Access Control (RBAC) components and functional specification in EJB. The results indicate that the EJB specification falls short of supporting even Core ANSI RBAC. EJB extensions dependent on the operational environment are required in order to support ANSI RBAC required components. Other vendor-specific extensions are necessary to support ANSI RBAC optional components. Fundamental limitations exist, however, due to the impracticality of some aspects of the ANSI RBAC standard itself. This paper sets up a framework for assessing implementations of ANSI RBAC for EJB systems.

INTRODUCTION

The American National Standard for Information Technology Role-Based Access Control (ANSI RBAC) (ANSI, 2004) is a specification of an access control system in which permissions are associated with roles, and users are assigned to appropriate roles. RBAC is an approach to address the needs of commercial enterprises better than lattice-based mandatory access control (MAC) (Bell & LaPadula, 1975) and owner-based discretionary access control (DAC) (Lampson, 1971). A

DOI: 10.4018/978-1-4666-2482-5.ch011

role can represent competency, authority, responsibility, or specific duty assignments. The ANSI RBAC standard consists of two main parts: the RBAC Reference Model, and the RBAC System and Administrative Functional Specification. Both parts cover four components: the minimum set of features included in all RBAC systems (*Core RBAC*), role hierarchies (*Hierarchical RBAC*), static constraint relations (*Static Separation of Duty Relations*), and dynamic constraints (*Dynamic Separation of Duty Relations*). A major purpose of RBAC is to facilitate access control administration and review.

Many papers propose ways to support or implement RBAC using commercial technologies, e.g., Oracle (Notargiacomo, 1995), NetWare (Epstein & Sandhu, 1995), Java (Giuri, 1998), DG/UX (Meyers, 1997), J2EE (Zhang, Sheng, Niu, Wang, & Zhang, 2006; Bindiganavale & Ouyang, 2006), object-oriented systems (Barkley, 1995), object-oriented databases (Wong, 1997), MS Windows NT (Barkley & Cincotta, 1998), enterprise security management systems (Awischus, 1997). Evidence of RBAC becoming a dominant access control paradigm is the approval of the American National Standard Institute (ANSI) RBAC Standard (ANSI, 2004) in 2004.

At the same time, commercial middleware technologies–such as Common Object Request Broker Architecture (CORBA) (OMG, 1999), COM+ (Oberg, 2000), Enterprise Java Beans (EJB) (DeMichiel, Yalçinalp, & Krishnan, 2001)– matured, with distributed enterprise applications routinely developed with the use of middleware. Each middleware technology, however, comes with its own security subsystem (Eddon, 1999; OMG, 2002; Hartman, Flinn, & Beznosov, 2001), sometimes dependent on and specific to the underlying operating system (OS). For instance, COM+ security (Eddon, 1999) is tied into Microsoft Windows OS and its services.

The ability of a particular middleware technology to support specific types of access control policy is an open and practical question. It is not a simple question for the following three reasons.

First, different middleware technologies and their subsystems are defined in different forms and formats. For example, CORBA is specified in the form of open application programming interfaces (APIs), whereas EJB is defined through APIs as well as the syntax and semantics of the accompanying extensible markup language (XML) files used for configuring the EJB container. COM+ is defined through APIs as well as graphical user interfaces (GUI) for configuring the behavior of a COM+ server. The variations in the form, terminology, and format of the middleware definitions lead to the difficulty of identifying the correspondence among the (security and other) capabilities of any two middleware technologies.

Second, the capabilities of the middleware access controls are not defined in the terms of any particular access control model. Instead, the controls are defined in terms of general mechanisms which are supposed to be adequate for the majority of cases, and could be configured to support various access control models. Designed to support a variety of policy types, as well as large scale and diverse distributed applications, the controls seem to be a result of engineering compromises between, among others, perceived customer requirements, the capabilities of the target runtime environment, and their expected usage. For example, CORBA access controls are defined in the terms of the principal's *attributes*, *required*, and *granted rights*, whereas EJB controls are defined using *role mappings* and *role-method permissions*. Assessing the capability of middleware controls to enforce particular types of authorization policies is harder due to the mismatch in the terminology between the published access control models and abstractions directly supported by the controls.

Third, the security subsystem semantics in commercial middleware is defined imprecisely, leaving room for misinterpretation. We clarify the semantics of the security subsystem and analyze its ability to support ANSI RBAC for one particular industrial middleware technology–EJB.

In this paper, we define the protection state of the access control subsystem of EJB. Our definitions offer precise and unambiguous interpretation of the middleware access controls. The language of the middleware protection state enables the analysis of the access control system on the subject of its support for specific access control models. To demonstrate the utility of the protection state definitions and to aid application developers and owners, we analyzed the degree to which EJB supports the family of role-based access control (RBAC) models as defined by ANSI RBAC Standard (ANSI, 2004).

We have formalized the authorization-related parts of EJB v.3.0 (DeMichiel & Keith, 2006) into a protection state configuration through studying its description and specifications. Then, we used the protection state configuration to analyze EJB in regards to its support for ANSI RBAC. When possible, we showed how the corresponding ANSI RBAC construct can be expressed in the language of the EJB protection state. In cases when support for a specific ANSI RBAC feature required implementation-dependent functionality, we explicitly stated what needed to be implemented by the middleware developers, or configured by the security administrators. When we could not identify the means of supporting an ANSI RBAC feature, we stated so. We have summarized the results of our analysis at the end of the paper.

Our analysis suggests that the EJB specification is not capable of fully supporting even the required Core RBAC component in order for it to be ANSI RBAC compliant. This is due to the fact that the EJB specification relies on (1) the operational environment to provide the management of user accounts, and the run-time environment to manage (2) user sessions, and (3) role activation. While these limitations can be easily worked around through vendor-specific

and implementation dependent extensions, each EJB implementation would have to be evaluated for ANSI RBAC separately. In order to provide standard support for administering and reviewing user accounts, their roles and their sessions, the corresponding administrative interfaces would need to be added to EJB, which would be contrary to the emerging practice of "outsourcing" such functions to enterprise-wide single sign-on and identity management solutions.

This paper establishes a framework for implementing and assessing implementations of ANSI RBAC using EJB. The results provide directions for EJB developers supporting ANSI RBAC in their systems, and criteria for users and application developers for selecting those EJB implementations that support both required and optional components of ANSI RBAC.

The rest of the paper is organized as follows: In the next section, we provide an overview of ANSI RBAC and EJB. We then discuss related work. The following section formally defines the protection state of the EJB access control subsystem. Then we discuss how an ANSI RBAC based access policy maps to the EJB protection state, and we provide an example. Following that, we discuss the results of our analysis. We present our conclusion in the last section of the paper.

BACKGROUND

This section provides the background to ANSI RBAC and EJB Security that is necessary in order to understand the rest of the paper. Readers familiar with both can skip directly to the next section.

Overview of ANSI RBAC

Role-Based Access Control (RBAC) was introduced more than a decade ago (Ferraiolo & Kuhn, 1992; Sandhu, Coyne, Feinstein, & Youman, 1996). Over the years, RBAC has enjoyed significant attention. Many research papers have been written on topics related to RBAC, and in recent years, vendors of commercial products have started implementing various RBAC features in their solutions.

The National Institute of Standards and Technology (NIST) initiated a process to develop a standard for RBAC to achieve a consistent and uniform definition of RBAC features. An initial draft of a standard for RBAC was proposed in the year 2000 (Sandhu, Ferraiolo, & Kuhn, 2000). A second version was later publicly released in 2001 (Ferraiolo, Sandhu, Gavrila, Kuhn, & Chandramouli, 2001). This second version was then submitted to the International Committee for Information Technology Standards (INCITS), where further changes were made to the proposed standard. Lastly, INCITS approved the standard for submission to the American National Standards Institute (ANSI). The standard was later approved in 2004 (ANSI, 2004). The ANSI RBAC standard consists of two main parts, as described in the following sections.

Reference Model

The RBAC Reference Model defines sets of basic RBAC elements, relations, and functions that the standard includes. This model is defined in terms of four major RBAC components as described in the following sections. Figure 1 depicts these RBAC components.

Core RBAC

Core RBAC defines the minimum set of elements required to achieve RBAC functionality. At a minimum, core RBAC must be implemented in RBAC systems. The other components described below, which are independent of each other, can be implemented separately.

Core RBAC elements are defined as follows (ANSI, 2004, pp.4-5):

Definition 1 [Core RBAC]

- *USERS, ROLES, OPS, and OBS (users, roles, operations, and objects respectively)*
- $UA \subseteq USERS \times ROLES$, a many-to-m*any mapping user-to-role assignment relation.*
- *assigned_users*
  $(r : ROLES) \rightarrow 2^{USERS}$, the mapping of role r onto a set of users. Formally, assigned_users
  $(r) = \{u \in USERS \,|\, (u, r) \in UA\}$.
- $PRMS = 2^{(OPS \times OBS)}$, the set of *permissions.*

Figure 1. ANSI RBAC sets, relations, and main functions

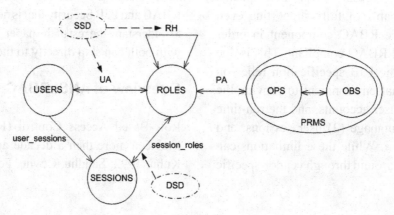

○ $PA \subseteq PERMS \times ROLES$, a many-to-many *mapping permission-to-role assignment relation.*

○ *assigned_permissions* $(r : ROLES) \to 2^{PRMS}$, the mapping of role r onto a set of permissions. Formally: assigned permissions $(r) = \{p \in PRMS \big| (p,r) \in PA\}$.

○ $Op(p : PRMS) \to \{op \in OPS\}$, the permissio*n to operation mapping, which gives the set of operations associated with permission p.*

○ $Ob(p : PRMS) \to \{ob \in OBS\}$, the permissio*n to object mapping, which gives the set of objects associated with permission p.*

○ $SESSIONS$ = *the set of sessions.*

○ *session_users* $(s : SESSIONS) \to USERS$, the mapping of session s onto the corresponding user.

○ *session_roles* $(s : SESSIONS) \to 2^{ROLES}$, the mapping of session s onto a set of roles. Formally, session_roles $(s_i) \subseteq \{r \in ROLES \big| (session\_users(s_i), r) \in UA\}$.

○ *avail_session_perms* $(s : SESSIONS) \to 2^{PRMS}$, the permissions available to a user in a session =

$$\bigcup_{r \in session\_roles(s)} assigned\_permissions(r).$$

Hierarchical RBAC

This component adds relations to support role hierarchies. Role hierarchy is a partial order relation that defines seniority between roles, whereby a senior role has at least the permissions of all of its junior roles, and a junior role is assigned at least all the users of its senior roles. A senior role is also said to "inherit" the permissions of its junior roles.

The standard defines two types of role hierarchies. These types are shown in Figure 2, and are defined as follows:

- **General Role Hierarchies:** Provide support for arbitrary partial order relations to serve as the role hierarchy. This type allows for the multiple inheritances of assigned_permissions and users; that is, a role can have any number of ascendants, and any number of descendants.

- **Limited Role Hierarchies:** Provide more restricted partial order relations that allow a role to have any number of ascendants, but is limited to only one descendant.

In the presence of role hierarchy, the following is defined, where $r_{senior} \geq r_{junior}$ indicates that r_{senior} inherits all permissions of r_{junior}, and all users of r_{senior} are also users of r_{junior}:

- *authorized_users* $(r) = \{u \in USERS \big| r' \geq r, (u, r') \in UA\}$

Figure 2. Examples of Hierarchical RBAC

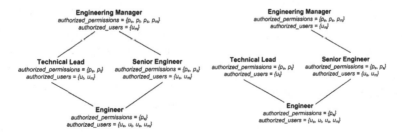

is the mapping of role *r* onto a set of users.

- *authorized_permissions*

$$(r) = \{p \in PRMS \,|\, r \geq r', (p, r') \in PA\}$$

is the mapping of role *r* onto a set of permissions.

Constrained RBAC

The Static Separation of Duty (SSD) Relations component defines exclusivity relations among roles with respect to user assignments. *The Dynamic Separation of Duty (DSD) Relations* component defines exclusivity relations with respect to roles that are activated as part of a user's session.

Functional Specification

For the four components defined in the RBAC reference model, the RBAC System and Administrative Functional Specification define the three categories of various operations that are required in an RBAC system. These categories are defined as follows:

The category of *administrative operations* defines the operations required for the creation and maintenance of RBAC element sets and relations. Examples of these operations are listed below. A complete list of these operations, as well as their formal definitions is included in the standard.

- Core RBAC administrative operations include AddUser, DeleteUser, AddRole, DeleteRole, AssignUser, GrantPermission, and so on.
- Hierarchical RBAC administrative operations include AddInheritance, DeleteInheritance, AddAscendant, and AddDescendant.
- SSD Relations administrative operations include CreateSsdSet, AddSsdRoleMember, SetSsdSetCardinality, and so forth.

- DSD Relations administrative operations include CreateDsdSet, AddDsdRoleMember, SetDsdSetCardinality, and so on.
- The administrative reviews category defines the operations required to perform administrative queries on the system. Examples of Core RBAC administrative review functions include RolePermissions, UserPermissions, SessionRoles, and RoleOperationsOnObjects. Other operations for other RBAC components can be found in the standard.

The system level functionality category defines operations for creating and managing user sessions and making access control decisions. Examples of such operations are CreateSession, DeleteSession, AddActiveRole, and CheckAccess.

Overview of EJB Security

In this section we provide an overview of EJB architecture, the main components of an EJB system, as well as the declarative and runtime aspects of EJB systems.

EJB

This section provides a brief and informal overview of Enterprise Java Beans (EJB). More information can be found in the corresponding EJB specification. Readers familiar with EJB are advised to proceed to the EJB Security Subsystem section.

The EJB standard (DeMichiel & Keith, 2006) defines an architecture for developing and deploying server-side components written in Java programming language. EJB architecture specifies the contracts that ensure the interoperability between various EJB components, clients, and deployment environments. These contracts ensure that an EJB product developed by one vendor is compatible with an EJB product provided by another vendor.

EJB architecture, similar to other middleware technologies, allows application developers to implement their business logic without having to handle transactions, state management, multithreading, connection pooling, and other platform-dependent deployment issues.

EJB architecture consists of the following basic parts. These parts are also shown in

Figure 3 for ProductBean, an example Enterprise Java Bean.

- **Enterprise Java Bean:** A server-side software component that is composed of one or more Java objects. The enterprise bean exposes certain interfaces that allow clients to communicate with the bean in compliance with the EJB specification. This is shown in Figure 3 as ProductBean. The EJB specification (DeMichiel & Keith, 2006) defines three main types of enterprise beans: *entity*, *session* (which include stateful and stateless session beans), and *message-driven* beans. Depending on the type of the enterprise bean, its functionality ranges from a mere object-oriented abstraction of an entity that exists in persistent storage (such as a record in a database), to a web service implementing certain business logic.

- **EJB Container:** Provides services–such as persistence, concurrency, bean lifecycle, resource pooling, and security–to the enterprise beans it hosts. Multiple enterprise beans typically exist inside a single container. The container vendor provides necessary tools, which are specific to their container, to help in the deployment of enterprise beans, as well as runtime support for the deployed bean instances.

- **EJB Server:** Provides the runtime environment to one or more containers. Since EJB specification does not explicitly define the separation of roles between containers and servers, they are usually inseparable and come as one system.

- **EJB Client:** A software component that invokes methods on the Enterprise Java Bean. The EJB architecture allows a variety of client applications to utilize the business logic that the beans provide. Servlets or Java Server Pages (JSP), Java standalone applications or applets are common types of EJB clients. EJBs can also be clients of other EJBs. CORBA-based applications, which are not necessarily developed in Java, may also be clients of EJBs. All EJB clients access enterprise beans' logic through predefined protocols and software

Figure 3. Basic parts of EJB architecture for an example Enterprise Java Bean Product

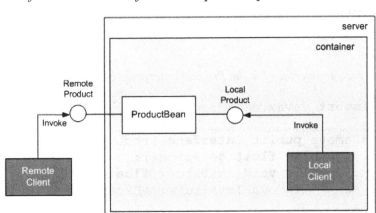

interfaces. These interfaces define the methods that can be invoked on the bean.

- **Remote Business Interface:** Java interfaces that are provided by the Enterprise Java Bean and marked with the @Remote Java language metadata annotation. (DeMichiel & Keith, 2006) The EJB container tools handle the generation of the required logic in order to support remote access to methods defined by this interface.

- **Local Business Interface:** A Java interface that is provided by the Enterprise Java Bean and that supports local access. Clients that utilize this type of interface have to be collocated in the same Java Virtual Machine (JVM) as the Enterprise Java Bean.

Although Enterprise Java Beans are written in Java programming language, fully compliant EJB deployment environments support the Internet Inter-ORB Protocol (IIOP) (OMG, 2004), leveraging IIOP and the Common Secure Interoperability Protocol Version 2 (CSIv2) (OMG, 2004) capabilities, which allow CORBA clients to access enterprise bean objects, and which can be written in languages other than Java.

- **Declarative Part:** Defining remote and local interfaces as well as implementing the business logic in EJB is as easy as in standard Java. Figure 4 shows an example of an enterprise bean remote interface definition, and Figure 5 illustrates an example of

the corresponding implementation for that interface.

In EJB 3.0, the metadata annotations defined in Java Development Kit (JDK) 5.0 and later are used to create annotated Enterprise Java Beans. The tools provided by the EJB Container vendors utilize these annotations to automatically generate proper Java classes as well as other required EJB interfaces.

As an alternative to metadata annotations, a bean developer can also specify transactional, security, and other requirements for the application using the *deployment descriptor*—an XML file with predefined syntax that holds all the explicit metadata for the assembly. The descriptor can be later augmented and altered by an application *assembler* and *deployer*, which play specific roles in the life cycle of enterprise beans predefined by the EJB specification.

- **Runtime Part:** While the remote object model for EJB components is based on the Remote Method Invocation (RMI) API (ORACLE, 2007), all invocations between J2EE components are performed using IIOP. The use of the RMI remote invocation model over the IIOP protocol is usually referred to as RMI-IIOP. When EJB components use the RMI-IIOP (mandatory for EJB 2.0 and higher), the standard mapping of the EJB architecture to CORBA enables interoperability with multi-vendor

Figure 4. Defining a remote interface for the Product enterprise bean (Product.java)

```
import javax.ejb.Remote;

@Remote public interface Product {
    public float getPrice();
    public void setPrice( float newPrice )
        throws InvalidPriceException;
};
```

Figure 5. Implementing the remote interface for the Product enterprise bean (ProductBean.java)

```java
import javax.ejb.Stateful;

@Stateful public class ProductBean implements Product {
    private float price = 0;

    public float getPrice() {
        return price;
    }

    public void setPrice( float newPrice ) {
        if ( price < 0 ) {
            throw new InvalidPriceException();
        }

        price = newPrice;
    }
}
```

ORBs, other EJB servers, and CORBA clients written in languages other than Java.

Because of the IIOP, the same object reference used for CORBA is used in the EJB. The similarities between CORBA and EJB lie in their use of a secure channel, as well as their client and server security layer architectures. For a more detailed explanation of EJB technology, please refer to Roman, Sriganesh, and Brose (2005).

EJB Security Subsystem

The EJB protection architecture is conceptually simple: When the client program invokes a method on a target EJB object, the identity of the subject associated with the calling client is transmitted to the EJB object's container. The container checks whether the calling subject has a right to invoke the requested method. If so, the container permits the invocation of the method.

- **Client Security Service:** Because of the use of IIOP and CSIv2, the responsibilities of an EJB client security service (CSS) are similar to those of a CORBA CSS:

1. Creating a secure channel with the target security service (TSS), and

2. Obtaining the user's authenticated credentials or passing username and password over the CSIv2 context to TSS, as well as

3. Protecting request messages and verifying response messages.

Treated by the EJB specification as an integral part of the server container, a TSS establishes and maintains a secure channel with clients, verifies authenticated credentials or performs client authentication itself, implements message protection policies, and performs access checks before an invocation is dispatched to an enterprise bean. Depending on the application configuration, which is done through the deployment descriptor, the container associates the runtime security context of the dispatched method either with the identity of the calling client or with some other subject. Other security-related responsibilities of a container include the following:

- Isolating the enterprise bean instances from each other and from other application components running on the server,
- Preventing enterprise bean instances from gaining unauthorized access to the system information about the server and its resources,

- Ensuring the security of the persistent state of the enterprise beans,
- Managing the mapping of principals on calls to other enterprise beans, or on access to resource managers, according to the defined security policy,
- Allowing the same enterprise bean to be deployed independently multiple times, each time with a different security policy.
- **Implementation of Security Functions:** The security parts of the EJB specification focus largely on authentication and access control. The specification relies on CSIv2 for message protection, and it leaves support for security auditing to the discretion of container vendors. We describe the EJB access control architecture later.
- **Authentication:** User authentication is either performed by the client's infrastructure (such as Kerberos), or by the EJB server itself. In the latter case, the EJB server receives user authentication data (only username and password for CSIv2 level 0) or credentials from a client and authenticates the client using a local authentication service, which is not predefined by the specification. Once the container authenticates the client (or verified their credentials), it enforces access control policies. The notion of a *principal* is used in the EJB specification to refer to authenticated clients.
- **Administration:** Some of the security administration tasks of EJB servers are performed through changes in deployment descriptors. This includes the definition of security roles, method permissions, and the specification of security identity, either delegated or predetermined, for dispatching calls to bean methods. Other tasks, such as mapping users to roles, specifying message protection, administering an audit, and authentication mechanisms, are beyond the scope of the EJB specification, and are therefore left up to the vendors of container products and deployment tools.

RELATED WORK

Over the past decade, there has been no shortage of papers proposing ways to support RBAC. Most of this work, however, is about support for RBAC96 (Sandhu et al., 1996), which defines the reference models for plain, hierarchical, and constrained RBAC, but does not specify the functions to be supported by an RBAC implementation. The paucity of analysis or proposals for supporting ANSI RBAC is not surprising, given the fact that the standard was published in 2004. Because of the lack of research on support for ANSI RBAC, and because of the significant similarities between RBAC96 and ANSI RBAC, we review related work on supporting or implementing RBAC96 in operating systems, databases, web applications, and distributed systems, including middleware. Since the mainstream operating systems, with the exception of Solaris (Sun Microsystems Inc., 2000), do not provide direct support for RBAC, researchers and developers have been employing either groups (e.g., Sandhu & Ahn, 1998; Ahn & Sandhu, 2001), or user accounts (e.g., Faden, 1999; Chalfant, 2003) to simulate roles. This choice determines whether more than one role can be activated in a session. Role hierarchies are either not supported (Faden, 1999; Sun Microsystems Inc., 2000), or are simulated by maintaining additional system files with the role hierarchy and various book-keeping data (Sandhu & Ahn, 1998; Ahn & Sandhu, 2001). None of the implementations we reviewed support static SoD. Just one case of dynamic SoD comes as a side-effect with those implementations that simulate roles with user accounts (Faden, 1999; Chalfant, 2003): the role set in this DSoD is equal to the set of all roles in the system, and the cardinality of the role set is exactly one. In other words, any session can have only one role activated at any given time; the current role is deactivated when another role is activated.

We analyzed DB2 (Tran & Mohan, 2006) and MySQL (MySQL AB, 2007), and updated the analysis of RBAC support in commercial database management systems (DBMS)—conducted by Ramaswamy and Sandhu (1998)—with the latest versions of the corresponding systems. Commercial DBMS continue to have the most advanced support for RBAC96. Informix Dynamic Server v7.2 (IBM, 2005), IBM DB2 (Tran & Mohan, 2006), Sybase Adaptive Server v11.5 (Sybase Inc., 2005), and Oracle Enterprise Server v8.0 (Baylis, Lane, & Lorentz, 2003) directly support roles and role hierarchies. Only Oracle and Sybase allow users to have more than one role activated at any time, though. On the other hand, Informix also provides limited support for dynamic SoD, and Sybase features support for both types of SoD.

In RBAC implementations for client-server systems, including Web applications, roles are either "pushed" from the client to the server in the form of attribute certificates or HTTP cookies (Gutzmann, 2001; Park, Sandhu, & Ahn, 2001; Robles, Choi, Yeo, & Kim, 2008), or "pulled" by the server from a local or remote database (Bartz, 1997; Ferraiolo, Barkley, & Kuhn, 1999; Park et al., 2001; Chadwick & Otenko, 2002; Zhou & Meinel, 2004). The former enables selective activation of roles by users, and the latter simplifies the implementation of client authentication, but activates all of the assigned roles for the user. However, Web implementation of NIST RBAC (Ferraiolo et al., 1999) has a hybrid design, which allows the user to select the roles to be "pulled" by the server. A number of implementations use a database, possibly accessible through the Lightweight Directory Access Protocol (LDAP) (Wahl, Howes, & Kille, 1997) front-end to store role and other information (Bartz, 1997; Gutzmann, 2001; Park et al., 2001; Zhou & Meinel, 2004). Role hierarchies are only supported by some implementations, using either manual assignment of permissions of junior roles to senior ones (Park et al., 2001), additional files (Giuri, 1999), a database (Ferraiolo et al., 1999) or an LDAP server (Chadwick & Otenko, 2002; Zhou & Meinel, 2004). JRBAC-WEB (Giuri, 1999) and RBAC/Web (Ferraiolo et al., 1999) also support both types of SoD.

The work most relevant to ours addresses support for RBAC in middleware. Ahn (2000) outlines a proposal for enforcing RBAC policies for distributed applications that utilize Microsoft's Distributed Component Object Model (DCOM) (Brown & Kindel, 1998; Microsoft, 1998). His proposal employs the following elements of Windows NT's architecture: (1) a registry for storing and maintaining the role hierarchy and permission-to-role assignment (PA); (2) user groups for simulating roles and maintaining user-to-role assignment (UA); and (3) a custom built security provider that follows the RBAC model to make access control decisions, which are requested and enforced by the DCOM run-time. Since the support for role hierarchy is indicated, but not explained, by Ahn (2000), we assume that the Windows NT registry can be used to encode the hierarchy so that the RBAC security provider can refer to it while making authorization decisions. Similar to the proposals for RBAC support in operating systems, the use of OS user groups for simulating roles enables activation of more than one role. Yet, as with the pull model in client-server systems, all assigned roles are activated, leaving no choice for the user. Ahn (2000) does not indicate support for any kind of SoD, nor does he explain how RBAC policies can be enforced consistently and automatically in a multi-computer deployment of DCOM-accessible objects.

RBAC-JaCoWeb (Westphall & da Silva Fraga, 1999; Obelheiro & da Silva Fraga, 2002) utilizes the PoliCap (Westphall, da Silva Fraga, Wangham, Obelheiro, & Lung, 2002) policy server to implement CORBASec specification in a way that supports RBAC. PoliCap holds all data concerning security policies within a CORBASec policy domain, including users, roles, user-to-role and role-to-permission assignments, role hierarchy relations, and SoD constraints. Most of the authorization policy enforcement is performed by an RBAC-JaCoWeb CORBA security interceptor. At the time of the client binding to a CORBA object, the interceptor obtains necessary data from the PoliCap server and instantiates CORBASec-compliant DomainAccessPolicy and Required-Rights objects containing the privilege and control attributes appropriate for the application object. When the client makes invocation requests later, the access decisions are then performed based on the local instances of these objects. Initially, the client security credentials object—created as part of the binding—has no privilege attributes, only AccessId, which is obtained from the client's X.509 certificate used in the underlying SSL connection. If the invocation cannot be authorized with the current set of client privilege attributes, the interceptor "pulls" additional role attributes from the PoliCap server. Only those roles that are (1) assigned to the user, (2) necessary for the invocation in question to be authorized, and (3) not in conflict with any DSoD constraints are activated. These role attributes are added to the client's credentials and are later re-used on the server for other requests from the same principal. The extent to which RBAC-JaCoWeb conforms to the CORBASec specification is unclear (Westphall & da Silva Fraga, 1999; Obelheiro & da Silva Fraga, 2002). Nevertheless, RBAC-JaCoWeb serves as an example of implementation-specific extensions to CORBAsec that enable better support for RBAC advanced features, such as role hierarchies and SoD, which—as will be seen from the results of our analysis—cannot be supported without extending a CORBASec implementation with additional operations.

EJB Protection State

In this section, we first introduce the EJB access control architecture. Then, we formally define a configuration of the EJB protection state.

EJB Access Controls

An EJB container controls access to its beans at the level of an individual method on a bean class, although not a bean instance. That is, if different instances of the same bean have different access control requirements, they should be placed in different application assemblies, which are defined by JAR files. This means that the scope of the EJB's policy domain is the application assembly.

The EJB access control architecture provides two ways for enforcing access control decisions. One approach, known in EJB terminology as declarative security, is to configure the container to enforce an authorization policy. The other is achieved by coding authorization decision and enforcement logic into the bean methods. In the former case, access permissions of principals are defined either using deployment descriptors, or through code annotations. The declarative approach decouples business logic from security logic. In the latter approach, known as programmatic security, the application developers employ methods called IsCallerInRole and getCallerPrincipal to obtain the information about the caller in order to enforce those access control policies, which cannot be expressed using the declarative approach.

Authorization to invoke the enterprise bean's methods is enforced by the container. It grants or denies clients' requests to execute the methods in conformance with access control policies described in the deployment descriptor and/or through the bean's metadata annotations. Since the bean's metadata annotations are equivalent in the expressiveness to the policies supported by the deployment descriptor, we use only the latter in the rest of the paper. Access control decisions are based on the security roles (or just "roles" for short) of the principal, who represents the calling client. The security role is defined in the EJB specification as "a semantic grouping of permissions that a given type of users of the application must have in order to successfully use the application" (DeMichiel & Keith, 2006, p. 456). As defined by the specification, there are three types of deployment descriptor sections relevant to the declarative access control: security-role, method-permission, and exclude-list. The exclude-list section lists those methods that cannot be called by any principal, no matter which roles the principal has. Figure 6 uses Unified Modeling Language (UML) (OMG, 2007a, 2007b) notation to summarize the relationships among authorization-related sections of the deployment descriptor and the elements of an EJB application. In the rest of this section, we describe syntax and semantics of the two other sections.

Each security-role section lists a role with optional human-readable unstructured description of the role. This role can be referenced in other sections of the deployment descriptor. In essence, these sections define a set of roles for an EJB application.

The assignment of permissions to roles is done in method-permission sections. Such sections list roles permitted to invoke one or more methods. When the special role name is "unchecked" it can be used to indicate that all the roles are permitted to invoke the listed method(s). Each method is defined by the name of the bean class, method name, and, optionally, the formal parameter types to distinguish methods with overloaded names. The special method name "*" refers to all methods on a given bean.

An example of an assignment done through method-permission sections is shown in Table 1. The first row illustrates an assignment of a permission to invoke method m_1 on bean b_1 $(b_1.m_1)$ to role r_1. The second row shows how several roles $(r_1$ and $r_2)$ can be granted permissions to invoke any of the listed methods $(b_1.m_2$ and $b_1.m_4)$. This means that any principal that has any of these two roles can invoke any of these two methods. The last row provides an example of using "unchecked" and "*" keywords. It states that any principal can invoke method $b_2.m_1$ as well as any method on bean b_3. The overall set of methods a principal can invoke on a given EJB application is the union of

Figure 6. Relationships among the sections of deployment descriptor used for expressing access control policy and the elements of an EJB application

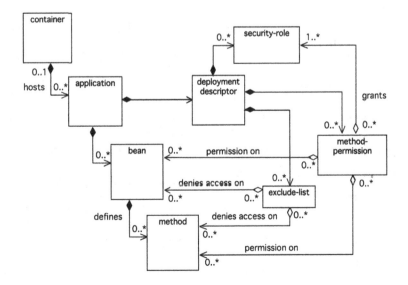

all the methods the principal's roles are permitted to invoke. For example, if a deployment descriptor contains only the three method-permission sections listed in Table 1, then a principal with role r_2 is granted permission to invoke methods $b_1.m_2$, $b_1.m_4$, $b_2.m_1$, and any method on bean b_3.

If a method (1) is not listed in any of the method-permission and exclude-list sections of a deployment descriptor, and (2) has no @Deny-All annotation in the code, then it is accessible by any principal—according to Section 17.3.2.3 of the EJB specification (DeMichiel & Keith, 2006), methods with unspecified permissions must be treated by the container as "unchecked." For instance, if $b_1.m_3$ is such a method then any principal would be able to invoke it.

Even though the syntax of the method-permission section allows the listing of more than one role and method, we will assume without the loss of generality that each section contains only one role and one method, as shown in the first row of Table 1. It is easy to define an algorithm for converting any number of method-permission sections in a deployment descriptor to this form. This assumption will simplify the definition of the protection state and the algorithm for making access control decisions in the following section.

In addition to the above deployment descriptor sections, EJB server vendors (or container providers) define container-specific sections of deployment descriptors that map users and/or groups to roles. Table 2 shows additional deployment

descriptor sections for major commercial EJB servers. Since the notions of users, groups, and the mapping from them to roles are lacking from the EJB v3.0 specification, these vendor-specific additions to the EJB system will not be used for defining the EJB protection state.

Formalization of the Protection State

In this section, we formalize the semantics of the EJB access control architecture.

Definition 2 [EJB Protection State]. *A configuration of an EJB system protection state is a tuple (R,B,M,MP,X) interpreted as follows:*

- ○ *R is a set of roles defined in the assembly-descriptor part of the deployment descriptor provided with the EJB application. These roles are defined using the security-role tags. This set also includes the special role "unchecked".*

- ○ *B is a set of enterprise beans listed in the enterprise-beans section of the deployment descriptor.*

Table 1. Examples of method-permission sections of EJB deployment descriptor. For the sake of clarity, the data representation is converted from XML notation to human-understandable form, with each row corresponding to an individual section

Roles	Methods
r_1	$b_1.m_1$
r_1, r_2	$b_1.m_2, b_1.m_4$
"unchecked"	$b_2.m_1, b_3.*$

Table 2. Additional authorization-related sections used in deployment descriptors of commercial EJB servers

App. Server	Section(s)	Comments
Oracle	users, groups	A security-role-mapping XML tag maps logical roles defined in the application deployment descriptor to entities defined in the users and groups sections
Sun ONE	principal-name, group-name	A security-role-mapping tag defines mapping between principal-names and roles, and/or between group-names and roles
BEA Web-Logic	principal-name	A security-role-assignment XML tag declares mapping between principal-names and roles
IBM Web-Sphere	Users, groups	Tools establish user-group memberships and mapping between groups and roles

○ *OPS is a set of methods defined by the enterprise beans of the application. Members of this set are denoted as m_i. The set also includes special method "*" for any bean defined by the application and signifying any method on that bean; for example, $OPS = \{m_1, m_2, ...\} \cup \{*\}$*

○ *$M \subseteq B \times OPS$ is the set of available uniquely identifiable methods. Members of this set are denoted $b_i m_j$.*

○ *$MP \subseteq R \times M$ is a many-to-many permission assignment of EJB application roles to invoke methods, as specified in method-permission sections of the application's deployment descriptor.*

○ *$X \subseteq M$ is a subset of methods-defined by exclude-list sections of the deployment descriptor-invocation of which is denied to any role.*

Note that the implementations of EJB containers and servers commonly have extensions to the deployment descriptors, which enable defining sets of users and groups, as well as assigning them to roles. Such vendor-specific extensions result in additional elements of the protection state. However, all elements defined in Definition 2 are present in any EJB implementation compliant with the specification. When analyzing EJB support for RBAC in the following section, we will identify additional elements of EJB protection state that are necessary for the support.

Given the protection state of an EJB application, Algorithm 1 defines the outcome of an access control decision. First, a check is performed on the membership of the requested method in the list of blocked methods. If the method is found in the list, then access is denied. If not, then the method permissions are checked for every role of the principal and the special role "unchecked." If no appropriate element is in *MP*, then access is denied.

ANALYSIS OF SUPPORT FOR ANSI RBAC

As described in the section titled Overview of ANSI RBAC, the ANSI RBAC Reference Model defines four major components. In order for a system to conform to ANSI RBAC, Core RBAC must be implemented at a minimum. An ANSI compliant RBAC system can also implement Hierarchical RBAC, which defines hierarchies of roles in addition to everything Core RBAC does. The other two optional components of the standard, Static Separation of Duty (SSD) and Dynamic Separation of Duty (DSD), define relations among roles with respect to user assignments as well as role activation in user sessions.

We first examine the extent to which an EJB protection state—as formalized in Definition 2 – can support each of the four ANSI RBAC model components (Algorithm 1). We then provide an example that illustrates the abilities of an EJB system to support ANSI RBAC. Following that, we analyze the degree to which the structures defined in EJB specification support the functional specification of ANSI RBAC. In the Discussion section, we then discuss the results of our analysis.

Reference Model

Core RBAC

Various Core RBAC data elements are mapped readily into EJB using the sets defined in the EJB Protection State section. For example, the *ROLES* set in RBAC maps directly to *R*, which defines the EJB security roles; RBAC objects (*OBJ*) are equivalent to EJB beans (*B*); RBAC operations (*OPS*) are represented by EJB *OPS*. The representation of other relations defined in Core RBAC is outside the scope of the EJB standard, as we will discuss later in this section. We first define Core RBAC in the language of the EJB protection system more formally as follows:

Algorithm 1. Authorization decision in EJB. Decide authorization for principal invoking method m_j on bean b_i, where $r_1, r_2, \ldots r_n \in R$, and $b_i.m_j \in M$

```
Authorize(p : 2^R, b_i.m_j : M) → {allow, deny}
if   b_i.m_j ∈ X then
    return deny
end if
for all  r ∈ p ∪ {"unchecked"} do
    if  (r, b_i.m_j) ∈ MP ∨ (r, b_i*) ∈ MP  then
        return allow
    end if
end for
return deny
```

Definition 3 [Core RBAC in EJB]. *Core RBAC in the language of EJB is defined by the EJB system protection state outlined in Definition 2, as well as the following additional elements:*

- *USERS is the set of users, where members of this set are defined in the operational environment of the EJB system.*
- *ROLES = R, is the set of roles as defined in Definition 2.*
- *OBS = B is a set of enterprise beans.*
- *UA = USERS × ROLES is a many-to-many assignment of users to roles.*
- *assigned_users*
  $(r : ROLES) = \{u \in USERS \,|\, (u,r) \in UA\}$
  is a function that returns the set of users in USERS that are assigned to the given role r.
- *PRMS ⊆ M − X is a set of permissions to invoke EJB methods provided that these methods do not exist in the exclusion set X. The existence of $b_i.m_j$ or $b_i.*$ in PRMS rovides permission to invoke a specific method m_j, or all methods on bean b_i, respectively.*
- *PA ⊆ PRMS × ROLES, a many-to-many assignment of permissions to roles.*

- *assigned_permissions*
  $(r : ROLES) = \{p \in PRMS \,|\, (p,r) \in PA\}$,
  is a function that returns the set of permissions in PRMS that are assigned to the given role r.
- $Op(p : PRMS) \rightarrow \{op \in OPS\}$, a function *that returns a set of operations that are associated with the given permission p.*
- $Ob(p : PRMS) \rightarrow \{ob \in OBS\}$, a function *that returns a set of objects that are associated with the given permission p.*
- *SESSIONS is a set of sessions for a specific application. Members of this set are mappings between authenticated users and their activated roles for a specific EJB application.*
- *session_users*
  $(s : SESSIONS) \rightarrow USERS$,
  the mapping of session s onto the corresponding user.
- *session_roles*
  $(s : SESSIONS) \rightarrow 2^{ROLES}$,
  the mapping of session s onto a set of roles. Formally: session_roles
  $(s_i) \subseteq \{r \in ROLES \,|\, (session\_users(s_i), r) \in UA\}$.
- *avail_session_perms*
  $(s : SESSIONS) \rightarrow 2^{PRMS}$,

the permissions available to a user in a session =

$$\bigcup_{r \in session\_roles(s)} assigned\_permissions(r) \cdot$$

In order to support Core RBAC in EJB systems, Definition 3 identifies additional elements to those identified in Definition 2. These additional elements are related to users and sessions. In the rest of this section we discuss how elements of Definition 3 are or can be supported in an EJB system.

Although the EJB standard (DeMichiel & Keith, 2006) does not mandate how users must be supported in an EJB system, various implementations of EJB servers and containers implement extensions to deployment descriptors. These extensions provide support for adding users to the system, as well as mapping those users to roles. The *USERS* set in Definition 3 abstracts this support; however, this support is implementation-dependent. By the same token, support for *UA* and *assigned_users* is also implementation-dependent.

The *SESSIONS* set is another element of Definition 3. In relation to support for users, the EJB standard does not specify a mapping of authenticated users to roles, or more precisely, role activation. Hence, EJB server's support for sessions is outside the scope of the EJB standard and is implementation-dependent. Similarly, in order to fully support Core RBAC, EJB implementations' support for session-related functions such as *session_users*, *session_roles*, and *avail_session_perms* are outside the scope of the EJB standard.

On the other hand, the sets *ROLES*, *OPS*, and *OBS*; the relations *PRMS* and *PA*; and the functions *Op* and *Ob* are all supported by the EJB standard as these can be readily obtained from the deployment-descriptor.

To summarize, about half the elements of ANSI Core RBAC can be provided by any implementation compliant with the EJB standard; however, support for *USERS*, *UA*, *assigned_us-*

ers, *SESSIONS*, *session_users*, *session_roles*, and *avail_session_perms*, which relate to users and sessions, if provided, can only be implementation-dependent.

Hierarchical RBAC

The Hierarchical RBAC component specifies two types of role hierarchies: general and limited. Both types are formally defined using elements of Core RBAC. In addition to role hierarchies, Hierarchical RBAC defines two functions: *authorized_users* and *authorized_permissions*. Although the EJB standard does not provide direct support for Hierarchical RBAC, an EJB implementation can still emulate both types of role hierarchies. The rest of this section discusses ways of emulating Hierarchical RBAC in EJB.

EJB server administrative tools can be modified in order to support role hierarchy. First, the administrative tools must maintain hierarchy relationships between roles in a repository. Second, the tools must ensure that when method permissions are granted to a certain role in a deployment descriptor, those method permissions are also appropriately and consistently granted to all senior roles. Finally, the administrative tools must also keep track of whether permission has been directly assigned to a role, or if the role inherited this permission through a role hierarchy. No special run-time support for role hierarchies would then be needed. This approach is similar to the ones used in Ahn and Sandhu (2001) and Sandhu and Ahn (1998) in order to support role hierarchy in various operating systems.

An alternative is an approach in which inherited permissions are determined at run-time. This approach would require the EJB server—or more specifically the Target Security Service (TSS) described earlier—to examine the role hierarchy repository during run-time. A certain role is then granted permission to invoke a specific method not only based on direct permission-to-role assignment, but also based on permissions granted to a junior role. In addition to a repository that maintains role hierarchy relationship, a run-time computation of inherited permissions would be required. A similar approach is adopted in (Ferraiolo et al., 1999) for Common Gateway Interface (CGI) based Web applications, and in (Giuri, 1999) for Java Authentication and Authorization Service (JAAS) (ORACLE, 2001) based access control.

With either of the above approaches, support for this role hierarchy–and the *authorized_users* and *authorized_permissions* functions required for Hierarchical RBAC–is implementation-dependent and is not specified by the EJB standard.

Constrained RBAC

The Constrained RBAC component introduces separation of duty relations to the RBAC reference model. As with Hierarchical RBAC, these relations are defined in terms of Core RBAC constructs. In essence, SSD constrains user-to-role assignment (*UA* set and *assigned_users* function) and the role hierarchy (*RH* set and *authorized_users* function). DSD, on the other hand, constrains the role activation (*SESSIONS* set and *session_roles* function). Since user accounts, role hierarchies, and role activation are beyond the scope of EJB, the Constrained RBAC component, if supported, would have to be implementation-dependent.

Example

In this section, we present an example that illustrates the abilities of an EJB system to support ANSI RBAC. As discussed in the previous section, the EJB standard does not provide direct support for role hierarchy; however, emulation of such support is possible as discussed earlier, and is straightforward. Hence, role hierarchy is not illustrated in this example.

The example in this section consists of a simple system that maintains employee and engineering project records in an engineering company. The system allows different users to perform various operations on the project and employee records, based on the users' roles in the company. The system handles the manipulation of various records through enterprise beans of two types: EngineeringProject and Employee. These enterprise beans are depicted in Figure 7. The figure shows the methods that can be invoked on the beans. The system also defines seven different user roles. Based on these roles and according to the policies listed in Figure 8, users are allowed to invoke various methods on a specific EJB. These roles are defined as follows:

- *Employee* represents a company employee.
- *Engineering Department* represents an employee of the engineering department.
- *Engineer* performs various engineering tasks in the company.
- *Product Engineer* is responsible for managing a product line.
- *Quality Engineer* is a quality assurance engineer.
- *Project Lead* oversees and leads the development of a project.
- *Director* is an engineering department director.

The access control policy that defines what actions each role is allowed to perform are summarized in Table 3, where a check mark ("√") denotes a granted permission for a specific EJB role to execute the corresponding enterprise bean method. Table 4 shows an example of system users, and their group memberships. Tables in Figure 9 show examples of user-to-role and group-to-role assignments. The following is a formalization of this example system's protection state as in Definition 2.

- R = { Employee, Engineering Department, Engineer, Product Engineer, Quality Engineer, Project Lead, Director}

Figure 7. Example EngineeringProject and Employee session beans

```
+-------------------------------+        +-------------------------------+
|      << Session Bean >>        |        |      << Session Bean>>         |
|     EngineeringProject         |        |          Employee              |
+-------------------------------+        +-------------------------------+
| + makeChanges()                |        | + getBasicInfo()               |
| + reviewChanges()              |        | + assignToProject()            |
| + inspectQuality()             |        | + unassignFromProject()        |
| + reportProblem()              |        | + reportProblem()              |
| + closeProblem()               |        | + addExperience()              |
| + createNewRelease()           |        | + getExperience()              |
| + getDescription()             |        | + fire()                       |
| + close()                      |        +-------------------------------+
+-------------------------------+
```

- B = { EngineeringProject, Employee }
- OPS = { makeChanges, reviewChanges, inspectQuality, reportProblem, closeProblem, createNewRelease, getDescription, close, getBasicInfo, assignToProject, unassignFromProject, addExperience, getExperience, fire}
- M = { EngineeringProject.makeChanges, EngineeringProject.reviewChanges, EngineeringProject.inspectQuality, EngineeringProject.reportProblem, EngineeringProject.closeProblem, EngineeringProject.createNewRelease, EngineeringProject.getDescription, EngineeringProject.close, Employee.getBasicInfo, Employee.assignToProject, Employee.unassignFromProject, Employee.addExperience, Employee.getExperience, Employee.fire }

- MP = { (Employee, Employee.getBasicInfo),
(Employee, Employee.getExperience),
(Engineering Department, EngineeringProject.reportProblem),
(Engineering Department, EngineeringProject.getDescription),
(Engineering Department, Employee.getBasicInfo),
(Engineering Department, Employee.getExperience),
(Engineer, EngineeringProject.makeChanges),
(Engineer, EngineeringProject.reviewChanges),
(Engineer, Employee.getBasicInfo),
(Engineer, Employee.getExperience),
(Product Engineer, EngineeringProject.createNewRelease),

Figure 8. Authorization policy for the example EJB system describing what actions are allowed. All other actions are denied.

1. Anyone in the organization can look up an employee's basic information, such as their name, department, phone number, and office location.
2. Everyone in the engineering department can get a description of and report problems regarding any project and look up experience of any employee.
3. Engineers, assigned to projects, can make changes and review changes related to their projects.
4. Quality engineers, in addition to being granted engineers' rights, can inspect the quality of projects to which they are assigned.
5. Product engineers, in addition to possessing engineers' rights, can create new releases.
6. The project lead, in addition to possessing the rights granted to product and quality engineers, can also close problems.
7. The director, in addition to being granted the rights of project leads, can manage employees (assign them to projects, un-assign them from projects, look up experience, add new records to their experience, and fire them) and close projects.

Table 3. Permission-to-role assignment for the example

Roles	Methods													
	EngineeringProject Bean								*Employee Bean*					
	make-Changes()	review-Changes()	in-spect-Quality()	re-port-Prob-lem()	closeP-rob-lem()	creat-eNe-wRe-lease()	get-De-scrip-tion()	close()	get-Ba-sicIn-fo()	as-sign-To-Pro-ject()	unas-sign-From-Pro-ject()	ad-dEx-peri-ence()	getEx-peri-ence()	fire()
Em-ploy-ee									√				√	
Engi-neer-ing De-part-ment				√		√			√				√	
Engi-neer	√	√							√				√	
Prod-uct Engi-neer						√			√				√	
Qual-ity Engi-neer			√						√				√	
Proj-ect Lead					√				√				√	
Direc-tor								√	√	√	√	√	√	√

(Engineering Department, Employee.getBasicInfo),

(Engineering Department, Employee.getExperience),

(Quality Engineer, EngineeringProject.inspectQuality),

(Quality Engineer, Employee.getBasicInfo),

(Quality Engineer, Employee.getExperience),

(Project Lead, EngineeringProject.closeProblem),

(Project Lead, Employee.getBasicInfo),

(Project Lead, Employee.getExperience),

(Director, EngineeringProject.close),

(Director, Employee.getBasicInfo),

(Director, Employee.assignToProject),

(Director, Employee.unassignFromProject),

(Director, Employee.addExperience),

(Director, Employee.getExperience),

(Director, Employee.fire) }

- $X = \Phi$

The R and B sets contain the roles and beans defined in the system. *OPS* defines all operations available to various roles. These methods are further qualified by the M set, where each method is qualified with the name of the bean for which it is

Table 4. Example users, groups, and group membership

User	Group
Alice	accounting
Bob	hardware
Carol	software
Dave	software
Eve	software
Fred	management

defined. The *MP* set represents Table 3, and *MP* is a many-to-many permission assignment of EJB application roles to invoke defined methods. These permissions are listed in the method-permission sections of the application's deployment descriptor. This example does not require any methods to be in the exclude-list sections of the deployment descriptor for the application; hence, set *X* is empty.

We use the above formalization of the example system's protection state in order to support the ANSI Core RBAC reference model. Considering Definition 3, the content of *ROLES*, *OPS*, and *OBS* is straightforward. The rest of the sets are defined as follows.

- *USERS* = { Alice, Bob, Carol, Dave, Eve, Fred, accounting, hardware, software, management }
- *UA* = { (Alice, Employee), (Bob, Engineer), (Carol, Quality Engineer), (Dave, Product Engineer), (Eve, Project Lead), (Fred, Director), (hard-

ware, Engineering Department), (software, Engineering Department), (Bob, Engineering Department), (Carol, Engineering Department), (Dave, Engineering Department), (Eve, Engineering Department)}

- *PRMS* = *M*
- *PA* = *MP*

The EJB 3.0 standard does not specify how EJB roles should be mapped to the user groups and accounts that exist in the bean's operational environment. This makes the *USERS* and *UA* sets dependent solely on the EJB container's operational environment, and the way users are managed there. For example, the *UA* set contains assignments that exist only due to user-group memberships. In this example, Carol is assigned to the *Engineering Department* role through her software group membership.

Functional Specification

This section reports on the results of our analysis of the support that the EJB standard (DeMichiel & Keith, 2006) can provide for ANSI RBAC system and administrative functional specifications. For the purpose of this analysis, we examined every function specified in Section 6 of the ANSI publication (2004) on the subject of its support by an EJB container conforming to the EJB standard.

Results of our examination suggest that the software interfaces that the EJB standard mandates are insufficient for implementing most of ANSI

Figure 9. Example EJB system role mappings

User	Role
Alice	Employee
Bob	Engineer
Carol	Quality Engineer
Dave	Product Engineer
Eve	Project Lead
Fred	Director

(a) User-to-role assignment

Group	Role
hardware	Engineering Department
software	Engineering Department

(b) Group-to-role assignment

RBAC functions as is. Furthermore, the XML data structures needed in the EJB deployment descriptor are incapable of fully supporting an ANSI RBAC compliant system. These data structures can provide support for implementing a limited number of Core RBAC functions. Other system and administrative Core RBAC functions, as well as all additional functions for Hierarchical and Constrained RBAC, cannot be supported without extending an EJB system implementation beyond what the EJB standard defines.

The following is an examination of various Core RBAC functions and their level of support in the EJB standard.

AddUser, DeleteUser operations allow users to be added to the USERS set and to be removed from it. In an EJB environment, these are realized in a implementation-dependent manner. For example, the IBM WebSphere Application Server (Sadtler et al., 2004) allows EJB application deployers to use various user registries to maintain the *USERS* set. WebSphere can be configured to use the local operating system user accounts, an LDAP (Wahlet al., 1997) server, or a custom user registry.

AddRole, DeleteRole add roles to and delete roles from the RBAC system. EJB data structures provide direct support for implementing these functions. They can be implemented by adding or removing a role definition using the security-role tags in the assembly-descriptor section of the deployment descriptor file.

AssignUser, DeassignUser allow assignment relationships to be established between roles and users. Similar to *AddUser* and *DeleteUser*, these operations need to be implemented in an implementation-dependent manner.

GrantPermission, RevokePermission allow invocation permissions to be granted to, or revoked for, a certain role. These operations can be implemented by adding or removing the corresponding method-permission section of the deployment descriptor.

CreateSession, DeleteSession, AddActiveRole, DropActiveRole allow for the creation and deletion of sessions, as well as activation of user roles. In an EJB environment, these operations are likely to be implemented in a proprietary manner and would differ from one EJB application server to another.

CheckAccess make an access control decision. The Authorize method in Algorithm 1 can be used to implement CheckAccess.

AssignedUsers, AssignedRoles return users assigned to a given role, and roles assigned to a given user, respectively. Since these functions are not supported in EJB 3.0, they need to be provided by the EJB application server.

Advanced Review Functions for Core RBAC

RolePermissions returns the permissions granted to a given role. This function can be implemented by examining the method-permission sections, where method permissions are granted to roles.

UserPermissions returns permissions assigned to users. Given the permissions assigned to roles (using the *RolePermissions* function), and knowing the roles the user is assigned to (using *AssignedUsers*), the implementation of this function is straightforward.

SessionRoles, SessionPermissions return the roles and permissions associated with a specific user session. These can be provided by the EJB application server assuming that the server implementation already supports the notion of sessions.

RoleOperationsOnObject, UserOperationsOnObject return a set of operations that can be invoked on an object given a certain role or a certain user, respectively. The operations that a certain role is permitted to invoke can be obtained directly from the method-permission sections of the deployment descriptor. The operations that a user is permitted to invoke, on the other hand, can be obtained given the implementation of the *RoleOperationsOnObject* as well as the *AssignedRoles* functions.

Table 5 provides a summary of the above results. The table classifies support for ANSI Core RBAC functions in two main categories. The first category contains functions that are supported directly by EJB data structures, whereas the second category identifies the supplemental components that must be implemented in an EJB system—outside the scope of the EJB specifications—in order to support the specified ANSI Core RBAC functions. These components are identified as related to user management, session and role activation. The user management related components are required to handle the addition/deletion of users from the system, as well as user-to-role assignments. On the other hand, the session and role activation related components are required to handle the management of user sessions and activation of permissions.

Discussion

The results of our analysis suggest that EJB functionality – as defined through the data structures and interfaces – falls short of fully supporting ANSI RBAC without resorting to vendor-specific extensions. Even in the case of Core RBAC alone – the mandatory part of any compliant implementation of ANSI RBAC – there are two major causes of this inadequacy.

The two major limitations of EJB are its lack of the notion of user accounts and support for their management (i.e., adding, deleting, (un)assigning to/from roles), as well as the lack of support for user sessions and role activation. According to our analysis, which is summarized in Table 5, this limitation results in two thirds of Core RBAC functions being dependent on vendor-specific extensions (see column "Additional Required Components"). The architects of EJB might have intentionally left the notion of user and support for user management as well as session and role activation beyond the scope of the specification. In order to provide standard support for administering and reviewing user accounts, their roles and their

sessions, the corresponding administrative interfaces would need to be added to EJB. However, such a revision would be contrary to the emerging state of practice for application systems.

The notable trend in IT systems design is to "outsource" the functionality for administering user accounts, and in some cases permissions, to single sign-on (SSO) (Pashalidis & Mitchell, 2003) solutions for new applications (Goth, 2005) and to identity management (IdM) solutions for existing applications (Buell & Sandhu, 2003). As a result, user accounts, and sometimes permissions, are administered across multiple application instances and types "outside" of the applications themselves. Therefore, an application system can only be successfully evaluated for compliance with ANSI RBAC when the application is considered together with the corresponding SSO or IdM solution. This condition makes evaluation of support for ANSI RBAC prohibitively expensive for systems designed to work in conjunction with multiple SSO or IdM solutions, as the evaluation would have to be performed for every combination of the system and the supporting SSO/IdM. Defining a separate ANSI RBAC profile for SSO/IdM solutions is a possible alternative to explore.

The other limitations of the EJB specification relate to Hierarchical and Constrained RBAC components of ANSI RBAC. The EJB specification does not define support for either role hierarchies or separation of duty. We sketch approaches for supporting the two components. However, additional data must be maintained outside of the standard deployment descriptor in order to implement role hierarchies.

CONCLUSION

In this paper, we analyzed support for ANSI RBAC by EJB 3.0 compliant systems. Specifically, we defined a configuration of the EJB protection system in precise and unambiguous terms using set theory. Based on this configuration definition, we

Table 5. Functions defined by ANSI Core RBAC and their support by EJB data structures

Core RBAC Functions	Additional Required Components		
	EJB Data Structures Support	User Management	Sessions and Role Activation
Administrative Commands			
AddUser		√	
DeleteUser		√	
AssignUser		√	
DeassignUser		√	
AddRole	√		
DeleteRole	√		
GrantPermission	√		
RevokePermission	√		
Supporting System Functions			
CreateSession			√
DeleteSession			√
AddActiveRole			√
DropActiveRole			√
CheckAccess	√		
Review Functions			
AssignedUsers		√	
AssignedRoles		√	
Advanced Review Functions			
RolePermissions	√		
SessionPermissions			√
UserPermissions		√	
SessionRoles			√
RoleOperationsOnObject	√		
UserOperationsOnObject		√	

formally specified the semantics of authorization decisions in EJB. We analyzed support for various ANSI RBAC components in EJB, and illustrated our discussion with an example.

Our analysis shows a mismatch between the access control architectures of EJB and ANSI RBAC. Although the specification of access controls in EJB does employ roles, it does not fully support even Core ANSI RBAC. The limitations are mainly due to the lack of support of (1) user accounts and their management, (2) user sessions,

and (3) role activation. While these limitations can be easily worked around through vendor-specific and implementation dependent extensions, each EJB implementation would have to be evaluated for ANSI RBAC separately. In order to provide standard support for administering and reviewing user accounts, their roles and their sessions, the corresponding administrative interfaces would need to be added to EJB, which would be contrary to the emerging practice of "outsourcing" such functions to enterprise-wide single sign-on and identity management solutions.

To support this rising trend, it is possible to explore extending the ANSI RBAC standard, as well as the EJB standard to define profiles for supporting SSO/IdM solutions. This would also require exploring options for providing proper support for role activation and deactivation in order to adhere to the principle of least privilege. Clearly, activating the roles assigned to a user all at the same time violates this principle. On the other hand, allowing one role to be active at a time would not provide proper role activation support because the user may need the permissions assigned to more than one role in order to invoke a certain operation, in the absence of role hierarchy, for example. Other issues to explore include whether role activation should occur upon user authentication or upon method invocation, when roles should be deactivated, and whether roles should be activated with or without user intervention.

This paper establishes a framework for analyzing support for ANSI RBAC in EJB implementations. The results provide directions for EJB developers implementing ANSI RBAC in their systems, and criteria application owners in selecting such EJB implementations that support required, and optional components of ANSI RBAC.

REFERENCES

Ahn, G.-J. (2000). Role-based access control in DCOM. *Journal of Systems Architecture, 46*(13), 1175–1184. doi:10.1016/S1383-7621(00)00017-5

Ahn, G.-J., & Sandhu, R. (2001). Decentralized user group assignment in Windows NT. *Journal of Systems and Software, 56*(1), 39–49. doi:10.1016/S0164-1212(00)00084-4

ANSI. (2004). *ANSI INCITS 359-2004 for role based access control*. Retrieved from http://intelligrid.ipower.com/IntelliGrid_Architecture/New_Technologies/Tech_ANSI_INCITS_359-2004_Role_Based_Access_Control_(RBAC).htm

Awischus, R. (1997). Role based access control with security administration manager (SAM). In *Proceedings of the Second ACM Workshop on Role-Based Access Control* (pp. 61-68). New York, NY: ACM Press.

Barkley, J. (1995). Implementing role-based access control using object technology. In *Proceedings of the First ACM Workshop on Role-Based Access Control* (pp. 93-98). New York, NY: ACM Press.

Barkley, J., & Cincotta, A. (1998). Managing role/permission relationships using object access types. In *Proceedings of the Third ACM Workshop on Role-Based Access Control* (pp. 73-80). New York, NY: ACM Press.

Bartz, L. S. (1997). hyperDRIVE: Leveraging LDAP to implement RBAC on the web. In *Proceedings of the ACM Workshop on Role-Based Access Control* (pp. 69-74). New York, NY: ACM Press.

Baylis, R., Lane, P., & Lorentz, D. (2003). *Oracle database administrator's guide*. Retrieved from http://otn.oracle.com/pls/db10g/db10g.homepage

Bell, D. E., & LaPadula, L. J. (1975). *Secure computer systems: Unified exposition and multics interpretation* (Technical Report No. ESD-TR-75-306). Bedford, MA: MITRE.

Bindiganavale, V., & Ouyang, J. (2006, September). Role based access control in enterprise application-security administration and user management. In *Proceedings of the IEEE International Conference on Information Reuse and Integration*, Waikoloa Village, HI (pp. 111-116). Washington, DC: IEEE Computer Society.

Brown, N., & Kindel, C. (1998). *Distributed component object model protocol-DCOM/1.0*. Retrieved from http://www.ietf.org/proceedings/43/I-D/draft-brown-dcom-v1-spec-03.txt

Buell, D., & Sandhu, R. (2003). Identity management. *IEEE Internet Computing, 7*(6), 26–28. doi:10.1109/MIC.2003.1250580

Chadwick, D. W., & Otenko, A. (2002). The PERMIS X.509 role based privilege management infrastructure. In *Proceedings of the Seventh ACM Symposium on Access Control Models and Technologies* (pp. 135-140). New York, NY: ACM Press.

Chalfant, T. M. (2003). *Role based access control and secure shell - a closer look at two Solaris™ operating environment security features*. Redwood Shores, CA: Sun BluePrints™ OnLine.

DeMichiel, L. G., & Keith, M. (2006). *JSR-220: Enterprise JavaBeans 24 specification, version 3.0: EJB core contracts and requirements (Specification No. v.3.0 Final Release)*. Retrieved from http://jcp.org/aboutJava/communityprocess/pfd/jsr220/index.html

DeMichiel, L. G., Yalçinalp, L. Ü., & Krishnan, S. (2001). *Enterprise JavaBeans specification, version 2.0*. Retrieved from http://java.sun.com/products/ejb/docs.html

Eddon, G. (1999). The COM+ security model gets you out of the security programming business. *Microsoft Systems Journal, 1999*(11).

Epstein, J., & Sandhu, R. (1995). Netware 4 as an example of role-based access control. In *Proceedings of the First ACM Workshop on Role-Based Access Control* (pp. 71-82). New York, NY: ACM Press.

Faden, G. (1999). RBAC in UNIX administration. In *Proceedings of the Fourth ACM Workshop on Role-Based Access Control* (pp. 95-101). New York, NY: ACM Press.

Ferraiolo, D. F., Barkley, J. F., & Kuhn, D. R. (1999). A role-based access control model and reference implementation within a corporate intranet. *ACM Transactions on Information and System Security, 2*(1), 34–64. doi:10.1145/300830.300834

Ferraiolo, D. F., & Kuhn, R. (1992). Role-based access controls. In *Proceedings of the 15th NIST-NCSC National Computer Security Conference*, Baltimore, MD (pp. 554-563).

Ferraiolo, D. F., Sandhu, R., Gavrila, S., Kuhn, D. R., & Chandramouli, R. (2001). Proposed NIST standard for role-based access control. *ACM Transactions on Information and System Security, 4*(3), 224–274. doi:10.1145/501978.501980

Giuri, L. (1998). Role-based access control in Java. In *Proceedings of the Third ACM Workshop on Role-Based Access Control*, Fairfax, VA (pp. 91-99). New York, NY: ACM Press.

Giuri, L. (1999). Role-based access control on the Web using Java. In *Proceedings of the Fourth ACM Workshop on Role-Based Access Control* (pp. 11-18). New York, NY: ACM Press.

Goth, G. (2005). Identity management, access specs are rolling along. *IEEE Internet Computing, 9*(1), 9–11. doi:10.1109/MIC.2005.16

Gutzmann, K. (2001). Access control and session management in the HTTP environment. *IEEE Internet Computing, 5*(1), 26–35. doi:10.1109/4236.895139

Hartman, B., Flinn, D. J., & Beznosov, K. (2001). *Enterprise security with EJB and CORBA*. New York, NY: John Wiley & Sons.

IBM. (2005). *IBM informix dynamic server administrator's guide*. Retrieved from http://www-306.ibm.com/software/data/informix/pubs/library/ids100.html

Lampson, B. W. (1971). Protection. In *Proceedings of the Fifth Princeton Conference on Information Sciences and Systems* (p. 437).

Meyers, W. J. (1997). RBAC emulation on trusted dg/ux. In *Proceedings of the Second ACM Workshop on Role-Based Access Control* (pp. 55-60). New York, NY: ACM Press.

Microsoft. (1998). *DCOM architecture*. Retrieved from http://www.microsoft.com/NTServer/

MySQL AB. (2007). *MySQL*. Retrieved from http://www.mysql.com

Notargiacomo, L. (1995). Role-based access control in oracle7 and trusted oracle7. In *Proceedings of the First ACM Workshop on Role-Based Access Control* (pp. 65-69). New York, NY: ACM Press.

Obelheiro, R. R., & Fraga, J. S. (2002). Role-based access control for CORBA distributed object systems. In *Proceedings of the IEEE International Workshop on Object-Oriented Real-Time Dependable Systems* (p. 53). Washington, DC: IEEE Computer Society.

Oberg, R. J. (2000). *Understanding & programming COM+: A practical guide to Windows 2000 DNA*. Upper Saddle River, NJ: Prentice Hall.

OMG. (1999). *The common object request broker: Architecture and specification*. Needham, MA: Object Management Group.

OMG. (2002). *Common object services specification, security service specification v1.8*. Needham, MA: Object Management Group.

OMG. (2004). *Common object request broker architecture: Core specification v3.0.3*. Needham, MA: Object Management Group.

OMG. (2007a, February). *Unified modeling language: Infrastructure, v2.1.1*. Needham, MA: Object Management Group.

OMG. (2007b, February). *Unified modeling language: Superstructure, v2.1.1*. Needham, MA: Object Management Group.

ORACLE. (2001). *Java authentication and authorization service (JAAS)*. Retrieved from http://java.sun.com/products/jaas/

ORACLE. (2007). *Remote method invocation*. Retrieved from http://java.sun.com/javase/technologies/core/basic/rmi/index.jsp

Park, J. S., Sandhu, R., & Ahn, G.-J. (2001). Role-based access control on the web. *ACM Transactions on Information and System Security, 4*(1), 37–71. doi:10.1145/383775.383777

Pashalidis, A., & Mitchell, C. J. (2003, July 9-11). A taxonomy of single sign-on systems. In R. Safavi-Naini & J. Seberry (Ed.), *Proceedings of the Eighth Australasian Conference Information Security and Privacy*, Wollongong, Australia (LNCS 2727, pp. 249-264).

Ramaswamy, C., & Sandhu, R. (1998). Role-based access control features in commercial database management systems. In *Proceedings of the 21st NIST-NCSC National Information Systems Security Conference* (pp. 503-511).

Robles, R., Choi, M.-K., Yeo, S.-S., & Kim, T. Hoon. (2008, October). Application of role-based access control for web environment. In *Proceedings of the International Symposium on Ubiquitous Multimedia Computing* (pp. 171-174). Washington, DC: IEEE Computer Society.

Roman, E., Sriganesh, R. P., & Brose, G. (2005). *Mastering enterprise javabeans* (3rd ed.). Indianapolis, IN: Wiley.

Sadtler, C., Clifford, L., Heyward, J., Iwamoto, A., Jakusz, N., & Laursen, L. B. (2004). *IBM websphere application server v5.1 system management and configuration websphere handbook series*. Armonk, NY: IBM International Technical Support Organization.

Sandhu, R., & Ahn, G.-J. (1998). Decentralized group hierarchies in UNIX: An experiment and lessons learned. In *Proceedings of the 21st NIST-NCSC National Information Systems Security Conference* (pp. 486-502).

Sandhu, R., Coyne, E., Feinstein, H., & Youman, C. (1996). Role-based access control models. *IEEE Computer, 29*(2), 38–47. doi:10.1109/2.485845

Sandhu, R., Ferraiolo, D., & Kuhn, R. (2000). The NIST model for role-based access control: Towards a unified standard. In *Proceedings of the Fifth ACM Workshop on Role-Based Access Control* (pp. 47-63). Application of role-based access control for web environment.

Sun Microsystems Inc. (2000). *RBAC in the Solaris™ operating environment.* Retrieved from http://www.sun.com/software/whitepapers/wp-rbac/wp-rbac.pdf

Sybase Inc. (2005). *System administration guide: Volume 1 - Adaptive server enterprise 15.0.* Retrieved from http://infocenter.sybase.com/help/topic/com.sybase.help.ase_15.0.sag1/sag1.pdf

Tran, S., & Mohan, M. (2006). *Security information management challenges and solutions.* Retrieved from http://www.ibm.com/developerworks/db2/library/techarticle/dm-0607tran/index.html

Wahl, M., Howes, T., & Kille, S. (1997). *RFC 2251: Lightweight directory access protocol (v3).* Retrieved from http://www.ietf.org/rfc/rfc2251.txt

Westphall, C. M., & da Silva Fraga, J. (1999, December). A large-scale system authorization scheme proposal integrating Java, CORBA and web security models and a discretionary prototype. In *Proceedings of the Latin American Network Operations and Management Symposium,* Rio de Janeiro, Brazil (pp. 14-25). Washington, DC: IEEE Computer Society.

Westphall, C. M., da Silva Fraga, J., Wangham, M. S., Obelheiro, R. R., & Lung, L. C. (2002). PoliCap - proposal, development and evaluation of a policy service and capabilities for CORBA security. In *Proceedings of the IFIP TC11 17th International Conference on Information Security* (pp. 263-274).

Wong, R. K. (1997). RBAC support in object-oriented role databases. In *Proceedings of the Second ACM Workshop on Role-Based Access Control* (pp. 109-120). PoliCap - proposal, development and evaluation of a policy service and capabilities for CORBA security.

Zhang, F., Sheng, X., Niu, Y., Wang, F., & Zhang, H. (2006). The research and scheme of RBAC using J2EE security mechanisms. In. *Proceedings of the SPIE Conference on Broadband Access Communication Technologies, 6390,* 63900L.

Zhou, W., & Meinel, C. (2004, Feb). Implement role based access control with attribute certificates. In *Proceedings of the 6th International Conference on Advanced Communication Technology* (Vol. 1, pp. 536-541). Washington, DC: IEEE Computer Society.

This work was previously published in the International Journal of Secure Software Engineering, Volume 2, Issue 2, edited by Khaled M. Khan, pp. 25-52, copyright 2011 by IGI Publishing (an imprint of IGI Global).

Chapter 12

Performance Evaluation of Secure Key Deployment and Exchange Protocol for MANETs

Alastair Nisbet
Massey University, New Zealand

M. A. Rashid
Massey University, New Zealand

ABSTRACT

Secure Key Deployment and Exchange Protocol (SKYE) is a new encryption Key Management Scheme (KMS) based on combination of features from recent protocols combined with new features for Mobile Ad Hoc Networks (MANETs). The design focuses on a truly ad hoc networking environment where geographical size of the network, numbers of network members, and mobility of the members is all unknown before deployment. Additionally, all key management is performed online making it distinct from most other implementations. This paper attempts to describe the process of development of the protocol and to more thoroughly discuss the simulation software design used to evaluate the performance of the proposed protocol. Simulation results show that security within the network can be increased by requiring more servers to collaborate to produce a certificate for the new member, or by requiring a higher trust threshold along the certificate request chain. SKYE works well within the limitations set by entirely online network formation and key management.

INTRODUCTION

Ad Hoc networks are distinguished from infrastructure networks in that the network members, or nodes, communicate directly with each other rather than through a fixed access point. They differ from a mesh network in that a truly ad hoc network is created 'on the fly' for a specific, sometimes spontaneous purpose, and is often disbanded soon after its usefulness has ended. Whilst a mesh network may consist of many stationary nodes, an ad hoc network will often be

DOI: 10.4018/978-1-4666-2482-5.ch012

very dynamic, with nodes frequently joining or leaving the network and with some nodes mobile throughout the network. It is this very dynamic nature of this type of network that creates such difficulties in implementing robust security.

Security implies control, whether it is by physical control of the network or control by some member or members who have power to control who may join the network. With a fixed wireless infrastructure, generally an access point or multiple access points will be preconfigured to control the network. These access points may be connected to a LAN or may simply act as a conduit for one node to communicate with another node. By forcing all communications to pass through an access point, even when nodes may be located within direct communication distance, the access point can maintain control over the network.

Security for MANETs includes five attributes: availability, authentication, confidentiality, integrity and non-repudiation. In an ad hoc environment, to achieve these five attributes firstly requires that any member of the network must be able to be identified. This is vital if malicious members are to be identified and permanently ejected from the network. A non-changeable identity can be linked to some unique physical attribute of the device such as the CPU serial number, meaning once that attribute is recorded, the node's behaviour can be monitored and if necessary the node's permission to join the network can be revoked. Additionally, robust encryption of the data is needed to prevent nodes reading messages intended only for an authorized recipient. This is especially necessary because of the nature of wireless communications. Generally, wireless devices transmit their messages omnidirectionally; meaning other similar devices within radio range can read the message. With radio ranges of at least several hundred metres for most wireless standards, preventing messages reaching unintended recipients is almost impossible to prevent. Therefore, encryption is one of the best methods for protecting the message from these unauthorized nodes. Whilst the data may be captured by unauthorized nodes, without the appropriate decryption key the message will remain unreadable and therefore secure. To encrypt and decrypt messages in a network, encryption keys must be created, distributed and when necessary revoked. Whilst several protocols have been proposed for these types of networks, one important aspect of the design is that it is both effective and efficient. Effectiveness can be measured by how well the protocol achieves its goal. The main goal is to create and distribute certificates to requesting nodes as they wish to join the network. Therefore, the success rate of the requests is a good measure. For efficiency, the measure is how the network performs as security is increased. Inevitably higher security will lead to a reduced success rate for certificate requests, and it is the impact on increasing security that can be used as a measure of efficiency.

There are two distinct encryption methods: symmetric key encryption where the same key is used for encryption and decryption, and asymmetric encryption where a public key is freely given out and is used to encrypt a message and a private key known only to the recipient is used to decrypt the message. Symmetric encryption is less computationally draining, but for total privacy of data it requires nodes to share the same secret key. This key creation and exchange can be done securely before network deployment or can be performed dynamically as required. Asymmetric encryption is robust, but requires the use of a Certificate Authority (CA) often called a Trusted Third Party, to create and distribute certificates validating the identities and the keys bound to those identities. Finding an efficient way to create and maintain an easily contactable CA is very challenging, especially when nodes in the network are mobile. However, with a truly ad hoc network where members have no prior knowledge or prior contact with each other, implementing control over the network is extremely difficult. The challenge in this area is to allow a highly dynamic network formation where all security is implemented after network formation.

This paper describes the development and testing, through simulation, of a newly developed encryption key management protocol that is designed for highly dynamic ad hoc networks. Following a discussion of general security in networks in the introductory section, next we investigate and critically review the important relevant MANET protocols. The process of development of the protocol is then described. This includes a brief discussion of the types of applications that this protocol may be best suited for. Next, the simulation environment setup and testing is discussed followed by simulation and results. A Conclusion is then presented in the following section, which can be drawn from the results as to the efficiency of the protocol and the effectiveness of the security that it provides.

Following is a critical review of several relevant MANET key management protocols. A review of these protocols shows where some of the design features for SKYE were derived from.

RELATED WORK

A partially distributed Threshold Certificate Authority Scheme has been proposed whereby a significant advantage is tolerance to intrusion of the Certification Authority (Zhou & Haas, 1999). The private CA is distributed over several nodes designated as server nodes. The threshold for the number of server nodes required is k (threshold) out of n (total nodes) nodes. When a node requires a certificate, each server node generates a partial signature using its private key. A server designated as a combiner node then collects all of the partial signatures and combines them to produce a valid signed certificate. This certificate is then securely passed to the requesting node. Periodic updates of the certificates are used to counter any possible attacks that may have compromised a server. The robustness for the scheme comes

from distributing the responsibility for certificate generation to several server nodes, meaning that a number of server nodes must be compromised within a limited time frame before enough useful information can be gleaned. The major drawback to this scheme is that the initial configuration, including which nodes shall act as servers, must be done prior to network boot strapping offline. One further problem with the scheme is that of periodic updating of the certificates. Whilst adding security to the protocol, it requires synchronisation of the nodes to ensure their certificates have been updated and old certificates are entered on the CRL. This adds considerable message overhead to the network using up valuable bandwidth and draining battery power.

An extension of this protocol was proposed by Yi and Kravets (2003). This scheme called Mobile Certificate Authority (MOCA) deals with the CA problem by distributing the CA functionality. CA nodes are selected by displaying the best physical security and computational ability. For example, a powerful laptop computer would be better suited to CA responsibility than a computationally and battery power limited PDA. Furthermore, the responsibility of combining the partial certificates into a full certificate is moved from combiner nodes to the requesting node. This adds robustness as the requesting nodes no longer rely on the combiner nodes being available. In Zhou and Haas's scheme flooding is used to request certificate services. In MOCA, a new protocol is proposed that sends request messages in a unicast format directly to the server nodes. However, if server nodes are not immediately available then the protocol reverts to flooding. This adds efficiency to the communications freeing up bandwidth for other communications, but requires nodes to maintain an extra routing table to that of the underlying routing protocol. This adds complexity and itself requires extra messages for management of the routing tables.

A slight modification to the MOCA protocol produced a scheme called Secure & Efficient Key

Management (SEKM) (Wu et al., 2007). In this modification the servers in MOCA instead form a multicast group to add efficiency to updating of secret shares and certificates. The node broadcasts a request for certificate services to a server group, with the first server to receive the request generating a partial signature and then forwarding the request to k + a servers. Only k partial signatures are required with the additional ones used as redundancy in case one is corrupted or lost. Whilst adding efficiency to the MOCA protocol, it is essentially a minor modification to gain a slight improvement in efficiency. One drawback to the proposed scheme is that it does not describe how the first receiving server should identify that it is the first and advise other servers of the fact.

Whilst MOCA and SEKM use partially distributed CA schemes, Kong et al have suggested a fully distributed threshold CA scheme called Ubiquitous Security Support (Kong et al., 2001). Here, all nodes in the network get a share of the private CA key. A coalition of k one-hop neighbours combines to provide CA functionality. It does not require an underlying routing protocol to assist with this but does require at least k one-hop neighbours. For this reason, mobility of the nodes may actually assist with functionality of the CA. The nodes in the network earn trust from other nodes when they prove that they hold a valid certificate, and holding a certificate allows the node to hold a share of the CA private key. The major drawback of this scheme is that it requires offline configuration of certificates for the initial nodes that instigate the network. Further, the threshold value k may be difficult to choose. A low value of k means that an intruder needs to compromise fewer nodes to obtain useful key information. A higher value of k makes intrusion more difficult but requires a higher number of nodes to be easily reachable for key management services. Limiting communications for certificate services to one-hop neighbours is bandwidth efficient and therefore good for scalability, but for a smaller network where nodes may only have one neighbour, this can mean CA services are unavailable.

A further protocol that utilises a fully distributed CA is that proposed by Zhu et al. (2005). Called Autonomous Key Management, this scheme is similar to Ubiq when there are only a few nodes in the network. However, as the network grows in numbers, a hierarchy of key shares is utilised. Instead of receiving a share, the new nodes receive a share of the share of the CA private key. The root CA private / public key pair is bootstrapped by a group of neighbours through distributed verifiable secret sharing (Rosario et al., 2007). Each of the n neighbours chooses a secret value and distributes shares of this to the other neighbours using a (k, n) secret sharing scheme. Whilst the distribution of the shares is contributory, the derivation of the shares is not. To counter too few nodes requiring compromising to discover the key, the shares are split and distributed to more nodes as the numbers grow. This adds a higher level of security to the scheme, but a major drawback is that authentication of nodes is done offline prior to network initialisation.

In an effort to devise a scheme that is fully distributed and therefore in the spirit of true ad hoc networking, Capkun et al developed Self-Organised Key Management (Capkun et al., 2003). It is essentially a Pretty Good Privacy (PGP) scheme adapted to ad hoc networks (Zimmerman 1994). All nodes are equal and generate their own private / public key pairs, distributing their certificates to nodes that they trust. The certificates are stored within each node rather than relying on a central repository. The scheme assumes that trust is transitive, meaning that if a trusts b and b trusts c, then a can also trust c. The nodes merge their certificate repositories and attempt to find a verifiable chain of certificates. Certificates may be revoked either explicitly by the issuer, or implicitly after an expiration time. Renewing a certificate requires contact with the issuer which may not always be possible in a mobile network. Periodic exchanges of certificates with neighbouring nodes occur, but this synchronization of exchanges and renewal of certificates is not defined in the protocol. Additionally, certificate expiry requires that a constant renewal of certificates is required, and along with a constant certificate exchange with neighbours means that the scheme does not scale well. Further, Byzantine nodes (misbehaviour by colluding nodes) could compromise a single node to gain information about several certificates. If a node can legitimately join the network, then it could maliciously issue certificates to other malicious nodes allowing them to legitimately join the network and freely be given certificate information of other nodes. This lack of scalability and reliance on transitive trust makes this scheme suffer from fairly poor security.

Yi and Kravets combined their MOCA protocol with certificate chaining to develop a new protocol called Composite Key Management (Yi & Kravets 2004). CKM attempts to take the best points of both protocols and eliminate the poorer points by providing higher security than PGP alone and increased availability of the CA in the MOCA scheme. Nodes certified by the CA can themselves issue certificates. Nodes must first request a certificate from a CA node, but if a CA node is unavailable then a certificate holding node can take over the certificate issuing duty. One major modification to the two schemes that it is derived from is that the certificates themselves contain a confidence value reflecting the confidence that the issuer has in the node. Confidence is measured from no confidence being a 0 to total confidence being a 1. Each node in the issuing chain multiplies the existing confidence by its confidence level and replaces the value in the certificate with that calculated confidence. In this way, the final confidence value in the certificate reflects the average confidence of all the nodes along the chain. A threshold value for confidence and therefore whether a certificate is issued can be preset for the network, with a higher value requiring more trust for a node to join. This scheme provides better security and greater availability

of the CA than the schemes from which it was derived, but the protocol does not describe how revocation of a certificate should be done. Additionally, the problem of bootstrapping the network with no initial trust is dealt with by configuring the initial nodes offline. This is unsuitable for a truly ad hoc network where all key management tasks must be performed after network formation.

THE PROPOSED SKYE PROTOCOL

One consideration when designing a protocol is that it must be practical. There is a balance between features of the design and the efficiency at which the protocol can operate at. Generally, as security is increased the complexity of the protocol also increases. More complexity will mean higher battery drain of the devices and more latency in performing the task. A very secure protocol may simply be unworkable in practice, and a very basic protocol may be so insecure as to be unusable. The goal of this protocol is to provide a key management scheme suitable for a truly ad hoc network with a high number of members with large geographical size. Any node can join the network meaning malicious nodes will inevitably become members. To counter this, monitoring of behaviour is required.

The process for the design of SKYE was to thoroughly review the previous relevant protocols and note any that showed promise for this type of network. The many previous designed were narrowed down to a few, and their positive attributes noted. Any negative attributes were noted in an effort to avoid any features that may be detrimental. Additionally, possible uses for the protocol were also identified early on. Whilst the uses may include military, educational, public and any other use involving a rapid deployment of a network, two possible applications stood out. The first of these is disaster relief and recovery where disaster victims may be able to establish a network for communications where other communication infrastructure has failed. If there is a large area affected by some natural disaster with all communications cut off, then people inside the disaster area could form an ad hoc network using computers or PDAs and can begin communicating with neighbours. As the networks grow, pockets of smaller networks join with other networks to eventually form a large network where every node can connect to every other node using intermediate nodes to pass on messages. When help arrives in the form of rescue workers, they can join the established network and immediately send and receive vital information about the disaster area and the victims. Additionally, outside communication may be possible so long as at least one node in the network is connected to the outside word, possibly through the Internet. Even in this type of scenario, security is vital for several reasons. Firstly, some messages may be highly confidential and must remain private from all but the intended recipient. Secondly, if any node can join the network but never be excluded, a misbehaving node could seriously upset the running of the network by excessive message sending, failing to pass on messages or sending false messages. It is desirable then to have a protocol in place that can efficiently provide all three key management functions: key creation, key exchange and key revocation.

The second application that SKYE may be suitable for is ad hoc networking within a vehicular environment. Called Vehicular Ad hoc Networking (VANET), inter-vehicular communication instigated on-the-fly requires similar attributes to the protocol's goal. That is, rapid setup of an unplanned network that allows anyone entry, but enforces strict controls so that any misbehaviour can be identified, reported and if necessary result in permanent exclusion from the network. VANET networks are designed to improve road safety by providing communication between vehicles so that drivers may be influenced in their behaviour, such as slowing down, exercising greater care, or choosing alternative routes (Plobl et al., 2006). This type of highly dynamic network requir-

ing moderate security but a very efficient key management infrastructure may be another ideal application for this protocol.

By looking at the type of scenario the protocol may be used for, the following desirable characteristics can be identified and their incorporation into the protocol is described.

1. Any node should be able to join the network. No prior knowledge or offline configuration should be necessary:

The combination of not having any offline configuration but using digital certificates to bind keys to identities leads to self certification of nodes or servers issuing certificates to nodes. Using a certificate authority requires a choice of how many servers should be required before a certificate can be issued. In the MOCA protocol around 10-20% of nodes are designated as servers and of those 15-20 were required to be contacted for KM services. However, this assumes that the network begins with 100 nodes or so as any less would mean that not enough servers are available to provide certificate services. With the network beginning with a single node and growing dynamically, the current protocol utilises a minimum server's required threshold but overrides that rule until enough servers are present to meet the threshold.

2. Key management messages should be the least number possible to provide the service.

The number of messages utilises more bandwidth than the size of the messages, so larger messages but less of them is desirable. Additionally, a choice of encryption should be available to save battery power where possible. From a security standpoint, some messages do not require high security, or perhaps any security. Encryption and decryption calculations require considerable CPU usage. For messages that require little or no privacy, it is therefore desirable to send them unencrypted or with lower encryption saving valuable battery power. This leads to the desirable functionality of ranking messages with a corresponding security level and using the appropriate encryption for the level. There should be three levels of security for messages similar to that used for military communications. That is, unclassified where no encryption is used, classified using symmetric encryption and secret utilising PKI.

3. Keys should only be exchanged with nodes that the sender needs to communicate with.

Exchanging keys with only those nodes that it is necessary for communication saves considerable key management overhead. The sender first selects the security level, open, symmetric or asymmetric encryption. The process is then:

a. Sender checks with closest server that the receiver has a valid certificate.
b. Server first checks sender's certificate and then replies with confirmation of receiver's certificate.
c. Sender requests communication with receiver and sends his certificate details and symmetric key if level 2 security is selected.
d. Receiver checks with closest server that the sender has a valid certificate.
e. Server first checks receiver's certificate and then replies with confirmation of sender's certificate.
f. Receiver replies to sender and communication begins.

4. All nodes should be able to communicate with all other authorised nodes in the network.

Provided the communicating nodes are part of the same network, the routing protocol employed should ensure that contact can be made between the two nodes. Only nodes holding valid certificates can exchange messages, but nodes that have not

yet been issued certificates can pass on certificate issuance requests. If this were not permitted, no requests could ever be forwarded to a server.

5. Certificates binding keys to nodes identities should be used for high security.

The use of digital certificates binding keys to the node's identity raises two points. Firstly, the identity of the node must positively identify it and must not be able to be changed or spoofed. It is assumed that a reliable method for binding identities to nodes is in place. Secondly, digital certificates must be created, issued and stored. Additionally, a certificate revocation list (CRL) must be maintained up-to-date and readily available to all nodes at all times. To avoid offline configuration self certification is employed where the nodes create their own certificates permanently bound to their identity. This complies with the truly ad hoc nature of the design where all nodes may join the network initially. To ensure robustness against attack, redundancy, which provides fault tolerance and high availability, a distributed CA using threshold cryptography is employed. The CA will comprise of k nodes out of n nodes in the network. A subset of the k nodes must combine to provide CA services.

6. If a node misbehaves, it should be identified and if necessary permanently excluded from the network.

To eject a node from the network, misbehaviour must be identified and noted. Neighbouring nodes are responsible for monitoring each other's behaviour. Each node joins the network with total trust. The trust is measured from full trust of 1 to very low trust of 0.1. Each instance of malicious behaviour identified reduces the trust in that node from the accuser of 0.1. The trust level is used when a node requests a certificate. The trust level along the certificate chain is calculated along with the attenuation factor (0.1 for every hop along the chain) and this final calculation is used by a server to decide whether a certificate should be issued or not. This method assumes that the likelihood of a node being compromised is equal for every node in the network with probability p. The length of the chain to the server is d. Therefore, the probability that the chain has not been compromised is $(1-p)^{(d-1)}$. The calculated level is compared with the network threshold required. If it is at or above the threshold a certificate is issued. If below the threshold the request is refused and the node must make another request (Yi & Kravets, 2004). Nodes that detect misbehaviour advise the CA of their accusations against a node.

A threshold of accusations within a time limit must be received by the CA before a node is ejected. To eject a node, the node's identity is added to the CRL and a broadcast message with the nodes identity and the revocation status is sent to all nodes.

7. A single node should not have the power to eject another node.

A threshold of accusations is required to eject a node ensuring that no single node can maliciously eject any other node.

8. An excluded node should still receive vital information

Any messages deemed unclassified such as messages about rescue efforts or warnings of impending danger in a disaster situation are sent unencrypted and can be read by all nodes, including those ejected or those who are not currently authenticated.

9. The network should be highly scalable.

For a network to be highly scalable, nodes must be able to communicate at the same time without interfering with others communication. With a maximum radio range of approximately 300 metres it is envisaged that with a widely dispersed network only limited numbers of nodes will be within range of each other. The scalability of the network therefore uses the limited radio range of the devices along with the key exchange on a demand basis to assist with scalability.

10. The network should handle mobility of nodes efficiently.

Mobility of the nodes should present no problems with the key management as key exchange is on a demand basis and network wide protocols are employed where geographic relocation of the nodes will make no difference to the keys employed providing the node remains within the same network. Additionally, the CA will be dispersed and the same number of CA servers will need to be contacted for certificate servers wherever the node may be. Therefore, mobility of the nodes will effectively be transparent to the members of the network, including the CA servers.

One major difficulty with MANET security is the dynamic nature of the nodes, both in mobility and in often joining and leaving networks frequently. This raises the problem of nodes not being able to rely on a single node for the network being available at all times to every member. One method to increase availability of the CA is to replicate the CA several times so that there are several nodes acting as a standalone CA, all sharing their data whenever an update to their certificate repositories is made. This simply and efficiently solves the problem of CA availability and makes the CA more robust against failure by providing redundancy. However, if several nodes share all the certificate information for the entire network, this makes an attacker's task much easier. Instead of having a single node to mount a successful attack against, the attacker now has a choice of several nodes to attack. A successful attack against any one of the CA nodes will provide the attacker with all the information about encryption keys and certificates for all nodes in the network. A pragmatic approach to this problem is to divide the information amongst more than one node. For example, if five nodes are required to collaborate to form a CA, then each of those nodes holds one fifth of the information about a certificate and key. An attacker must successfully compromise all five nodes before the information can be combined to disclose the secret keys. This is far more difficult for an attacker to achieve and therefore far more robust from a security standpoint. This method of using threshold cryptography, where the threshold is the number of CA nodes that must collaborate to provide CA services, is used in SKYE.

SKYE SIMULATION ENVIRONMENT

Once the protocol design was finalised, a suitable test bed was sought to perform simulations. There are several wireless network simulators available, many of them at no cost or with an educational licence for students. A requirement for the simulations was to have a network simulator that would display the simulations in real time as they were run, would be very fast as many simulations would be needed to be run consecutively, and needed to be relatively simple to modify as many different experiment parameters would be changed.

Matlab was extensively used in developing the simulation model for SKYE. Approximately 3.2% of MANET simulation studies use Matlab (Kurkowski et al., 2005). Matlab is primarily a statistical software package which is designed to work with large, multi-dimensional matrices. After initial hesitation about its suitability, it was quickly found that its ease of use was a major advantage. It uses the Pascal programming language which is quite similar to C. Its ability to deal with large matrices was of significant benefit when considerable numbers of calculations were required very quickly. Finally, Matlab's ability to plot nodes with a single 'Plot' command made viewing the simulation as it progressed fairly simple. Matlab was therefore chosen as the simulation software and the task of constructing the simulator began.

The first task was to decide on what parameters would be measured. The purpose of the protocol is to create and issue certificates to joining nodes.

Therefore, the success rate of this process was the primary objective. The many variable parameters such as 'Servers Required' and 'Trust Required' could then be manipulated and the change in outputs observed. The trends that developed as these variables were changed is the measure of performance, and exact performance was not necessary. Primarily, such things as bit error rate and signal attenuation were not necessary and these would have little effect on the trends. This would save considerable work to implement with little or no benefit.

The first step in beginning software coding was to decide on the area of the simulations. With a likely use of disaster relief in mind, a 2500m square area was considered suitable. The next task was to plot nodes on the grid. Matlab includes several random number generators and one of these was used to place nodes randomly on the grid. Simply choosing 2 random numbers between 0 and 2500 gave the x and y coordinates. Using the plot command, the graphical representation for this was easily displayed. Next was to decide on the radio range of the nodes. A likely technology for such an implementation is the IEEE 802.11 suite of protocols. With 802.11g being the most common currently, the range of this protocol of 300 metres was used. To represent this range graphically a circle around the node was made.

The next step was to include mobility for some of the nodes. Again the PRNG was used to randomly select a percentage of nodes that would be mobile. Initially the 'Straight Line Model' for mobility was used. The nodes randomly select a direction and move at a constant speed before striking a boundary. They then randomly select a new direction and so on. Whilst this is a simple model, it is generally not considered realistic. More appropriate is the Random Waypoint Mobility Model (Johnson & Maltz, 1996; Hyytiä & Virtamo, 2007). In this model, a node moves for a random time in a straight line, then pauses for a set time and then moves off in another random direction.

The steps are (see Box 1):

This model was used with a varied figure for speed and pause time. For example, if 20kmh was

Box 1.

```
    Note current coordinates (x, y)
    Randomly select destination coordinates (x¹, y¹)
    Randomly select speed
Speed = (minspeed < speed < maxspeed)
    Calculate step to destination for the speed (x², y²)
    Calculate distance from (x², y²) to (x¹, y¹)
    If distance less than step distance:
Move to (x¹, y¹)
else
Move to (x², y²)
    end
```

used, the node would randomly choose a speed between 20kmh and 29kmh and then pause for a random time of between 0 and 10 seconds. The highest speed was always 9kmh above the input speed. Here again the graphical abilities of Matlab proved invaluable as a minor problem was found that would not have been identified otherwise. On occasion, a node would continue off the grid in a straight line. This was quickly found to be a rounding error where the node would miss its waypoint, and was easily corrected.

Once the nodes were placed and moving correctly, the next step was to begin communications. This became a quite complex implementation as the distance from every node to every other node needed to be constantly calculated and updated. A large 2-dimensional matrix was used to store the identity of every node and the distance to every other node. This was then used as a lookup table as the nodes were cycled through and the distance checked. If a node was within radio range of another node, then a green line was drawn between them indicating direct communication was possible. If a node was out of range of every other node, then a circle at 300 metres was drawn around the node.

The steps are (see Box 2):

The update cycle for the network was set at one second, meaning all new calculations of position and separation distance were performed every second.

The simulation time was set to 10 minutes as this was a reasonable time for the network to begin from a single node and grow to a reasonable size. This led to the question of growth rate for the network. Again, the possible implementation was looked at and it was decided that initially nodes would join quickly. A growth rate of 30 nodes per minute was used, with a node leaving rate of 10 nodes per minute. This gave a net growth of 20 nodes per minute. The telecommunications industry was looked at for the best way to simulate growth rates. In this industry, a Poisson distribution is used to give more realistic performance. In this type of distribution, random numbers are used that approximate the growth rate. For example, a linear rate of one node per second for 5 seconds would look like {1 1 1 1 1}, whereas a Poisson distribution may give something similar to {1 0 0 3 1}. This gives minor bursts and lulls in the joining activity. Matlab can create the Poisson distribution using the Poisson.M function. The output was saved to text files to be read during simulation time.

Finally, the routing of messages, both for certificate request messages and inter-node communication was needed. Nodes were set to send messages to another node in the same network at a rate of one message every 10 seconds. This would require the steps of checking certificates with servers, sending the request to communicate and receiving an acceptance. At times, these messages would necessarily hop along several nodes to reach their destination. The reason for the mes-

Box 2.

```
For x = 1 to (num_of_nodes – 1) (ignore self)
    Lookup distance table Node(x)
    If table value is less than 301 metres
    NodeID.Neighbours = NodeID.Neighbours + 1
    Draw line from NodeID to NeighbourID
    end
end
If NodeID.Neighbours < 1
    Draw green circle at 300 metre distance around node
end
```

sages was to give malicious nodes an opportunity to misbehave resulting in an accusation to a server. If more than 5 accusations were received against a node within 1 minute, the node was permanently ejected from the network. Ejected nodes were shown by a black diamond. The protocol was best suited to an on-demand routing protocol such as DSR. Fully implementing DSR would be a very time-consuming task and so a slimmed down version was written. This is effectively a breadth-first search where a node wishing to find a route to another node in the same network will first ask all its neighbours if it is the target node. If not, they will all ask their neighbours and so on. Once found, the reverse route is sent back to the requester and this is also sent to the target node. This requires only one route discovery for 2 nodes to utilise. Once again the ability to display the graphics was invaluable, both to check that the optimum route was being found and to display messages traversing the network by displaying the route with red lines. This also allowed certificate requests to be viewed where the request to server, inter-server communication, and return of the certificate could all be watched. Nodes waiting for certificates had green labels with their ID and nodes with certificates were assigned red labels. The graphical abilities were constantly viewed as a check of performance and proved a very valuable asset at many stages.

However, when viewing the simulations a severe degradation in performance occurred. A 600 second simulation took on average around 4 minutes without graphics and almost ½ an hour with graphics. For this reason the graphics could be simply switched off for multiple simulations. The input for the simulations came from a text file. Each line contained all of the simulation parameters meaning they could very simply be changed. Initial simulation runs gave baseline figures that showed what parameters were suitable for testing. For example, any more than 5 servers was found to degrade success rate to an

unacceptably low level, therefore only 1-5 servers was simulated. It was necessary to cut down the number of simulations required as much as possible to achieve an acceptable time frame for the simulations. Ultimately aver 50 000 simulations were run on 2 computers taking almost 6 weeks. With all the initial simulation runs, modifications to the protocol and final simulation runs, the total number of simulations reached closer to 100000.

SIMULATIONS

Each simulation scenario is run several times and the results averaged for each run. A node mobility of 20% of nodes was selected as a baseline with each node having an equal chance of being mobile. The speed was set at a minimum with the maximum 10kmh above that, so for example a speed of 20kmh meant that nodes randomly chose a speed between 20-29kmh. The simulation begins with one randomly placed node on the grid, growing and shrinking dynamically with 30 nodes per minute randomly added and 10 nodes per minute randomly leaving.

Each node had an equal chance of mobility and being either added to or removed from the network. A malicious node threshold of 6% of the nodes was chosen based on crime statistics. This figure is deliberately low as malicious behaviour is predicted to be rare. The figure for the percentage of malicious nodes in the network caused some difficulty. Data on malicious behaviour in ad hoc networks is very scarce and the type of use for the network and therefore the potential members could vary widely. For example, an educational setting could expect little or no malicious behaviour, but military use in a hostile environment may see many attempts at attacking the network. For the purpose of the simulation, malicious behaviour involves nodes failing to pass on every third message. This resulted in the trust in that node from the previous node being reduced by 0.1. The node would then make an accusation against the malicious node to one of the servers. If 5 accusations were received within 60 seconds, the malicious node was permanently ejected from the network.

The steps are (see Box 3):

Following (Yi & Kravets, 2004), the calculation of trust is performed as follows. Each node receiving a certificate request to pass on multiplies the current calculation by its trust in the previous node in the chain. If the previous node has misbehaved, it is assumed the following node has noted this by both reducing its trust by 0.1 and making an accusation to a server. When this request reaches the server, it takes the trust calculation and multiplies it to the power of the number of hops less 1. This calculation is compared with the trust threshold required (0.1 to 0.9) and if equal to or above, a certificate is returned to the requester.

Additionally, 20 messages per second utilising symmetric encryption were sent between random nodes in the same network. This required a high level of messages meaning malicious nodes had frequent opportunity to misbehave and therefore disrupt certificate requests or be ejected.

With a radio communication range of 300 metres and node placed at random, inevitably several networks will form. With node mobility and some

nodes leaving and joining the networks at random locations, networks will also divide into smaller networks or join into larger networks. Therefore, there is an initial network node count, a maximum network node count during the simulation and a final network node count. A seed value for the random generator was used resulting in similar networks for each simulation run. Each scenario was run several times with a different seed value, resulting in a very different network formation, and the results averaged. This was useful for comparison as the simulation runs appeared identical with node placement and mobility.

Figure 1 shows the network scenario generated after 200 seconds of simulation time forming 8 networks. The nodes with a large circle around them (representing 300 metres) are out of range of another node. Node 257 in the middle just above half way (represented by a diamond) has been ejected from the network.

The simulation has now run for the full 600 seconds and ends with a single large network as depicted in Figure 2. The smaller circles around the diamonds show the 18 malicious nodes that have been ejected.

Results were collected for certificate success and the parameters altered to view the decline in success of those requests. Additionally, the trust threshold was raised to see what effect that had on success rate. Both of these changes impacted certificate request success by reducing it. However, degradation in performance was not significant until a threshold was reached. This threshold is approximately 5 servers required with a trust threshold value of 0.6. Any more than 5 servers were so significant as to be impractical, and raising the trust threshold along the certificate chain above 0.6 also degraded performance to an unacceptable level. These figures give a guide as to the suitable default setting for a network, with the option to modify those setting according to security needs. Table 1 shows the fixed parameters used for the simulation runs.

Box 3.

```
Previous node does not pass message on
 Contact server with accusation and offending Node.ID
 The Server:
 NodeID.Accusations = NodeID.Accusations + 1
 Sum Accusations <= 60 seconds

If > threshold (eg: 3)
 Contact (servers threshold – 1) servers with ejection
 intention
 If >= servers threshold agree
 Broadcast revocation with NodeID
        Servers remove certificate from Valid Certificate
        List
        Servers enter Certificate in Revoked Certificate
        List
 end
 end
```

Figure 1. Simulation snapshot at 200 seconds

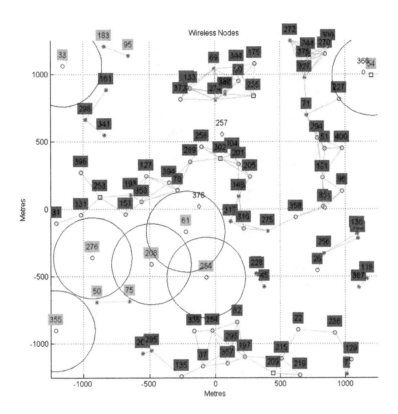

Security within networks could be increased, either by requiring a higher threshold of trust for the certificate request message, or by requiring more servers to be contacted to receive a certificate, or a combination of both. As more servers are required, the placement of those servers be-comes more critical to the efficiency of the running of the networks. Servers must be easily and quickly contactable, both for initial issuance of a certificate and key, and to check a communicating party holds a valid certificate. Whilst many protocols choose servers based on their superiority of processing power over lesser nodes, the placement of those servers to other nodes has not been closely examined. Therefore, further simulations to test the effectiveness of choosing various server locations compared to other nodes were performed. A new server may be required to replace a server that has left the network, or as the network grows new servers are added to the network to maintain the correct percentage of servers. Three different server placements were tested (dubbed the server rule). The differences in both successful certificate issuance and in hops to receive certificates are compared.

Table 1. Simulation parameters

Simulation Area (metres square)	2500
Simulation Time (seconds)	600
Radio range (metres)	300
Node begin	0
Node Growth rate	30
Node Leave rate	10
Node Minimum Speed Kmh	0-100
Percent Mobile	0-100
Trust Threshold	0.1 – 0.9

Figure 2. Simulation snapshot at 600 seconds

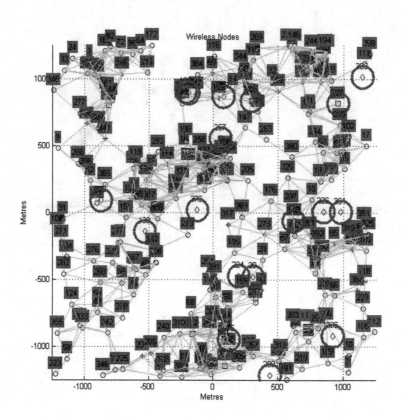

Server locations are:

1: The node with the most neighbours.
2: The node with the least neighbours.
3: Randomly chosen nodes.

The process of choosing a node based on location was simple for random choice. However, the other rules required that nodes advise servers of how many neighbours they have. The server would then rank servers and non-servers in order by how many neighbours they had. If a new server was required, then if the 'Most' rule was in force, the non-server with the most number of neighbours would convert to a server. The 'Least' rule required a similar process but with the non-server with the least number of neighbours.

Results

The very tunable properties of the protocol mean that the scheme deals very effectively with mobile nodes and with splitting and merging of networks. Often, several smaller networks would form and then merge together into a large, single network. The placement of the servers would become more critical as the network grew larger and greater distances were traversed from server to server.

Mobility has shown to make a slight difference in increasing certificate request success. However, malicious behaviour has shown a significant effect in certificate request failures resulting in a node making more than one request for a certificate. Therefore, the ability of this protocol to handle mobile nodes and to identify misbehaving nodes and then permanently eject them are desirable features helping to stabilise the network and maintain robustness against misbehaving nodes. The following tables show the results for the networks where 20% of nodes are mobile, and those mobile are moving at 20-29kmh.

Comparison of the three tables shows the difference the rule for selecting server locations makes to the percentage of certificate requests that are successful. Table 2, Table 3, and Table 4 show the difference in successful request percentage that choosing the location for the servers provides. Whilst there is little difference for very low or very high trust thresholds, threshold requirements in the 0.3 to 0.7 range show that choosing a node

with the most neighbours to become a server is best, with random placement only slightly less successful and with least neighbours providing the poorest result. The following graph shows the comparison with 3 servers required and 20% of nodes mobile at 20-29kmh.

Figure 3 shows that when 3 or more servers are required for a certificate, the placement of the servers has a noticeable impact on the efficiency of the protocol. Once again it is the trust threshold values in the middle range where the effect is most noticeable. Here, nodes with the most number of neighbours taking on a server role proved

Table 2. Results for mobile nodes 20kmh– most neighbours

Servers / Trust	0.1	0.2	0.3	0.4	0.5	0.6	0.7	0.8	0.9
1	98	97	92	89	78	53	40	16	4
2	93	91	82	74	67	30	16	7	2
3	83	78	74	53	37	16	8	3	1
4	76	72	57	42	23	9	4	2	1
5	69	62	51	28	13	5	2	1	0

Table 3. Results for mobile nodes 20kmh– least neighbours

Servers / Trust	0.1	0.2	0.3	0.4	0.5	0.6	0.7	0.8	0.9
1	98	96	96	92	83	57	39	15	4
2	90	87	81	69	49	49	12	5	2
3	81	79	67	47	27	9	5	2	1
4	72	69	55	33	17	5	2	1	0
5	67	62	46	22	11	3	1	1	0

Table 4. Results for mobile nodes 20kmh – random placement

Servers / Trust	0.1	0.2	0.3	0.4	0.5	0.6	0.7	0.8	0.9
1	97	96	93	85	82	51	40	15	4
2	92	90	85	75	58	29	17	7	2
3	82	79	69	52	32	16	7	3	1
4	76	72	58	38	20	8	4	2	0
5	70	63	44	24	12	4	2	1	0

Figure 3. 3 Servers, 20% mobile, most v least v random rules

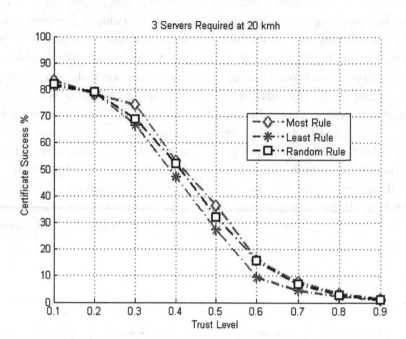

to be the most effective. Conversely, those with the least number of neighbours proved to be the worst choice. This is because nodes placed nearer the centre of the network, on average, required fewer hops to reach. Additionally, if all servers were located near the centre of the network, then they tended to be close together. This made inter-server communication very efficient, and as the server threshold was increased the inter-server closeness made certificate issuance more and more efficient. The distance to the first server became less important than the distance from first server to the other servers.

Having to inform new nodes of the number of servers in the network creates more management messages using up valuable network time. A blind request requires no management messages prior to request but may lead to multiple requests for a certificate before enough servers are present and a certificate is issued. Results showed that when only two servers are required, a blind or informed request made no difference to the success rate. This is because a network will always have at least two members and if two servers are required, it will always have at least two. However, if more

than two servers are required, blind requests can become considerable in number and may result thousands of refusals. Therefore, for more than two servers, the extra overhead of informing new nodes of the number of servers currently in the network is warranted.

As the required trust calculation made by the server for a certificate request is raised, the percentage of certificates refused increases. Additionally, requiring more servers to be contacted requires a longer certificate chain. An increase in the length of the certificate chain (hops) increases the likelihood of the chain encountering a malicious node and therefore a failure.

Table 5 shows 5 servers required and trust thresholds of 0.3, 0.5, 0.7 and 0.9. Requiring 5 servers provides high security, but couple this with a high certificate chain threshold and certificate refusals approach 100%. Therefore, both the trust level and the number of servers has a significant impact on success rate.

These results also show the considerable advantage in success ratio with an informed request versus a blind request for more than 2 servers required. Simulations were run to identify the

Table 5. Certificate success with 5 servers required – most rule

Trust Threshold	0.3	0.5	0.7	0.9
Success % Blind	8.2	5.7	2.2	0.3
Success % Informed	53.4	15.7	3.1	0.3
Average hops	26	22	14	7
Maximum Hops	80	51	27	10

impact of mobility on the success ratio of certificates. The following figures show the results of the simulations for similar networks with server rule Most and informed requests. Figure 4 shows all nodes stationary, whilst Figure 5 shows 20% of nodes in the network mobile at 100kmh.

These results show that as the nodes in the network increase in speed, the successful certificate issuance ratio increases. This is because the routes to the servers change fairly rapidly meaning a refused initial request will result in a re-request likely taking a different path to a server and therefore having a renewed chance of success.

Figure 6 shows some nodes mobile at relatively slow speeds. This could represent slow driving or perhaps boats navigating a flooded area. Comparing this with figure 4 where all nodes are stationary, the mobility of even a small percentage of nodes has an increase in certificate issuance success, especially in the mid trust thresholds of 0.3 - 0.8.

The trust threshold ensures increased security but at the cost of requests more likely to fail as hop counts for certificates increases. The mobility of nodes assists in this scenario as nodes and servers may move closer to each other reducing the number of hops required and increasing the chance of success with each retry. The hops for a successful certificate request necessarily reduce as very long hops will always result in a refusal. Here, the informed requests results in considerably less requests and much shorter hops to receive the certificate. The optimum trust level was found to be in the region of 0.4 to 0.5. Therefore, the security level required for the network should be considered carefully as increasing security of KMS services by increasing the trust threshold has a severe impact on KMS message performance.

Figure 4. Network with stationary nodes

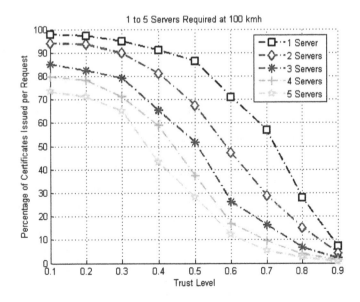

Figure 5. Network with 20% mobile at 100kmh

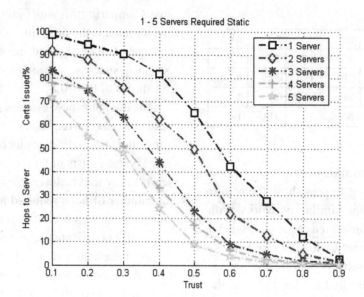

CONCLUSION

In this paper, we presented the performance of the proposed Secure Key Deployment and Exchange (SKYE) encryption Key Management Scheme

(KMS) based on simulation. Recent schemes have been examined in order to utilize promising features of these protocols combined with new features to provide a new protocol. Simulations have shown that security within the network can

Figure 6. Graph of certificate success for 1 – 5 Servers required with server rule Most and 20% nodes mobile at 20kmh

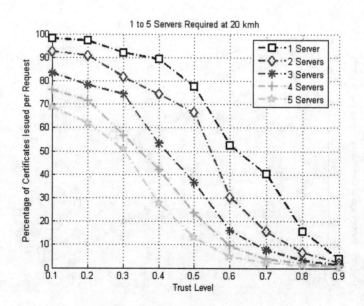

be increased by requiring more servers to collaborate to produce a certificate for the new member, or by requiring a higher trust threshold along the certificate request chain. Results show that the location of nodes designated as servers within the network has an impact on the likelihood of a successful issuance of a certificate. Three different locations for servers relative to other nodes was experimented with and results show that for more than a single server required for a certificate, the node with the most number of neighbours is the best choice.

Designing the simulation was a significant step in showing the performance of the protocol. The ability to simply and quickly alter the input results and watch the change in performance was extremely helpful, both in checking that the protocol, was performing as expected and in making minor alterations to the protocol when needed such as with the server location rule.

SKYE works well within the limitations set by entirely online network formation and key management. The simulator has proven to be a very valuable tool in showing the performance of SKYE and easily allowing changes to parameters and protocol rules. Further changes to both the protocol and to the simulator are planned. Firstly, the server rules will be enhanced so that groups of servers will be located using the current server rules. For example, if 5 servers are required, then up to 5 servers will be located as neighbours and the group of servers will be located according to the current rules, rather than an individual server. The simulator would benefit from implementing such attributes as signal attenuation, bit error rates and at least one fully functional routing algorithm. This would enhance the simulator's realism to where it could be used for other wireless network simulations that require a more fully functioning simulator.

REFERENCES

Capkun, S., Buttyan, L., & Hubaux, J. P. (2003). Self-Organized Public-Key Management for Mobile Ad Hoc Networks. *IEEE Transactions on Mobile Computing, 2*(1), 52–64. doi:10.1109/TMC.2003.1195151

Gennaro, R., Jarecki, S., Krawczyk, H., & Rabin, T. (2007). Secure Distributed Key Generation for Discrete-Log Based Cryptosystems. *J. Cryptology, 20*(1), 51–83. doi:10.1007/s00145-006-0347-3

Hyytiä, E., & Virtamo, J. (2007). Random Waypoint Mobility Model in Cellular Networks. *Wireless Networks, 13*(2), 177–188. doi:10.1007/s11276-006-4600-3

Johnson, D. B., & Maltz, D. A. (1996). Dynamic Source Routing in Ad Hoc Wireless Networks. In Imielinski & Korth (Eds.), *Mobile Computing* (Vol. 353, pp. 153-181). Dordrecht, The Netherlands: Kluwer Academic Publishers.

Kong, J., Zerfos, P., Luo, H., Lu, S., & Zhang, L. (2001). Providing Robust and Ubiquitous Security Support for Mobile Ad-hoc Networks. In *Proceedings of the Ninth International Conference on Network Protocols (ICNP2001)* (pp. 251-260).

Kurkowski, S., Camp, T., & Colagrosso, M. (2005). MANET simulation studies: the incredibles. *SIGMOBILE Mob. Comput. Commun. Rev., 9*(4), 50–61. doi:10.1145/1096166.1096174

Plobl, K., Nowey, T., et al. (2006, April). Towards a security architecture for vehicular ad hoc networks. Availability, Reliability and Security. In *Proceedings of the First International Conference on Availability, Reliability and Security (ARES)*.

Rosario, G., & Jarecki, S. (2007). Secure Distributed Key Generation for Discrete-Log Based Cryptosystems. *Journal of Cryptology, 20*(1), 51–83. doi:10.1007/s00145-006-0347-3

Wu, B., & Wu, J. (2007). Secure and Efficient Key Management in Mobile Ad Hoc Networks. *Journal of Network and Computer Applications, 30*, 937–954. doi:10.1016/j.jnca.2005.07.008

Yi, S., & Kravets, R. (2003). MOCA: Mobile Certificate Authority for Wireless Ad Hoc Networks. In *Proceedings of the Annual PKI Research Workshop Program,* MD (pp. 65-79).

Yi, S., & Kravets, R. (2004). Composite key management for ad hoc networks. In *Proceedings of the First Annual International Conference on Mobile and Ubiquitous Systems: Networking and Services (MOBIQUITOUS 2004)* (pp. 52-61).

Zhou, C., & Buttyan, S. L. (2003). Self-Organized Public-Key Management for Mobile Ad Hoc Networks. *IEEE Transactions on Mobile Computing, 2*(1), 52–64. doi:10.1109/TMC.2003.1195151

Zhou, C. S., & Buttyan, L. (2003). Self-Organized Public-Key Management for Mobile Ad Hoc Networks. *IEEE Transactions on Mobile Computing, 2*(1), 52–64. doi:10.1109/TMC.2003.1195151

Zhou, L., & Haas, Z. (1999). Securing Ad Hoc Networks. *IEEE Network, 13*(6), 24–30. doi:10.1109/65.806983

Zhu, B., & Bao, F. (2005). Efficient and robust key management for large mobile ad hoc networks. *Computer Networks, 48*(4), 657–682. doi:10.1016/j.comnet.2004.11.023

Zimmerman, P. (1994). *PGP User's Guide.* Cambridge, MA: MIT.

This work was previously published in the International Journal of Secure Software Engineering, Volume 2, Issue 1, edited by Khaled M. Khan, pp. 1-21, copyright 2011 by IGI Publishing (an imprint of IGI Global).

Chapter 13
JavaSPI:
A Framework for Security Protocol Implementation

Matteo Avalle
Politecnico di Torino, Italy

Alfredo Pironti
INRIA, France

Davide Pozza
Teoresi Group, Italy

Riccardo Sisto
Politecnico di Torino, Italy

ABSTRACT

This paper presents JavaSPI, a "model-driven" development framework that allows the user to reliably develop security protocol implementations in Java, starting from abstract models that can be verified formally. The main novelty of this approach stands in the use of Java as both a modeling language and the implementation language. The JavaSPI framework is validated by implementing a scenario of the SSL protocol. The JavaSPI implementation can successfully interoperate with OpenSSL, and has comparable execution time with the standard Java JSSE library.

1. INTRODUCTION

Security protocols are distributed algorithms that run over untrusted networks with the aim of achieving security goals, such as mutual authentication of two protocol parties. In order to achieve such goals, security protocols typically use cryptography.

It is well known that despite their apparent simplicity it is quite difficult to design security protocols right, and it may be quite difficult to find out all the subtle flaws that affect a given protocol logic. Research on this topic has led to the development of specialized formal methods that can be used to rigorously reason about protocol logic and to prove that it does really achieve its

DOI: 10.4018/978-1-4666-2482-5.ch013

intended goals under certain assumptions (e.g., Blanchet, 2009).

One problem that remains with this solution is the gap that exists between the abstract protocol model that is formally analyzed and its concrete implementation written in a programming language. The latter may be quite different from the former, thus breaking the validity of the formal verification when the final implementation is considered.

In order to solve this problem two approaches have been proposed. On one hand, model extraction techniques (e.g., O'Shea, 2008; Bhargavan, Fournet, Gordon, & Tse, 2008; Backes, Maffei, & Unruh, 2010; Chaki & Datta, 2009), automatically extract an abstract protocol model that can be verified formally, starting from the code of a protocol implementation. On the other hand, code generation model-driven techniques (e.g., Pironti & Sisto, 2007; Kiyomoto, Ota, & Tanaka, 2008; Almeida, Bangerter, Barbosa, Krenn, Sadeghi, & Schneider, 2010; Bhargavan, Corin, Deniélou, Fournet, & Leifer, 2009; Balser, Reif, Schellhorn, Stenzel, & Thums, 2000; Song, Perrig, & Phan, 2001), automatically generate a protocol implementation, starting from a formally verified abstract model. In either case, if the automatic transformation is formally guaranteed to be sound, it is possible to extend the results of formal verification done on the abstract protocol model to the corresponding implementation code.

Model-driven development (MDD) offers the advantage of hiding the complexity of a full implementation during the design phase, because the developer needs only focus on a simplified abstract model. Moreover, since the implementation code is automatically generated, it is possible to make it immune from some low-level programming errors, such as memory leakages, that could make the program vulnerable in some cases but that are not represented in abstract models.

However, MDD usually requires a high level of expertise, which limits its adoption, because formal languages used for abstract protocol mod-

els are generally not known by code developers, and quite different from common programming languages. For example, the user needs to know the formal spi calculus language in order to properly work with the Spi2Java framework (Pironti & Sisto, 2007).

Our motivation is to solve this problem and make MDD approaches more affordable. To achieve this, our contribution is the proposal of a new framework, based on Spi2Java, called *JavaSPI* (http://typhoon5.polito.it/javaspi/), where the abstract protocol model is itself an executable Java program.

This little but significant difference grants several different improvements over frameworks like Spi2Java:

- It is not necessary to learn a new completely different modeling language anymore (Java is also used as a modeling language);
- Standard Java Integrated Development Environments (ides), to which the programmer is already familiar, can be used to develop the security protocol model like it was a plain Java program, making full use of IDE features such as code completion, or live compilation;
- It is possible to debug (or *simulate*) the abstract model using the same debuggers Java programmers are used to;
- Thanks to Java annotations, information about low-level implementation choices and security properties can be neatly embedded into the abstract model.

The viability of the proposed approach is validated by a case study where interoperable client and server sides of a specific SSL scenario are implemented. The interoperability capabilities are demonstrated by running alternatively the client and the server against the OpenSSL 0.98o corresponding implementations, while the performances of the generated code are compared against the Oracle's Java official implementation of SSL contained in the JSSE library.

The rest of the paper is organized as follows. Section 2 analyzes related work and Spi2Java in particular, highlighting its main limitations. Then, Section 3 illustrates the JavaSPI framework in detail, while Section 4 reports about the SSL case study. Finally, Section 5 concludes.

2. BACKGROUND AND RELATED WORK

Model-driven development of security protocols based on formal models has been experimented using various languages and tools. One of the most comprehensive approaches is Spi2Java, which enables semi-automatic development of interoperable Java implementations of standard protocols (Pironti & Sisto, 2007).

In this framework, protocols are modeled in spi calculus, a formal domain-specific process algebraic language. A spi calculus protocol model can be automatically analyzed in order to formally verify that there are no possible attacks on the protocol under the modeling assumptions made. For this to be done, the protocol expected goals must be formally specified too. The formal analysis can be done, for example, by the automatic theorem prover ProVerif (Blanchet, 2009), whose input language is a superset of spi calculus.

Once the abstract model has been successfully analyzed, and it has been shown that it is free from logical flaws, it can be refined up to the point that a Java implementation can be derived for each protocol role.

During this refinement step, the abstract model must be enriched with all the missing protocol aspects that are needed in order to get a concrete and interoperable Java implementation:

1. Concrete Java implementations of cryptographic algorithms with their actual parameters
2. Java types to be used for terms

3. Concrete binary representations of messages and corresponding Java implementations of marshaling functions

In the Spi2Java framework, the spi calculus model and this refinement information are kept in two separate but coupled files. When a change to the model is done, it is under the user's responsibility to keep the coupled refinement file up to date, which is error prone and time consuming. By keeping refinement information neatly integrated in the source code as Java annotations, JavaSPI also solves these engineering issues.

In addition to Spi2Java, other approaches based on code generation are documented in literature (e.g., Kiyomoto, Ota, & Tanaka, 2008; Almeida, Bangerter, Barbosa, Krenn, Sadeghi, & Schneider, 2010; Bhargavan, Corin, Deniélou, Fournet, & Leifer, 2009; Balser, Reif, Schellhorn, Stenzel, & Thums, 2000; Song, Perrig, & Phan, 2001), but they present the same or larger limitations.

Other researchers have explored the model extraction approach (e.g., O'Shea, 2008; Bhargavan, Fournet, Gordon, & Tse, 2008; Backes, Maffei, & Unruh, 2010; Chaki & Datta, 2009). These techniques, like JavaSPI, do not expose the programmer to specialized formal specification languages, but they lack the model-driven approach, so that all the code must be written manually by the programmer.

For example, the Elyjah framework (O'Shea, 2008) requires a full Java implementation to be developed, before a model can be extracted and verified. In contrast, with JavaSPI, the programmer only writes a simplified Java model of the protocol, from which a code generator generates the full implementation. The abstract Java model developed with JavaSPI enables features such as symbolic execution of the protocol, and the use of Java annotations keeps implementation and verification details neatly separated from the Java model. These features are inherently difficult to achieve in Java model-extraction frameworks such as Elyjah.

In Bhargavan, Fournet, Gordon, and Tse (2008), model extraction is performed on full implementations written in F#. The F# implementation can be linked either to a concrete or to a symbolic library of cryptographic and communication primitives, which enables protocol symbolic simulation, just like when the JavaSPI abstract Java model is executed. However, in Bhargavan, Fournet, Gordon, and Tse (2008) there is no neat distinction between protocol logic and lower-level details such as cryptographic algorithms and parameters or data marshaling. Moreover, in Bhargavan, Fournet, Gordon, and Tse (2008) programs are written in F#, which is far less known than Java, thus making the tool of lesser impact to common developers.

Other researchers have focused on different model-driven approaches, starting from UML representations of security protocols (e.g., Jürjens, 2005; Basin, Doser, & Lodderstedt, 2006). While UML modeling is agreed to be an essential design phase in very large scale software projects, it is often the case that the UML modeling overhead is deemed too expensive for the typical application size of a security protocol, thus being not accepted by the average security protocol implementer.

3. THE JAVASPI FRAMEWORK

The main contributions of this paper are the development of the JavaSPI framework and also the implementation of a case study, which will be described later in Section 4.

JavaSPI has been designed as a set of tools and utilities that enable the user to model a cryptographic protocol by following the workflow shown in Figure 1: basically, the user is intended to develop abstract models in the form of typical Java applications, but using a specific library which is part of the JavaSPI framework, named *SpiWrapperSim*, which contains a set of basic data types along with the networking and cryptographic primitives.

The logical execution of the protocol can be simulated by simply debugging the abstract code. The protocol security properties can be formally verified by using the JavaSPI *Java-ProVerif* converter that produces an output compatible with the ProVerif tool.

Once a model has been properly designed, it can be refined by adding implementation information by means of Java annotations, as defined in the SpiWrapperSim library.

Figure 1. The complete workflow provided by JavaSPI

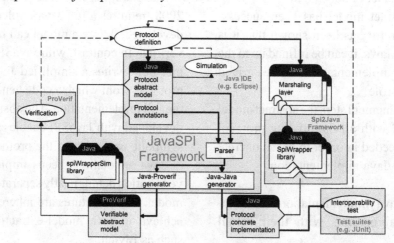

From the annotated Java model a concrete implementation of the protocol can be generated by using the JavaSPI *Java-Java* converter.

The entire JavaSPI framework and tools described in this paper have been completely developed from scratch: still, some architectural choices have been made to allow re-use of parts of the Spi2Java framework.

3A. Developing the Abstract Model

The JavaSPI framework includes a Java library, called SpiWrapperSim, which can be used to write abstract security protocol models as Java applications and to simulate them.

Models that can be expressed in this way are instances of the class of models that can be described by the input language of ProVerif. Based on this, the framework provides the *Java-ProVerif* tool that transforms a Java model into the corresponding ProVerif model, which can be analyzed by ProVerif. Note that differently from (Bhargavan, Fournet, Gordon, & Tse, 2008), here the ProVerif model is not extracted from the Java code, rather the model, expressed in the Java syntax, is translated into the ProVerif syntax. A Java model differs from the final Java implementation because it is as abstract as the ProVerif model.

Moreover, the Java model can also be executed like any regular Java application. Its execution in fact simulates the underlying model that it describes, thus giving the user the possibility to debug the abstract model. In this execution messages are represented symbolically, and input/output operations are implemented by exchanging symbolic expressions over in-memory channels behaving according to the classical spi calculus semantics.

In order to get a Java program that models a protocol in this way, the user must write Java according to a particular programming pattern. Only the SpiWrapperSim library can be used for cryptographic and input/output operations, and some restrictions on the Java language constructs that can be used for the description of each process apply. These restrictions, documented in the library JavaDoc, naturally lead the user to develop models in the right way.

A protocol role (a "process") is represented by a class that inherits from the library class *spiProcess*. In this way, the common code needed for simulation that is the context of the protocol algorithm is hidden inside the superclass. Moreover, objects derived from *spiProcess* are allowed to use some protected methods that enable common operations, like the parallel instantiation of sub-processes.

The class that inherits from *spiProcess* must define the *doRun()* method, which is the abstract description of the protocol role.

Any message, complex at will, can be represented by an immutable object belonging to a class that inherits from the *Packet* library class. The fields of this class are the fields of the message. The class must be made immutable by declaring all fields as final. This is necessary as, in spi calculus, each variable can be bound only once. Using mutable Java objects would be possible but it would then entail more complex relationships between the Java code and the underlying model.

The only class types the user is allowed to instantiate are the ones provided by the SpiWrapperSim library, plus the ones used as arguments of methods of such classes (e.g., *String*). The primitive type *int* is also admitted, but only for loop flow control, with the constraint that each loop must be bounded and the bound must be known at compile time.

Conditional statements are possible only with equality tests (via the *equals()* method) and with tests on the return values of certain operations of the library.

SpiWrapperSim is very similar to the SpiWrapper library that provides the implementations of the spi calculus cryptographic and communication operations in the Spi2Java framework. This is a precise architectural choice that greatly facilitates the last development step, i.e., the refinement of the abstract model into a concrete implementation.

Indeed, the implementation code is based on the SpiWrapper library.

As showed in Figure 2, thanks to this choice even the syntax used in the two codes is very similar; the main difference is that the abstract model lacks many implementation details, like the encryption algorithms of each cryptographic function call, or the marshaling functions (whose implementation is included in the "SR"-suffixed classes in the example showed).

Within the SpiWrapperSim library a set of annotations was also developed, which can be used during refinement to assign, for each object, its implementation details. As annotations do not affect the simulation phase, they can be specified later on, just before generating the concrete implementation.

By using this technique the implementation details and the code both reside on the same file: this means that JavaSPI is not affected by the

sync problems described previously for Spi2Java. Moreover, each annotation has a scope and a default value, so that it is not necessary to specify each implementation detail for each object used in the code, but it is possible to specify just the implementation details that differ from the default values.

By following the intended workflow, the Java model can be converted into a ProVerif compatible model, or a concrete Java implementation can be derived from the Java model.

The next two subsections will cover these two cases.

3B. Java-ProVerif Conversion and Formal Verification

The mapping from Java to ProVerif syntax is based on simple rules, developed in this work along with the corresponding converter, that are informally

Figure 2. An example of how four lines of the abstract model are converted into the corresponding concrete implementation and ProVerif syntax

Java Abstract Model

```
1 Message m = new Identifier("Secret Message");
2 Nonce n = new Nonce();
3 SharedKey s = new SharedKey(n);
4 SharedKeyCiphered<Message> mk =
      new SharedKeyCiphered<Message>(m,s);
```

Java Concrete Implementation

```
1 Message m = new IdentifierSR("Secret Message");
2 Nonce n = new NonceSR("8");
3 SharedKey s = new SharedKeySR(n, "DES", "64");
4 SharedKeyCiphered mk =
      new SharedKeyCipheredSR(m, s, "DES,
          "1234567801g=", "CBC",
          "PKCS5Padding", "SunJCE");
```

ProVerif Model

```
1 new m1;
2 new n2;
3 let s4 = SharedKey(n2) in
4 let mk6 = SymEncrypt(s4, m1) in
```

exemplified in Table 1. Each Java statement that may occur in a *doRun* method is mapped to a corresponding ProVerif equivalent piece of code. For simplicity, the table does not include the name mangling algorithm, which is needed in order to

Table 1. A significant portion of the conversion mapping between the java model and the proverif model

Statement	Java	ProVerif
Fresh	Type a = new Type();	New a;
Assign	Type a = b;	let a = b in
Hashing	Hashing a = new Hashing(b);	let a = H(b) in
Send	cAB.send(a);	out(cAB, a);
Receive	Type a = cAB.receive(Type.class);	in(cAB, a);
Shared-Key	SharedKey key = new SharedKey(a);	let key = SharedKey(a) in
Encrypt	SharedKeyCiphered <Type> a = new SharedKeyCiphered <Type>(b, key);	let a = SymEncrypt(key, b) in
Decrypt	Type a = b.decrypt(key);	let a = SymDecrypt(key, b) in
Error handled Decipher	ResultContainer<Type> c= a.decrypt_w(key); if (c.isValid()) { Type b = c.getResult(); ...} else { ... }	let b = SymDecrypt(key, a) in (...) else (...)
Packet Comp.	PacketType m = new PacketType(a, b, ...);	let m = (a, b, ...) in
Packet Split	Type a = b.getField();	let a = b_getField in (*)
Match Case	If (a.equals(b)) { ...} else { ... }	If a = b then (...) else (....)
Start	SpiProcess a = new Client(c, d, ...); SpiProcess b = new Server(e, f, ...); start(a, b);	(Client(c, d, ...) | Server(e, f, ...))

Type stands for any class name, PacketType stands for any user-defined Packet class name, Field stands for any field name in a Packet class, while a... f and key stand for variable names.

(*) Variable b_getField is created in ProVerif code during a Packet splitting phase which is automatically generated after any Decrypt or Receive statement that produces a Packet object.

disambiguate variable names in ProVerif, and whose outcome is shown in Figure 2.

Conversion of loops requires special handling. ProVerif does not support unbounded loops natively, but they can be easily encoded as recursive processes. However, ProVerif often experiences termination problems when loops encoded as recursive processes are used. Because of this limitation of the verification engine, the restriction of having only bounded loops was introduced in the Java modeling language, so that the conversion tool can perform loop unrolling in order to eliminate loops.

The fields of a Java Packet object are translated into nested pairs. In order to facilitate code translation and readability, a new variable is introduced in ProVerif for each field. For example, let us consider a class called MyPacket with three fields called *a*, *b* and *c*, all of type Nonce: the following Java code receives a message of type MyPacket and extracts its three fields, as presented in Box 1.

This group of four Java instructions is converted into the following ProVerif code, presented in Box 2.

By using this technique the converter is forced to write, in ProVerif, more code lines than with the Java syntax, but this disadvantage is overcome by the fact that this technique totally hides to ProVerif the additional complexity that custom packet types could cause, thus avoiding the risk to generate diverging code.

There is also another particular characteristic of ProVerif which actually needs to be taken into consideration: its syntax does not allow writing any expression *after* an *if/else* statement. This poses some limits to the Java-ProVerif conversion, as it generates some situations in which a simple rule-based mapping is not feasible.

The naïve solution of forbidding the users to write Java code after an if/else statement is not acceptable, because it would limit the expressiveness freedom a Java developer usually has and exploits. For this reason, a pre-parsing Java algorithm has been developed, to inline all the

Box 1.

```
MyPacket p = channel.receive(MyPacket.class);
Nonce a = p.getA();
Nonce b = p.getB();
Nonce c = p.getC();
```

Java code appearing after an if/else branch, so that it can be more easily mapped to ProVerif syntax statements. This operation, again, generates a ProVerif file that can be more complex than the Java model, but this can be considered an acceptable tradeoff, as in this way it is not necessary to limit the developer too much. Moreover, ProVerif files are not meant to be read by any developer. They just need to be used with the corresponding verification tool.

Translating plain Java models into ProVerif is not enough to enable automatic verification of security properties: two types of information need to be added

- The initial attacker knowledge
- The security properties that have to be checked.

By default, the initial attacker knowledge is automatically generated this way: constants shared by the communication actors are considered public

Box 2.

```
in(channel1, p2);
(* Packet expansion *)
let p2_getA3 = GetLeft(p2);
let tmp4 = GetRight(p2);
let p2_getB5 = GetLeft(tmp4);
let p2_getC6 = GetRight(tmp4);
(* Variable assignment *)
let a7 = p2_getA3;
let b8 = p2_getB5;
let c9 = p2_getC6;
```

constant data, and the communication channels are considered public free names.

However sometimes some communication protocols may work in a slightly different way for various reasons: for example, two actors may share a common secret symmetrical key which must be considered unknown to the attacker.

For this reason, the user can have control over the initial attacker knowledge, by overriding the default behavior by means of a single annotation, called *@pVarDef(PRIVATE|PUBLIC)*. This annotation can be scoped to a single variable or to an entire block of code: in this case every variable declared inside the code block inherits the *pVarDef* property of the block, unless a more specific, inner-scoped annotation affects the variable declaration.

With these simple rules it is possible to express very complex initial attacker knowledge bases with a very small effort: in fact, in a simple protocol, the files that model the actor behaviors do not need these annotations. The *pVarDef* annotation is just added to the instancer process, by defaulting its variables as *PUBLIC*. Changing this behavior just implies adding few annotations on some variables in the instancer, when these variables must be considered *PRIVATE*.

Note that the *pVarDef* annotation has a direct influence on how the ProVerif code is generated: every *PUBLIC* variable is declared as a free or constant term (whether the variable is a channel or any other data type), which are particular elements globally available throughout the entire protocol code. As this behavior is not logically the same of the Java model, a particular variable renaming technique has been applied in order to avoid name conflicts.

A specific annotation set has been developed within the JavaSPI library to express security properties. These annotations are then processed during conversion to ProVerif and translated into corresponding queries in the output ProVerif code.

A variable can be marked as *@Secret* in order to specify that ProVerif should verify its syntactic secrecy. For instance:

```
@Secret
Nonce DHPrivate = new Nonce();
```

The corresponding ProVerif generated code will look like this:

```
(* Secrecy queries *)
query attacker:DHPrivate21.
```

If the *@Secret* term is a compound term or anyway a term that needs to be constructed over another one, the translation becomes slightly more complex: in fact, as ProVerif cannot directly verify the secrecy of variables, but only of fresh names or terms built upon them, the ProVerif query that will be generated regards the entire composition of the term, along with queries about the secrecy of any ground term involved in the composition. For this reason, during verification some false alerts may be reported by ProVerif, for example when a complex secret term is composed of a mix of secret and publicly available terms: in such cases the secrecy verification of public terms will certainly fail.

In the current version of the JavaSPI framework the task of recognizing such false alerts and safely ignore them is left to the user. In fact, the bigger goal of interpreting ProVerif output to consistently report it to the user into the JavaSPI environment is a major ongoing effort that is scheduled to be included in the next version of the framework. Within this bigger goal, automatic recognition of such false alerts is a planned feature.

In order to verify authentication properties, instead, it is possible to use correspondence assertions. In JavaSPI, a process can raise an event by calling the *event(String name, Message... data)* method provided by the *SpiProcess* class, where *name* specifies the name of the event, and *data* the set of variables associated to that event.

This method has no effect in the code, but it is translated to a corresponding event in ProVerif. Once the event sets are defined it is possible to use them to write some interrogations: for example, the reachability of every event, which increases the confidence in the model correctness, is automatically queried, while in order to check other more complex properties a set of annotations was developed: for example, the correspondence between events, such as "if *event(n1,x,y,...)* happened, then *event(n2,x,y,...)* must have happened before" can be specified by the *@PEvinj* annotation, associated with the instantiation process class, as demonstrated in Box 3.

This technique can be used to write more advanced queries, by extending the number of events in a *PEvinj* clause to three or more, or by combining multiple *PEvinj* annotations by using another annotation, called *PInjList*, like in this example:

```
@PInjList({
@PEvinj({"n1","n2","n3"}),
@PEvinj({"m1", "m2"})
})
...
```

As a design choice, all the queries are written by using just the name of the events, without referencing also the data associated with the event calls (as opposed to what ProVerif does): by default, the exact comparison of all the parameters will be verified. This design choice allows queries to be stated in a very simple form, even if it slightly reduces the overall expressive power. Note that this

Box 3.

```
@PEvinj({"n1", "n2"})
public class Master extends SpiProcess ...
```

slightly reduced expressiveness did not prevent nor made more complex the development of the SSL case study.

With this set of techniques a user can express the main part of basic ProVerif queries. There is still the possibility, however, that the user needs to write a more complex interrogation, not expressible with just these annotations. For this reason a particular annotation has been provided to enable the user to directly write a custom query with the ProVerif syntax. This, however, is an advanced feature that can just be used by experienced developers who actually know the ProVerif query syntax: for this reason, it is a feature of little interest for the purposes of this paper, and it will not be discussed in more detail.

3C. Implementation Generation

The last development stage is the automatic generation of the protocol implementation code from the model. As SpiWrapperSim is similar to the library used for the concrete implementation, there is a strict correspondence between the abstract code (the model) and the concrete code (the implementation). The implementation aspects that are missing in the abstract model can all be specified by means of annotations.

One of such aspects is the choice of the marshaling functions to be used for each object. A default marshaling mechanism based on Java serialization is provided by a library called *spiWrapperSR*, which extends spiWrapper. The user however can provide custom implementations of the marshaling functions. This is a key factor

enabling development of interoperable implementations of standard protocols, where the specific marshaling functions to be used are specified by the protocol standard.

Another key feature of JavaSPI enabling interoperability is the ability of resolving Java annotations values either statically at compile time, or dynamically at run time, like in this example presented in Box 4.

Here it is possible to notice how the algorithm name for the key "k" is not directly hardcoded in an annotation, but this value will change at run time by assuming the value of the "algorithm" variable..

This technique is particularly useful to implement, as example, protocols featuring algorithms negotiation.

The last thing that needs to be performed is to specify how the various constants of the protocol have to be initialized. Since in general different actors of a protocol may need different constants, the user can specify, for each actor, a piece of code that initializes every parameter before calling the protocol method in the proper way.

The initialization code must be written into the *doInit* method, which overrides the one in the *SpiProcess* class. The code inside *doInit* is neither considered during simulation nor in ProVerif verification, but it will be replicated verbatim in the concrete Java implementation. This technique avoids the need of modifying the generated code at all. To integrate the generated code into a bigger security-aware application only its interfaces will be needed.

Box 4.

```
Identifier algorithm = channel.receive(Identifier.class);
@Algo(Type=Types.varname, value="algorithm")
SharedKey k = new Sharedkey(n);
```

4. THE SSL CASE STUDY

In order to validate the proposed JavaSPI approach, a simplified but interoperable implementation of both the client and server sides of the SSL handshake protocol has been developed.

The considered scenario, depicted in Figure 3, can be logically divided into four different phases:

1. Client and server exchange two "hello" messages which are used to negotiate protocol version and ciphersuites.
2. The server authenticates itself to the client by sending its certificate *s_cert*.
3. Diffie-Hellman (DH) key exchange is performed; note that the server DH parameters are signed by the server.
4. Finally, the session is completed by the exchange of encrypted "Finished" messages.

For simplicity, in the considered scenario both the developed client and server only support version 3.0 of the protocol with DSA server certificate. Other ciphersuites or other protocol features such as session resumption or client authentication are not considered. Indeed, the goal is to validate the methodology with a minimal, yet significant example, rather than provide a full reference implementation of the SSL protocol.

The SpiWrapperSim library has been used to develop the abstract model of the SSL protocol. This includes eight new Packet classes representing the structures of the different types of exchanged messages and a client and a server SpiProcess classes. In addition, an "instancer" process called *Master* that just runs an instance of client and server in parallel has been added in order to simulate protocol execution. Figure 4 provides a code excerpt of the Java SSL model, while the complete version of the code is available online (http://typhoon5.polito.it/javaspi).

After defining the model the following properties have been expressed and successfully verified:

*   Secrecy of the client and server DH secret values.
*   Server authentication, expressed as an injective correspondence between the correct termination of the two processes: each time a client correctly terminates a session, agreeing on all relevant session data and the server identity, a server must have started a session, agreeing on the same session data and on the server identity.

Finally, in order to get interoperability, a custom marshaling library compliant with the SSL standard has been developed.

Besides setting the marshaling layer, it was also necessary to specify by means of annotations the needed cryptographic details, such as algorithms and related parameters. In the sample SSL protocol both compile time and run time resolution features of JavaSPI have been exploited. Even if this protocol implementation uses many "hardcoded" parameters, like the ciphersuites and the key strengths, other information is only known at run time: for example, the initialization vectors used for shared key encryption are calculated from the shared secret, thus they change at each run.

As shown by the code excerpt in Figure 5, static details can be specified once, on the head of the class, while dynamic details and special cases are specified just before each variable needing them.

Figure 3. SSL message exchange in the selected scenario

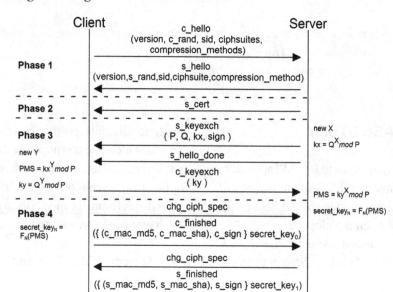

Figure 4. An excerpt of the SSL protocol abstract model

Server.java

```
class Server extends SpiProcess { ...
  @Override void doRun(final Channel c,
    final Identifier SSL_VERSION3_0, ...)
  {
    final Pair<Identifier, DHHashing> c_key_exch =
      c.receive(Pair.class);
    final DHHashing c_DHy = c_key_exch.getRight();
    final Triplet PMSp =
      new Triplet(c_DHy, DH_x, DH_P);
    final DHHashing common_key =
      new DHHashing(PMSp);
    ...
  }
}
```

Master.java

```
class Master extends SpiProcess {
  @Override void doRun() {
    ...
    final Client c = new Client( ... );
    final Server s = new Server( ... );
    start(c, s);
  }
}
```

In the sample code, the initialization vector is computed by applying a hash function and is stored in variable c_write_iv. Then, an annotation specifies that the initialization vector for the ciphered message received in variable c_encrypted_Finish is the value in variable c_write_iv.

The amount of required annotations does not burden the code too much: the SSL example required about 60 annotations in total (client + server), which amounts to about 10% of the whole model size. To make this measure significant, default values were not crafted to suite the SSL example, rather the scoping feature of annotations was exploited, so that SSL-specific default values could be annotated just once at the class scope.

The generated client and server implementations have been successfully tested for interoperability against OpenSSL 0.9.8o.

Performance Considerations

One claimed disadvantage of code generation techniques is that as the code is automatically generated it will never be as optimized as it is possible to do by manually writing the code.

Nonetheless, with cryptographic protocols it is often the case that the main computing effort lies in the computation of cryptography: for this reason the possible overhead due to potential code inefficiency is often negligible with respect to the overall computing time.

In order to experimentally confirm this claim, we compared the performance of the SSL client implementation generated with JavaSPI to the performance of a corresponding code into the JSSE library, which is the Oracle's Java official implementation of SSL. The two codes have been executed against the same SSL server, based on the OpenSSL application. To ensure that the two clients are effectively performing the same operations, a custom Certificate validator has been written for the JSSE implementation in order to treat the certificates in the same way they are treated by the JavaSPI SSL implementation. As a further check, some network packet sniffing has been preliminarily performed in order to ensure that the same ciphersuites were used, and the same messages were exchanged.

Finally, in order to run the two applications in the same environment and limit random components in the measurements, the tests were run keeping every communication local, thus eliminating random network latencies. Moreover, the two implementations were run in the same Java virtual machine a thousand times and the mean execution time and its standard deviation were computed. Since in the first run a Java program is affected by the Java class loader latency, the

Figure 5. An excerpt of the Java model with annotations on it

```
@SharedKeyA(Algo="3DES", Strength="168")
@SharedKeyCipheredA("Algo="3DES", Mode="CBC")
public class Server extends spiProcess {
   ...
   final Hashing c_write_iv = new Hashing(PA3);
   ...
   @Iv(type=Types.varName, value="c_write_iv")
   final SharedKeyCiphered
     <Pair<Pair<Hashing, Hashing>, Hashing>>
     c_encrypted_Finish =
       c.receive(SharedKeyCiphered.class);
   ...
```

time of the first run has been excluded, while all other measurements have been used to compute mean and standard deviation values.

The obtained results demonstrate that the processing times of the two implementations are nearly the same; the performance difference between the two implementations is just about 5% in favor of the JSSE code.

As stated before, the explanation of this fact is that both the pieces of code are using exactly the same cryptographic library (JCA) and the DSA signature check and DH modular exponentiation performed in the SSL protocol take the main part of the total protocol execution time. It is likely that the JSSE implementation is much more optimized than the JavaSPI auto-generated code, but this performance boost just affects a very small portion of the total execution time.

In conclusion, the performance results show us a very small difference between an optimized version of the code, written by hand, and an automatically generated implementation. This inefficiency might be considered non negligible in some particular cases, but in any other situation having an implementation with an high level of trustworthiness and correctness can greatly balance this small performance penalty.

5. CONCLUSION

The JavaSPI framework enables model-driven development of security protocols based on formal methods without the need to know specialized formal languages. Knowledge of a formal language is replaced by knowledge of a Java library and of a set of language restrictions, which is easier to learn for Java experienced programmers. Moreover, standard IDEs can be used to develop the Java model, with the benefit of having access to all the development features offered by such IDEs.

This could potentially enable any common developer to perform formal verifications of security protocols. Even if this can be considered a usability improvement, in some situations this can be considered a dangerous feature, as developers who are completely new to the modeling world could generate wrong formal proofs by simply verifying wrong queries. Anyway, even in these environments, JavaSPI could still be of great use as it simplifies the interaction between modelers and developers by forcing the two categories to speak "the same language".

The proposed approach, along with the provided toolchain and libraries, enables (i) interactive simulation and debugging of the Java model, via standard Java debuggers available in all common IDEs; (ii) automatic verification of the protocol security properties, via the de-facto standard ProVerif tool; and (iii) automatic generation of interoperable implementation code, via a custom tool, driven by Java annotations embedded into the model files.

Compared to similar frameworks, like Spi-2Java, JavaSPI is easier to use, while retaining the nice feature of enabling fast development of protocol implementations with high integrity assurance given by the linkage between Java code and verified formal models.

Future work includes focusing on the formalization of the relationship between Java and spi calculus semantics, in order to get a soundness proof for the Java code, once the ProVerif model is verified.

From an engineering point of view, porting the ProVerif verification results directly to the Java model and better engineering the way security properties are expressed in Java could further improve usability and accessibility of the proposed framework. Moreover, further tests could be performed in order to demonstrate that quite every Java developer is able to design and validate a communication protocol by just reading the framework documentation.

REFERENCES

Almeida, J., Bangerter, E., Barbosa, M., Krenn, S., Sadeghi, A., & Schneider, T. (2010). A certifying compiler for zero-knowledge proofs of knowledge based on sigma-protocols. In *Proceedings of the European Symposium on Research in Computer Security* (pp. 151-167).

Backes, M., Maffei, M., & Unruh, D. (2010). Computationally sound verification of source code. In *Proceedings of the 17th ACM Conference on Computer and Communications Security* (pp. 387-398).

Balser, M., Reif, W., Schellhorn, G., Stenzel, K., & Thums, A. (2000). Formal system development with KIV. In *Proceedings of the 3rd International Conference on Fundamental Approaches to Software Engineering: Held as Part of the European Joint Conferences on the Theory and Practice of Software* (pp. 363-366).

Basin, D., Doser, J., & Lodderstedt, T. (2006). Model driven security: from UML models to access control infrastructures. *ACM Transactions on Software Engineering and Methodology, 15*(1), 39–91. doi:10.1145/1125808.1125810

Bhargavan, K., Corin, R., Deniélou, P., Fournet, C., & Leifer, J. (2009). Cryptographic protocol synthesis and verification for multiparty sessions. In *Proceedings of the Computer Security Foundations Symposium* (pp. 124-140).

Bhargavan, K., Fournet, C., Gordon, A., & Tse, S. (2008). Verified interoperable implementations of security protocols. *ACM Transactions on Programming Languages and Systems, 31*(1), 1–61. doi:10.1145/1452044.1452049

Blanchet, B. (2009). Automatic verification of correspondences for security protocols. *Journal of Computer Security, 17*(4), 363–434.

Chaki, S., & Datta, A. (2009). ASPIER: An automated framework for verifying security protocol implementations. In *Proceedings of the Computer Security Foundations Symposium* (pp. 172-185).

Jürjens, J. (2005). *Secure systems development with UML*. New York, NY: Springer.

Kiyomoto, S., Ota, H., & Tanaka, T. (2008). A security protocol compiler generating C source codes. In *Proceedings of the International Conference on Information Security and Assurance* (pp. 20-25).

O'Shea, N. (2008). Using Elyjah to analyse Java implementations of cryptographic protocols. In *Proceedings of the Conference on Foundations of Computer Security, Automated Reasoning for Security Protocol Analysis and Issues in the Theory of Security* (pp. 221-226).

Pironti, A., & Sisto, R. (2007). An experiment in interoperable cryptographic protocol implementation using automatic code generation. In *Proceedings of the IEEE Symposium on Computers and Communications* (pp. 839-844).

Song, D. X., Perrig, A., & Phan, D. (2001). AGVI - Automatic generation, verification, and implementation of security protocols. In *Proceedings of the 13th International Conference on Computer Aided Verification* (pp. 241-245).

This work was previously published in the International Journal of Secure Software Engineering, Volume 2, Issue 4, edited by Khaled M. Khan, pp. 34-48, copyright 2011 by IGI Publishing (an imprint of IGI Global).

Chapter 14
A Systematic Empirical Analysis of Forging Fingerprints to Fool Biometric Systems

Christian Schwarzl
Vienna University of Technology and SBA Research, Austria

Edgar Weippl
Vienna University of Technology and SBA Research, Austria

ABSTRACT

This paper serves to systematically describe the attempts made to forge fingerprints to fool biometric systems and to review all relevant publications on forging fingerprints to fool sensors. The research finds that many of the related works fail in this aspect and that past successes could not be repeated. First, the basics of biometrics are explained in order to define the meaning of the term security in this special context. Next, the state of the art of biometric systems is presented, followed by to the topic of security of fingerprint scanners. For this, a series of more than 30,000 experiments were conducted to fool scanners. The authors were able to reproduce and keep records of each single step in the test and to show which methods lead to the desired results. Most studies on this topic exclude a number of steps in producing a fake finger and fooling a fingerprint scanner are not explained, which means that some of the studies cannot be replicated. In addition, the authors' own ideas and slight variations of existing experiment set-ups are presented.

INTRODUCTION

The study focuses on the issue of security of fingerprint scanners. Fingerprint scanners are used to improve identification and authentication of users to the operating system; moreover, they are used to confirm critical transactions in software systems. For the overall security of a software system it is essential for its engineers to understand the strengths and limitations of fingerprints when used for authentication. While many successful attacks have been described most papers

DOI: 10.4018/978-1-4666-2482-5.ch014

are not so precise as to allow other researchers to replicate the same experiment. This paper summarizes previous attacks and documents all steps in a detailed way. Software engineers will benefit from this study as they can use our paper as a scaffold for similar research.

There are a number of studies that have reported that fingerprint scanners can be outwitted with extremely basic technologies (Chaos Computer Club, 2004; Kaseva & Stén, 2003; Matsumoto et al., 2002). Although the approach and materials used in these studies may differ, all share certain common features: procedures are described only superficially, whereby in a few cases one gets the impression that such imprecision is entirely intentional: Some steps are mentioned in merely a brief statement, with no precise description of the procedure or of the materials and instruments used. *Our contribution is, thus, to establish a reproducible, quantifiable approach to assessing the security of fingerprint scanners* – a security-critical component in many systems. The lack of detailed descriptions in many of the reviewed papers make some steps seem much simpler and easier than they actually are. The impression thus arises that it is extremely simple to deceive a fingerprint scanner.

The study examines whether a person of average practical and technical abilities using the appropriate tools can successfully recreate "false fingers" to fool fingerprint scanners. We also examined whether a slight adaptation of the methods used in the relevant articles may be successful. Moreover, we explain why a possible success depends on the scanner used or the device's scanning method. All of these experiments are carried out under scientific conditions, and the methods are tested to determine whether success can be

counted on every time, only occasionally. With the help of all of these experiments, an attempt is made to answer the question of the security of fingerprint scanners.

QUALITY MEASURES

To enable a certain comparison between various products, particular guidelines and measurement parameters are required. For biometric systems, as a rule, performance is measured by the following error rates:

One of the most important measurements in a biometric system is the *False Accept Rate (FAR)*. This states the frequency with which non-authorized people are accepted as authorized and hence given access to the system (Bromba, 2008a).

Similar in importance to the *False Accept Rate is the False Rejection Rate (FRR)*. It is, in fact, the exact opposite of the FAR and states the frequency with which an authorized person is not granted entrance/access. Although it is often perceived as annoying when a biometric characteristic is not immediately accepted, this does not compromise the confidentiality of a system, but rather impacts availability

The *False Identification Rate (FIR)* states the frequency with which a biometric characteristic is, recognized, but assigned to the wrong person. This error can obviously occur only in systems that use a biometric characteristic as identifier and not for authentication. What must also be taken into account is that the FIR is associated with the number of stored biometric references. This measure is thereby only conditionally an indicator of a possible security risk. The *Failure to Enroll Rate* has relevance only during the enrollment phase. It provides the percentage of people who are unable to enroll.

Should a person be rejected by the system, this affects the previously mentioned FRR. However, a so-called *Failure to Acquire* error might be present. This occurs when a biometric characteristic is not correctly recognized.

THE FINGERPRINT

The fingerprint is certainly one of the most well-known biometric characteristics. Unfortunately, fingerprints are often associated solely with their use in law enforcement, which has negatively burdened their application (Wikipedia, 2010b) (Figure 1).

A fingerprint is the print of the so-called epidermal ridges on the finger tip. The endings and bifurcations of these ridges are identified as minutiae points. The pattern that arises from these minutiae points is a randotypical feature and can be assigned to an individual. Even identical twins have different fingerprints. For the purposes of comparison in law enforcement, as well as in biometrics, not only the fine features (minutiae points) are used, but also the pore structure and

the so-called rough features (Wikipedia, 2010b; Blomme, 2003).

- **Loop:** The most commonly appearing feature is the so-called loop, whereby differentiation is made between the left and right loops, according to the direction in which the ridges wind (Figure 2).

- **Whorl:** A further widespread feature is the so-called whorl. In this, the epidermal ridges form either spirals or concentric rings (Figures 3 and 4).

- **Arches:** Arches are far less common than loops and whorls. With this feature, one or more epidermal ridges form(s) an arch over one or several others (Figure 5).

Depending on the type of acquisition/scanning device, fingerprint systems either store the entire print in the data base and use it for comparison, or algorithms are applied to the image of the fingerprint, which recognize the rough and fine features, extract them, and then store only these

Figure 1. Market shares of the various biometric systems (Wikipedia, 2010c)

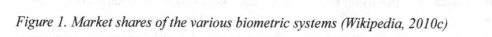

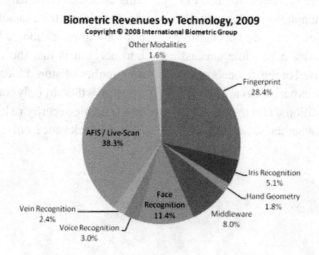

Figure 2. Left loops (Faber, 2010)

features. The advantage is that less data is stored and a comparison of two fingerprint samples is faster. It also creates trust of users as the fingerprint cannot be reproduced on the basis of the stored features (Petermann & Sauter, 2002).

There are several methods for acquiring/scanning a fingerprint. An optical sensor or a capacitive sensor can be used. Likewise, there are acquisition/scanning devices that operate on the basis of ultrasound technology. There are, additionally, other devices that have thermal sensors.

Figure 3. Spirals (Faber, 2010)

Figure 4. Concentric rings (Faber, 2010)

Figure 5. Arches (Faber, 2010)

Optical Sensors

Acquisition/scanning by means of an optical sensor is a relatively intuitive method of fingerprint acquisition/scanning. Stated simply, the finger is photographed by a camera. This occurs by placing the finger on a prism surface. The scanner illuminates this surface with a light source, usually LEDs. The camera records the image of the finger lines through the different light reflections of the epidermal ridges lying on the surface and the furrows or valleys found between them, which do not touch the support. Here, it is necessary to differentiate whether the scanner uses an optical reflexive or an optical scattering sensor. With the former, the lines on the finger are represented because a total reflection occurs from all areas that do not touch the support surface. The epidermal ridges of the fingerprints are, on the contrary, photocopied as dark surfaces, as they disturb the total reflection of light. With an optical scattering sensor, the reverse is true, a different incidence of light and camera arrangement results in the scattering of the emitted light to those places where the finger touches the support surface. Through this, an inverted image of the finger lines emerges in which the epidermal ridges are represented as light and the furrows as dark (Bromba, 2009; Harris, 2002).

Optical transmissive sensors offer a different possibility. Here, the finger lies on a light-circuit board and is x-rayed by a light source. In most cases, with these scanners, the finger is x-rayed on the back side of the finger by a light source. There are, however, versions of this scanner in which the light sources are mounted on the edges of the scanner, whereby the light hits the finger on the side (Mainguet, 2009a). The support surface prevents the sensor from being touched and at the same time enables an appropriate support so that the light reaches the sensor without loss (Bromba, 2009).

All of the optical sensors cited here could also be built as slide sensors, also known as stripe sen-

sors. In this case, the scanner, which comprises simply a row of sensors, is smaller than the surface to be scanned. In order to scan a fingerprint, the user must therefore move his or her finger over this row of sensors. The sensors thus scan the entire finger bit by bit and subsequently put together the fingerprint from the individual bits of scanned data (Bromba, 2009).

The aforementioned optical scanner types all have the common disadvantage that the finger has to be laid onto a surface for authentication. For example, latent prints are left on such sensors and there are certain concerns on the part of users as to how hygienic the process is. There are, however, also scanner systems that have a non-contact optical sensor. With such systems, there is no prism; instead, the finger is photographed directly. However, this type of scanner is only partly non-contact as here, too, devices must be available to put the finger in the right position and to maintain the correct distance from the scanner. In this way, latent prints are indeed prevented, but the description as non-contact is only partly justified (Bromba, 2009; Mainguet, 2009a). A further disadvantage arises through minor influencing of the scanner by impurities found on the scanner surface or on the user's finger. Wounds and scars can also lead to problems in recognizing a person.

Advantages of optical sensors are, mainly, their high degree of maturity as well as their high picture quality. A further advantage, mainly in comparison with capacitive scanners, is optical scanners' lack of sensitivity to an electrostatic discharge, which can easily occur when people are charged with frictional electricity.

Capacitive Sensors

Whereas with optical sensors a picture of the finger lines is created with the help of a light source that x-rays or photographs the finger, capacitive sensors use the skin's conducting abilities to generate a corresponding picture (Marcialis & Roli, 2008). With capacitive sensors, there is one electrode for each pixel. The scanner thus comprises a multitude of electrodes. The finger laid on the device forms the second electrode whereby a great number of condensers are created. The dielectric (isolating level between the two electrodes of a condenser) is water or air depending on whether an epidermal ridge is lying on it or not. If there is no ridge on an electrode (a pixel), then the dielectric is air, whereby the capacity is less than for electrodes that hit upon an epidermal ridge. A capacitive scanner graphically depicts this difference in capacity giving rise to a picture of the finger lines (Bromba, 2009; Wikipedia, 2010d).

A special form of capacitive sensor is the so-called luminescent capacitive sensors. In this case, optical sensors employ a picture sensor chip to register the picture of the finger's lines. However, the picture is not generated with the help of a light source, but rather, based on the same principle as other capacitive scanners. The only difference is that with these scanners an electroluminescent film is used with a transparent electrode. The finger serves here again as a counter electrode. The electroluminescent film now illuminates those areas where there are epidermal ridges more strongly as the electrical field is the strongest in these areas. In this way, again a picture of the finger lines emerges, which is registered by the picture sensor chip (Bromba, 2009).

Like optical scanners, capacitive scanners can also be built as swipe sensors. The difference once again is that the user must move his or her finger over the row of sensors. Here, too, the individual data is put together again as a total picture.

A serious disadvantage of capacitive scanners, however, is their susceptibility to electrostatic discharge. A person can, for example, become charged with static electricity simply by walking across a carpet. This electrical charge can discharge upon touching the scanner and damage it (Mainguet, 2009a; Wikipedia, 2010e).

Ultrasound Systems

Ultrasound systems operate according to a principle similar to optical scanners with the difference being that instead of emitting electromagnetic waves of the visible spectrum (light), they emit acoustic waves in the ultrasound realm. An ultrasound scanner is thus built from a series of transceivers that present a combination of transmitter and receiver. These send a short ultrasound impulse and then immediately switch to receive mode to receive the echo reflected by the finger. The signals thus received are subsequently converted into a corresponding image (Optel, 2002).

One of the greatest advantages of ultrasound systems is that the ultrasound waves penetrate the topmost layer of skin (epidermis) and thereby read the fingerprint from the underlying layer of skin (dermis) (Mainguet, 2009a). A further advantage of ultrasound systems arises from precisely this property: they are not affected by epidermal injuries or impurities (Optel, 2002). Disadvantages of this type of fingerprint scanner are the high cost of production and the duration of a scan procedure, which can take up to a few seconds (Mainguet, 2009a).

Thermal Sensors

Thermal sensors consist of a pyroelectric material that transforms temperature differences into electrical potential. Yet what is measured in this is not the difference in temperature between the epidermal ridges and the furrows. Instead, the sensor registers temperature changes that are cause by the contact of the sensor's surface with the finger, and are clearly defined. In those places where the skin does not touch the sensor (furrows), the temperature remains nearly constant. Through this difference, the scanner can acquire a picture of the fingerprint lines. A limitation does arise in such scanners in that the temperature of the finger and that of the scanner surface align within a fraction of a second, so that it is only possible to acquire a picture within a brief moment. For this reason, thermal scanners are built as swipe scanners compelling the user to move his or her finger over the scanner. In this way, the scanned area of the finger remains on the sensor for a brief time only and the scanner is able to capture the fingerprint.

SECURITY OF FINGERPRINT SCANNERS

The following section provides details on the reliability of a system's security by means of a fingerprint scanner, that is, how good the FAR and the FRR actually are when the attempt is made to penetrate the system with a dummy. This is meant to show if it is possible, and if so, how difficult it is to fool a fingerprint scanner. For this purpose, tests with various scanners were made. The goal was to outwit the scanner with prepared fingerprint dummies in order to gain access to the system protected by the scanner. In contrast to the already existing articles such as (Blommé, 2003; Chaos Computer Club, 2004; Marcialis & Roli, 2008; Feltin, 2002; Bergadano, Gunetti, & Picardi, 2002; Hein & Mahrla, 2004; Kaseva & Stén, 2003; Kleine-Albers, Tokar, & Uhe, 2006; Matsumoto et al., 2002; Thalheim, Krissler, & Ziegler, 2002; Van der Putte & Keuning, 2000). We precisely document the materials and instruments used in the tests. This will facilitate readers' reconstruction of the results, as well as a possible reproduction of the tests or individual steps therein.

Fingerprint Scanners Used

In the experiments, several fingerprint scanners were used to derive the most general possible statements from the tests. Only a few of the hitherto studies mention exactly which scanners were

fooled. For that reason, the tests have been carried out on a device with an optical full surface sensor as well as one with a capacitive swipe sensor in order to cover both possible scanner designs:

- Microsoft Fingerprint Reader (optical full surface scanner)
- Digitus Desktop Biometric Fingerprint Reader (capacitive swipe scanner)

Microsoft Fingerprint Reader

This device is a full surface optical fingerprint scanner. With the software (Digital Persona) delivered with the device, the scanner can be used to log onto the system by fingerprint or to log onto diverse websites storing and encrypting the username and password with the fingerprint. The device affordable for a typical home user (at the time of writing, it was approx. 40 Euro).

Digitus Desktop Biometric Fingerprint Reader

The Digitus Fingerprint Reader was selected for similar reasons as the Microsoft Fingerprint Reader: the device is inexpensive to purchase (at the time of writing, approx. 35 Euro) and readily available. A further aspect was the construction of the device; the second test device should have capacitive sensors and be constructed as a swipe scanner. This is important because on today's laptop market an increasing number of products are equipped with such a scanner.

Similar to Microsoft Fingerprint Reader, unfortunately no technical data or reference values, such as FAR or FRR, are delivered along with this device. Admittedly, some of these data can be gathered from the manufacturer's homepage (Digitus, 2010). A False Accept Rate (FAR) for the Digitus Fingerprint Reader of less than 1:100000 and a recognition time of less than one second are hereby given.

Fingerprint Taking

In order to fool a fingerprint scanner, one naturally has to have a dummy (aka as artificial finger), which should have the same characteristics as the natural finger of the person that one wants to impersonate (aka the victim). The most fundamental characteristic to be recreated is the structure of the finger itself—its epidermal ridges. Many fingerprint scanners do not work with the entire fingerprint, but instead, only with the so-called minutiae points. Yet since it is difficult to recreate these alone, as a rule, the entire print is remolded.

Normally, one must therefore first try to gain hold of an object that the victim has previously touched and thereby left fingerprints on. In this, naturally the type and texture of the object plays a decisive role. Furthermore, care should be taken that the object has been touched exclusively by the victim to avoid processing a fingerprint from an entirely different person in the further course of the operation, which for obvious reasons is not desirable. Additionally, the object should be one that that the victim has not touched too often, or the problem may arise that individual fingerprints overlap making it difficult to obtain any useable fingerprints.

Influence of the Surface Texture on the Taking of Fingerprints

As already mentioned, the texture of the acquired object is crucial. Depending on the surface, one must decide on the process (powder or steam) for making the fingerprint visible, or decide whether the surface of the object even allows obtaining a fingerprint with simple means. As an easy, basic rule, one can say that objects with smooth surfaces, such as various glass surfaces (for example, drinking glasses), as well as metal surfaces (for example, door handles) are much more suitable for taking fingerprints than rough or patterned surfaces. In such cases, one can often only obtain partial prints.

In addition, the color of the object should be as uniform as possible to facilitate digitizing of the print in a further step.

Graphite Powder

Clearly the most common method for making fingerprints appear is to sprinkle the fingerprint with graphite powder (Chaos Computer Club, 2004), as occurs in law enforcement and can be seen frequently in films. This was also one of the methods used in this study for making fingerprints visible. The reason for this was that the application of this method is not difficult to learn and with a bit of practice, entirely useful results can be achieved. A further reason important for this study was the ready availability of graphite powder, which is used, for example, to grease door locks.

In order to make a fingerprint visible with this method, a bit of graphite powder must be carefully distributed on the spot where one detects, or at least suspects the fingerprint to be located. A soft hairbrush is best suitable for application of the powder. Here, it is important not to press down too much on the brush when distributing the powder or the fingerprint will smear and be rendered unusable. Once the powder is distributed, one carefully blows away the extra powder from the object. Although this process proves less trivial than initially imagined, with a bit of practice it is possible to use this method and extract satisfactory fingerprints with graphite powder. For all of the tests using graphite powder, the powder Graphit from the firm Pressol (no. 10 589) was used.

Steaming with Cyanoacrylate

This method of making fingerprints visible is meanwhile also well known from different police shows on television. In these series, the object on which the fingerprint is suspected is steamed with a chemical in an airtight chamber and after a certain time, the fingerprint becomes visible. The chemical cyanoacrylate (Chaos Computer Club, 2004) is, for example, an ingredient in many types of super glue. Fingerprints can thus be made visible with little effort in that one turns a cover of sorts over the spot where the fingerprint is suspected. On the inside of this cover, a bit of superglue is applied. One can therewith steam a fingerprint using such a simple method.

Making fingerprints visible by this method rests on a chemical process in which the chemical's steam reacts to the fat residues from the fingerprint (attach to the fat particles). The sediments of this chemical visible on the fat residues thus deliver a usable fingerprint.

This method, too, requires some practice as it is easy to apply too much glue in which case it will drop down from the cover onto the surface, rendering the fingerprint useless. In addition, it is important to assure that the seal made by the cover over the appropriate spot is as airtight as possible, or in most cases, the desired result will fail to materialize. After several attempts, one can already judge quite accurately how much glue to use and how to choose a cover and what it should be made of. In the context of this study, we used Super Glue 1200 from the firm Wiko as well as the glue Superkleber from the firm Loctite. Both delivered nearly identical results.

Digitizing Fingerprints

After the fingerprints have been taken from the acquired object, or made visible, they must be digitized to enable further processing on the computer. Therefore, depending on the method used, it may be necessary to mirror the acquired fingerprint. It may also be necessary to digitally enhance the picture of the fingerprint. To do all of this, the fingerprint must first be digitized. Two different methods, which will be described later in greater detail, were used in order to achieve this in the tests. One problem encountered with all of

the methods presented is the correct recording of the size of the print. For this, it makes sense to place a ruler to the side and under the print when photographing so that one can later derive also the size of the print. Without this information, it becomes much more difficult to print out the fingerprint correctly for producing a mold for the dummy.

Photographing Fingerprints

A simple method for digitizing a fingerprint is to photograph it (Chaos Computer Club, 2004). At first this sounds quite simple, but in the execution it is not as easy as it seems. For example, one must consider that when collecting a fingerprint, it is advantageous for the object to have a smooth surface but when photographing the fingerprint, this surface can become a disadvantage as smooth surfaces usually reflect light strongly. If the use of a flash is required, then one must take care that the flash does not hit the surface directly as this commonly leads to reflections.

In the tests, several digital cameras were used to photograph the fingerprints:

- Sony Cybershot DSC-T3 (snapshot camera)
- LeicaDigilux 1 (compact camera)
- Nikon D300 (digital reflex camera)

At first, the attempt was made to take the photos freehand as it cannot be assumed that the average user has a tripod. However, it soon became apparent that the epidermal ridges (or minutiae points) of the fingerprints have too fine of a pattern, which easily become fuzzy and blurred in freehand photos. For that reason, in the later course of the tests, a tripod and a repro table were used to make precise photos of the fingerprints. An attempt was thus made to take photos of various fingerprints on different backgrounds. All photos were taken under normal interior lighting conditions with the device's own flash or with an external flash (for the Nikon D300, only). The shutter speeds necessary for interior lighting (without a flash) were, however, too long, and most of the photos were blurry. Use of a flash was a problem in that it created a reflection on the glass surface holding the fingerprint. Therefore the photos on the repro table were shot using two daylight lamps (5300 Kelvin) without a flash.

Furthermore, the photos of the prints were taken in color and (to the extent that the camera allowed) in black-and-white, or grayscale. In the later course of the tests, however, it proved advantageous to photograph the prints in color as otherwise pictorial information is lost already in the recording.

Scanning in Fingerprints

A further method for digitizing a fingerprint that has been made visible is to scan the print (Chaos Computer Club, 2004). In the tests carried out, two types of scanners were used—two desktop scanners and a slide scanner. The object on which the print is located must have a flat surface and cannot exceed a certain maximum size (or a potential maximum weight). With the slide scanner, these limitations are even stricter as it must be possible to stretch the object to be scanned into a slide frame. Thus, as a rule, after the fingerprint has been made visible, it is necessary to remove it with an adhesive film (or adhesive tape) and subsequently stick this to a backing film and continue to work with that. The backing film can then be cut appropriately for all necessary forms and sizes so that it fits, for example, into a slide frame. However, this method has the disadvantage that gathering the print with adhesive film must be successful on the first attempt, as usually, the original print is destroyed. This was less of a problem, as in most cases we worked with cooperative victims. In the case of an unsuspecting victim, however, one often has only one single useable fingerprint, which means that destroying it would present a serious problem.

Desktop Scanner

For this, we used two devices: the ScanJet 5300c from Hewlett-Packard with an optical resolution of 1200 dpi and the Pixma M610 from Canon.

The advantage of using a desktop scanner as opposed to a slide scanner is that even larger surfaces can be scanned directly. Although here, care must be taken that the print is not wiped away when placed onto the scanner. If the object on which the fingerprint is found is not flat or small enough, however, then also here the fingerprint first has to be collected on adhesive film and then applied to a backing film. In consideration of the mentioned danger of wiping away the fingerprint, such a procedure is likewise advisable for small, flat objects.

Slide Scanner

The slide scanner used was the Coolscan V ED from Nikon. An advantage over desktop scanners is, for one, the very high resolution (optical resolution of 4000 ppi), but mainly that the print to be scanned cannot slip since it is stretched in the slide frame and thereby automatically lies flat. At the same time, this presents a disadvantage as all objects on which prints are found that should be scanned, must first be put in the correct form and size (slide frame). Here, care must be taken that the print is not retrospectively contaminated, smeared, or distorted when stretched into the slide frame.

Processing Digitized Fingerprints

The retouching or enhancing of the digitized fingerprints is not mentioned in detail in any of the related work. In digitizing the prints, as a rule, the contrast between the epidermal ridges that are made visible and the background is not strong enough, which means that there is not enough contrast distinguishing the spaces between the epidermal ridges from the rest of the fingerprint in a print of the fingerprint that has not been edited by means of an appropriate program. It is essential to have sufficient contrasts as one must print the obtained fingerprint on film, so that the interstitial spaces are translucent. With poor contrast, it can occur that the interstitial spaces are not colorless, but rather, depicted as gray tones and correspondingly printed. A further problem can arise if the fingerprint has no uniform background color, but instead, is present on a photo, for example, or for other reasons it is possible to see several colors or structures (for instance, wood). In this case, a further retouching would be necessary to separate the fingerprint from the background. In the following, we will examine the programs used in the attempt to improve the fingerprints and will show which methods are more promising and which less promising for doing so. Here we will look only at digitized pictures of prints with a uniform background.

Retouching Methods

Before dealing with the issue of the method and achievable results of concrete programs, sketched out in brief in the following sections are the basic operations that were used in the tests (Kleine-Albers, Tokar, & Uhe, 2006). Most of these methods proved very useful in the tests, with the exception of sharpening of contours (in Adobe Photoshop). One could, of course, also achieve useful results with other methods. The methods presented here, however, made it possible to achieve the desired results in nearly all of the pictures. Some of the methods also proved essential in the production of a useful result picture. For example, in general, thresholding is indispensable for obtaining a printable black-and-white version of the image.

Gray Level Adjustment/ Histogram Adjustment

The gray level (also called histogram level) adjustment creates an increase in the contrast of grayscale images (Wikipedia, 2010f; Kleine-Albers, Tokar, & Uhe, 2006). This rests on the fact that in such pictures, often only a minimum range of possible grayscale values from the entire range of gray values is present. Through gray level adjustment, the gray values present are extended to the entire possible range of gray values, whereby gray values that were previously close together now lie far from one another, thus increasing the contrast. This operation also facilitates further processing of the image, as it is easier to select the individual areas based on the gray values.

High Pass Filter

A high pass filter is applied to a frequency spectrum and allows only a certain part of this spectrum to pass through (Barthel, 2007). Applied to a picture, only those parts of the picture that lie above a defined border frequency can pass through while all areas of the image that lie below this frequency are heavily muted. Put simply, in this way, the high pass filter emphasizes strong contrasts thereby suppressing a gradual change in gray values.

Thresholding (Conversion To A Binary Image)

Conversion to a binary image generates a black-and-white picture from a gray level or color image. This occurs through so-called thresholding (Wikipedia, 2010g). In this, the user sets a threshold value defining a point from which the gray level or color values of the picture are to be mapped as black or white. This is necessary as the fingerprint must be printed on a film for etching on circuit boards in order to produce a mold for a dummy. For this purpose, the image must be composed solely of black (light impermeable) parts and white (or transparent) parts that allow light through.

Sharpening of Contours

In this operation, a program attempts to automatically find contours in the picture and sharpen them, while all other areas are left in their current state (Kleine-Albers, Tokar, & Uhe, 2006). Since a fingerprint consists of epidermal ridges, a program that has this function should be able to easily detect these as contours, permitting fast, satisfactory results. In the course of the tests, however, it turned out that this operation only rarely led to the desired result.

Processing with Simple Graphics Programs

Since this work is also meant to test whether it is possible to produce dummies using simple means, this section also tests simple programs in terms of their suitability for processing digitized fingerprints. The concrete programs tested here were Paint and Gimp, as Paint is delivered with Windows and Gimp with many Linux distributions. In addition, a further graphics program, Paint.net, was tested. This program can be downloaded for free from the Internet, and is thereby also available to all users.

Processing with Paint

The Paint program quickly confirmed what was already suspected before proceeding with the tests. The program is not sufficiently suited for an adequate processing of the images and does not allow for a histogram or gray level adjustment or for conversion to a binary image through thresholding. Thus, after just a few tests the program could be definitively excluded as a possibility for processing the images.

Processing with GIMP

In contrast to Paint, Gimp (Gimp, 2010) is not a simple drawing program, but a digital image editing program. In practice, useful results can be achieved through two processes (Kleine-Albers, Tokar, & Uhe, 2006): First, through the operation find contours (with LaPlace, algorithm) with a subsequent inversion and second, by adapting

of the color curves in the dialogue field curves. In both processes, thresholding is carried out as a final step.

Figure 6 shows the picture before the start of the process in a state before any alterations of any kind have been carried out (raw state).

In a first step, the dialogue curves are called up (Figure 7), which presents the histogram of the image and in which the color curves can be altered. With the help of this function, dark colors can be intensified and light colors toned down in order to obtain a better contrast (Figure 8).

Subsequently, the picture was converted into black-and-white by means of thresholding. For this, a threshold value is defined via the corresponding dialogue (Figure 9 and Figure 10).

Now, the second process will also be illustrated. To facilitate a better comparison, we worked here again only with Figure 6 . In this process, the first step was to call up the function "find edges" (Figure 12). Selected here was the algorithm LaPlace. Applying these filters onto the

Figure 6. Initial image

Figure 7. Achieved changes

picture generated a negative image, the edges of this found by the algorithm were highlighted (Figure 13). Compensation was made for this by subsequently performing an inversion. Finally, as in the previously described process, here, too, a thresholding was applied to convert the image to a binary image, which also brought a slight improvement .

Processing with Paint.net

Used in all of the processing steps in this study was Paint.net version 3.36. In practice, two approaches were found that facilitated significant improvement of the picture of the finger's lines. Here, too, we used Figure 6 as initial image. First a conversion to a black-and-white image was carried out. The conversion to black-and-white

Figure 8. Correction of the color curve

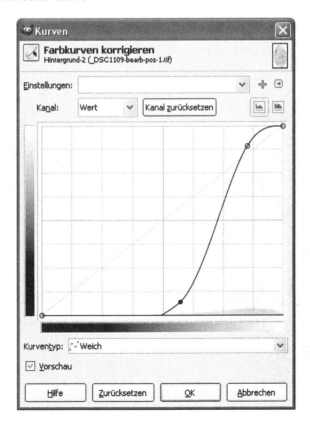

Figure 9. Thresholding

took place automatically here, and the result is shown in Figure 14.

Subsequently, a color level adjustment was carried out by means of the option "levels," under "adjustments" (Figure 16). This operation enables

obtaining significantly better contours as compared with the black-and-white image (Figure 15).

Finally, an additional posterization was carried out. However, the improvements achieved by this

Figure 10. End result

Figure 11. Inversion

Figure 12. Filter "find edges"

Figure 13. Result

Figure 14. Conversion to black-and-white in Paint.net

Figure 15. Results of color adjustment

were hardly visible to the naked eye (Figure 17 and Figure 18).

Another version of this process is to use the option "curves" under the menu item "adjustments". It is possible to have the dark areas depicted even darker and the light areas even lighter. In our example, a satisfactory result was obtained using the curve shown in Figure 19 and Figure 20. Subsequently, a posterization is carried out here, too. The achieved improvements are, once again, barely perceptible.

Processing with Professional Graphics Programs

In contrast to the last section, we tested also the possibilities for retouching a digitized fingerprint with professional graphics programs.

Processing with Adobe Photoshop

One of the most widespread graphics programs is Adobe Photoshop. In this study, the images were retouched using the version Adobe Photoshop CS 3. We first converted the image to a gray-value image (function "grayscale" or by setting the levers of the individual color channels appropriately). It turned out that this was not absolutely necessary and editing could also be carried out directly on the color photo.

At first, experiments were undertaken on the individual images to determine which image applications and filters would lead to the best results. In the first tests with significant results, the filter "sharpening of contours" was simply applied several times (Kleine-Albers, Tokar, & Uhe, 2006). Although this did indeed lead to the improvement of several images, the results achieved were not nearly as positive as we hoped.

Better results were later obtained using the function "color correction" (gray level adjustment), if the images were processed using this function and finally converted into binary images via "thresholding" (threshold value process) (Kleine-Albers, Tokar, & Uhe, 2006). In most cases, this led to satisfactory results. Similarly positive results were obtained by using a high pass filter with a successive thresholding process (Kleine-Albers, Tokar, & Uhe, 2006). It was not possible to determine which of these two methods

Figure 16. Color level adjustments in Paint.net

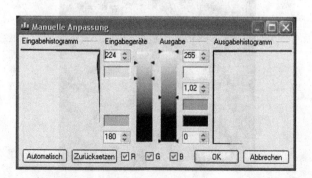

Figure 17. Results of the posterization

led to a better image in each case, as this varied in the tests from image to image.

In Figure 21, the image can be seen before the individual steps in the editing process. The only process that the image has undergone is the removal of the irrelevant image parts (those that are not part of the fingerprint). In this phase, the structures are very faint and not very recognizable. Nonetheless, in the histogram of the image it is possible to see that most of the colors lie very close together.

Thus, for the first step, a histogram scaling was carried out (Figure 22). In Photoshop, this operation can be achieved through color correction. The small area of the scale, which holds the most color parts, can be spread over the entire scale, making the granulation of the color differences finer and the histogram thereby flatter.

Figure 23 shows the effect of the histogram scaling on the image of the fingerprint. The colors present are now much more intense and the structures, too, are more recognizable.

For the further processing of the fingerprint image and the printing on film required in this, the fingerprint must be converted to a binary image. This occurs as previously explained through the use of the so-called thresholding process. For this, a reference value is chosen for the given color values in the picture. As a result of the operation, all color values that are higher than the reference value are illustrated in white in the image; all values that are lower are illustrated in black. Figure 24 shows the selection of the reference point. In this way, the reference value can be defined in the relevant dialogue box by either entering a concrete value or positioning the arrow below the histogram. In this, it proved helpful to activate the preview option and simply try out different ways of finding the ideal reference point for the respective image.

Figure 25 ultimately shows the result of the thresholding and, at the same time, the final result of image editing: a fingerprint image in which clearly structured epidermal ridges can be recognized and which, through conversion to a binary image, consists of the colors black-and-white only. It can therefore be printed out and used for the exposure of a circuit board.

The high pass filter can be used as an alternative to this procedure. This process, as a rule,

Figure 18. Posterizein Paint.net

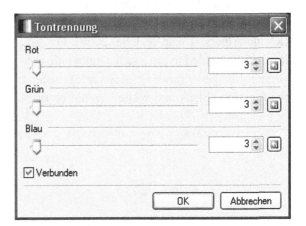

Figure 19. Result after adjustment of the curve

leads to similarly favorable and in part even better results. Furthermore, its application is much easier. In order to edit an image in Photoshop with this procedure, the high pass filter must simply be applied to the original image (in this case, again the picture from Figure 21: Image and histogram) (filter -> special filter -> high pass). Subsequently, here, too, thresholding can be used to create a binary image (image -> application -> threshold value) that is suitable for further editing (Figure 26 and Figure 27).

Another method of attaining a suitable result in Photoshop is to convert to a grayscale image (Kleine-Albers, Tokar, & Uhe, 2006). For this, it is recommended to not use the automatic conversion (image -> mode -> gray scale). Instead, the function "black-and-white" should be used,

so that the user can define which color channels should be lightened (whiter) and which darkened (Figure 28 and Figure 29). Afterwards, the black-and-white image necessary in the further course of the experiment can be produced using thresholding (Figure 30).

Editing with Adobe Lightroom

For all of the tests carried out with Lightroom, version 2.3 was used. With Lightroom it is not possible to apply a filter or thresholding to a photo of a fingerprint. After several attempts, possibilities were indeed found to improve the quality of a fingerprint image and to correspondingly enhance the image.

The initial image was also converted into a grayscale image. Here, it is necessary to mention that the option for carrying out this conversion was not immediately recognizable could be discovered only after quite some time (Figure 31 and Figure 32).

When this step has been completed, Lightroom offers a multitude of possibilities to further enhance the image. However, what all of these options have in common is that they require a great deal of finesse and patience. Lightroom did not support thresholding (conversion to a pure black-and-white image.

Exposure time and black saturation can be increased or decreased by using the appropriate levers. By further increasing the black saturation, the dark finger lines become clearly visible; the remainder of the image (the furrows of the finger line image) are, however, practically white through the increased light exposure. By adjusting the brightness and contrast levers, in most cases the result can be further improved somewhat. The

Figure 20. Function "curves" in Paint.net

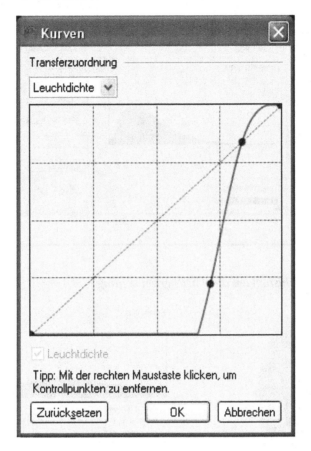

quality of the image likewise increases slightly by raising the "clarity" option lever (Figure 33 and Figure 34).

A further possibility to enhance the image is to apply a gradation curve. For this, it is not pos-

sible to change the curve manually in Adobe Lightroom. Instead, the gradation curve is created in four stages: "depth," "dark color values," "light color values," and "lights," whereby the

Figure 21. Image and histogram before editing

Figure 22. Histogram scaling

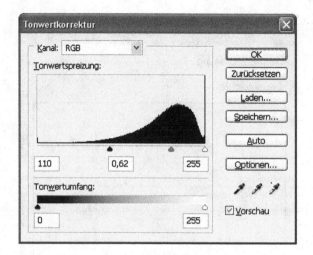

Figure 23. Fingerprint and histogram after histogram scaling

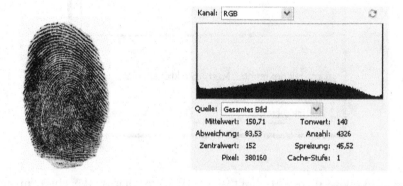

Figure 24. Thresholding--determining the reference point

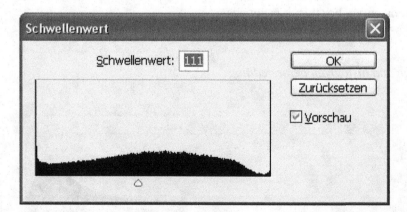

Figure 25. Final result of image processing

Figure 26. Final result after thresholding

Figure 27. High pass filter

Figure 28. Conversion to grayscale

Figure 29. Dialogue box "black and white"

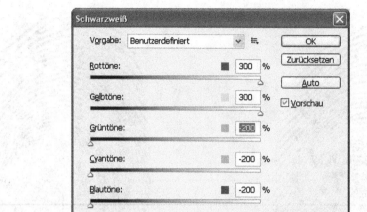

gradation curve must be applied in each of these stages (Figure 35 and Figure 36).

The result can be improved even more when, in addition to the application of the gradation curve, a color level adjustment is performed using the levers below the curve. Through this, some grayscales are eliminated from the image, which creates a more clearly recognizable difference between ridges and furrows of the finger's line image (Figures 37 and 38).

Processing with Capture NX 2

Capture NX (version 2.0.1) is an image processing program from Nikon that is intended primarily for photo editing. At first glance the software did not seem especially suited for the retouching of fingerprint images, because it does not offer any processing options that correspond with a thresholding process. The function "convert to black-and-white" was used from the start in processing color photos. This application option did not allow the user to set the desired threshold

Figure 30. Final result after thresholding

Figure 31. Conversion to grayscale

Figure 32. Raw image

value that indicates from which color code the pixels should be converted into black-and-white; nevertheless, it does create a black-and-white image, which is essential for further editing and use as a template for the circuit board.

Consequently, with Capture NX there were two ways of enhancing the finger line image: for one, by applying a high pass filter, similar to that in Photoshop, for another, through the editing function "color values and curves," which corresponds approximately to the use of the "curves" function in GIMP.

Based on Figure 39, first the adjustment "convert to black-and-white" was carried out, whereby brightness and contrast had to be individually adjusted for each image. In the example here, satisfactory results were obtained with a brightness value of -66 and contrast value +19, as can be seen in Figure 40 and Figure 41.

A high pass filter could now be applied to the obtained binary image (Figure 42 and Figure 43).

A satisfactory result was obtained by changing the settings of the setting option "color values and curves" in the binary image created through the black-white conversion (Figure 44) to achieve a better contrast (Figure 45).

Figure 33. Default settings levers

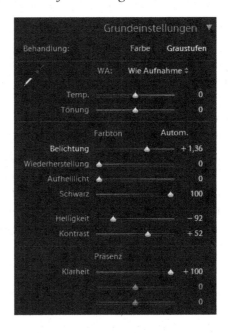

Figure 34. Achieved result

Creating a Model for Fingerprint Dummies

In order to produce fingerprint dummies, first of all, a model must be made with the help of which, the dummies can then ultimately be cast. Assumed in the experiments was, first of all, a cooperative victim (Matsumoto et al., 2002; Van der Putte & Keuning, 2000; Bromba, 2009), which is why also Fimo models and wax models were used in the tests. For this, one can naturally ignore all of the hitherto cited points (acquiring the fingerprint and processing it) and begin directly with building the dummy model. Nonetheless, creating a model from an unsuspecting victim was set as a greater goal (Matsumoto et al., 2002; Van der Putte & Keuning, 2000; Chaos Computer Club, 2004). For this, all of the phases described in the previous sections are necessary to enable model creation.

Creating a Model from Modeling Clay

In the tests, the products Fimo Classic and Fimo Soft from the firm Eberhard Faber GmbH (Faber, 2010) were used as modeling clays as these are readily available and can be easily fired in a hot-air oven for hardening. The production of clay models with a cooperative victim is therefore extremely simple. The "victim" simply has to press a finger firmly enough into a piece of modeling clay which must then be fired according to the instructions (for Fimo Classic and Fimo Soft approx. 30 minutes at 110 degrees Celsius). However, it is important that the finger is not pressed too firmly into the clay as that will make the dummy harder to cast, as more material will be required for pouring out the form, whereby the dummy will take longer to dry and often becomes difficult to separate from the form. Also important is that the finished Fimo mold is fired on a level foundation or the model may possibly become twisted during the firing process thus making it unusable.

Figure 35. Gradiation curve settings

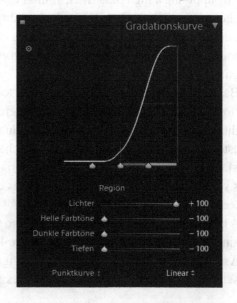

Figure 36. Result of change

Figure 37. Result of gray level adjustment

Creation of Wax Models

The production of models from wax proceeds similar to the procedure with modeling clay. Only the wax must first be heated and the victim's finger must be pressed in the warm wax, which hardens by cooling. Nonetheless, this procedure proved less suitable as the wax model, even in a hardened state, could still be distorted too easily. It also proved to be a hindrance that the finger had to be pressed into the wax until the model had hardened to prevent the wax from running together after removal of the finger. Used in the tests was wax from candles made with stearin from the firm Gala—World of Candles.

Also important in the production of this type of model is that the wax has already cooled slightly before the finger is pressed into it, as otherwise, the cooperative victim might suffer slight burns to the finger when producing the model.

Figure 38. Gray level adjustment

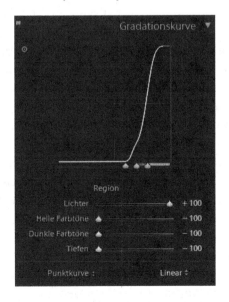

Figure 39. Initial image for Capture NX

Production of Models by Printing on Film

The production of a model by a simple printout of the fingerprint onto a film was attempted because it was cited in a well-known article from the CCC (Chaos Computer Club) as a simple option for faking fingerprints (Chaos Computer Club, 2004). Here, the theory was that by printing a fingerprint onto an overhead transparency using a laser printer, the deposits of the printer would generate enough structure to be able to create a dummy directly from the transparency using wood glue. After several attempts with two different printers (LaserJet 1015 from Hewlett-Packard, LaserJet 4 from Hewlett-Packard) and three different types of overhead transparencies (Overhead Laser Transparencies no. 3552 from Avery Zweckform, LaserJet Transparency Film no. C2936A from Hewlett-Packard, and Lumocolor Laser Printer Film no. 634 LA A4 from Staedtler), this option for the production of dummies turned out to be unrealistic. Not nearly enough structures were generated in any of the tests to enable the production of usable dummies. For that reason, this approach was rejected for use in further tests.

Production of Dummies from Silicon

A further option for the production of dummies was to press the finger in hardening silicon. As a sealant, silicon adapts quite well to all possible forms and contours. However, after just a few attempts it became obvious that this would not work for the creation of models. If the finger is pressed too early in the silicon mass, then the mass does indeed adjust to the finger, but remains stuck so tightly that it is not possible to pull the finger out without destroying the fingerprint. On the contrary, if one waits long enough until the surface of the mass has dried a bit so that it no longer sticks to the finger, it is already too late as the dried surface of the mass no longer adapts to the contours of the finger, meaning that no print is created. For that reason, also this idea was abandoned and no further attempts were made to produce models from silicon. In further tests silicon was used only in the casting of dummies.

Figure 40. Setting the black and white conversion

Figure 41. Results of conversion

Production of Models by Etching Circuit Boards

A further possibility for creating models, which was also frequently mentioned in the already existing papers on the topic, is the etching of (photosensitive) circuit boards (also known as PCBs) (Sandström, 2004; Van der Putte & Keuning, 2000). Used in the tests was one-sided photosensitive base material from the firm Bungard. Such circuit boards are also readily available to amateurs at electrical supplies shops. All of the other utensils needed in the course of production (UV tubes, developer, and etching liquid) can also be purchased at regular electrical supplies shops.

This procedure was originally developed to include the help of a template in the creation of a circuit pattern out of copper on circuit boards for electronic devices. Since the copper circuit pattern on the base material could turn out to be about as thin as the epidermal ridges of fingerprints, this etching process was also of interest for the tests in the context of this study.

As in the production of circuit boards, for the creation of fingerprint models, several steps have to be carried out (Krijnen, 2008):

- Exposing the circuit board
- Developing the photosensitive layer
- Etching the circuit board
- Rinsing and drying the circuit board

When these steps have been successfully completed, a circuit board has been created with a "circuit pattern" displaying the negative image of a fingerprint.

Exposing the Circuit Boards

In order to create a model from circuit boards, first the processed image must be printed out on a film. This film is then applied to the photosensitive side of the circuit board and attached in such a way that it cannot slip. Afterwards, the side of the circuit board thus prepared is treated with UV light, whereby the non-black parts of the fingerprint on the film allow the UV light to pass through thus exposing

Figure 42. Setting the high pass filter

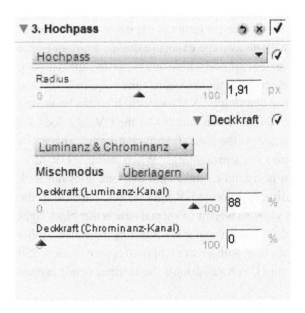

Figure 43. High pass filter results

the photo layer in these areas. Depending on the available financing, either an exposure device or, if that is not foreseen in the available budget, a simple UV fluorescent tube with a corresponding support can be used. In the tests carried out in the framework of this study, an 8W UV tube from the firm Phillips was used. Apart from the costs, there is also a difference between the two possibilities in terms of exposure time. Whereas with an average exposure device a circuit board can be exposed within one to two minutes (in part, even less), the exposure time required with the use of a single UV fluorescent tube can be as long as ten to fifteen minutes, as the UV tube does not beam on the plate directly, but rather, also emits into the surroundings. When using a UV tube, it is crucial to make sure that one does not look directly into the UV light, as it is harmful to the eye. Also worthy of special note is that black light does not present a UV light in the sense of this study as with a wave length of approximately 350 nm (UV-A radiation), the desired result cannot

be achieved. In order to efficiently carry out an exposure, a UV light of approximately 250 nm or less (UV-C radiation) is required.

When exposing the circuit board it is necessary to note the type of photosensitive material attached to the circuit board. Here, a differentiation is made between negative photoresist and positive photoresist. If a negative photoresist is used, then exposed parts remain preserved, whereas with positive photoresist, precisely these parts are etched in the further production process. The fingerprint must be printed out appropriately to ensure that with the template, either the epidermal ridges (positive photoresist) or the gaps between them (negative photoresist) are exposed. Negative photoresist was used in the experiments for this study.

In the tests, the UV light source was applied at different distances from the exposure-ready circuit boards, and set at different exposure times. Proving optimal in the tests was the use of only one UV tube at a distance of nearly 30 cm and an exposure time of 20 to 30 minutes. One can, indeed, decrease the distance to the circuit board in order to save time, however, if the distance is less, the change in degree of radiation of the circuit board is correspondingly faster, and the exposure time must be held much more precisely. Thus, with a distance of 5 centimeters, the difference between the circuit board being overexposed or not is a matter of just a few second, whereas at a distance of 30 centimeters, 5 extra minutes of exposure time have little effect. The combinations of distances and exposure times tried out in the tests can be seen in Table 1.

The exposure was carried out on 40 circuit boards. As can be seen in the table, in the tests some of the circuit boards were exposed for too long, which is why only 35 of the original 40 circuit boards were available for further processing.

Figure 44. Color values and curves settings

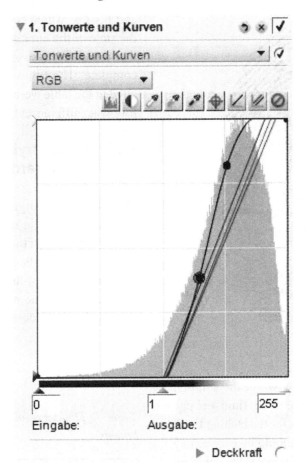

Developing of the Photosensitive Material

After exposure of the circuit board, the photosensitive material must still be developed. For this, a developing solution must be mixed and the circuit boards must be stirred therein for a few minutes. This causes the exposed parts to stand out clearly and secures those parts that should remain preserved when etching.

In the tests on which this study is based, 10 g of caustic soda (sodium hydroxide) dissolved in a liter of water was used as developer. The average developing time of the circuit boards was four minutes, depending also on the degree of exposure. Thus, circuit boards that had been exposed longer could be developed faster than those exposed to the UV radiation for a shorter time.

Etching of the Circuit Boards

Like for developing, a solution for etching was also mixed, in which the circuit boards were placed. Then, the circuit boards had to be carefully stirred in the solution until all non-developed parts had dissolved. When etching, care must be taken that etching solution should be heated and the temperature should be maintained during the

Figure 45. Fingerprint after adjustment

the attempt was made to not waste any of the circuit boards, which is why after the given times, the state of the circuit board was assessed, but it then remained in the solution until the etching was complete. The times and etching temperatures cited in the table were used in these tests, and the following differences hereby established (Table 2).

Rinsing and Drying of the Circuit Board

The rinsing and drying of the circuit board is summarized here in one step, as these steps are simply included for the sake of thoroughness. The circuit board must be entirely rinsed after etching to ensure that all of the etching fluid is removed and that no residue remains. Finally, the board must be dried in order to continue working with it.

entire etching process. How warm the solution should be, depends on the etching fluid and can be found on the instructions for the etching fluid. As a rule, the temperature should be between 35 and 55 degrees Celsius. The cooler the solution, the longer the etching process. To maintain the temperature of the etching solution, it is useful to place the dish with the etching fluid in a water bath in which the water is heated or in which warm water is constantly flowing in. The duration of the etching varies according to the etching fluid and base material, as well as the temperature of the etching solution, and can take up to 45 minutes. Care must be taken as most etching fluids are poisonous and therefore must be disposed of as hazardous waste.

Ammonium persulfate was used as etching fluid in the tests performed for this study. A total of 35 circuit boards were etched at different temperatures. For 10 of the boards, the temperature was 30° Celsius, for ten it was 40° Celsius, and for the remaining 15 circuit boards, the etching temperature was raised to 50° Celsius. Naturally,

Table 1. Distance and time in exposing circuit boards

Distance from circuit board (cm)	Exposure time (hours)	Remarks
50	2	Exposure time much too long—the entire circuit board (including covered parts) was exposed.
50	1	Exposure time to long—also covered parts were, in part, exposed.
50	0.5	Exposure time too short resulting in etching of parts of the covered area.
30	1	Exposure time too long—also covered parts were, in part, exposed.
30	0.5	Circuit board exposure complete
30	0.16	Exposure time too short resulting in etching of parts of the covered area.
5	0.5	Exposure time too long
5	0.16	Circuit board properly exposed

Table 2. Temperature and duration of etching of circuit boards

Etching temperature (C)	Etching time (minutes)	Remarks
30°	15	Etching period clearly too short—photosensitive layer barely dissolved
30°	25	Noticeable improvement as compared with 15 minutes—although still too brief
30°	45	Photosensitive layer well dissolved—etching of circuit board complete
40°	15	Etching period too short—circuit board not entirely etched
40°	25	In rare cases is time period too brief, in most cases, etching of the circuit board is complete.
40°	45	The entire time of 45 minutes was never fully used as all circuit boards were already completely etched before the end of the time period.
50°	15	In two tests, 15 minutes were already sufficient to finish the etching of the circuit boards, all others required more time.
50°	25	In all but 3 of the test runs, all circuit boards could be etched within 25 minutes at 50° Celsius.
50°	45	Only 3 circuit boards required more than 25 minutes at 50° Celsius, the proposed 45 minutes were, however, not required.

Casting Dummies

When a model has been created, it can be used to produce an "artificial finger". To achieve this, various materials were used in this process, which in part are also mentioned in other literature (Chaos Computer Club, 2004; Matsumoto et al., 2002; Marcialis & Roli, 2008; Sandström, 2004; Van der Putte & Keuning, 2000). Here, attention was primarily on differences between the various materials.

Casting with Wood Glue

Molding the prints with wood glue worked very well in the experiments. However, care should be taken not to use too much glue so as to prevent long drying times. For this reason, it is not advisable to use wood glue to fill a too deeply formed model in which the finger was pushed too firmly into the modeling clay. The glue dries too slowly in such a model and in most cases it is very difficult to free the dummy from the model without damaging it.

A further disadvantage of wood glue dummies is that they become rigid and stiff after a short time, and can thereby be used only under certain conditions; they also break easily. Depending on the amount of glue and the storage location, the time that elapses before breakage of the dummy can vary from a few days to several weeks.

Casting with Silicon

Silicon also appeared suitable for producing dummies due to its qualities and texture, thus it was examined more closely in the experiments (Van der Putte & Keuning, 2000). It nonetheless became evident during the tests that it is necessary to take care in terms of the kind of silicon used. Thus, for example, it was not possible to produce dummies when testing with a type of silicon used in construction work (Classic Bausilikon [construction silicon] made by Ayrton for Obi), as this did not dry out properly and had too little cohesion. This led to two problems: on the one hand, the dummies frequently tore when being freed from the molds; on the other hand, they remained sticky and never dried completely, rendering them unusable. Therefore, a different silicon sealing compound was used in further tests (the transparent silicon Neutral 120 made by Ramsauer Dichtstoffe).

One advantage of silicon over wood glue is that it remains flexible also after drying, which means that silicon dummies are usable for a longer period. The surface of the silicon mass also dried out faster.

However, it was not really possible to determine whether the entire compound had already dried. A further difficulty when using silicon is filling the molds. This can be done easily enough using a silicon injection gun, but care must be taken that the silicon is well distributed and that the surface of the mold is completely covered. If this is not the case, it may result in the compound not taking on the contours of the model, making the resulting dummy thereby unusable. A further problem can result from the silicon mass in part binding too firmly with the mold, so that upon freeing the dummy, parts of the compound remain stuck to the mold, tearing holes in the dummy, likewise rendering it unusable. To counteract this, it may be helpful to rub some greasy cream into the molds before filling them. However, care must be taken to apply the cream very thinly so that the silicon can still assume the contours of the model.

Casting with Gelatin (Blommé, 2003; Matsumoto et al., 2002; Sandström, 2004)

When producing dummies using gelatin, care must be taken to use the correct type of gelatin. The experiments thus showed that significant differences exist between instant gelatin (Instant Gelatin 30 g from Haas was used) and the use of gelatin leaves (here, "Gelatin weiß 12 Blatt" from Dr. Oetker was used). It was not possible to produce dummies with instant gelatin by following the manufacturer's preparation instructions, as the gelatin thus produced tore too easily, making it nearly impossible to free a complete dummy from the mold without destroying it in the process. In contrast, gelatin leaves enabled the creation of very good dummies when following the manufacturer's instructions. They could be easily freed from the mold, and also dried very quickly. The relevant experiments with instant gelatin showed that better results can be obtained by disregarding the manufacturer's instructions and using less water than indicated. Thus, instead

of the suggested 250 ml, just 30 to 40 ml was used. Care had to be taken with both kinds of gelatin to ensure, if possible, that no bubbles formed in the substance as otherwise this would lead to an unusable dummy.

One frequently cited positive aspect of gelatin is that the dummy can be eaten after the finger scanner has been successfully deceived, thus destroying any evidence. At the same time, the edibility of gelatin is also a disadvantage, as, like other foods, gelatin tends to develop mold. Dummies made of gelatin can thus only be used shortly after they are made and cannot be kept for any long period of time for later use. A further disadvantage is that gelatin dummies tend to melt and dissolve when heated. In the tests, body warmth proved sufficient for this to occur, which means that a corresponding dummy can only be attached to a finger for a short period of time before it begins to melt and become unusable.

Another problem that may arise when producing dummies using gelatin is that the gelatin becomes highly liquid after coming to a boil. While this may be an advantage with models made of modeling clay, as the gelatin fits the model exactly, this feature turns into a problem, for instance, when one wishes to cast models etched from circuit boards. The gelatin often runs off too much, making it advisable to limit the area to be cast; for example, by creating a border with adhesive tape, thus preventing the gelatin from running off.

Casting of Dummies with Melted Gummi Bears

When discussing the casting of dummies from gelatin, several articles mention that gelatin is the material from which gummi bears are made. Although it is not explicitly stated in any of the studies that gummi bears were melted and used for experiments to produce dummies, it seemed logical to also conduct an experiment using this material. Hence, several test runs involved melting Goldbären made by Haribo and then attempting to pour the resulting viscous compound into the molds. In the first attempts, the gummi bears were dissolved without the need to add other substances. However, it quite quickly became apparent that this undertaking was doomed to failure as the compound was too sticky. So even filling the models caused problems, and removing the dummies after the compound had dried proved impossible. The compound had coalesced too greatly with the model, making it then also very difficult to clean the model molds.

In a second experiment, an attempt was made to overcome the problem by dissolving the gummi bears in five teaspoonfuls of water. The resulting compound was indeed less sticky and more fluid. Filling the models was then possible without further complications. However, freeing the dummies from the molds once again proved problematic. The dummy could be detached from the mold, but it ripped apart too easily and was thus destroyed.

Casting with Wax

A further possible method of making a dummy is to pour a model using wax. Here, too, the wax used came from quality candles containing stearin from Gala—World of Candles. To produce the corresponding dummies, hot wax had to be dripped into the finished model mold. However, it soon became apparent from the tests that while wax adapts well to the model, it is almost impossible to free the hardened wax from the model without destroying the wax dummy at the same time. The few dummies that could be freed from the model proved, moreover, to be too hard for any actual use. For this reason, no further experiments were done using wax dummies.

Casting with Handicraft Glue

Another material that is suitable for producing fingerprint dummies is handicraft glue. Used for this purpose was the glue Bastelkleber no. 47735 manufactured by UHU. The characteristics of this glue are similar to those of wood glue, meaning that similar disadvantages also apply. For example, it is also difficult to ascertain whether the dummy is fully dried out when using handicraft glue.

One advantage over wood glue, however, is that dummies made with handicraft glue remain flexible for a longer time and thereby do not crack so quickly.

Testing the Dummies

At the beginning of the experiments, a multitude of dummies were made using a combination of the options explained in the previous sections. Work was conducted with a test person as an assenting victim and Fimo polymer clay as well as wax models were produced. Also, the scenario of an unsuspecting victim was played out, in which the test person leaves behind fingerprints on a glass surface. The fingerprints were made visible using the previously described means and methods, digitized, then edited with a graphics program, printed out, and finally etched onto a circuit board as a template. More than one test person was drawn upon, of course, and also the fingerprints of a man and a woman were used for both the polymer clay and wax models and for the exposing of circuit boards to ensure that the results remained applicable in general rather than enabling statements to be made only about one special fingerprint. Also, in this way an attempt was made to exclude gender-specific differences that could influence the test results. One such difference, for example, would be the more subtle epidermal ridges of a female test person, which may lead to problems with correct recognition (Optel, 2002).

In order to etch the model from the circuit board, used was a combination of all above-mentioned variants of making the fingerprint visible, through to the digitization of the same to the subsequent editing of it on a PC. Thus, some of the fingerprints were processed on a glass plate using graphite powder, with the rest being steamed in using cyanoacrylate. Unfortunately, it was not possible to carry out both methods on one and the same fingerprint. The fingerprints that were made visible were both photographed and taken off with adhesive film, and then scanned in. In this process, all previously mentioned cameras and scanners were used. All of the resulting digitized images of the fingerprints were reworked (with the programs in section 4.4) so as to represent the lines of the fingers more clearly and thus enable the creation of good templates for exposing the circuit boards. The models created in this way were then printed out on film, with only the best models subsequently being used for additional experiments.

The methods used in the individual working steps described in the previous sections could now be combined in diverse ways. For example, a single fingerprint can be made visible in two ways. There are then, in turn, two options for digitizing this (taking a photograph or scanning). The digitized fingerprint can be retouched in any of the introduced programs (whereby there are, in turn, several ways of editing in many of the programs). In the first ten tests in which all of these combinations were tried out, at least ten film templates were thus created from the fingerprint left behind by the test person; in the case of particularly good quality prints, as many as eighteen templates. After the initial attempts it soon became clear that the fastest image editing was achieved with Adobe Photoshop, and also the best results. This experience was taken into consideration in later tests, which explains why the acquired fingerprints were edited exclusively in Adobe Photoshop.

With the film templates that resulted from this, the circuit boards were exposed and then developed and etched. The production of models from modeling clay and wax presented no problems and entailed little effort.

It would not be possible to make general statements about the usefulness of the models if there were only one dummy of each kind, therefore, various examples were made from the wax and Fimo polymer clay models. Although several examples had already been made of the molds on circuit boards, all the production phases were run through a number of times, as findings were also to be made concerning the individual steps in acquiring, digitizing, and reworking the fingerprints. The results and findings of these experiments can be read about in the corresponding sections of this study.

Subsequently, it was attempted to create dummies from all finished models (out of modeling clay, wax, and circuit boards) using wood glue, silicon, and also gelatin. Here too, several dummies were made from every model and material to facilitate accurate statements concerning the models. Here, too, specific information concerning the usability of individual materials for making dummies, or about the findings gained during the tests can be read in the relevant sections.

Since several dummies were made in the tests, as just described, these of course had to be likewise tested on the fingerprint scanners in order to find out whether the scanners can, in fact, be deceived as easily as predicted in other articles (Chaos Computer Club, 2004; Kaseva & Stén, 2003; Matsumoto et al., 2002; Marcialis & Roli, 2008). In order to maintain a clearer overview during the tests, each model produced was labeled. Also, the created dummies were labeled and a note was made from which model they had been cast.

Tests with "Microsoft Fingerprint Reader"

First, the Microsoft Fingerprint Reader was examined more closely and thoroughly tested. This scanner does not contain any kind of "Life and Well" detection so it cannot *per se* distinguish between natural and artificial fingers.

Initially, the fingerprints of the test persons were entered into the computer system by means of the scanner as reference prints for a particular user account, allowing the people in question to register in the system by briefly placing a finger on the surface of the scanner. The delivered software

"DigitalPersona" (version 2.0.1.1843) was used for this purpose.

After the prints were stored in the system, the most primitive variant of deception was attempted. For this, a test person attempted to register with a fingerprint that was not recorded in the system as his or hers. Here, in most cases, an enrolled person used a finger matching the one enrolled, but on the other hand. All these attempts failed, as was expected.

Subsequently, an attempt was made by another person to register onto the system using one of the dummies produced as described. For each dummy 20 attempts were made in order to eliminate the element of chance, and to ensure that the login had taken place due to the dummy and not some other randomly occurring error.

In the experiments with the cooperative victim, it quickly became evident in the course of the tests that some models created dummies able to achieve better results than the dummies created from other models. Thus, retrospectively, it was ascertained that some models made of polymer clay and wax had clearly lost some of their shape in the production process, which was not evident at first glance.

Otherwise, success was definitely achieved during the attempts at deception in this test setup. The test person was able, for example, to fool the Microsoft Fingerprint Reader and thereby gain access to the system in nearly half the cases with dummies made of wood glue and handicraft glue, around one third of those made with silicon, and also with one or two gelatin dummies made from polymer clay models. The performance of dummies made from wax molds was not as good, as many molds were destroyed by dummy material that remained stuck to them.

The test persons mentioned in the tables can be characterized as follows:

- Test person 1—TP1—male, aged 26
- Test person 2—TP2—female, aged 23

The "deceived" column indicates the total number of successful deceptions of the scanner with dummies from a model of the test person shown. The same applies for the two columns, "not deceived" and "no reaction." The last column shows, as a percentage, how often the dummies of a particular test person could deceive the scanner, whereby here, experiments in which the scanner did not react to the dummy were not counted (Table 3, Table 4, Table 5, Table 6, Table 7, Table 8, Table 9, and Table 10).

On the other hand, experiments set up on the basis of an unknowing victim were incapable of producing such results. Of all such attempts undertaken, the test person was able to access the system just three times, once with the help of a gelatin dummy and twice with the help of a handicraft glue dummy. None of the other dummies produced from circuit board models could register comparable success despite the great number of experiments and dummies. The following tables show a summary of the test results. A compilation of the concrete results of the series of tests will not be displayed individually, as no success of any kind was achieved (Table 11, Table 12, Table 13, and Table 14).

Table 3. Test statistics—Fimo polymer clay—wood glue—assenting victim - MS

Test person	Models used	Dummies created	Deceived	Not deceived	No reaction	%
TP1	12	33	167	214	279	43.8
TP2	12	33	157	213	290	42.4

Table 4. Test statistics—Fimo polymer clay—handicraft glue—assenting victim—MS

Test person	Models used	Dummies created	Deceived	Not deceived	No reaction	%
TP1	11	32	163	200	277	44.9
TP2	12	33	143	211	306	40.4

Table 5. Test statistics—Fimo polymer clay—silicon—assenting victim—MS

Test person	Models used	Dummies created	Deceived	Not deceived	No reaction	%
TP1	11	27	69	221	250	23.8
TP2	12	29	92	215	273	30

Table 6. Test statistics—Fimo polymer clay—gelatin—assenting victim—MS

Test person	Models used	Dummies created	Deceived	Not deceived	No reaction	%
TP1	11	32	18	242	380	6.9
TP2	12	33	10	255	395	3.8

Table 7. Test statistics - Wax—Wood glue—assenting victim—MS

Test person	Models used	Dummies created	Deceived	Not deceived	No reaction	%
TP1	6	16	52	116	152	30.9
TP2	6	13	26	101	133	20.5

Table 8. Test statistics - Wax—Handicraft glue—assenting victim—MS

Test person	Models used	Dummies created	Deceived	Not deceived	No reaction	%
TP1	6	16	38	120	162	24.1
TP2	6	16	36	130	154	21.7

Table 9. Test statistics—wax—silicon—assenting victim—MS

Test person	Models used	Dummies created	Deceived	Not deceived	No reaction	%
TP1	6	14	25	98	157	20.3
TP2	6	15	18	110	172	14.1

Table 10. Test statistics—wax—gelatin—assenting victim—MS

Test person	Models used	Dummies created	Deceived	Not deceived	No reaction	%
TP1	6	18	19	150	191	11.2
TP2	6	18	0	171	189	0

Table 11. Test statistics—circuit board—wood glue—unknowing victim—MS

Test person	Models used	Dummies created	Deceived	Not deceived	No reaction	%
TP1	21	60	0	308	892	0
TP2	21	61	0	288	932	0

Table 12. Test statistics—circuit board—handicraft glue—unknowing victim—MS

Test person	Models used	Dummies created	Deceived	Not deceived	No reaction	%
TP1	18	70	2	416	982	0,05
TP2	19	55	0	304	796	0

Table 13. Test statistics—circuit board—silicon—unknowing victim—MS

Test person	Models used	Dummies created	Deceived	Not deceived	No reaction	%
TP1	17	51	0	313	707	0
TP2	17	51	0	324	696	0

Table 14. Test statistics—circuit board—gelatin—unknowing victim—MS

Test person	Models used	Dummies created	Deceived	Not deceived	No reaction	%
TP1	21	80	1	367	1233	0.3
TP2	21	63	0	254	1006	0

Tests with "Digitus Fingerprint Reader"

The second test device was the Digitus Fingerprint Reader; since this is a scanner with capacitive sensors, the dummy material must at least offer a minimum of conductivity, so that the scanner reacts to the fake finger. However, the conductivity of human skin can be very easily simulated by the test person spreading a small amount of saliva on the dummy (Sandström, 2004).

Here, too, as with the first test device, the first step was the simplest test scenario of the test person attempting to access the system using a non-registered finger. All attempts to fool the scanner failed here, too, as expected.

Also in the tests with this device, twenty attempts were made with each fingerprint dummy to log onto the system. Since the tests of the two scanners were not carried out in direct succession, at the time point for the tests with this device, some wood glue dummies had already cracked. Most of the gelatin dummies had also already gone off by this stage and were thereby no longer usable. Although the attempt was still made to use these dummies, further dummies were produced as a replacement for those that were, for one reason or another, simply bad or no longer usable, so as to provide a better comparison with the other device.

Here, too, tests took place in two steps. Also for this device, chosen first was the variant involving a cooperative victim. In contrast to the first device, however, no positive results of any kind could be registered. The device also only reacted to many

of the fingerprint dummies once they had been slightly wetted with saliva as previously described (Sandström, 2004), and even then not every time. Nonetheless, the test person was unable to register successfully on the system, whether with wood glue or handicraft glue dummies, silicon or gelatin dummies. A summary of test results can be gleaned from the following tables. Individual test results are not listed in detail as none of the attempts to log onto the system with one of the dummies was successful.

The significance of the individual columns and the characterization of the test persons is the same as with the tests of the Microsoft Fingerprint Readers (Table 15, Table 16, Table 17, Table 18, Table 19, Table 20, Table 21 and Table 22).

Table 15. Test statistics—Fimo polymer clay—Wood glue—assenting victim—Digitus

Test person	Models used	Dummies created	Deceived	Not deceived	No reaction	%
TP1	11	32	0	58	582	0
TP2	12	33	0	86	574	0

Table 16. Test statistics—Fimo polymer clay—handicraft glue—assenting victim—Digitus

Test person	Models used	Dummies created	Deceived	Not deceived	No reaction	%
TP1	11	32	0	185	455	0
TP2	12	33	0	177	483	0

Table 17. Test statistics—Fimo Polymer clay—silicon—assenting victim—Digitus

Test person	Models used	Dummies created	Deceived	Not deceived	No reaction	%
TP1	11	32	0	48	592	0
TP2	12	33	0	36	624	0

Table 18. Test statistics—Fimo Polymer clay—gelatin—assenting victim—Digitus

Test person	Models used	Dummies created	Deceived	Not deceived	No reaction	%
TP1	11	32	0	156	484	0
TP2	12	33	0	143	517	0

Table 19. Test statistics—wax—wood glue—assenting victim—Digitus

Test person	Models used	Dummies created	Deceived	Not deceived	No reaction	%
TP1	6	14	0	37	243	0
TP2	6	13	0	42	218	0

Table 20. Test statistics—wax—handicraft glue—assenting victim—Digitus

Test person	Models used	Dummies created	Deceived	Not deceived	No reaction	%
TP1	6	15	0	66	234	0
TP2	6	18	0	89	271	0

Table 21. Test statistics—wax—silicon—assenting victim—Digitus

Test person	Models used	Dummies created	Deceived	Not deceived	No reaction	%
TP1	6	18	0	31	329	0
TP2	6	16	0	29	291	0

Table 22. Test statistics—wax—gelatin—assenting victim - Digitus

Test person	Models used	Dummies created	Deceived	Not deceived	No reaction	%
TP1	6	17	0	65	275	0
TP2	6	18	0	82	278	0

Also for the second experiment set-up in which the scenario was based on an unknowing victim, no successes were registered. Thus, it was not possible for the test person to deceive the scanner and thereby illegally register with the system using any of the dummies produced with circuit board models. Here too, the following tables show only a summary. A table showing the specific results in detail was not created due to the unsuccessful tests (Table 23, Table 24, Table 25 and Table 26).

CONCLUSION

According to the literature reviewed in this paper, it initially appeared relatively easy to deceive a fingerprint scanner. Articles such as the one by Chaos Computer Club (2004) gave the impression that a biometric system could be tricked in no time at all, and required only the simplest materials to pull off the deception. Other studies (e.g., Matsumoto et al., 2002) make similar claims and describe the ease with which a "dummy" finger can be made and used to fool a fingerprint scanner.

Table 23. Test statistics—circuit board—wood glue—unknowing victim – Digitus

Test person	Models used	Dummies created	Deceived	Not deceived	No reaction	%
TP1	21	59	0	174	1006	0
TP2	21	63	0	207	1053	0

Table 24. Test statistics - Board – Handicraft glue – Unknowing victim – Digitus

Test person	Models used	Dummies created	Deceived	Not deceived	No reaction	%
TP1	19	57	0	203	937	0
TP2	21	61	0	263	957	0

Table 25. Test statistics—circuit board—silicon—unknowing victim—Digitus

Test person	Models used	Dummies created	Deceived	Not deceived	No reaction	%
TP1	19	57	0	165	975	0
TP2	20	60	0	153	1047	0

Table 26. Test statistics—circuit board—gelatin—unknowing victim—Digitus

Test person	Models used	Dummies created	Deceived	Not deceived	No reaction	%
TP1	21	63	0	197	1063	0
TP2	21	63	0	249	1011	0

A goal of our research was to not only review existing attacks but to reproduce them and to document the results more precisely than the original papers. Thus, while all essential points are investigated, we could not reproduce some of the results. The experiments also showed that fingerprints are certainly not forgery-proof. They can most certainly be copied. Thus, it is relatively easy, and was also achieved in these experiments, to produce a functional fingerprint dummy. If an attempt is made to copy the fingerprint of a third party without that person's consent the success rates are much lower compared to cooperating victims. In this context, it is generally assumed that an object of some kind is available that provides a perfect print. In reality, however, many

factors influence the quality of the print (Bromba, 2009). For example, if possible, only this person should have touched the object, otherwise it is uncertain whose fingerprint is being processed. Also, the person should not have touched the object too many times or else the prints will overlap or smudge. The object's surface also plays a certain role. Furthermore, it must be kept in mind that if possible, the object to be used should be portable. If one takes a fingerprint from, e.g., a door handle, it is rarely possible to do so without being noticed or leaving behind traces (graphite powder or residual cyanoacrylate).

Another important point to bear in mind is whether the procedure of copying a fingerprint is being carried out for the first time, or whether one has already gathered experience in using the materials. The time required to create a dummy naturally changes accordingly. Experiments have shown that a beginner in this area with little or no experience requires a relatively long time to create a dummy. If work is carried out with an cooperating victim, it is easily possible for a beginner to make a dummy. The only aspect of making a dummy that depends on experience is the exact timing of when it hardens. Thus, the time required for making dummies with an assenting victim—i.e., the time that an experienced person takes—is only marginally less than that needed for a beginner. Exact data on the duration of the dummy production cannot be provided as this depends greatly on the materials used in each case. Thus, a beginner as well as an experienced tester must expect the production of a Fimo polymer clay model to take around 30 minutes. Creating a wax model can be achieved in nearly 10 minutes. The time required for the dummy to dry is naturally dependent on the material used and the thickness of the dummy (the amount of material used). Here, as already mentioned, an experienced tester has the advantage of being able to better assess the drying time of the dummy.

If one assumes an experiment set up with an unsuspecting victim, then certainly the time varies between a beginner and a tester with sufficient experience. Thus, a tester with no prior knowledge must first ascertain how a latency print can be made clearly visible, and, for instance, what must be watched out for when using graphite powder. He or she must also try out the methods for enhancing a digitized fingerprint to see which methods hold greater promise of success and which less. Also, the exposing and etching of circuit boards are certainly more difficult for someone who has not yet worked with such materials and chemicals. Thus, a beginner can easily expose a circuit board either for too long or too short a time. Here, a tester with relevant experience and prior knowledge of this subject has a clear advantage. Simply rendering a fingerprint visible is carried out faster by a practiced person. The latter also saves much time by knowing which programs and which methods within those programs to utilize in order to successfully retouch an image. Finally, time can be saved through experience in exposing and etching a circuit board. In all, a beginner must reckon with a good ten hours to produce the first dummy. If, on the other hand, one knows what to look out for in terms of individual processing steps, then a time investment of around three hours (i.e., time required after repeated action) can be expected. It can thus occur that the time and effort were in vain in cases where the dummy does not work at all. In the experiments we undertook, we were forced to arrive at this conclusion: with one single exception, none of the dummies created within the scenario of an unsuspecting victim was able to fool the scanner.

The experiments conducted for this study thus show that many previous studies of the topic have treated it at a very superficial level and merely show that a scanner can be fooled with the help of an assenting victim. In consideration of the experiments carried out, other articles, such as that published by the Chaos Computer Club, seem to have been aimed at stirring up the public so that biometric systems are also questioned critically rather than being seen as absolutely secure. Nonetheless, the experiments also showed that fingerprint scanners are not as easy to deceive as the source literature led us to assume at the outset of the study.

REFERENCES

Barthel, K. U. (2007). *Bildmanipulation II: Filter.*

Bergadano, F., Gunetti, D., & Picardi, C. (2002, November). User authentication through keystroke dynamics. *ACM Transactions on Information and System Security, 5*(4), 367–397. Retrieved from http://doi.acm.org/10.1145/581271.581272. doi:10.1145/581271.581272

Bicz, W. O. (2010). *Fingerprint structure imaging based on an ultrasound camera.* Retrieved from http://www.optel.com.pl/article/english/article.htm

Biomedical Signal Analysis Laboratory. (2010). *Liveness Detection in Biometric Devices.* Retrieved from http://people.clarkson.edu/~biosal/research/liveness.html

Blommé, J. (2003). *Evaluation of biometric security systems against artificial fingers.*

Bromba, M. (2002). *Biometrie und Sicherheit.* Retrieved from http://www.bromba.com/knowhow/biosich.htm

Bromba, M. (2008, February 5). *Über die Unbrauchbarkeit der Biometrie.* Retrieved from http://www.bromba.com/knowhow/KleineAnleitung.htm

Bromba, M. (2008, February 16). *Biometrie FAQ.* Retrieved from http://www.bromba.com/faq/biofaqd.htm

Bromba, M. (2009). *Fingerprint FAQ.* Retrieved from http://www.bromba.com/faq/fpfaqd.htm

Campell, E. D. (1998). *Fingerprints & Palmar-Dermatoglyphics.* Retrieved from http://www.edcampbell.com/PalmD-History.htm

Chaos Computer Club. (2004, October 9).*Wie können Fingerabdrücke nachgebildet werden?* Retrieved from http://www.ccc.de/biometrie/fingerabdruck_kopieren.xml?language=de

Cremerius, R., & Snurnikov, L. (2006). *Biometrie und Datenschutz.* Retrieved from http://waste.informatik.hu-berlin.de/Lehre/ss06/SE_ueberwachung/vortrag5.pdf

Daugman, J. (2004). *How Iris Recognition Works.* Retrieved from http://www.cl.cam.ac.uk/users/jgd1000/csvt.pdf

Daugman, J. (2004). How Iris Recognition Works. *IEEE Trans. CSVT, 14*(1), 21–30.

Daugman, J. (2007). New methods in iris recognition. *IEEE Trans. Systems, Man. Cybernetics B, 37*(5), 1167–1175. doi:10.1109/TSMCB.2007.903540

Digitus. (2010). *Digitus USB Fingerprint Reader.* Retrieved from http://www.digitus.info/en/products/accessories/?c=1215&p=3577

Faber, E. (2010). *Eberhard Faber Gmbh.* Retrieved from http://www.eberhardfaber.de/

Feltin, B. (2002). *Information Assurance Using Biometrics.*

Gimp. (2010). *GNU Image Manipulation Program.* Retrieved from http://www.gimp.org/

Haluschak, B. (2009, January). *Biometrie Grundlagen - Vom Fingerprint bis zur Gesichtserkennung. Tec Channel.* Retrieved from http://www.tecchannel.de/sicherheit/identity_access/402320/grundlagen_mehr_sicherheit_mit_biometrie/index.html

Harris, T. (2002, September). *How Fingerprint Scanners work.* How stuff works. Retrieved from http://computer.howstuffworks.com/fingerprint-scanner.htm

Hein, S., & Mahrla, M. (2004). *Überwindungsszenarien für biometrische Systeme.* Retrieved from http://www2.informatik.huberlin.de/Forschung_Lehre/algorithmenII/Lehre/SS2004/Biometrie/09Ueberwindung/Ueberwindung/index.html

International Biometric Group. (2005). *Independent Testing of Iris Recognition Technology.*

International Biometric Group. (2008). *Biometrics Market and Industry Report 2009 - 2014.* Retrieved from http://www.biometricgroup.com/reports/public/market_report.php

ISO/IEC Group 1. (2010). *Harmonized Biometric Vocabulary.* Retrieved from http://www.3dface.org/media/vocabulary.html

Kaseva, A., & Stén, A. (2003, March). *Fooling Fingerprint Scanners.*

Kent, J. (2005, March 31). *Malysia car thieves steal finger. BBC News.* Retrieved from http://news.bbc.co.uk/1/hi/world/asia-pacific/4396831.stm

Kleine-Albers, D., Tokar, D., & Uhe, P. (2006). *Versuch: Fingerabdruck (Teil 2).* Retrieved from http://dka.web-republic.de/ downloads.html?eID=dam_frontend_push&docID=570

Krijnen, K. (2008). *PCB Etching.* Retrieved from http://sfprime.net/pcb-etching/index.htm

Leyden, J. (2002, May). *Gummi bears defeat fingerprint sensors. The Register.* Retrieved from http://www.theregister.co.uk/2002/05/16/gummi_bears_defeat_fingerprint_sensors/

Mainguet, J.-F. (2009). *Retinal.* Retrieved from http://pagespersoorange.fr/fingerchip/biometrics/types/retinal.htm

Mainguet, J.-F. (2009). *Fingerprints.* Retrieved from http://pagespersoorange.fr/fingerchip/biometrics/types/fingerprint.htm

Mainguet, J.-F. (2010). *Movies & Biometrics.* Retrieved from http://pagespersoorange.fr/fingerchip/biometrics/movies.htm

Manhart, K. (2002, January). *Sicher durch Biometrie. Tec Channel.* Retrieved from http://www.tecchannel.de/sicherheit/identity_access/401777/sicher_durch_biometrie/index.html

Marcialis, G. L., & Roli, F. (2008). Fingerprint verification by decision-level fusion of optical and capacitive sensors. In *Proceedings of the International Workshop on Biometric Authentication (BioAW04).* DOI: 10.1007/b99174

Matsomoto, T. (2002). Importance of Open Discussion on Adversarial Analysis for Mobile Security Technologies. A Case Study for User Identification.

Matsumoto, T. (2002). *Impact of Artificial "Gummy".* Fingers on Fingerprint Systems.

Medical Discoveries. (2010). *Retinography.* Retrieved from http://www.discoveriesinmedicine.com/Ra-Thy/Retinography.html

Optel. (2002). *Comparing Ultrasound with Conventional Finger-Scan Technologies.* Retrieved from http://www.optel.pl/article/deutsch/comparing.htm

Österreichischer Nationalrat. (2009). *Der Reisepass mit Fingerabdruck kommt.* Retrieved from http://www.parlament.gv.at/PG/PR/JAHR_2009/PK0023/PK0023.shtml

Petermann, T., & Sauter, A. (2002). *Biometrische Identifikationssysteme.* Retrieved from http://www.tab.fzk.de/de/projekt/zusammenfassung/ab76.pdf

Ross, A., Jain, A., & Pankanti, S. A. (2010). *Hand Geometry Based Verification System.* Retrieved from http://biometrics.cse.msu.edu/hand_proto.html

Sandström, M. (2004). *Liveness Detection in Fingerprint Recognition Systems*.

Schneider, B. (1998, August). *Biometrics: Truths and Fictions. Crypto-Gram*. Retrieved from http://www.schneier.com/crypto-gram-9808.html#biometrics

Schneider, B. (1999, August). *Biometrics: Uses and Abuses*. Retrieved from http://www.schneier.com/essay-019.html

Schneider, B. (2002, May).*Fun with Fingerprint Readers. Crypto-Gram*. Retrieved from http://www.schneier.com/crypto-gram-0205.html#5

Thalheim, L., Krissler, J., & Ziegler, P.-M. (2002, November). *Körperkontrolle - Biometrische Zugangssicherung auf die Probe gestellt* (p. 114).

Turk, M. A., & Pentland, A. P. (1991). *Face Recognition Using Eigenfaces*.

Van der Putte, T., & Keuning, J. (2002). *Biometrical Fingerprint Recognition: Don't get your fingers burned*. Retrieved from http://cryptome.org/fake-prints.htm

Wikipedia. (2009). *Microsoft Fingerprint Reader*. Retrieved from http://en.wikipedia.org/wiki/Microsoft_Fingerprint_Reader

Wikipedia. (2010a). *Biometrics*. Retrieved from http://en.wikipedia.org/wiki/biometrics

Wikipedia. (2010b). *Fingerprint*. Retrieved from http://en.wikipedia.org/wiki/Fingerprint

Wikipedia. (2010c). *AFIS*. Retrieved from http://en.wikipedia.org/wiki/

Wikipedia. (2010d). *Capacitor*. Retrieved from http://en.wikipedia.org/wiki/Capacitor

Wikipedia. (2010e). *Electrostatic discharge*. Retrieved from http://en.wikipedia.org/wiki/Electrostatic_discharge

Wikipedia. (2010f). *Histogram Equalization*. Retrieved from http://en.wikipedia.org/wiki/Histogram_equalization

Wikipedia. (2010g). *Thresholding (image processing)*. Retrieved from http://en.wikipedia.org/wiki/Thresholding_%28image_processing%29

Wikipedia. (2010h). *Iris Recognition*. Retrieved from http://en.wikipedia.org/wiki/Iris_recognition

Wikipedia. (2010i). *Retinal Scan*. Retrieved from http://en.wikipedia.org/wiki/Retinal_scan

Wikipedia. (2010j). *Eigenfaces*. Retrieved from http://en.wikipedia.org/wiki/Eigenface

Wikipedia. (2010k). *Speaker Recognition*. Retrieved from http://en.wikipedia.org/wiki/Speaker_recognition

This work was previously published in the International Journal of Secure Software Engineering, Volume 2, Issue 1, edited by Khaled M. Khan, pp. 40-83, copyright 2011 by IGI Publishing (an imprint of IGI Global).

Chapter 15
Integrating Patient Consent in e–Health Access Control

Kim Wuyts
Katholieke Universiteit Leuven, Belgium

Riccardo Scandariato
Katholieke Universiteit Leuven, Belgium

Griet Verhenneman
Katholieke Universiteit Leuven, Belgium

Wouter Joosen
Katholieke Universiteit Leuven, Belgium

ABSTRACT

Many initiatives exist that integrate e-health systems on a large scale. One of the main technical challenges is access control, although several frameworks and solutions, like XACML, are becoming standard practice. Data is no longer shared within one affinity domain but becomes ubiquitous, which results in a loss of control. As patients will be less willing to participate without additional control strategies, patient consents are introduced that allow the patients to determine precise access rules on their medical data. This paper explores the consequences of integrating consent in e-health access control. First, consent requirements are examined, after which an architecture is proposed which incorporates patient consent in the access control service of an e-health system. To validate the proposed concepts, a proof-of-concept implementation is built and evaluated.

INTRODUCTION

To date, medical data are shared with a single affinity domain (e.g. hospital, group practice, etc.). Because medical information is very sensitive, its controlled access represents a key security requirement. This is also reflected by several legislations like the US Health Insurance Portability and Accountability Act and the EU Data Protection Directive. In this respect several frameworks and solutions, like XACML (Moses, 2005), are already standard practice.

DOI: 10.4018/978-1-4666-2482-5.ch015

Currently, many initiatives have emerged that aim toward integrating e-health systems on a larger scale. Well-known examples are the Integrating the Healthcare Enterprise consortium (IHE), the UK National Health System, and the European epSOS project. These initiatives aim at creating a unified Electronic Health Record (EHR) containing patient data provided by a wide range of health-care professionals. As scale increases, e.g. when regional or national e-health systems will be fully operational, data will no longer be contained in a single affinity domain and it will become harder for patients to stay in control of how data is used. This results in concerns for the patient who will be less eager to participate in a ubiquitous e-health system.

Moreover, projects like Google Health and Microsoft HealthVault have successfully introduced the idea of the Personal Health Record (PHR) that is a medical file containing health data provided by the patients themselves. Patients are also more and more engaged with online communities (e.g., PatientsLikeMe) where they can provide and share personal health information with peers. We are at the verge of a deeper and tighter integration among different systems (large scale EHR, PHR, communities), which demands for greater and greater control from the user perspective. Once more, it is simply no longer realistic to expect the patient to outsource the control over her own data to care providers (like hospitals) and service provider (like Google) altogether, especially in a converged environment where many stakeholders are involved.

To counter these concerns, electronic patient consents bear the promise of enabling a user-centric access to own medical data and hence re-establish the trust of the patients. Patient consents are user-defined (often complex) rules providing directives on how access to own data should be regulated. Although this is a crucial part of e-health access control systems (as required by compliance to laws and regulations), the related work is rather limited. Furthermore, the literature is even more inadequate for what concerns the integration of user directives (like patient consents) into the standard practice access control.

As its main contribution, this paper explores the options for representing patient consents and incorporating their directives into the access control decision process. The legal requirements concerning patient consent (with focus on European legislation) are presented first. On top of the results of the legal analysis, we propose a format for representing patient consents and outline the lifecycle governing them, e.g., with respect to their creation and revocation. Finally, we suggest both a policy evaluation algorithm and a reference authorization architecture that incorporates patient consents at its core. The reference architecture extends the XACML authorization model, which is the de facto standard for authorization. In particular, we suggest integrating consents via a Policy Information Point (PIP) interacting with a Policy Decision Point (PDP) that enforces the suggested evaluation algorithm. An implementation of the proposal is presented at the end of the paper, together with an extensive evaluation. As a case study for the evaluation, the prototype implementation is instantiated in the context of XDS, which is an EHR proposal for cross-enterprise data sharing set forward by IHE. XDS is highly promising in the health care sector and is endorsed by key industrial players like Microsoft and IBM, which makes the illustration more relevant.

PATIENT CONSENT

Sharing patient data on a large scale has a big impact on the patient's privacy. Therefore, it is important that the patients themselves are also given the ability to determine rules concerning the access rights of their own data. This section is divided in a conceptual part and a more technical part. The first part provides an introduction to basic consent concepts and motivates the importance of patient consents. The second part derives from the legal analysis technical constraints for the format of a consent and its management (storage, access, etc.).

Background: Consent Terminology

In order to obtain a mutual understanding of some key concepts regarding patient consent, this section provides an overview of useful consent terminology.

In the US, patient consent is used to protect the patient's individually identifiable health data, also known as *protected health information* (PHI), which includes information that is created or received by a covered entity, including a health care provider, and relates to the past, present, or future physical or mental health, or condition of an individual, or relates to payment for an individual's health care, or relates to the provision of health care in the past, present, or future, and identifies an individual or could be used for identifying an individual (U. S. Department of Health and Human Services, 2003).

In Europe, patient consent is used to control the *processing of personal data* which is any operation or set of operations that is performed upon personal data, whether or not by automatic means, such as collection, recording, organization, storage, adaptation or alteration, retrieval, consultation, use, disclosure by transmission, dissemination or otherwise making available, alignment or combination, blocking, erasure or destruction (European Communities, 1995).

The *controller* concept is a typical European concept used to describe the natural or legal person, public authority, agency or any other body which alone or jointly with others determines the purposes and means of the processing of personal data (European Communities, 1995). A controller can for example be the health care provider or health association who uploaded the patient data to the system. Next thereto, the *processor*

is the natural or legal person, public authority, agency or any other body which processes personal data on behalf of the controller (European Communities, 1995). This could for example be the e-health system or associated personnel (e.g. system administrators). The *receiver* or recipient is the natural or legal person, public authority, agency or any other body to whom data are disclosed (European Communities, 1995). The *data subject* is the patient himself whose health data are being processed.

Patient Consent Relevance

User empowerment in general, and patient consents specifically, become more and more important. This section highlights two important factors which influence the necessity of (a clear view on) user consents: legislation and the user's perspective towards empowerment.

Legal Analysis

The European Data Protection Directive (DPD) (European Communities, 1995) states that processing of personal sensitive data is prohibited unless a) the processing is necessary for the protection of the vital interests of the data subject, b) the processing is necessary for purposes of preventive medicine, medical diagnosis, provision of care or treatment or c) the data subject has given his explicit, written consent to the processing of the data (art. 7) (The DPD also describes some additional situations when processing of sensitive data is allowed, however, these are of minor importance for this paper). The American Health Insurance Portability and Accountability Act (HIPAA) (U. S. Department of Health and Human Services, 1996) describes a similar rule stating the "necessity of the individual's written authorization for any use of disclosure of protected health information that is not treatment, payment or health care operations", illustrating the need for patient consent. Another rule in HIPAA states that "individuals have the right to request restriction of use or disclosure of protected health information for treatment, payment or health care operations, disclosure to persons involved in the individual's health care or payment for health care, or disclosure to notify family members or others about the individual's general condition, location or death". This rule clearly illustrates the need for a negative patient consent to allow the patients to limit access to their personal health data.

In order to be valid, consent needs to fulfill five requirements. Article 2(h) of the DPD defines consent as follows: *"any freely given, specific, and informed indication of the data subject's wishes, by which the data subject signifies his agreement to personal data relating to him being processed"*. The DPD's definition clearly indicates 3 conditions: the consent must be specific, informed and freely given. *"Freely given"* implies that the data subject should not be forced into a consent, but that it is a voluntary decision. *"Informed"* refers to the information that needs to be provided to allow the data subject to understand all the benefits and disadvantages of providing a certain consent. *"Specific"* refers to the content of a consent, which should describe a well-defined, concrete situation, instead of allowing everyone access to anything in one general consent. This paper will only focus on the specificity of the consent, by defining the required set of attributes. A more extensive discussion about the legal challenges concerning patient consent, can be found in Verhenneman (2010).

User's Perspective

Users become more aware of the possibilities of technology and embrace these new opportunities. However, they are also concerned with the downside of this evolution: their own privacy. Think of the protests when Facebook changed their privacy policies overnight (BBC News, 2009). Users want to know what happens with their data and should be in control of who can access it. This becomes especially important when sensitive information, like health data, is involved.

This awareness causes the shift from paper-based, and even orally obtained consents, with limited room for personalization of consents, to a digital setting where users can create their own consents.

Not only will the user want to control data he created, more importantly he will also want to control access to data a third party created of him (e.g. a tagged picture uploaded by a friend to a social network, or a patient's medical file created by a doctor).

Consent Structure

Access control technology has evolved, and authorization is no longer a static decision based on the user's identity and the application he is trying to use. Many more factors make decisions shift from static to dynamic concepts. Also, predefined generic rules are extended with user-specific rules. A tradeoff needs to be made between simplicity and expressiveness when dealing with access control policies. Either only a very limited set of rules can be expressed that are easy to create and maintain, or, a very rich set of rules can be expressed, which are more challenging to create and maintain and might require additional (meta) data to become part of the system. Evidently the aim is to use a set of expressive policies which are still easy to manage and maintain, and do not require too much additional information from the system. This tradeoff will clearly depend on the requirements of the system, and thus it needs to be clearly stated what type of rules, and more precisely, what type of patient consents need to be expressed. Unfortunately, there is currently no clear-cut comprehension of the consent subject matter.

This section describes a proposal for this missing consent structure. The Data Protection Directive and, to a lesser extent, the Health Information Portability and Accountability Act were used as basis to create the set of minimal attributes. The structure is also illustrated by the domain model in Figure 1. Evidently, this list can be custom-

Figure 1. Domain model of patient consent

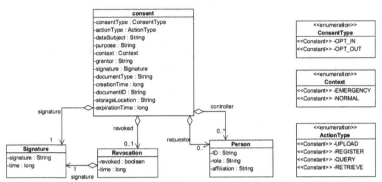

ized to the system's needs by expanding it with additional attributes or only selecting a limited set of features.

A first important attribute is the *consent type* which can be either positive to allow certain actions or negative to prohibit actions. Although legally conceived as a positive reply to a request to process data, it could also express a negative attitude towards a certain processing action. The *action type* is another key feature, because different actions will correspond to different access rules. A consent can be created to allow a user to upload certain patient information to a repository, or to allow the registration of metadata at the system's registry. Similarly, consents can be created to determine the access for querying metadata at the registry or retrieving patient data from a repository. A straight-forward consent attribute is the *data subject*, which, in e-health systems, represents the patient. As legally defined, all actions and collected data should be assigned a *purpose*. A consent should only be created for a specific purpose, e.g. statistical analysis for cancer prevention. The *context* attribute describes the circumstances in which the consent should be applied. Two main contexts can be distinguished: general (in most cases) and emergency (in life-or-death situations). In some cases, it can be that the patient herself is incapable of making access control decisions. In that case, a legal guardian will be responsible for the creation of the patient's

consents. In order to track the creator of each consent, a *grantor* attribute can be used. The patient's or grantor's (digital) *signature* is also required to ensure that the consent is genuine. The *document type* enables the consent to only focus on one particular type of information (e.g. prescriptions or psych reports). If a patient decides that her consent should no longer be used, the consent can be *revoked* (consents should not be removed for auditing purposes). In order for the revocation to be valid, the patient's or grantor's (digital) signature is required. The *creation time* of the document is also an important attribute. Since in most cases it is legally required to store health data for a minimum number of years, the consent to do so should be treated equally. After this period, the consents can be removed, on the condition that the consent was already revoked. The creation time can be used to (automatically) determine whether a consent can be deleted.

The attributes described above are the strict minimum for creating patient consents, it is however recommended to extend this set. Clearly, the more attributes are combined, the more expressive consents can be created. Three attributes describe the document's *controller*: the controller's identifier, the controller's role (e.g. pharmacist, GP), and the controller's organization or affiliation (e.g. hospital, pharmacy). This allows the patient to specify consents for a particular document creator, e.g. only allow sharing his medical documents created by doctor X with the e-health system. Similarly, attributes concerning the *requestor* of the documents can be added to the consent: the receiver's identifier, the receiver's role and the receiver's organization. To make the consents document-specific, the *document identifier* can also be added to the consent. Also the document's *storage location* can be used as consent feature to, for example, only allow access to documents which are stored in a trusted repository. Last but not least, also time-related information can be added to a consent, which can replace the revocation attribute since the time-related attributes are more fine-grained. Consents can be only temporarily applicable (e.g. allowing a replacing physician only access for the time of replacement or sharing a document for only 2 weeks). Therefore, an *expiration time* can be added to a consent.

An example is a consent valid for a one year period, created by patient John Smith, that allows pharmacist Michaels to access John's medication history, controlled by John's general practitioner, Dr. Hibbert, to enable conflicting medication resolution. It will have the following attributes: *"opt-in"* (consent type), *"retrieve"* (action type), *John's SSN* (data subject), *"check for medication habits and possible interferences"* (purpose), *"normal"* (context), *John's SSN* (grantor), *John's digital signature* (signature), *"medication history"* (document type), *"05.05.2010 12:35"* (creation time), *"05.05.2011 12:35"* (expiration time), *Dr. Hibbert's care provider ID* (controller ID), *"GP"* (controller role), *pharmacist Michaels' care provider ID* (receiver ID), *"pharmacist"* (receiver role). Note that in this example document ID and storage location are not used.

Consent Management

This section elaborates further on the two different types of consent, positive and negative, and their lifecycle.

Consent Lifecycle

The proposed lifecycle management slightly differs from the current situation, because currently positive consents are handled on paper and negative consents are only oral agreements, thus the possibilities are more restricted. Currently, the main driver of the consent lifecycle is the controller, because no applications exist which allows the patient to handle consents himself. In the proposed version, the focus will shift toward the patient.

As indicated in the legal analysis section, the sharing of medical information is forbidden unless one of the exemptions - amongst which consent - applies. To allow access, the patient will need to sign a consent indicating he agrees upon the sharing of certain data. These consents extend the access control rules, and are therefore called positive consents. Also negative consents are introduced, which will overrule the internal policies, because the patient's privacy is considered as more important.

In principle, only the patients themselves should be involved in the consent lifecycle. However, it should be possible for the document controller to create and revoke consent too, at least on behalf of the patient. This could for example be necessary when the patient prefers to create or revoke his consent through the health care practitioner because the patient simply prefers the assistance of the health care professional or because the patient does not yet have internet access. The same rules could be necessary to allow a trusted representative other that the health care practitioner to assist the patient. In both cases the consent needs, evidently, to be validated by the patient himself through a (digital) signature. A third situation in which also a representative should be able to create or revoke consents is when the patient is mentally incapable and needs to be represented by a legal guardian. This scenario is however of minor importance to the paper since it can be assumed that the legal guardian was assigned the same rights as the patient himself. The different actions of the consent lifecycle are illustrated by use case diagrams in Figure 2.

- **Creation:** In theory, a consent can only be created by the patient himself, but, as already indicated above, it should also be possible for the controller to create a consent when the patient instructs him thereto. The controller can draft the consent document which will be signed by the patient to validate it. The controller will upload the signed consent to the consent service. If the patient creates the consents himself, the system can provide consent templates to facilitate the creation. Clearly, a consent will only be considered binding if it is signed by the data subject.
- **Retrieval:** Both the controller and data subject are allowed to retrieve their corresponding consents.
- **Revocation:** When the patient decides that a consent is no longer accurate, the consent can be revoked. A revoked consent will continue to be stored for audit purposes, but will not be taken into account for access control decisions. Only the data subject can revoke consents. If necessary, the controller can assist in the revocation, yet again on the condition it is signed by the patient.
- **Alteration:** Alterations as such will not be allowed. Jurisprudence suggests that a consent should be preserved for evidence purposes. The old consent therefore needs to be revoked and a new consent needs to be created, or, if possible, the old consent remains unchanged and an additional consent is created which results, when combined with the original consent, in the desired rules.

- **Deletion:** On-demand deletion of consents is, similar to alteration, and for the same reason not allowed. When the health data for which the consent was given are however destroyed, it is preferred to delete the consent too, because sensitive personal data, like consents, must be minimized as much as possible (art. 6 in (European Communities, 1995), and (U. S. Department of Health and Human Services, 2003)).

PATIENT CONSENT INTEGRATION

In order to enforce patient consents, they will need to be integrated in an access control system. This section starts with an introduction to the basics of XACML. Second, a proposal is made to integrate consents in the access control system using PIPs. Also, an alternative solution strategy is discussed. Finally, an algorithm is proposed that defines how both the patient consent rules and the general practice e-health rules can be combined to obtain integrated authorization enforcement.

Background: XACML Basics

Attribute-based access control (ABAC) (Yuan & Tong, 2005) is becoming the new standard, since role-based access control (RBAC) no longer adheres to the growing complexity of rules expressiveness. As highlighted by Yuan and Tong, ABAC is more manageable and scalable than RBAC, because if policies become more fine-grained and require more attributes, the roles and permissions grow exponentially in RBAC. Also, environment attributes are not explicitly supported in RBAC. Although several extensions of RBAC exist (Barkley, Beznosov, & Uppal, 1999; Al-Kahtani & Sandhu, 2003) that try to address these issues, the solutions are still limited by the drawbacks of general RBAC.

Figure 2. Consent lifecycle

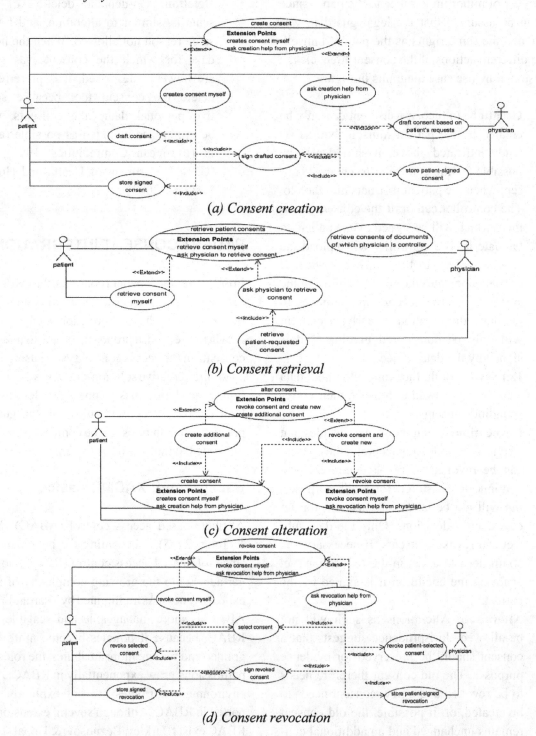

(a) *Consent creation*

(b) *Consent retrieval*

(c) *Consent alteration*

(d) *Consent revocation*

Extensible Access Control Markup Language (XACML) (Moses, 2005) is an OASIS standard that is designed for defining ABAC policies and automating their use. It is a specification that defines an XML schema for an extensible access-control policy language and access control dataflow. As shown in Figure 3, four main components characterize the access control system: a *Policy Administration Point* (PAP) which is responsible for providing policies that will be enforced; a *Policy Decision Point* (PDP), responsible for evaluating the applicable policies and returning authorization decisions; a *Policy Information Point* (PIP), an application specific component that acts as a source of attribute values needed by the PDP for making decisions; and a *Policy Enforcement Point* (PEP), responsible for protecting the resources. When a subject tries to access a resource, the PEP enforces the authorization decision. When the request is allowed, it is forwarded. When the request is denied, it is evidently not forwarded, however an error message can be returned. Furthermore,

the *context handler* separates the application environment from the XACML specifics.

A policy is a collection of related rules which are joined according to the selected rule-combining algorithm. A rule is characterized by a condition on one hand, and an effect on the other hand, as illustrated in Figure 4. If the condition is met, the effect is executed. The condition is determined by 4 main concepts. The *subject* represents the requestor, the *resource* represents the data which is targeted, the *action* describes the activity performed on the resource and the *environment* represents additional information which is independent of the subject, resource and action. The effect represents the intended consequence of the rule (permit or deny).

Patient Consent Integration through PIP

Based on interviews with health professionals and industrial partners, we have identified five high-level requirements regarding user empow-

Figure 3. XACML data-flow model (Moses, 2005)

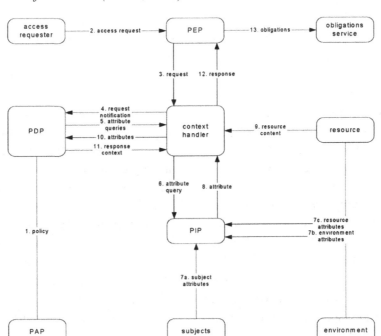

Figure 4. ABAC rule representation

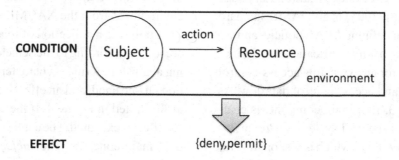

erment. 1) jurisprudence suggests that consents need to be stored for liability purposes; 2) support needs to exist to create, alter (revoke) and retrieve consents; 3) the system needs to be able to deal with a growing set of consents; 4) actions in the consent lifecycle should be controlled, as described in the consent management section; 5) in order to support user empowerment, consents need to be integrated in the access control system.

Founded on these requirements, we have introduced four architectural components. Based on the first three requirements, we have opted to store the consents in a *database*, independent of the access control system. Because it is legally required to store consents, and a database is designed to support large data sets and also support easy addition, retrieval and alteration of data, this choice is rather straight-forward. Second, a *consent management service* provides an interface for handling the lifecycle of the consents. Supported actions are, as defined by the second requirement, consent creation, retrieval, and revocation. Third, the *access control service* is integrated in the consent management service to control the allowed actions, as determined in the fourth requirement. Finally, and most importantly, the consents are integrated in the access control system using a *consent-specific PIP*, based on the fifth requirement. In order for the PDP to determine whether a request should be granted based on a patient's consent, the consent PIP is contacted, which retrieves the corresponding consents from the database and informs the PDP whether or not a matching consent has been found. The exact algorithm applied by the access control system is detailed in the following sections.

Patient Consent Integration Alternative

It would also be possible to convert the patient consents in policy rules which are directly fed to the appropriate PDP, however, we have opted not to do so based on the requirements described above. First, for evidence purposes, keeping the consents in a database meets the suggestions made by jurisprudence sufficiently. Second, there is a technical drawback when using XACML policies to express consents: whenever there is a change to a consent or its lifecycle, the policy changes, which requires dynamic policy (re)deployment at the PDP (when using standard sunXACML implementation, this means downtime because the PDP needs to be redeployed). Also it is not straight-forward to locate and remove a policy when the corresponding consent is revoked. Third, all single patient consent rules need to be combined as one large rule set which can be analyzed by the access control system, as indicated by the fifth requirement. This joining can become rather complex, because, for example, a distinction has to be made between opt-in and opt-out and the order of applicability will need to be determined. This will be easier to manage when storing the consents in a database and implementing the combination logic in the responsible PIP, than fitting it all in one large XACML rule set, especially when consents will often be added or removed. Finally, when the size of the policy set grows, the performance of the standard (sunXACML) PDP decreases, while a database is designed to handle a large set of data. However several XACML extensions exist that try to tackle the performance issues (Liu, Chen, Hwang, & Xie, 2008; Marouf, Shehab, Squicciarini, & Sundareswaran, 2009; Saldhana, 2010).

Patient Consent Integration Algorithm

Clearly, patient consent will not be the only input used by the access control system. A set of standard practice rules forms the basis for the access control system. These are predefined rules based on the current best practice (e.g. pharmacists are allowed to retrieve a patient's prescriptions, but nurses are not). These rules are a general representation of legislation and internal (e.g. hospital) policies, and, in principle, do not specify an individual patient or health care provider. Patients can extend (opt-in) or restrict (opt-out) the standard practice rules by creating consents. One of the challenges regarding patient consent integration is determining the algorithm that the access control system should apply in order to merge the predefined standard practice rules with the patient consents.

As an initial method, we suggest to implement the algorithm illustrated in Figure 5. The dashed alternatives in the top part of the figure can be omitted. User-defined restrictions are applied first (negative consents), then the standard practice rules are evaluated, and finally, extensions are considered (positive consents). The check of negative consents needs to occur first, because they will overrule both standard practice rules and positive consents, as the patient's privacy is priority in consent-centric systems. If a match is found, the request is immediately denied, if not, the request is mapped against the standard practice rules. If a standard practice rule corresponding to the request exists, the access is granted, else, the positive consents are examined. Notice that standard practice rules are assumed to be positive only, which is common practice according to our experience in e-health projects. If a positive consent exists allowing the request, access will be granted. If not, access is denied and the evaluation stops. Although this algorithm is intended for requests in a normal context, the same algorithm can be applied in case of emergency. However, when an emergency occurs, it should be taken into account that a negative consent of the patient can be overruled to, for example, protect his vital interest or those of a third person.

Clearly, the simplified algorithm favors the user's preferences over the needs of other stake-

Figure 5. Consent integration algorithm

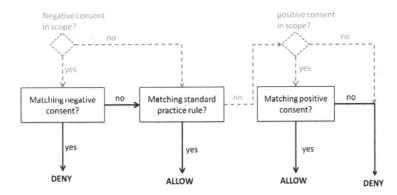

holders, like care providers. As a mitigation, the dashed part in Figure 5 can be used. It allows healthcare providers to determine the scenarios when users may influence the access control rules. These terms are predefined and determine the scope when consent should be considered by the authorization system. Negative consents narrow the access rules and can thereby obstruct the patient's medical treatment. Healthcare providers can define the appropriate scope when these access limitations can be allowed, for example, for non-emergency situations and for health care providers who do not deal with life-or-death situations, e.g. allowing patients to opt-out of sharing certain medication information with a specific doctor (for example, because the doctor is a relative). Similar scoping can be implemented for positive consents. Although in theory, a patient should be allowed to share his medical data with whomever he pleases; from an ethical perspective it is useful to provide some basic rules to help protect the patient's privacy. An example can be to only allow a patient to share his medication history with his pharmacist, but not with his physiotherapist. In the more general case, all positive consents, negative consents and standard practice rules applicable to the access request must be fetched and fed to a knowledge-based reasoner. This option is however not implemented.

PATIENT CONSENT INTEGRATION: THE XDS CASE STUDY

To validate the proposed integration strategy, a proof of concept implementation was created and tested. The IHE XDS reference architecture has been used as basis to build our own architecture, as XDS is becoming a widely accepted standard for e-health applications.

Background: XDS Architecture

Integrating the Healthcare Enterprise (IHE) is an initiative designed by health care professionals and industry to stimulate the integration of information systems of healthcare institutions by profiling existing open standards. Its main objectives are to improve communication between the various information systems which will result in an increase of efficiency and quality of care, and to ensure that healthcare professionals have access to all of their patients' clinical data in any place, at any time, and on any device. IHE provides a set of Integration Profiles, which profile existing open standards to solve an interoperability problem.

One of the most popular IHE profiles (IHE International, 2010) describes the Cross-Enterprise Document Sharing (XDS) reference architecture.

This profile is also integrated in the Microsoft Connected Health Framework (Microsoft, 2009), which presents a set of best practices, based on Service-Oriented Architecture that assist in the creation of e-health architectures, and development guidelines both for the business and technical framework.

The reference architecture is illustrated in Figure 6 and exists of one (or more) *document repository* that contains the actual data, a *document source* that provides information to the repository, a *document registry* which stores the metadata of the information stored in the repositories, a *document consumer* who can retrieve information and a *patient identity source* that provides the list of valid patient identifiers.

Consent Integrated in XDS Architecture

Figure 7 shows a possible setup that integrates consents in the access control system of an XDS architecture. The XACML authorization service has been plugged into the XDS architecture and

Figure 6. Cross-enterprise document sharing (XDS) reference architecture (IHE International, 2010)

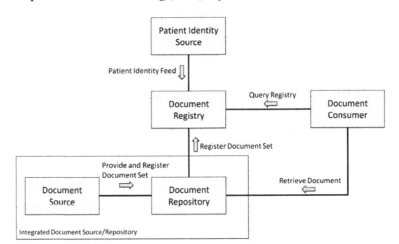

is extended with the consent services that were described earlier. This architecture exists of one central registry, and a set of distributed repositories (e.g. hospitals or regional data storage centers). The users of the platform can be both document providers and consumers. The identity provider is responsible for both the patients' and the health professionals' authentication.

If a user wants to access certain medical information, he accesses the client application which queries the registry. The registry returns a set of links that correspond to the query. Based on these results, the application fetches the requested in-

Figure 7. Patient consent in practice: setup

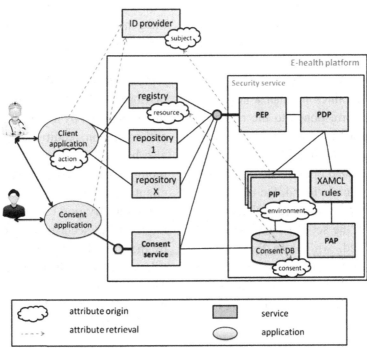

formation from the corresponding repositories. Before the registry and repositories execute the request, they contact the security service to verify whether the action is allowed. The PDP verifies whether the request should be granted by checking the policy rules, and, if required, contacts the PIP to retrieve additional attributes. The algorithm applied by the security service is described in the following section.

The security service is situated as interceptor in the back-end, because it is responsible for the protection of the dataflow and thus needs to be located as close to the data as possible. Additional services can be added to secure the applications, but this is not within the scope of this paper.

Consent Integration Algorithm Applied in XACML

As shown in Figure 7, the registry and repositories act as clients to the security service. Every time they receive a request, they verify with the security service whether this request is allowed. The rules applied by the security service are described in a XACML policy file which is evaluated by the PDP.

The policy and rule combining algorithm applied to the policy set is "first-applicable", indicating that the first matching policy will be applied and thus the policy file clearly reflects each step of the algorithm described earlier.

First, a policy examines whether a negative consent exists that corresponds to the request. Because the PDP does not have access to this information, the corresponding PIP is contacted which retrieves all related opt-out consents from the database. If a match is found, the request is denied, else the PDP continues the evaluation of the policies. Second, the set of general practice policies are examined, which are the current best practice rules (e.g. a GP has access to the medication history documents of the patients he is assigned to). If attributes are missing, the PIP

is contacted to retrieve the necessary information. When a matching policy is found, the request is granted (assuming only positive general practice rules are expressed). If not, a third type of rule is examined, which will grant the request if an opt-in consent exists (which is check by a PIP). If no matching consent exists, the final policy rule is executed which states that the request is denied.

Attribute Origin

The different attributes used to express a consent have already been discussed earlier, but it still needs to be determined how the corresponding request attributes should be acquired to check whether a consent matches a request. The attributes can be categorized according to the general concepts of attribute-based access control. *Subject* attributes include the requestor ID, role and affiliation. *Resource* attributes include the storage location, the document ID and type, the data subject, and the controller ID, role and affiliation. *Action*-related attributes are the action type, purpose and context. *Environment* attributes are all related to time and include the creation time and expiration time. Similar categorization exists for the general practice rules, but this is not within the scope of this paper.

As shown in Figure 7, the request attributes, represented as clouds, are scattered among the platform. Subject attributes are retrieved from the ID provider by the client application for basic authentication. Additional subject attributes can also be retrieved later on by the PIP if they are required. Action attributes are determined by the client application. Resource attributes are located in the registry, and can be sent together with the request to the security service, or can be retrieved by the PIP when required. The environment attributes are directly retrieved from the system. The consents themselves will also be retrieved by the PIP if required by the PDP.

PIP Attribute Retrieval

Whenever the PDP requires attributes for policy evaluation that are not provided, the appropriate PIP is contacted. For each type of attribute, a distinct PIP is implemented which contains the necessary logic to retrieve the missing attribute and return the corresponding result to the PDP. For example, the consent PIP uses the available request attributes to search for corresponding consents in the database. The PIP then informs the PDP of the presence or absence of the required consent.

Implementation Details

The concepts discussed in this paper have been implemented in a proof of concept for an interdisciplinary project that enables sharing of medical information between different healthcare providers (pharmacists, GPs, hospitals, etc.). The project focuses on the integration of patient consents, therefore only a basic set of standard practice rules has been implemented, using following attributes: user ID, user role, patient ID, controller ID, controller role, resource ID, resource type and action type.

The platform is composed of a set of distributed repositories containing medical data, and one central registry which stores the metadata of all medical files, as shown in Figure 7. Multiple applications can be developed on top of the e-health platform.

The consent repository has been implemented as a basic MySQL database, which includes a subset of the attributes defined earlier. The consent management service and the security service are implemented in Java, and use Hibernate (King et al., 2011) to easily communicate with the database in an object-oriented way. XStream (n. d.) is used to transfer patient consents in XML format between the consent service and the consent client.

The access control mechanism is handled using XACML (Moses, 2005), and authentication is integrated using SAML (Ragouzis et al., 2008). The policy has been implemented according to the algorithm described earlier by applying the concepts of first-applicable.

EVALUATION

As described in the algorithm section, four types of requests exist which either match a positive consent, a negative consent, a (positive) standard practice rule, or match nothing at all. To make the performance tests more meaningful, a distinction has been made between these types corresponding to the XACML policy.

This implementation was used in a proof-of-concept of an industrial project, thus it has already been extensively tested.

Also, the security system has been subjected to a series of tests where the set of request attributes were pseudo-randomized. On the one hand, the tests needed to be randomized to check a large range of attributes, on the other hand, it needed to be possible to predict the outcome to verify the requests, therefore only a limited set of parameters was randomized (with upper boundaries) to obtain variation within the tests without losing control over the expected results. Each of the four request categories have been tested. For each category, one attribute set has been selected, and the requestor ID and patient ID are (pseudo) randomized.

Third, a set of performance tests have measured the impact of adding consent rules to the general access control rules. Two settings were investigated: the base setting, where all rules are hard-coded as XACML policy and no consent database or PIP is used, and the implementation as discussed in the previous section, where patient consents are stored in a mySQL database.

The standard practice rules allow a GP to access medication records, prescriptions, patient summaries and aggregations, and allow pharmacists to access prescriptions. Patient consent is required when pharmacists retrieve medication records. This consent is provided for a set of patients and pharmacists (depending on the tested number of consents). Concerning negative consents, access to medication records will be denied to a set of GPs concerning a set of patient (again depending on the number of evaluated consents). The tests were run on 2 Intel Pentium computers with CPU 3.00 GHz and 1.00GB RAM. One computer deployed the security service and database, the second acted as multi-threaded client application.

Several factors have been made variable during the tests. First, the multi-threaded client simulated 1 to 5 clients concurrently accessing the security service. This is a realistic estimation for a proof-of-concept evaluation, as the clients of the security service are not the actual users of the system, but the repositories and registry, which are a relatively small set. The number of requests varies between 1 request/second to requests/second for each client, by varying the time of breaks between each request. Third, the number of consents in the database varies between 100 and 1000 negative and positive consents each, which is a sufficient upper boundary for this proof-of-concept evaluation, as only a simple mySQL database is used, and, in practice a dedicated database will be used to support the large number of consents.

Three main performance results are discussed in this section. First, a comparison is made between the different types of request, as they have a different impact on the performance. Second, the number of stored consents is compared, and third, the influence of the number of requests per second in relationship with the number of concurrent clients is discussed.

No performance optimizations have been implemented, so it was expected that the security service, which needs to contact the database for each request will have a slower response time than the base scenario. Figure 8 confirms this. The baseline has the best performance results. Second and third are the requests which do not correspond to any consent, which is quickly resolved by the database. The fourth line describes the performance of requests which correspond to one of the negative consents. To ease the query creation (because complex combinations of attributes are possible), only a limited set of attributes is fed to the database as query. The database returns the set of matching consents, which the PIP examines, to perform the more complex checks on the remaining consent set, which is time consuming. Finally, the top line represents those requests which match a positive consent. These requests have the slowest response time, and approximately double the results of the negative consent matches because first the negative consents need to be checked, which is already time consuming, and second, following the same procedures, the positive consents are checked.

The impact of increasing the number of consents is negligible, as shown in Figure 9. Clearly, extending the size of the database will not influence the general system's performance. This was to be expected, because one of the key features of a database is its ability to cope with large amounts of data.

It is also worth mentioning that as long as the time between two requests originating from the same client is 100 milliseconds or more, the response time remains constant when the number of clients grows, as shown in Figure 10. Also note that once the server CPU's saturation point has been reached, and the response time grows fast, the performance differences between the various

Figure 8. Comparison between base scenario and different types of requests (100000 requests/second (breaks of 0.01ms) per client, 500 positive consents and 500 negative consents in the database)

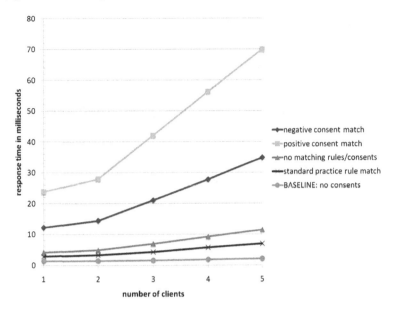

number of requests per second are negligible. As a side note, the slightly higher result of the 1request/second response time for 1 client is caused by the initialization of the service. This is also verified by the high standard deviation of this result (which, for simplicity reasons, is not depicted in the figure).

Figure 9. Comparison between number of consents in the database (all requests correspond to positive consents, 1000 requests/second (breaks of 1ms) per client

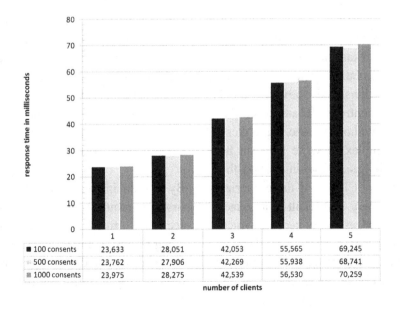

	1	2	3	4	5
■ 100 consents	23,633	28,051	42,053	55,565	69,245
500 consents	23,762	27,906	42,269	55,938	68,741
■ 1000 consents	23,975	28,275	42,539	56,530	70,259

number of clients

Figure 10. Comparison of break time between requests (all requests correspond to negative consents, 500 positive consents and 500 negative consents stored in the database)

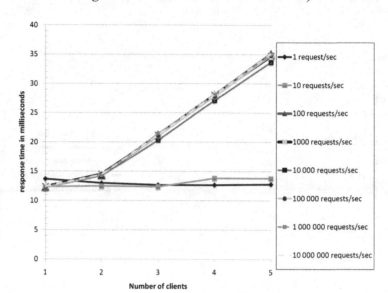

Optimizations

As mentioned before, no performance optimizations have yet been implemented, because it was only a proof-of-concept implementation. For production environments, we suggest a number of improvements.

First, the queries to the consent database can be optimized. Currently, the PIPs send a query that only specifies a limited set of attributes to the database and receive a large set of matches, which are then further examined using hibernate. This eases the implementation, because for several attributes different options need to be investigated (e.g. combination of controller ID and controller role, controller role without ID, etc.), and these queries become complex to write and can be error-prone; but this has a large impact on the system's performance. Clearly, if these queries are optimized, the query will result in an exact match and no post-processing is needed, which will drastically improve performance. This is confirmed by the results shown in Figure 8, because all 4 request types are examined by the

negative consent PIP, but only those requests of which the query results in a large matching set (requests corresponding to the positive and negative consents) have slow performance, while the requests which correspond to a small or empty set, have much better performance. Second, the query results can be cached by the system to avoid having to contact the database for similar queries. Third, when expanding the number of consents, it will be necessary to switch from a simple MySQL database to a dedicated database system with higher performance. Final, having a distributed setting of PEPs, PIPs and PDPs (Goovaerts, 2011) will spread the load, and will result in better performance.

Evaluation Summary

By introducing a database to store consents, the first three requirements described in the integration section are fulfilled. Figure 9 illustrates that by using a consent database, the performance is not influenced when the number of consents grow as requested by the third requirement. By using a PIP to retrieve matching consents for the PDP, consents can be easily integrated in the access control system, thus satisfying the fifth requirement. The evaluation has shown that, without optimization, the use of a PIP connected to a consent database introduces a performance decrease, as shown in Figure 8, however a number of optimization strategies have been suggested. Also, the size of the delay depends on the type of request and although consents are important for access control, a large number of requests will still correspond to the standard practice rules, as consents are used to introduce exceptions. As shown in Figure 8, the requests that match a standard practice rule only suffer from a minor performance overhead. The consent management service and corresponding application to handle the consent lifecycle, as described in the fourth requirement, were implemented but are not included in the evaluation, as they do not influence the performance of the general e-health system.

RELATED WORK

This section discusses work related to patient consents and its integration in the access control system. A distinction was made between work concerning consent modeling and technology that actually supports consents.

Patient-Consent Modeling

Cross-Enterprise Security and Privacy Authorization (XSPA) is an OASIS profile which focuses on the development of healthcare profiles of existing OASIS standards used to exchange interoperable security and privacy attributes within and between organizations. A mechanism to exchange privacy policies, consent directives and authorizations in an interoperable way, is required. The purpose of the XSPA profile is to focus on common requirements: allow parties to adopt a set of methods that will enable them to interoperate with other

parties. The XSPA HIMSS Interop Scenarios document (OASIS, 2009) gives an overview of some sample scenarios, of which the described attributes were used as inspiration for this paper. The XSPA scenarios do however not consider positive consents.

The BMA security policy is the first model for clinical information systems that includes consents (Anderson, 1996). It reflects best practice rules, medical ethics and actual privacy threats. It states that patients must be informed of the access control policy of a care team when they enroll, and they should be able to restrict access if they wish. The access control policy is based on access control lists that correspond to each clinical record. Whenever a name is added to the access control list, or when the responsibility of the list is transferred, the patient must be notified and his consent must be obtained (except in case of emergency). The primary control of this model is notification, together with access control lists. Although this paper has been the basis for patient consent integration, the consent structure is not discussed and no exact integration strategies are provided.

Influences of different types of consent (models) on clinical work and patient privacy are discussed in Coiera and Clarke (2004). Four different forms are identified: general consent, general consent with specific denial, general denial with specific consent and general denial. A patient consent can also have different functions: only as legal document, as audit trail or as gatekeeper for access control. Also some hints are provided for basic consent and security services. The authors also claim that a general approach to e-consent is needed; we believe that our paper can be a first step in this direction.

A decentralized approach for e-consent is presented in O'Keefe, Greenfield, and Goodchild (2005), which focuses on consents in asynchronous communication. They present the following set of consent attributes: a provider or facility identifier, a link to the consent it is replacing (optional), the access (grant, deny, grant in emergency), person to notify when emergency access override is invoked, time of consent creation and author of the consent. It is also important to note that the consents are attached to their corresponding health record entries and although health information can be shared among different facilities, revocation of consents is never propagated to other facilities, which is clearly a downside. Although these attributes already form a valuable basis for consent, our work has extended this set.

Katt et al. (2008) describe privacy and security requirements for IHE-based systems. A first requirement is the assignment of a specific role to each healthcare provider based on an electronic certificate (e.g. e-card). Second, access should only be allowed according to roles. Third, doctors are allowed access to all healthcare documents they created. Fourth, identifiable health information is only allowed to be used under consent of the patient for a specific purpose. Fifth, the patient is allowed to access all documents in his personal healthcare record; and finally, in addition to the general rules, the patient should be able to control the access to his personal record. Katt et al. (2008) thus make a clear distinction between general rules, which they refer to as "Rule-Base" and the patient's preferences. They however do not elaborate further on the integration of patient consents.

Technology Supporting User Consents

As stated earlier, technology already supports the use of user consents. This section highlights the key publications in this domain.

Cassandra (Becker & Sewell, 2004) is a trust management system which supports the tuning of the expressiveness of the policy language to address the tradeoff between expressive policies and efficiently computable policies. It is role-based with parameterized roles and actions. It supports role hierarchy and delegation, separa-

tion of duties, cascading revocation, automatic credential discovery and trust negotiation. Policies are expressed in Datalog (a prolog derivative). Cassandra uses six predicates to express rules: canActivate, hasActivated, permits, canDeactivate, isDeactivated and canRequestCredential. The activation and deactivation predicates are related to role-assignment, "canRequestCredential" defines the entities that are allowed to retrieve attribute-asserting credentials, and "permits" is used to express grant actions. Whenever an action occurs, the rule set is updated (e.g. a new role is added for a user, or a cascading deactivation of roles occurs). Cassandra also supports patient consents, which is enabled in two phases. First the clinician activates the consent request role, after which the patient can activate the consent. The proposed policy language is very expressive and can be used in a distributed setting (although it is not explained how the exchange of credentials between different domains occurs). Unfortunately only a limited prototype has been built which only supports "raw" Cassandra requests.

The consent-based framework (Russello, Dong, & Dulay, 2008) enables patients to control the disclosure of their medical data. The policies are based on the context, which is represented in terms of workflows. Obtaining consents is integrated in the workflows, where permissions are associated with tasks. In case of medical workflows, consent is implicitly assumed, and the patient can explicitly deny access if he wishes. For non-medical workflows, explicit consent is required, as an access deny is implicitly assumed. Two separate sets of policies are combined. The first set is subject-specific and represents the general workflow rules applied in hospitals. The other set is target-specific and is specified by the patients to control the privacy of their medical information. In our work, the workflow is separated from the access control system, but can be integrated by explicitly implementing need-to-know rules (based on treatment relationships) in the access control system (however this is not within the scope of this paper). Although the integration of consents in workflows is interesting, it can be restrictive, as the patient can only give his consent if this action is part of the workflow. Our solution is broader as it allows the patient to create both opt-in and opt-out consents for whatever resource, subject and action he wants, which enable true user empowerment (although, if required, this can be limited as discussed in the algorithm section). Also, the structure of the consents and rules is missing in the consent-based framework.

Jin, Ahn, Hu, Covington, and Zhang (2009) present a framework for patient-centric authorization. They claim that the patient should own his medical records and therefore be responsible for the access rights of it. They create a hierarchical structure for EHR documents and associate the objects with criteria such as data types, intended purposes and information sensitivities. Policies are specified according to a (set of) subject(s), a (set of) purpose(s) and a (set of) object(s) and the corresponding effect. They focus on discovery and resolution of policy anomalies which can occur when multiple policies apply to a request. A distinction is made between policy inconsistency and policy efficiency. The former anomalies include contradictions, exceptions and correlations, while the latter regard redundancy and verbosity. By comparing the type of match between policies and their effects, the anomaly type can be derived rather straight-forward. To resolve the anomalies, three resolution strategies are proposed: new authorization overrides, specific authorization overrides and deny overrides. A proof-of-concept implementation has been built to illustrate these concepts. The access control policies are divided in three types: break-glass consent, patient consent and default consent. The default consents describe the general access control rules, the break-glass consents described the general rules in case of emergency, and the patient consents are the rules introduced by the patient. The implementation settings are only limitedly discussed and no evaluation is provided.

The anomaly detection and resolution strategies however can be very useful to incorporate in our future work.

As illustrated in this section, technically many possibilities already exist to implement consent in health frameworks, unfortunately it is still unclear how and especially which rules should be implemented. This paper makes a first step in defining the policy content by providing a general overview of the required consent attributes which were derived from legislation, and also makes suggestions on how to integrate consent in standard practice access control. Future work is still needed to elaborate on the consent content.

DISCUSSION

Although the need-to-know principle is a key requirement in health care, it is currently not possible to technically support it in a distributed setting. The principle is based on the treatment relationship between the physician requesting the data and the corresponding patient. In a closed system (like a hospital) this can, in most cases, be achieved by tracking the patient's activity flow within the institution, although in several cases, an overrule system is necessary to support unforeseen situations. In a distributed system, where all types of health professionals can gain access to patient data, this treatment relationship is even more complex. If the need-to-know principle cannot be applied, the only viable (and legally accepted) solution is the use of patient consents.

Also, there are conflicting needs among the different stakeholders. While the patient wants his privacy protected by means of patient consent, the administrators of e-health systems are concerned with the added complexity and performance decrease. As shown in the evaluation section, the added complexity is negligible as consent enforcement will be centralized and thus not directly influence any local authorization systems. Also, as the central access control system will only be contacted by the data repositories, the performance overhead will still be manageable, especially when the suggested improvements are implemented.

This solution is also applicable to other systems if the number of clients using the security service (the number of repositories) stays rather limited, or if a distributed setup of the security service is applied where each local security service will contact the centralized patient consent database. The security service can also be used to manage service security, next to the data security that is described in this paper. Not only the actual data needs to be secured, also the back-end services should be protected from unauthorized used. As another extension, the patient consent system can also be applied in scenarios where user empowerment is not imposed by law, but just represents the user's preferences.

CONCLUSION

Patient consent is an essential concept in e-health systems. Unfortunately, the basics are still rather unstable and require further research which is the focus of this paper. This paper consists of two main contributions. First, we propose the structure of a patient's consent where all required attributes are listed, and its corresponding lifecycle describing the expected actors and actions regarding a consent. Second, necessary consent services are highlighted and integrated in an established e-health reference architecture. Finally, this architecture is validated by means of a performance evaluation of the proof-of-concept implementation.

Although this paper focuses on consents in an e-health environment, we believe that the contributions can be extended to the general user consent concept, because the main drivers for patient consent are not limited to e-health, but can be generalized to all scenarios which involve sensitive information. It is expected that the set of attributes will still require some minor tweaking to incorporate domain-specific information (e.g. an emergency context will not be relevant for banking or e-government applications), however, the general ideas can be easily translated to other domains.

ACKNOWLEDGMENT

This research is partially funded by the FP7-NESSoS project, the Interuniversity Attraction Poles Programme Belgian State, Belgian Science Policy, and by the Research Fund K.U. Leuven.

REFERENCES

Al-Kahtani, M. A., & Sandhu, R. (2003). Induced role hierarchies with attribute-based RBAC. In *Proceedings of the 8th ACM Symposium on Access Control Models and Technologies* (pp. 142-148).

Anderson, R. J. (1996). A security policy model for clinical information systems. In *Proceedings of the IEEE Symposium on Security and Privacy* (pp. 30-43). Washington, DC: IEEE Computer Society.

Barkley, J., Beznosov, K., & Uppal, J. (1999). Supporting relationships in access control using role based access control. In *Proceedings of the Fourth ACM Workshop on Role-Based Access Control* (pp. 55-65).

Becker, M. Y., & Sewell, P. (2004). Cassandra: Flexible trust management, applied to electronic health records. In *Proceedings of the 17th IEEE Workshop on Computer Security Foundations* (p. 139). Washington, DC: IEEE Computer Society.

Coiera, E., & Clarke, R. (2004). e-consent: The design and implementation of consumer consent mechanisms in an electronic environment. *Journal of the American Medical Informatics Association, 11*(2), 129–140. doi:10.1197/jamia.M1480

European Communities. (1995). *Directive 95/46/EC of the European Parliament and of the Council of 24 October 1995 on the protection of individuals with regard to the processing of personal data and on the free movement of such data.* Retrieved from http://old.cdt.org/privacy/eudirective/EU_Directive_.html

Goovaerts, T. (2011). *Distributed authorization middleware for service-oriented architectures.* Unpublished doctoral dissertation, Katholieke Universiteit Leuven, Leuven, Belgium.

International, I. H. E. (2010). *IHE integration profiles, revision 7.0, technical framework volume 1.* Retrieved from http://www.ihe.net/Technical_Framework/

Jin, J., Ahn, G. J., Hu, H., Covington, M. J., & Zhang, X. (2009). Patient-centric authorization framework for sharing electronic health records. In *Proceedings of the 14th ACM Symposium on Access Control Models and Technologies* (pp. 125-134).

Katt, B., Breu, R., Hafner, M., Schabetsberger, T., Mair, R., & Wozak, F. (2008). Privacy and access control for IHE-based systems. In *Proceedings of the 1st International Conference on Electronic Healthcare in the 21st Century.*

King, G., Bauer, C., Andersen, M. R., Bernard, E., Ebersole, S., & Ferentschik, H. (2011). *Hibernate reference documentation 3.6.1. final.* Retrieved from http://www.hibernate.org/

Liu, A. X., Chen, F., Hwang, J., & Xie, T. (2008). Xengine: A fast and scalable XACML policy evaluation engine. In *Proceedings of the ACM SIGMETRICS International Conference on Measurement and Modeling of Computer Systems* (pp. 265-276).

Marouf, S., Shehab, M., Squicciarini, A., & Sundareswaran, S. (2009). Statistics & clustering based framework for efficient XACML policy evaluation. In *Proceedings of the 10th IEEE International Conference on Policies for Distributed Systems and Networks* (pp. 118-125). Washington, DC: IEEE Computer Society.

Microsoft. (2009). *Connected health framework architecture and design blueprint, part 3 - technical framework.* Retrieved from http://www.interoperabilityshowcase.com/himss10/ docs/himss09examples/HIMSS09LeadershipWhitePaper-Microsoft.pdf

Moses, T. (2005). *eXtensible access control markup language version 2.0, specifications document.* Retrieved from http://www.oasis-open.org/committees/ tc_home.php?wg_abbrev=xacml

News, B. B. C. (2009). *Facebook faces criticism on privacy change.* Retrieved from http://news.bbc.co.uk/2/hi/technology/8405334.stm

O'Keefe, C., Greenfield, P., & Goodchild, A. (2005). a decentralized approach to electronic consent and health information access control. *Journal of Research and Practice in Information Technology, 37.*

OASIS. (2009). *HIMSS interop scenarios - demonstration of XSPA profile of SAML*. Retrieved from http://lists.oasis-open.org/archives/xspa/200901/msg00001.html

Ragouzis, N., Hughes, J., Philpott, R., Maler, E., Madsen, P., & Scavo, T. (2008). *Security assertion markup language (SAML) v2.0 technical overview, committee draft 02*. Retrieved from http://www.oasis-open.org/committees/download.php/27819/sstc-saml-tech-overview-2.0-cd-02.pdf

Russello, G., Dong, C., & Dulay, N. (2008). Consent-based workflows for healthcare management. In *Proceedings of the IEEE International Workshop on Policies for Distributed Systems and Networks* (pp. 153-161). Washington, DC: IEEE Computer Society.

Saldhana, A. (2010). *Xacml caching for performance*. Retrieved from http://community.jboss.org/wiki/ XACMLCachingforPerformance

U. S. Department of Health and Human Services. (1996). *Health insurance portability and accountability act*. Retrieved from http://www.hhs.gov/ocr/privacy/hipaa/understanding/index.html

U. S. Department of Health and Human Services. (2003). *Summary of the HIPAA privacy rule (HIPAA privacy)*. Retrieved from http://www.hhs.gov/ocr/privacy/hipaa/understanding/summary/privacysummary.pdf

Verhenneman, G. (2010). Consent, an instrument for patient empowerment? In *Proceedings of the 49th FITCE Congress*.

XStream. (n. d.). *About XStream*. Retrieved from http://xstream.codehaus.org

Yuan, E., & Tong, J. (2005). Attributed based access control (ABAC) for web services. In *Proceedings of the IEEE International Conference on web services*. Washington, DC: IEEE Computer Society.

This work was previously published in the International Journal of Secure Software Engineering, Volume 2, Issue 2, edited by Khaled M. Khan, pp. 1-24, copyright 2011 by IGI Publishing (an imprint of IGI Global).

Compilation of References

Abou-Assaleh, T., Cercone, N., Keselj, V., & Sweidan, R. (2004). Detection of new malicious code using n-grams signatures. In *Proceedings of the 2nd Annual Conference on Privacy, Security and Trust*, New Brunswick, Canada (pp. 193-196).

Abou-Assaleh, T., Cercone, N., Keselj, V., & Sweidan, R. (2004). N-gram-based detection of new malicious code. In *Proceedings of the 28th Annual International Computer Software and Applications Conference* (pp. 41-42).

Aderemi, A., & Seok-Won, L. (2010). Assimilating and optimizing software assurance in the SDLC: A framework and step-wise approach. *International Journal of Secure Software Engineering, 1*(4).

Ahn, G.-J. (2000). Role-based access control in DCOM. *Journal of Systems Architecture, 46*(13), 1175–1184. doi:10.1016/S1383-7621(00)00017-5

Ahn, G.-J., & Sandhu, R. (2001). Decentralized user group assignment in Windows NT. *Journal of Systems and Software, 56*(1), 39–49. doi:10.1016/S0164-1212(00)00084-4

Alam, M., Breu, R., & Breu, M. (2004). Model driven security for web services (MDS4WS). In *Proceedings of the 8th International Multitopic Conference* (pp. 498-505).

Alam, M., Hafner, M., & Breu, R. (2006). Constraint based role based access control (CRBAC) for restricted administrative delegation constraints in the SECTET. In *Proceedings of the International Conference on Privacy, Security, and Trust: Bridge the Gap between PST Technologies and Business Services*, Markham, ON, Canada.

Alam, M., Seifert, J. P., & Xinwen, Z. (2007). A model-driven framework for trusted computing based systems. In *Proceedings of the 11th IEEE International Enterprise Distributed Object Computing Conference* (pp. 75-75).

Alam, M., Breu, R., & Hafner, M. (2007). Model-driven security engineering for trust management in SECTET. *Journal of Software, 2*(1). doi:10.4304/jsw.2.1.47-59

Alam, M., Hafner, M., Breu, R., & Unterthiner, S. (2007). A framework for modelling restricted delegation of rights in the SECTET. *Computer Systems Science and Engineering, 22*, 289–305.

Alexander, I. (2003). Misuse cases: Use cases with hostile intent. *IEEE Software, 20*(1), 58–66. doi:10.1109/MS.2003.1159030

Al-Kahtani, M. A., & Sandhu, R. (2003). Induced role hierarchies with attribute-based RBAC. In *Proceedings of the 8th ACM Symposium on Access Control Models and Technologies* (pp. 142-148).

Alkussayer, A., & Allen, W. (2010). The ISDF framework: Towards secure software development. *Journal of Information Processing Systems, 6*(1). doi:10.3745/JIPS.2010.6.1.091

Allen, J. F. (1984). Towards a general theory of action and time. *Artificial Intelligence, 23*(2), 123–154. doi:10.1016/0004-3702(84)90008-0

Almeida, J., Bangerter, E., Barbosa, M., Krenn, S., Sadeghi, A., & Schneider, T. (2010). A certifying compiler for zero-knowledge proofs of knowledge based on sigma-protocols. In *Proceedings of the European Symposium on Research in Computer Security* (pp. 151-167).

Almendros-Jimenez, J. M., & Becerra-Teron, A., & Enciso-ba Nos, F. J. (2008). Querying xml documents in logic programming*. *Theory and Practice of Logic Programming, 8*(3), 323–361. doi:10.1017/S1471068407003183

Alshammari, B., Fidge, C., & Corney, D. (2009). Security metrics for object-oriented class designs. In *Proceedings of the 9th International Conference on Quality Software* (pp. 11-20). Washington, DC: IEEE Computer Society.

Anderson, R. (1993). Why cryptosystems fail. In *Proceedings of the 1st ACM Conference on Computer and Communications Security* (pp. 215-227).

Anderson, R. J. (1996). A security policy model for clinical information systems. In *Proceedings of the IEEE Symposium on Security and Privacy* (pp. 30-43). Washington, DC: IEEE Computer Society.

Anderson, R. (2001). *Security engineering: A guide to building dependable distributed systems*. New York, NY: John Wiley & Sons.

ANSI. (2004). *ANSI INCITS 359-2004 for role based access control*. Retrieved from http://intelligrid.ipower. com/IntelliGrid_Architecture/New_Technologies/Tech_ ANSI_INCITS_359-2004_Role_Based_Access_Control_(RBAC).htm

Anton, A. I., & Earp, J. B. (2004). A requirements taxonomy for reducing web site privacy vulnerabilities. *Requirements Engineering*, 9(3), 169–185. doi:10.1007/s00766-003-0183-z

Antonino, P., Duszynski, S., Jung, C., & Rudolph, M. (2010). Indicator-based architecture-level security evaluation in a service-oriented environment. In *Proceedings of the 4th European Conference on Software Architecture: Companion Volume* (pp. 221-228). New York, NY: ACM.

Anutariya, C., Chatvichienchai, S., Iwaihara, M., Wuwongse, V., & Kambayashi, Y. (2003). A rule-based xml access control model. In *RuleML* (pp. 35-48).

Apache Software Foundation. (2010). *The apache. http server project*. Retrieved from http://httpd.apache.org/

Araújo Neto, A., & Vieira, M. (2008). Towards assessing the security of DBMS configurations. In *Proceedings of the International Conference on Dependable Systems and Networks* (pp. 90-95).

Araújo Neto, A., Vieira, M., & Madeira, H. (2009). An appraisal to assess the security of database configurations. In *Proceedings of the 2nd International Conference on Dependability* (pp. 73-80).

Asnar, Y., Bonato, R., Giorgini, P., Massacci, F., Meduri, V., Riccucci, C., & Saidane, A. (2007). Secure and dependable patterns in organizations: An empirical approach. In *Proceedings of the IEEE International Conference on Requirements Engineering* (pp. 287-292).

Asnar, Y., Dalpiaz, F., Massacci, F., Nguyen, V. H., & Saidane, A. (2009). *Security and dependability engineering for ambient assisted living: A report on the research results by UniTN*. Retrieved from http://www.disi.unitn. it/~massacci/Download/SERENITY-MPEG.mpg

Asnar, Y., Moretti, R., Sebastianis, M., & Zannone, N. (2008). Risk as dependability metrics for the evaluation of business solutions: A model-driven approach. In *Proceedings of the 3rd International Workshop on Dependability Aspects on Data Warehousing and Mining Applications* (pp. 1240-1248).

Atkison, T. (2009). Applying randomized projection to aid prediction algorithms in detecting high-dimensional rogue applications. In *Proceedings of the 47th ACM Southeast Conference*, Clemson, SC (p. 23).

Atluri, V., & Gal, A. (2002). An authorization model for temporal and derived data: Securing information protals. *ACM Transactions on Information and System Security*, 5(1), 62–94. doi:10.1145/504909.504912

Awischus, R. (1997). Role based access control with security administration manager (SAM). In *Proceedings of the Second ACM Workshop on Role-Based Access Control* (pp. 61-68). New York, NY: ACM Press.

Backes, M., Maffei, M., & Unruh, D. (2010). Computationally sound verification of source code. In *Proceedings of the 17th ACM Conference on Computer and Communications Security* (pp. 387-398).

Baeza-Yates, R., & Ribeiro-Neto, B. (1999). *Modern information retrieval*. Harlow, UK: Addison-Wesley.

Bai, Y., & Varadharajan, V. (2003). On transformation of authorization policies. *Data & Knowledge Engineering*, *45*(3), 333–357. doi:10.1016/S0169-023X(02)00194-5

Balser, M., Reif, W., Schellhorn, G., Stenzel, K., & Thums, A. (2000). Formal system development with KIV. In *Proceedings of the 3rd International Conference on Fundamental Approaches to Software Engineering: Held as Part of the European Joint Conferences on the Theory and Practice of Software* (pp. 363-366).

Baral, C. (2003). *Knowledge representation, reasoning, and declarative problem solving*. Cambridge, MA: MIT Press. doi:10.1017/CBO9780511543357

Barkley, J. (1995). Implementing role-based access control using object technology. In *Proceedings of the First ACM Workshop on Role-Based Access Control* (pp. 93-98). New York, NY: ACM Press.

Barkley, J., & Cincotta, A. (1998). Managing role/permission relationships using object access types. In *Proceedings of the Third ACM Workshop on Role-Based Access Control* (pp. 73-80). New York, NY: ACM Press.

Barkley, J., Beznosov, K., & Uppal, J. (1999). Supporting relationships in access control using role based access control. In *Proceedings of the Fourth ACM Workshop on Role-Based Access Control* (pp. 55-65).

Barthel, K. U. (2007). *Bildmanipulation II: Filter.*

Bartz, L. S. (1997). hyperDRIVE: Leveraging LDAP to implement RBAC on the web. In *Proceedings of the ACM Workshop on Role-Based Access Control* (pp. 69-74). New York, NY: ACM Press.

Basin, D., Clavel, M., & Egea, M. (2011). A decade of model-driven security. In *Proceedings of the 16th ACM Symposium on Access Control Models and Technologies.*

Basin, D., Doser, J., & Lodderstedt, T. (2003). Model driven security for process oriented systems. In *Proceedings of the 8th ACM Symposium on Access Control Models and Technologies*, Como, Italy.

Basin, D., Doser, J., & Lodderstedt, T. (2006). Model driven security: From UML models to access control infrastructures. *ACM Transactions on Software Engineering and Methodology*, *15*(1), 39–91. doi:10.1145/1125808.1125810

Baskerville, R. L. (1999). Investigating information systems with action research. *Communications of the Association for Information Systems*, *2*(19), 1–32.

Baumhardt, F. (2006). *Common criteria - It security certification, or shiny sales sticker? (IN)Security architecture*. Retrieved from http://blogs.technet.com/fred/archive/2006/03/02/421014.aspx

Baylis, R., Lane, P., & Lorentz, D. (2003). *Oracle database administrator's guide*. Retrieved from http://otn.oracle.com/pls/db10g/db10g.homepage

Becker, M. Y., & Sewell, P. (2004). Cassandra: Flexible trust management, applied to electronic health records. In *Proceedings of the 17th IEEE Workshop on Computer Security Foundations* (p. 139). Washington, DC: IEEE Computer Society.

Bell, D. E., & LaPadula, L. J. (1975). *Secure computer systems: Unified exposition and multics interpretation* (Technical Report No. ESD-TR-75-306). Bedford, MA: MITRE.

Bergadano, F., Gunetti, D., & Picardi, C. (2002, November). User authentication through keystroke dynamics. *ACM Transactions on Information and System Security*, *5*(4), 367–397. Retrieved from http://doi.acm.org/10.1145/581271.581272. doi:10.1145/581271.581272

Bergeron, J., Debbabi, M., Desharnais, J., Erhioui, M. M., Lavoie, Y., Tawbi, N., et al. (2001). Static detection of malicious code in executable programs. In *Proceedings of the Symposium on Requirements Engineering for Information Security* (pp. 184-189).

Bergeron, J., Debbabi, M., Erhioui, M. M., & Ktari, B. (1999). Static analysis of binary code to isolate malicious behaviors. In *Proceedings of the IEEE 8th International Workshop on Enabling Technologies: Infrastructure for Collaborative Enterprises* (pp. 184-189).

Bertino, E., Braun, M., Castano, S., Ferrari, E., & Mesiti, M. (2000). Author-x: A java-based system for xml data protection. In *Proceedings of the IFIP Workshop on Database Security* (pp. 15-26).

Bertino, E., Jajodia, S., & Samarati, P. (1996). Supporting multiple access control policies in database systems. In *Proceedings of the IEEE Symposium on Research in Security and Privacy* (pp. 94-107).

Bertino, E., Bettini, C., Ferrari, E., & Samarati, P. (1998). An access control model supporting periodicity constraints and temporal reasoning. *ACM Transactions on Database Systems*, *23*(3), 231–285. doi:10.1145/293910.293151

Bertino, E., Buccafurri, F., Ferrari, E., & Rullo, P. (2000). A logic-based approach for enforcing access control. *Computers & Security*, *8*(2), 109–140.

Bertino, E., Carminati, B., & Ferrari, E. (2004). Access control for xml documents and data. *Information Security Technical Report*, *9*(3), 19–34. doi:10.1016/S1363-4127(04)00029-9

Bertino, E., Catania, B., Ferrari, E., & Perlasca, P. (2003). A logical framework for reasoning about access control models. *ACM Transactions on Information and System Security*, *6*(1), 71–127. doi:10.1145/605434.605437

Bertino, E., Jajodia, S., & Samarati, P. (1995). Database security: Research and practice. *Information Systems Journal*, *20*(7).

Best, B., Jurjens, J., & Nuseibeh, B. (2007). Model-based security engineering of distributed information systems using UMLsec. In *Proceedings of the 29th International Conference on Software Engineering*.

Betous-Almeida, C., & Kanoun, K. (2002). Stepwise construction and refinement of dependability models. In *Proceedings of the Conference on Dependable Systems and Networks* (pp. 515-524).

Beznosov, K. (2003). Extreme security engineering: On employing XP practices to achieve 'good enough security' without defining it. In *Proceedings of the First ACM Workshop on Business Driven Security Engineering*, Fairfax, VA.

Bhargavan, K., Corin, R., Deniélou, P., Fournet, C., & Leifer, J. (2009). Cryptographic protocol synthesis and verification for multiparty sessions. In *Proceedings of the Computer Security Foundations Symposium* (pp. 124-140).

Bhargavan, K., Fournet, C., Gordon, A., & Tse, S. (2008). Verified interoperable implementations of security protocols. *ACM Transactions on Programming Languages and Systems*, *31*(1), 1–61. doi:10.1145/1452044.1452049

Bicz, W. O. (2010). *Fingerprint structure imaging based on an ultrasound camera.* Retrieved from http://www.optel.com.pl/article/english/article.htm

Bindiganavale, V., & Ouyang, J. (2006, September). Role based access control in enterprise application-security administration and user management. In *Proceedings of the IEEE International Conference on Information Reuse and Integration*, Waikoloa Village, HI (pp. 111-116). Washington, DC: IEEE Computer Society.

Bingham, E., & Mannila, H. (2001). Random projection in dimensionality reduction: Applications to image and text data. In *Proceedings of the 7th ACM SIGKDD International Conference on Knowledge Discovery and Data Mining* (pp. 245-250).

Biomedical Signal Analysis Laboratory. (2010). *Liveness Detection in Biometric Devices.* Retrieved from http://people.clarkson.edu/~biosal/research/liveness.html

Blanchet, B. (2009). Automatic verification of correspondences for security protocols. *Journal of Computer Security*, *17*(4), 363–434.

Blanco, C., de Guzman, I. G. R., Fernandez-Medina, E., Trujillo, J., & Piattini, M. (2008). Automatic generation of secure multidimensional code for data warehouses: An MDA approach. In R. Meersman & Z. Tari (Eds.), *Proceedings of the International Conference of On the Move to Meaningful Internet Systems* (LNCS 5332, pp. 1052-1068).

Blanco, C., Fernandez-Medina, E., Trujillo, J., & Piattini, M. (2008, March 4-7). Implementing multidimensional security into OLAP tools. In *Proceedings of the 3rd International Conference on Availability, Security, and Reliability*, Barcelona, Spain.

Blanco, C., Pérez-Castillo, R., Hernández, A., Fernández-Medina, E., & Trujillo, J. (2009). Towards a modernization process for secure data warehouses. In T. B. Pedersen, M. K. Mohania, & A. M. Tjoa (Eds.), *Proceedings of the 11th International Conference on Data Warehousing and Knowledge Discovery*, Linz, Austria (LNCS 5691, pp. 24-35).

Blobel, B., & France, R. A. (2001). A systematic approach for analysis and design of secure health information systems. *International Journal of Medical Informatics*, *62*(2).

Blommé, J. (2003). *Evaluation of biometric security systems against artificial fingers.*

Boehm, B., & Basili, V. R. (2001). Software defect reduction top 10 list. *IEEE Computer, 34*, 135–137.

Boström, G., Wäyrynen, J., & Bodén, M. (2006). Extending XP practices to support security requirements engineering. In *Proceedings of the ACM International Workshop on Software Engineering for Secure Systems* (pp. 11-18).

Bresciani, P., Giorgini, P., Giunchiglia, F., Mylopoulos, J., & Perini, A. (2004). TROPOS: An agent-oriented software development methodology. *Journal of Autonomous Agents and Multi-agent Systems, 8*(3), 203–236. doi:10.1023/B:AGNT.0000018806.20944.ef

Breu, R., Hafner, M., Weber, B., & Novak, A. (2005, March 2-4). Model driven security for inter-organizational workflows in e-government. In M. Böhlen, J. Gamper, W. Polasek, & M. A. Wimmer (Eds.), *Proceedings of the International Conference on E-Government: Towards Electronic Democracy*, Bolzano, Italy (LNCS 3416, pp. 122-133).

Bromba, M. (2002). *Biometrie und Sicherheit.* Retrieved from http://www.bromba.com/knowhow/biosich.htm

Bromba, M. (2008, February 16). *Biometrie FAQ.* Retrieved from http://www.bromba.com/faq/biofaqd.htm

Bromba, M. (2008, February 5). *Über die Unbrauchbarkeit der Biometrie.* Retrieved from http://www.bromba.com/knowhow/KleineAnleitung.htm

Bromba, M. (2009). *Fingerprint FAQ.* Retrieved from http://www.bromba.com/faq/fpfaqd.htm

Brown, N., & Kindel, C. (1998). *Distributed component object model protocol-DCOM/1.0.* Retrieved from http://www.ietf.org/proceedings/43/I-D/draft-brown-dcom-v1-spec-03.txt

Buell, D., & Sandhu, R. (2003). Identity management. *IEEE Internet Computing, 7*(6), 26–28. doi:10.1109/MIC.2003.1250580

Busnel, P., El Khoury, P., Li, K., Saidane, A., & Zannone, N. (2008). S&D pattern deployment at organizational level: A prototype for remote healthcare system. *Electronic Notes in Theoretical Science, 244*, 27–39. doi:10.1016/j.entcs.2009.07.036

Byers, D., & Shahmehri, N. (2010). Unified modeling of attacks, vulnerabilities and security activities. In *Proceedings of the ICSE Workshop on Software Engineering for Secure Systems* (pp. 36-42). New York, NY: ACM.

Cachin, C., Camenisch, J., Dacier, M., Deswarte, Y., Dobson, J., Horne, D., et al. (2000). *Reference model and use cases* (Tech. Rep. No. IST-1999-11583). Retrieved from http://spiderman-2.laas.fr/TSF/cabernet/maftia/deliverables/D1.pdf

Campell, E. D. (1998). *Fingerprints & Palmar Dermatoglyphics.* Retrieved from http://www.edcampbell.com/PalmD-History.htm

Capkun, S., Buttyan, L., & Hubaux, J. P. (2003). Self-Organized Public-Key Management for Mobile Ad Hoc Networks. *IEEE Transactions on Mobile Computing, 2*(1), 52–64. doi:10.1109/TMC.2003.1195151

Castano, S., Fugini, M. G., Martella, G., & Samarati, P. (1994). *Database security.* Reading, MA: Addison-Wesley.

Center for Internet Security. (2008). *CIS benchmarks/scoring tools.* Retrieved from http://www.cisecurity.org

Chadwick, D. W., & Otenko, A. (2002). The PERMIS X.509 role based privilege management infrastructure. In *Proceedings of the Seventh ACM Symposium on Access Control Models and Technologies* (pp. 135-140). New York, NY: ACM Press.

Chaki, S., & Datta, A. (2009). ASPIER: An automated framework for verifying security protocol implementations. In *Proceedings of the Computer Security Foundations Symposium* (pp. 172-185).

Chalfant, T. M. (2003). *Role based access control and secure shell - a closer look at two Solaris™ operating environment security features.* Redwood Shores, CA: Sun BluePrints™ OnLine.

Chaos Computer Club. (2004, October 9).*Wie können Fingerabdrücke nachgebildet werden?* Retrieved from http://www.ccc.de/biometrie/fingerabdruck_kopieren.xml?language=de

Checkland, P., & Scholes, J. (1990). *Soft systems methodology in action.* New York, NY: John Wiley & Sons.

Chikofsky, E., & Cross, J. (1990). Reverse engineering and design recovery: A taxonomy. *IEEE Software, 7*(1), 13–17. doi:10.1109/52.43044

Chomicki, J., Lobo, J., & Naqvi, S. (2000). A logical programming approach to conflict resolution in policy management. In *Proceedings of the International Conference on Principles of Knowledge Representation and Reasoning* (pp. 121-132).

Christodorescu, M., & Jha, S. (2003). Static analysis of executables to detect malicious patterns. In *Proceedings of the 12th Conference on USENIX Security Symposium* (p. 12).

Chung, L., Nixon, B. A., Yu, E., & Mylopoulos, J. (2000). *Non-functional requirements in software engineering.* Boston, MA: Kluwer Academic.

Clavel, M., Silva, V., Braga, C., & Egea, M. (2008). Model-driven security in practice: An industrial experience. In *Proceedings of the 4th European Conference on Model Driven Architecture: Foundations and Applications* (pp. 326-337).

Cockburn, A. (2001). *Writing effective use cases.* Reading, MA: Addison-Wesley.

Coiera, E., & Clarke, R. (2004). e-consent: The design and implementation of consumer consent mechanisms in an electronic environment. *Journal of the American Medical Informatics Association, 11*(2), 129–140. doi:10.1197/jamia.M1480

Commission of the European Communities. (1993). *Information technology security evaluation manual (ITSEM).* Brussels, Belgium: Author.

Common Criteria. (1999). *Common criteria for information technology security evaluation: User guide.* Retrieved from http://www.commoncriteriaportal.org/files/ccfiles/CCPART2V3.1R2.pdf

Compagna, L., Khoury, P. E., Krausová, A., Massacci, F., & Zannone, N. (2009). How to integrate legal requirements into a requirements engineering methodology for the development of security and privacy patterns. *Artificial Intelligence and Law, 17*(1), 1–30. doi:10.1007/s10506-008-9067-3

Computer Emergency Response Team. (2011). *CERT statistics.* Retrieved from http://www.cert.org/stats/

Consortium, W. W. W. (1999). *Xml path language (xpath) version 1.0.* Retrieved from http://www.w3.org/TR/xpath

Consortium, W. W. W. (2008). *Extensible markup language (xml) 1.0* (5th ed.). Retrieved from http://www.w3.org/TR/REC-xml/

Control Engineering, U. K. (2010, 20 July). *'Stuxnet' Trojan Targets Siemens WinCC.* Retrieved from http://www.controlenguk.com/article.aspx?ArticleID=35267

Cooper, A. (1999). *The inmates are running the asylum: Why high tech products drive us crazy and how to restore the sanity* (2nd ed.). Upper Saddle River, NJ: Pearson Higher Education.

Corbin, J. M., & Strauss, A. L. (2008). *Basics of qualitative research: techniques and procedures for developing grounded theory.* Thousand Oaks, CA: Sage.

Crampton, J., & Khambhammettu, H. (2008). Delegation in role-based access control. *International Journal of Information Security, 7*, 123–136. doi:10.1007/s10207-007-0044-8

Cremerius, R., & Snurnikov, L. (2006). *Biometrie und Datenschutz.* Retrieved from http://waste.informatik.hu-berlin.de/Lehre/ss06/SE_ueberwachung/vortrag5.pdf

Crook, R., Ince, D., Lin, L., & Nuseibeh, B. (2002). Security requirements engineering: When anti-requirements hit the fan. In *Proceedings of the 10th International Requirements Engineering Conference* (pp. 203-205).

CVE. (2011). *Common vulnerabilities and exposures (CVE).* Retrieved from http://cve.mitre.org/

Dacier, M., & Deswarte, Y. (1994). Privilege graph: An extension to the typed access matrix model. In *Proceedings of the European Symposium on Research in Computer Security* (pp. 319-334).

Damiani, E., di Vimercati, S. D. C., Paraboschi, S., & Sama-rati, P. (2002). A fine-grained access control system for xml documents. *ACM Transactions on Information and System Security, 5*(2), 169–202. doi:10.1145/505586.505590

Damiani, E., Vimercati, S., Paraboschi, S., & Samarati, P. (2002). A fine grained access control system for XML documents. *ACM Transactions on Information and System Security*, 160–202.

Dardenne, A., van Lamsweerde, A., & Fickas, S. (1993). Goal-directed requirements acquisition. *Science of Computer Programming, 20*, 3–50. doi:10.1016/0167-6423(93)90021-G

Dasgupta, S., & Gupta, A. (1999). *An elementary proof of the Johnson-Lindenstrauss Lemma*. Berkley, CA: International Computer Science Institute.

Das, S. K. (1992). *Deductive databases and logic programming*. Reading, MA: Addison-Wesley.

Daugman, J. (2004). How Iris Recognition Works. *IEEE Trans. CSVT, 14*(1), 21–30.

Daugman, J. (2007). New methods in iris recognition. *IEEE Trans. Systems, Man. Cybernetics B, 37*(5), 1167–1175. doi:10.1109/TSMCB.2007.903540

Davis, J. (2009). *Open source SOA* (1st ed.). Stamfort, CT: Manning.

Defense Information Systems Agency. (2007). *Database - Security technical implementation guide, version 8, release 1*. Washington, DC: Author.

DeMichiel, L. G., & Keith, M. (2006). *JSR-220: Enterprise JavaBeans 24 specification, version 3.0: EJB core contracts and requirements (Specification No. v.3.0 Final Release)*. Retrieved from http://jcp.org/aboutJava/communityprocess/pfd/jsr220/index.html

DeMichiel, L. G., Yalçinalp, L. Ü., & Krishnan, S. (2001). *Enterprise JavaBeans specification, version 2.0*. Retrieved from http://java.sun.com/products/ejb/docs.html

Dempster, A. (2008). The dempster-shafer calculus for statisticians. *International Journal of Approximate Reasoning, 48*(2), 365–377. doi:10.1016/j.ijar.2007.03.004

den Braber, F., Hogganvik, I., Lund, M. S., Stølen, K., & Vraalsen, F. (2007). Model-based security analysis in seven steps - A guided tour to the CORAS method. *BT Technology Journal, 25*(1), 101–117. doi:10.1007/s10550-007-0013-9

Denning, D. E. (1976). A lattice model of secure information flow. *Communications of the ACM, 19*, 236–243. doi:10.1145/360051.360056

Department of Defense. (1985). *Trusted computer system evaluation criteria*. Washington, DC: Author.

Devanbu, P., & Stubblebine, S. (2000). Software engineering for security: A roadmap. In *Proceedings of the International Conference on the Future of Software Engineering* (pp. 201-211).

DHS. (2011). *Security in the software lifecycle*. Retrieved from http://home.himolde.no/~molka/lo205/booknotes-06/Security-Software-Lifecycle2006.pdf

Di Giacomo, V., Felici, M., Meduri, V., Presenza, D., Riccucci, C., & Tedeschi, A. (2008). Using security and dependability patterns for reaction processes. In *Proceedings of the 19th International Conference on Database and Expert Systems* (pp. 315-319).

di Vimercati, S. D. C., Marrara, S., & Samarati, P. (2005). An access control model for querying xml data. In *Proceedings of the 2005 workshop on Secure web services (SWS '05)* (pp. 36-42). New York: ACM.

Digitus. (2010). *Digitus USB Fingerprint Reader*. Retrieved from http://www.digitus.info/en/products/accessories/?c=1215&p=3577

Dobrica, L., & Niemelä, E. (2002). A survey on software architecture analysis methods. *IEEE Transactions on Software Engineering, 28*(7), 638–653. doi:10.1109/TSE.2002.1019479

Duszynski, S., Knodel, J., & Lindvall, M. (2009). SAVE: Software architecture visualization and evaluation. In *Proceedings of the European Conference on Software Maintenance and Reengineering* (pp. 323-324). Washington, DC: IEEE Computer Society.

Dybå, T., Dingsøyr, T., & Hanssen, G. K. (2007). Applying systematic reviews to diverse study types: An experience report. In *Proceedings of the 1st International Symposium on Empirical Software Engineering and Measurement* (pp. 225-234).

Eddon, G. (1999). The COM+ security model gets you out of the security programming business. *Microsoft Systems Journal, 1999*(11).

Elahi, G., & Yu, E. (2007). A goal oriented approach for modeling and analyzing security trade-offs. In C. Parent, K.-D. Schewe, V. C. Storey, & B. Thalheim (Eds.), *Proceedings of the 26th International Conference on Conceptual Modeling* (LNCS 4801, pp. 375-390).

Epstein, J., & Sandhu, R. (1995). Netware 4 as an example of role-based access control. In *Proceedings of the First ACM Workshop on Role-Based Access Control* (pp. 71-82). New York, NY: ACM Press.

European Communities. (1995). *Directive 95/46/EC of the European Parliament and of the Council of 24 October 1995 on the protection of individuals with regard to the processing of personal data and on the free movement of such data.* Retrieved from http://old.cdt.org/privacy/eudirective/EU_Directive_.html

eXtreme Programming. (2011). *A gentle introduction.* Retrieved from http://www.extremeprogramming.org/

Faber, E. (2010). *Eberhard Faber Gmbh.* Retrieved from http://www.eberhardfaber.de/

Faden, G. (1999). RBAC in UNIX administration. In *Proceedings of the Fourth ACM Workshop on Role-Based Access Control* (pp. 95-101). New York, NY: ACM Press.

Fagin, R., Halpern, J. Y., Moses, Y., & Vardi, M. Y. (1995). *Reasoning about knowledge.* Cambridge, MA: MIT Press.

Faily, S., & Fléchais, I. (2009). Context-sensitive requirements and risk management with IRIS. In *Proceedings of the 17th IEEE International Requirements Engineering Conference* (pp. 379-380).

Faily, S., & Fléchais, I. (2010). A meta-model for usable secure requirements engineering. In *Proceedings of the 6th International Workshop on Software Engineering for Secure Systems* (pp. 126-135).

Faily, S., & Fléchais, I. (2010). Barry is not the weakest link: Eliciting secure system requirements with personas. In *Proceedings of the 24th British HCI Group Annual Conference on People and Computers: Play is a Serious Business* (pp. 113-120).

Faily, S., & Fléchais, I. (2010). The secret lives of assumptions: Developing and refining assumption personas for secure system design. In R. Bernhaupt, P. Forbrig, J. Gulliksen, & M. Lárusdóttir (Eds.), *Proceedings of the 3rd Conference on Human-Centered Software Engineering* (LNCS 6409, pp. 111-118).

Faily, S., & Fléchais, I. (2010). Towards tool-support for usable secure requirements engineering with CAIRIS. *International Journal of Secure Software Engineering, 1*(3), 56–70. doi:10.4018/jsse.2010070104

Fan, W., Chan, C., & Garofalakis, M. (2004). Secure xml querying with security views. In *Proceedings of the 2004 ACM SIGMOD international conference on Management Data (SIGMOD 2004)*. New York: ACM Press.

Feltin, B. (2002). *Information Assurance Using Biometrics.*

Fernandez, E. B., France, R. B., & Wei, D. (1995). A formal specification of an authorization model for object-oriented databases. *Database Security, IX: Status and Prospects*, 95-109.

Fernandez, E. B., Gudes, E., & Song, H. (1995). A security model for object-oriented databases. In *Proceedings of the IEEE Symposium on Research in Security and Privacy* (pp. 110-115).

Fernandez-Medina, E., Jurjens, J., Trujillo, J., & Jajodia, S. (2009). Model-driven development for secure information systems. *Information and Software Technology, 51*, 809–814. doi:10.1016/j.infsof.2008.05.010

Ferraiolo, D. F., & Kuhn, R. (1992). Role-based access controls. In *Proceedings of the 15th NIST-NCSC National Computer Security Conference*, Baltimore, MD (pp. 554-563).

Ferraiolo, D. F., Cugini, J. A., & Kuhn, D. R. (1995). Role-based access control (rbac): Features and motivations. In *Proceedings of the 11th Annual Computer Security Applications.*

Ferraiolo, D. F., Barkley, J. F., & Kuhn, D. R. (1999). A role-based access control model and reference implementation within a corporate intranet. *ACM Transactions on Information and System Security*, 2(1), 34–64. doi:10.1145/300830.300834

Ferraiolo, D. F., Sandhu, R., Gavrila, S., Kuhn, D. R., & Chandramouli, R. (2001). Proposed NIST standard for role-based access control. *ACM Transactions on Information and System Security*, 4(3), 224–274. doi:10.1145/501978.501980

Fléchais, I. (2005). *Designing secure and usable systems.* Unpublished doctoral dissertation, University College London, London, UK.

Fléchais, I., Mascolo, C., & Sasse, M. A. (2007). Integrating security and usability into the requirements and design process. *International Journal of Electronic Security and Digital Forensics*, 1(1), 12–26. doi:10.1504/IJESDF.2007.013589

Food and Drug Administration. (2010). *Infusion pump software safety research at FDA.* Retrieved from http://www.fda.gov/MedicalDevices/ProductsandMedicalProcedures/GeneralHospitalDevicesandSupplies/InfusionPumps/ucm202511.htm

Fota, N., Kaaniche, M., & Kanoun, K. (1998). Dependability evaluation of an air traffic control computing system. In *Proceedings of the 3rd IEEE International Symposium on Computer Performance and Dependability* (pp. 206-215).

Gabillon, A. (2005). *A formal access control model for xml databases* (LNCS 3674, pp. 86-103). New York: Springer.

Gabor, H., & Istvin, M. (2000). Quantitative analysis of dependability critical systems based on UML statechart models. In *Proceedings of the 5th IEEE International Symposium on High Assurance Systems Engineering* (pp. 83-92).

Gamma, E., Helm, R., Johnson, R., & Glissades, J. (1994). *Design patterns: Elements of reusable object-oriented software.* Reading, MA: Addison-Wesley.

Ge, X., Paige, R. F., Polack, F. A. C., Chivers, H., & Brooke, P. J. (2006). Agile development of secure web applications. In *Proceedings of the 6th International Conference on Web Engineering* (pp. 305-312).

Gelfond, M., & Lifschitz, V. (1988). The stable model semantics for logic programming. In R. A. Kowalski & K. Bowen (Eds.), *Proceedings of the Fifth International Conference on Logic Programming* (pp. 1070-1080). Cambridge, MA. The MIT Press.

Gelfond, M. (1994). Logic programming and reasoning with incomplete information. *Annals of Mathematics and Artificial Intelligence*, 12, 98–116. doi:10.1007/BF01530762

Gennaro, R., Jarecki, S., Krawczyk, H., & Rabin, T. (2007). Secure Distributed Key Generation for Discrete-Log Based Cryptosystems. *J. Cryptology*, 20(1), 51–83. doi:10.1007/s00145-006-0347-3

Ghezzi, C., Jazayeri, M., & Mandrioli, D. (2003). *Fundamentals of software engineering.* Upper Saddle River, NJ: Prentice Hall.

Gimp. (2010). *GNU Image Manipulation Program.* Retrieved from http://www.gimp.org/

Giorgini, P., Massacci, F., & Zannone, N. (2005b). Security and trust requirements engineering. In A. Aldini, R. Gorrieri, & F. Martinelli (Eds.), *Proceedings of the Tutorial Lectures on Foundations of Security Analysis and Design III* (LNCS 3655, pp. 237-272).

Giorgini, P., Massacci, F., Mylopoulos, J., & Zannone, N. (2005). Modeling security requirements through ownership, permission and delegation. *International Journal of Information Security*, 5(4), 257–274. doi:10.1007/s10207-006-0005-7

Giuri, L. (1998). Role-based access control in Java. In *Proceedings of the Third ACM Workshop on Role-Based Access Control*, Fairfax, VA (pp. 91-99). New York, NY: ACM Press.

Giuri, L. (1999). Role-based access control on the Web using Java. In *Proceedings of the Fourth ACM Workshop on Role-Based Access Control* (pp. 11-18). New York, NY: ACM Press.

Goovaerts, T. (2011). *Distributed authorization middleware for service-oriented architectures.* Unpublished doctoral dissertation, Katholieke Universiteit Leuven, Leuven, Belgium.

Goth, G. (2005). Identity management, access specs are rolling along. *IEEE Internet Computing, 9*(1), 9–11. doi:10.1109/MIC.2005.16

Grégoire, J., Buyens, K., De Win, B., Scandariato, R., & Joosen, W. (2007). On the secure software development process: CLASP and SDL compared. In *Proceedings of the Third International Workshop on Software Engineering for Secure Systems* (p. 1).

Gutzmann, K. (2001). Access control and session management in the HTTP environment. *IEEE Internet Computing, 5*(1), 26–35. doi:10.1109/4236.895139

Hafner, M., Alam, M., & Breu, R. (2006, October 1-6). Towards a MOF/QVT-based domain architecture for model driven security. In O. Nierstrasz, J. Whittle, D. Harel, & G. Reggio (Eds.), *Proceedings of the 9th International Conference on Model Driven Engineering Languages and Systems*, Genova, Italy (LNCS 4199, pp. 275-290).

Hafner, M., Breu, M., Breu, R., & Nowak, A. (2005). Modelling inter-organizational workflow security in a peer-to-peer environment. In *Proceedings of the IEEE International Conference on Web Services.*

Hafner, M., & Breu, R. (2009). *Security engineering for service-oriented architectures.* Berlin, Germany: Springer-Verlag.

Haley, C. B. (2007). *Arguing security: A framework for analyzing security requirements.* Saarbrücken, Germany: VDM Verlag Dr Müller.

Haley, C. B., Laney, R., Moffett, J. D., & Nuseibeh, B. (2006). Arguing satisfaction of security requirements. In Mouratidis, H., & Giorgini, P. (Eds.), *Integrating security and software engineering: Advances and future visions* (pp. 16–43). Hershey, PA: Idea Group. doi:10.4018/978-1-59904-147-6.ch002

Haluschak, B. (2009, January). *Biometrie Grundlagen - Vom Fingerprint bis zur Gesichtserkennung. Tec Channel.* Retrieved from http://www.tecchannel.de/sicherheit/identity_access/402320/grundlagen_mehr_sicherheit_mit_biometrie/index.html

Harris, T. (2002, September). *How Fingerprint Scanners work.* How stuff works. Retrieved from http://computer.howstuffworks.com/fingerprint-scanner.htm

Hartman, B., Flinn, D. J., & Beznosov, K. (2001). *Enterprise security with EJB and CORBA.* New York, NY: John Wiley & Sons.

Haug, T. H. (2007). *A systematic review of empirical research on model-driven development with UML.* Unpublished master's thesis, University of Oslo, Oslo, Norway.

Haventools Software. (2009). *Heaventools: PE Explorer.* Retrieved from http://www.heaventools.net

Hein, S., & Mahrla, M. (2004). *Überwindungsszenarien für biometrische Systeme.* Retrieved from http://www2.informatik.huberlin.de/Forschung_Lehre/algorithmenII/Lehre/SS2004/Biometrie/09Ueberwindung/Ueberwindung/index.html

Henchiri, O., & Japkowicz, N. (2006). A feature selection and evaluation scheme for computer virus detection. In *Proceedings of the 6th International Conference on Data Mining* (pp. 891-895).

Hermann, G., & Pernul, G. (1999). Viewing business-process security from different perspectives. *International Journal of Electronic Commerce, 3,* 89–103.

Hope, P., McGraw, G., & Anton, A. I. (2004). Misuse and abuse cases: getting past the positive. *IEEE Security & Privacy, 2*(3), 90–92. doi:10.1109/MSP.2004.17

Hovemeyer, D., & Pugh, W. (2004). Finding bugs is easy. In *Proceedings of the Companion to the 19th Annual ACM SIGPLAN Conference on Object-Oriented Programming Systems, Languages, and Applications* (pp. 132-136). New York, NY: ACM.

Howard, M., & Leblanc, D. E. (2002). *Writing secure code* (2nd ed.). Sebastopol, CA: Microsoft Press.

Howard, M., & Lipner, S. (2006). *The security development lifecycle: SDL: A process for developing demonstrably more secure software.* Sebastopol, CA: Microsoft Press.

Hyytiä, E., & Virtamo, J. (2007). Random Waypoint Mobility Model in Cellular Networks. *Wireless Networks, 13*(2), 177–188. doi:10.1007/s11276-006-4600-3

IBM. (2005). *IBM informix dynamic server administrator's guide.* Retrieved from http://www-306.ibm.com/software/data/informix/pubs/library/ids100.html

IBM. (2011). *Rational software.* Retrieved from http://www-01.ibm.com/software/rational/

Iivari, J., Hirschheim, R., & Klein, H. K. (1998). A paradigmatic analysis contrasting information systems development approaches and methodologies. *Information Systems Research, 9*(2), 164–193. doi:10.1287/isre.9.2.164

International Biometric Group. (2005). *Independent Testing of Iris Recognition Technology.*

International Biometric Group. (2008). *Biometrics Market and Industry Report 2009 - 2014.* Retrieved from http://www.biometricgroup.com/reports/public/market_report.php

International Organization for Standardization (ISO). (1999). *ISO/IEC 13407: Human-centered design processes for interactive systems.* Geneva, Switzerland: ISO.

International Organization for Standardization. (2005). *ISO 27001: Information technology—Security techniques—Information security management systems—Requirements.* Retrieved from http://www.iso27001security.com/html/27001.html

International, I. H. E. (2010). *IHE integration profiles, revision 7.0, technical framework volume 1.* Retrieved from http://www.ihe.net/Technical_Framework/

ISO/IEC Group 1. (2010). *Harmonized Biometric Vocabulary.* Retrieved from http://www.3dface.org/media/vocabulary.html

Jackson, W. (2007). *Under attack: Common Criteria has loads of critics, but is it getting a bum rap?* Retrieved from http://www.gcn.com/print/26_21/44857-1.html

Jajodia, S., Samarati, P., Sapino, M. L., & Subrahmanian, V. S. (2001). Flexible support for multiple access control policies. *ACM Transactions on Database Systems, 29*(2), 214–260. doi:10.1145/383891.383894

Jensen, J., & Jaatun, M. G. (2011). Security in model driven development: A survey. In *Proceedings of the 5th International Workshop on Secure Software Engineering.*

Jin, J., Ahn, G. J., Hu, H., Covington, M. J., & Zhang, X. (2009). Patient-centric authorization framework for sharing electronic health records. In *Proceedings of the 14th ACM Symposium on Access Control Models and Technologies* (pp. 125-134).

Johnson, D. B., & Maltz, D. A. (1996). Dynamic Source Routing in Ad Hoc Wireless Networks. In Imielinski & Korth (Eds.), *Mobile Computing* (Vol. 353, pp. 153-181). Dordrecht, The Netherlands: Kluwer Academic Publishers.

Johnson, W. B., & Lindenstrauss, J. (1984). Extensions of Lipschitz mappings into a Hilbert space. *Contemporary Mathematics, 26,* 189–206.

Jones, R., & Rastogi, A. (2004). Secure coding: Building security into the software development life cycle. *Information Systems Security, 13*(5).

Jovanovic, N., Kruegel, C., & Kirda, E. (2006). Pixy: A static analysis tool for extracting web application vulnerabilities. In *Proceedings of the IEEE Symposium on Security and Privacy* (pp. 258-263).

Jürjens, J., Schreck, J., & Bartmann, P. (2008). Model-based security analysis for mobile communications. In *Proceedings of the 30th International Conference on Software Engineering.*

Jürjens, J., Schreck, J., & Bartmann, P. (2008). Model-based security analysis for mobile communications. In *Proceedings of the International Conference on Software Engineering* (pp. 683-692).

Jürjens, J. (2004). *Secure systems development with UML.* New York, NY: Springer.

Kang, M. G., Poosankam, P., & Yin, H. (2007). Renovo: A hidden code extractor for packed executables. In *Proceedings of the ACM Workshop on Recurring Malcode.*

Kanoun, K., & Spainhower, L. (2008). *Dependability benchmarking for computer systems.* Los Alamitos, CA: Wiley-IEEE Computer Society Press. doi:10.1002/9780470370506

Karppinen, K., Lindvall, M., & Yonkwa, L. (2008). Detecting security vulnerabilities with software architecture analysis tools. In *Proceedings of the IEEE International Conference on Software Testing Verification and Validation Workshop* (pp. 262-268). Washington, DC: IEEE Computer Society.

Kasal, K., Heurix, J., & Neubauer, T. (2011, January 4-7). Model-driven development meets security: An evaluation of current approaches. In *Proceedings of the 44th Hawaii International Conference on Systems Science*.

Kaseva, A., & Stén, A. (2003, March). *Fooling Fingerprint Scanners*.

Kaski, S. (1998). Dimensionality reduction by random mapping: Fast similarity computation for clustering. In *Proceedings of the IEEE World Congress International Joint Conference on Neural Networks and Computational Intelligence* (pp. 413-418).

Katt, B., Breu, R., Hafner, M., Schabetsberger, T., Mair, R., & Wozak, F. (2008). Privacy and access control for IHE-based systems. In *Proceedings of the 1st International Conference on Electronic Healthcare in the 21st Century*.

Kazman, R., Bass, L., Abowd, G., & Webb, M. (1994). SAAM: A method for analyzing the properties of software architectures. In *Proceedings of the 16ᵗʰ International Conference on Software Engineering* (pp. 81-90). Washington, DC: IEEE Computer Society.

Kent, J. (2005, March 31). *Malysia car thieves steal finger. BBC News.* Retrieved from http://news.bbc.co.uk/1/hi/world/asia-pacific/4396831.stm

Kephart, J. O., Sorkin, G. B., Arnold, W. C., Chess, D. M., Tesauro, G. J., & White, S. R. (1995). Biologically inspired defenses against computer viruses. In *Proceedings of the 14th International Joint Conference on Artificial Intelligence*, San Francisco, CA (pp. 985-996).

Keramati, H., & Mirian-Hosseinabadi, S. H. (2008). Integrating software development security activities with agile methodologies. In *Proceedings of the IEEE/ACS International Conference on Computer Systems and Applications* (pp. 749-754).

King, G., Bauer, C., Andersen, M. R., Bernard, E., Ebersole, S., & Ferentschik, H. (2011). *Hibernate reference documentation 3.6.1. final*. Retrieved from http://www.hibernate.org/

Kissel, R., Stine, K., Scholl, M., Rossman, H., Fahlsing, J., & Gulick, J. (2008). *Security considerations in the system development life cycle*. Gaithersburg, MD: NIST.

Kitchenham, B. (2004). *Procedures for performing systematic reviews*. Staffordshire, UK: Keele University.

Kiyomoto, S., Ota, H., & Tanaka, T. (2008). A security protocol compiler generating C source codes. In *Proceedings of the International Conference on Information Security and Assurance* (pp. 20-25).

Kleine-Albers, D., Tokar, D., & Uhe, P. (2006). *Versuch: Fingerabdruck (Teil 2)*. Retrieved from http://dka.web-republic.de/ downloads.html? eID=dam_frontend_push&docID=570

Kleppe, A. G., Warmer, J., & Bast, W. (2003). *MDA explained: The model driven architecture: Practice and promise*. Reading, MA: Addison-Wesley.

Kolmogorov, A. N. (1956). *Foundations of the theory of probability* (2nd ed.). Providence, RI: Chelsea Publishing.

Kong, J., Zerfos, P., Luo, H., Lu, S., & Zhang, L. (2001). Providing Robust and Ubiquitous Security Support for Mobile Ad-hoc Networks. In *Proceedings of the Ninth International Conference on Network Protocols (ICNP2001)* (pp. 251-260).

Krijnen, K. (2008). *PCB Etching*. Retrieved from http://sfprime.net/pcb-etching/index.htm

Kurimo, M. (1999). Indexing audio documents by using latent semantic analysis and SOM. *Kohonen Maps*, 363-374.

Kurkowski, S., Camp, T., & Colagrosso, M. (2005). MANET simulation studies: the incredibles. *SIGMOBILE Mob. Comput. Commun. Rev.*, 9(4), 50–61. doi:10.1145/1096166.1096174

Lampson, B. W. (1971). Protection. In *Proceedings of the Fifth Princeton Conference on Information Sciences and Systems* (p. 437).

Lamsweerde, A., & Letier, E. (2000). Handling obstacles in goal-oriented requirements engineering. *IEEE Transactions on Software Engineering, 26*(10), 978–1005. doi:10.1109/32.879820

Larochelle, D., & Evans, D. (2001). Statically detecting likely buffer overflow vulnerabilities. In *Proceedings of the 10th Usenix Security Symposium* (p. 14). Berkeley, CA: USENIX.

Laws, S., Combellack, M., Feng, R., Mahbod, H., & Nash, S. (2011). *Tuscany SCA in action*. Stamfort, CT: Manning.

Lewin, K. (1946). Action research and minority problems. *The Journal of Social Issues, 2*(4), 34–46. doi:10.1111/j.1540-4560.1946.tb02295.x

Leyden, J. (2002, May). *Gummi bears defeat fingerprint sensors. The Register*. Retrieved from http://www.theregister.co.uk/2002/05/16/gummi_bears_defeat_fingerprint_sensors/

Lifschitz, V. (2008). What is answer set programming? In *Proceedings of the 23rd national conference on Artificial intelligence (AAAI'08)* (p. 1594). Cambridge, MA: MIT.

Lin, J., & Gunopulos, D. (2003, May). Dimensionality reduction by random projection and latent semantic indexing. In *Proceedings of the Text Mining Workshop at the 3rd SIAM International Conference on Data Mining.*

Lin, L., Nuseibeh, B., Ince, D., Jackson, M., & Moffett, J. (2003). Introducing abuse frames for analysing security requirements. In *Proceedings of the 11th IEEE International Requirements Engineering Conference*, Monterey, CA (pp. 371-372).

Liu, A. X., Chen, F., Hwang, J., & Xie, T. (2008). Xengine: A fast and scalable XACML policy evaluation engine. In *Proceedings of the ACM SIGMETRICS International Conference on Measurement and Modeling of Computer Systems* (pp. 265-276).

Liu, L., Yu, E., & Mylopoulos, J. (2003). Security and privacy requirements analysis within a social setting. In *Proceedings of the 11th International Requirements Engineering Conference* (pp. 151-161).

Liu, N., Zhang, B., Yan, J., Yang, Q., Yan, S., Chen, Z., et al. (2004). Learning similarity measures in non-orthogonal space. In *Proceedings of the Thirteenth ACM International Conference on Information and Knowledge Management* (pp. 334-341).

Livshits, V. B., & Lam, M. S. (2005). Finding security errors in java programs with static analysis. In *Proceedings of the 14th Usenix Security Symposium* (pp. 271-286). Berkeley, CA: USENIX.

Lloyd, J., & Jürjens, J. (2009). Security analysis of a biometric authentication system using UMLsec and JML. In *Proceedings of the 12th International Conference on Model Driven Engineering Languages and Systems.*

Lodderstedt, T., Basin, D., & Doser, J. (2002). SecureUML: A UML-based modelling language for model-driven security. In J.-M. Jézéquel, H. Hussmann, & S. Cook (Eds.), *Proceedings of the 5th International Conference on the Unified Modeling Language* (LNCS 2460, pp. 426-441).

Maiden, N., & Jones, S. (2004). *The RESCUE requirements engineering process: An integrated user-centered requirements engineering process (Version 4.1)*. London, UK: City University.

Mainguet, J.-F. (2009). *Fingerprints*. Retrieved from http://pagespersoorange.fr/fingerchip/biometrics/types/fingerprint.htm

Mainguet, J.-F. (2009). *Retinal*. Retrieved from http://pagespersoorange.fr/fingerchip/biometrics/types/retinal.htm

Mainguet, J.-F. (2010). *Movies & Biometrics*. Retrieved from http://pagespersoorange.fr/fingerchip/biometrics/movies.htm

Manhart, K. (2002, January). *Sicher durch Biometrie. Tec Channel*. Retrieved from http://www.tecchannel.de/sicherheit/identity_access/401777/sicher_durch_biometrie/index.html

Mannila, H., & Seppänen, J. K. (2001). Finding similar situations in sequences of events. In *Proceedings of the 1st SIAM International Conference on Data Mining.*

Marceau, C. (2000). Characterizing the behavior of a program using multiple-length n-grams. In *Proceedings of the Workshop on New Security Paradigms* (pp. 101-110).

Marcialis, G. L., & Roli, F. (2008). Fingerprint verification by decision-level fusion of optical and capacitive sensors. In *Proceedings of the International Workshop on Biometric Authentication (BioAW04)*. DOI: 10.1007/b99174

Marouf, S., Shehab, M., Squicciarini, A., & Sundare-swaran, S. (2009). Statistics & clustering based framework for efficient XACML policy evaluation. In *Proceedings of the 10th IEEE International Conference on Policies for Distributed Systems and Networks* (pp. 118-125). Washington, DC: IEEE Computer Society.

Massacci, F., & Zannone, N. (2008). A model-driven approach for the specification and analysis of access control policies. In R. Meersman & Z. Tari (Eds.), *Proceedings of the Confederated International Conferences of On the Movie to Meaningful Internet Systems* (LNCS 5332, pp. 1087-1103).

Matsomoto, T. (2002). Importance of Open Discussion on Adversarial Analysis for Mobile Security Technologies. A Case Study for User Identification.

Matsumoto, T. (2002). *Impact of Artificial "Gummy".* Fingers on Fingerprint Systems.

McDermott, J. (2005). *Visual security protocol modeling.* Paper presented at the New Security Paradigms Workshop.

McDermott, J., & Fox, C. (1999). Using abuse case models for security requirements analysis. In *Proceedings of the 15th Annual Computer Security Applications Conference* (pp. 55-64).

McGraw, G. (2006). *Software security: Building security.* Reading, MA: Addison-Wesley.

McGraw, G., & Morrisett, G. (2000). Attacking malicious code: A report to the Infosec Research Council. *IEEE Software, 17*(5), 33–41. doi:10.1109/52.877857

Mead, N. R., Hough, E. D., & Steheny, T., II. (2005). *Security quality requirements engineering (SQUARE) methodology* (Tech. Rep. No. CMU/SEI-2005-TR-009). Pittsburgh, PA: Carnegie Mellon Software Engineering Institute.

Mead, N. R. (2006). Identifying security requirements using the security quality requirements engineering (SQUARE) method. In Mouratidis, H., & Giorgini, P. (Eds.), *Integrating security and software engineering* (pp. 44–69). Hershey, PA: Idea Group.

Meadows, C. (1991). Policies for dynamic upgrading. *Database Security, IV: Status and Prospects*, 241-250.

Medical Discoveries. (2010). *Retinography.* Retrieved from http://www.discoveriesinmedicine.com/Ra-Thy/Retinography.html

Meyers, W. J. (1997). RBAC emulation on trusted dg/ux. In *Proceedings of the Second ACM Workshop on Role-Based Access Control* (pp. 55-60). New York, NY: ACM Press.

Microsoft Corporation. (2011). *Microsoft SQL server 2005.* Retrieved from http://www.microsoft.com/sqlserver/en/us/default.aspx

Microsoft Corporation. (2011). *Microsoft Windows XP.* Retrieved from http://windows.microsoft.com/en-US/windows/products/windows-xp

Microsoft. (1998). *DCOM architecture.* Retrieved from http://www.microsoft.com/NTServer/

Microsoft. (2009). *Connected health framework architecture and design blueprint, part 3 - technical framework.* Retrieved from http://www.interoperabilityshowcase.com/himss10/ docs/himss09examples/HIMSS09LeadershipWhitePaper-Microsoft.pdf

Microsoft. (2011). *FxCop.* Retrieved September 6, 2011, from http://msdn.microsoft.com/en-us/library/bb429476.aspx

Moebius, N., Stenzel, K., & Reif, W. (2009). Generating formal specifications for security-critical applications - A model-driven approach. In *Proceedings of the ICSE Workshop on Software Engineering for Secure Systems* (pp. 68-74).

Moebius, N., Stenzel, K., Grandy, H., & Reif, W. (2009). Model-driven code generation for secure smart card applications. In *Proceedings of the Australian Software Engineering Conference.*

Moebius, N., Stenzel, K., Grandy, H., & Reif, W. (2009). SecureMDD: A model-driven development method for secure smart card applications. In *Proceedings of the International Conference on Availability, Reliability and Security.*

Moses, T. (2005). *eXtensible access control markup language version 2.0, specifications document.* Retrieved from http://www.oasis-open.org/committees/ tc_home. php?wg_abbrev=xacml

Mouratidis, H. (2004). *A security oriented approach in the development of multiagent systems: Applied to the management of the health and social care needs of older people in England.* Unpublished doctoral dissertation, University of Sheffield, South Yorkshire, UK.

Mouratidis, H., Jürjens, J., & Fox, J. (2006). Towards a comprehensive framework for secure systems development. In E. Dubois & K. Pohl (Eds.), *Proceedings of the 18th International Conference on Advanced Information Systems Engineering* (LNCS 4001, pp. 48-62).

Mouratidis, H., & Giorgini, P. (2007). Security attack testing (SAT)-testing the security of information systems at design time. *Information Systems, 32*(8), 1166–1183. doi:10.1016/j.is.2007.03.002

Mouratidis, H., & Giorgini, P. (Eds.). (2006). *Integrating security and software engineering: Advances and future visions.* Hershey, PA: Idea Group. doi:10.4018/978-1-59904-147-6

Murata, M., Tozawa, A., & Kudo, M. (2003). XML access control using static analysis. In *Proceedings of the ACM Conference on Computer and Communications Security* (pp. 73-84).

Murray, T., & Grove, D. (2008). Non-delegatable authorities in capability systems. *Journal of Computer Security, 16*, 743–759.

MySQL AB. (2007). *MySQL.* Retrieved from http://www.mysql.com

National Vulnerability Database. (2011). *Statistics.* Retrieved from http://web.nvd.nist.gov/view/vuln/statistics

News, B. B. C. (2009). *Facebook faces criticism on privacy change.* Retrieved from http://news.bbc.co.uk/2/hi/technology/8405334.stm

Nicolaysen, T., Sassoon, R., Line, M., & Jaatun, M. (2010). Agile software development: The straight and narrow path to secure software? *International Journal of Secure Software Engineering, 1*(3). doi:10.4018/jsse.2010070105

Niemela, I., Simons, P., & Syrjanen, T. (2000). Smodels: a system for answer set programming. In *Proceedings of the 8th International Workshop on Non-Monotonic Reasoning.*

Notargiacomo, L. (1995). Role-based access control in oracle7 and trusted oracle7. In *Proceedings of the First ACM Workshop on Role-Based Access Control* (pp. 65-69). New York, NY: ACM Press.

Nuseibeh, B. (2001). Weaving together requirements and architectures. *Computer, 34*(3), 115–117. doi:10.1109/2.910904

O'Keefe, C., Greenfield, P., & Goodchild, A. (2005). a decentralized approach to electronic consent and health information access control. *Journal of Research and Practice in Information Technology, 37.*

OASIS. (2009). *HIMSS interop scenarios - demonstration of XSPA profile of SAML.* Retrieved from http://lists.oasis-open.org/archives/xspa/200901/msg00001.html

OASIS. (2010). *OASIS web services security specification.* Retrieved May 10, 2010, from http://www.oasis-open.org/specs/index.php#wssv1.0

Obelheiro, R. R., & Fraga, J. S. (2002). Role-based access control for CORBA distributed object systems. In *Proceedings of the IEEE International Workshop on Object-Oriented Real-Time Dependable Systems* (p. 53). Washington, DC: IEEE Computer Society.

Oberg, R. J. (2000). *Understanding & programming COM+: A practical guide to Windows 2000 DNA.* Upper Saddle River, NJ: Prentice Hall.

OMG. (1999). *The common object request broker: Architecture and specification.* Needham, MA: Object Management Group.

OMG. (2002). *Common object services specification, security service specification v1.8.* Needham, MA: Object Management Group.

OMG. (2004). *Common object request broker architecture: Core specification v3.0.3.* Needham, MA: Object Management Group.

OMG. (2007a, February). *Unified modeling language: Infrastructure, v2.1.1.* Needham, MA: Object Management Group.

OMG. (2007b, February). *Unified modeling language: Superstructure, v2.1.1.* Needham, MA: Object Management Group.

OMG. (2010). *Executive overview - Model driven architecture.* Retrieved September, 2011, from http://www.omg.org/mda/executive_overview.htm

Optel. (2002). *Comparing Ultrasound with Conventional Finger-Scan Technologies.* Retrieved from http://www.optel.pl/article/deutsch/comparing.htm

Oracle Corporation. (2011). *MySQL community edition 5.* Retrieved from http://www.oracle.com/technetwork/database/express-edition/overview/index.html

Oracle Corporation. (2011). *Oracle 10g express edition.* Retrieved from http://www.oracle.com/technetwork/database/express-edition/overview/index.html

ORACLE. (2001). *Java authentication and authorization service (JAAS).* Retrieved from http://java.sun.com/products/jaas/

ORACLE. (2007). *Remote method invocation.* Retrieved from http://java.sun.com/javase/technologies/core/basic/rmi/index.jsp

O'Shea, N. (2008). Using Elyjah to analyse Java implementations of cryptographic protocols. In *Proceedings of the Conference on Foundations of Computer Security, Automated Reasoning for Security Protocol Analysis and Issues in the Theory of Security* (pp. 221-226).

OSOA. (2011). *Service component architecture (SCA).* Retrieved September 6, 2011, from http://www.osoa.org/display/Main/Service+Component+Architecture+Home

Österreichischer Nationalrat. (2009). *Der Reisepass mit Fingerabdruck kommt.* Retrieved from http://www.parlament.gv.at/PG/PR/JAHR_2009/PK0023/PK0023.shtml

OWASP. (2011). *Category: OWASP top ten project.* Retrieved from http://www.owasp.org/index.php/Category:OWASP_Top_Ten_Project

Papadimitriou, C. H., Raghavan, P., Tamaki, H., & Vempala, S. (2000). Latent semantic indexing: A probabilistic analysis. *Journal of Computer and System Sciences, 61*(2), 217–235. doi:10.1006/jcss.2000.1711

Park, J. S., Sandhu, R., & Ahn, G.-J. (2001). Role-based access control on the web. *ACM Transactions on Information and System Security, 4*(1), 37–71. doi:10.1145/383775.383777

Pashalidis, A., & Mitchell, C. J. (2003, July 9-11). A taxonomy of single sign-on systems. In R. Safavi-Naini & J. Seberry (Ed.), *Proceedings of the Eighth Australasian Conference Information Security and Privacy*, Wollongong, Australia (LNCS 2727, pp. 249-264).

Paulk, M. (2001). Extreme programming from a CMM perspective. *IEEE Software, 18*(6). doi:10.1109/52.965798

Peine, H., Jawurek, M., & Mandel, S. (2008). Security goal indicator trees: A model of software features that supports efficient security inspection. In *Proceedings of the 11th High Assurance Systems Engineering Symposium* (pp. 9-18). Washington, DC: IEEE Computer Society.

Perdisci, R., Lanzi, A., & Lee, W. (2008). Classification of packed executables for accurate computer virus detection. *Pattern Recognition Letters, 29*(14), 1941–1946. doi:10.1016/j.patrec.2008.06.016

Pernul, G., & Luef, G. (1992). Bibliography on database security. *SIGMOD Record, 21*(1). doi:10.1145/130868.130884

Petermann, T., & Sauter, A. (2002). *Biometrische Identifikationssysteme.* Retrieved from http://www.tab.fzk.de/de/projekt/zusammenfassung/ab76.pdf

Pironti, A., & Sisto, R. (2007). An experiment in interoperable cryptographic protocol implementation using automatic code generation. In *Proceedings of the IEEE Symposium on Computers and Communications* (pp. 839-844).

Plobl, K., Nowey, T., et al. (2006, April). Towards a security architecture for vehicular ad hoc networks. Availability, Reliability and Security. In *Proceedings of the First International Conference on Availability, Reliability and Security (ARES).*

Policarpio, S., & Zhang, Y. (2010). *An implementation of $A^{xml(T)}$: A formal language of authorisation for xml documents.*

PostgreSQL Global Development Group. (2011). *PostgreSQL 8.* Retrieved from http://www.postgresql.org

Python Software Foundation. (2010). *Python programming language.* Retrieved from http://www.python.org/

Ragouzis, N., Hughes, J., Philpott, R., Maler, E., Madsen, P., & Scavo, T. (2008). *Security assertion markup language (SAML) v2.0 technical overview, committee draft 02.* Retrieved from http://www.oasis-open.org/committees/download.php/ 27819/sstc-saml-tech-overview-2.0-cd-02.pdf

Ramaswamy, C., & Sandhu, R. (1998). Role-based access control features in commercial database management systems. In *Proceedings of the 21st NIST-NCSC National Information Systems Security Conference* (pp. 503-511).

Red Hat. (2011). *Enterprise Linux 5.* Retrieved from http://www.redhat.com/rhel/

Reddy, D. K. S., & Pujari, A. K. (2006). N-gram analysis for computer virus detection. *Journal in Computer Virology, 2*(3), 231–239. doi:10.1007/s11416-006-0027-8

Robertson, J., & Robertson, S. (2009, January 14). *Volere requirements specification template.* Retrieved from http://www.volere.co.uk/template.htm

Robertson, S., & Robertson, J. (2006). *Mastering the requirements process.* Reading, MA: Addison-Wesley.

Robles, R., Choi, M.-K., Yeo, S.-S., & Kim, T. Hoon. (2008, October). Application of role-based access control for web environment. In *Proceedings of the International Symposium on Ubiquitous Multimedia Computing* (pp. 171-174). Washington, DC: IEEE Computer Society.

Rodriguez, A., Fernandez-Medina, E., & Piattini, M. (2006). Security requirement with a UML 2.0 profile. In *Proceedings of the 1st International Conference on Availability, Reliability and Security.*

Rodriguez, A., Fernandez-Medina, E., & Piattini, M. (2006). Towards a UML 2.0 extension for the modeling of security requirements in business processes. In S. Fischer-Hübner, S. Furnell, & C. Lambrinoudakis (Eds.), *Proceedings of the 3rd International Conference on Trust and Privacy in Digital Business* (LNCS 4083, pp. 51-61).

Rodriguez, A., Fernandez-Medina, E., & Piattini, M. (2007). Towards CIM to PIM transformation: From secure business processes defined in BPMN to use-cases. In G. Alonso, P. Dadam, & M. Rosemann (Eds.), *Proceedings of the 5th International Conference on Business Process Management* (LNCS 4714, pp. 408-415).

Rodriguez, A., Fernandez-Medina, E., & Piattini, M. (2008). CIM to PIM transformation: A reality. In *Proceedings of the IFIP TC 8 WG 8.9 International Conference on Research and Practical Issues of Enterprise Information Systems II* (Vol. 255, pp. 1239-1249).

Roman, E., Sriganesh, R. P., & Brose, G. (2005). *Mastering enterprise javabeans* (3rd ed.). Indianapolis, IN: Wiley.

Rosario, G., & Jarecki, S. (2007). Secure Distributed Key Generation for Discrete-Log Based Cryptosystems. *Journal of Cryptology, 20*(1), 51–83. doi:10.1007/s00145-006-0347-3

Ross, A., Jain, A., & Pankanti, S. A. (2010). *Hand Geometry Based Verification System.* Retrieved from http://biometrics.cse.msu.edu/hand_proto.html

Rosson, M. B., & Carroll, J. M. (2002). *Usability engineering: scenario-based development of human-computer interaction.* New York, NY: Academic Press.

Rosson, M. B., & Carroll, J. M. (2008). Scenario-based design. In *The human-computer interaction handbook* (pp. 1041–1060). Mahwah, NJ: Lawrence Erlbaum.

Russello, G., Dong, C., & Dulay, N. (2008). Consent-based workflows for healthcare management. In *Proceedings of the IEEE International Workshop on Policies for Distributed Systems and Networks* (pp. 153-161). Washington, DC: IEEE Computer Society.

Sadtler, C., Clifford, L., Heyward, J., Iwamoto, A., Jakusz, N., & Laursen, L. B. (2004). *IBM websphere application server v5.1 system management and configuration websphere handbook series.* Armonk, NY: IBM International Technical Support Organization.

Safecode. (2011). *Software assurance: An overview of current industry best practices.* Retrieved from http://www.safecode.org

Saldhana, A. (2010). *Xacml caching for performance.* Retrieved from http://community.jboss.org/wiki/ XACMLCachingforPerformance

Salton, G., & Buckley, C. (1988). Term-weighting approaches in automatic text retrieval. *Information Processing and Management: an International Journal, 24*(5), 513–523. doi:10.1016/0306-4573(88)90021-0

Salton, G., Wong, A., & Yang, C. S. (1975). A vector space model for automatic indexing. *Communications of the ACM, 18*(11), 613–620. doi:10.1145/361219.361220

Sandhu, R., & Ahn, G.-J. (1998). Decentralized group hierarchies in UNIX: An experiment and lessons learned. In *Proceedings of the 21st NIST-NCSC National Information Systems Security Conference* (pp. 486-502).

Sandhu, R., Ferraiolo, D., & Kuhn, R. (2000). The NIST model for role-based access control: Towards a unified standard. In *Proceedings of the Fifth ACM Workshop on Role-Based Access Control* (pp. 47-63). Application of role-based access control for web environment.

Sandhu, R., Coyne, E., Feinstein, H., & Youman, C. (1996). Role-based access control models. *IEEE Computer, 29*(2), 38–47. doi:10.1109/2.485845

Sandia National Laboratories. (2011). *The information design assurance red team.* Retrieved from http://www.idart.sandia.gov/

Sandström, M. (2004). *Liveness Detection in Fingerprint Recognition Systems.*

Schell, R., & Heckman, M. (1987). Views for multilevel database security. *IEEE Transactions on Software Engineering, 13*(2).

Schneider, B. (1998, August). *Biometrics: Truths and Fictions. Crypto-Gram.* Retrieved from http://www.schneier.com/crypto-gram-9808.html#biometrics

Schneider, B. (1999, August). *Biometrics: Uses and Abuses.* Retrieved from http://www.schneier.com/essay-019.html

Schneider, B. (2002, May). *Fun with Fingerprint Readers. Crypto-Gram.* Retrieved from http://www.schneier.com/crypto-gram-0205.html#5

Schneier, B. (1999). Attack trees. *Dr. Dobb's Journal, 24*(12), 21–29.

Schneier, B. (2000). *Secrets & lies: Digital security in a networked world.* New York, NY: John Wiley & Sons.

Schultz, M., Eskin, E., Zadok, E., & Stolfo, S. (2001). Data mining methods for detection of new malicious executables. In *Proceedings of the IEEE Symposium on Security and Privacy* (pp. 38-49).

Schumacher, M., & Roedig, U. (2001). Security engineering with patterns. In *Proceedings of the 8th Conference on Pattern Languages for Programs*, Chicago, IL.

Schumacher, M. (2003). *Security engineering with patterns: Origins, theoretical models, and new applications.* Berlin, Germany: Springer-Verlag.

Secure Software. (2005). *The CLASP application security process.* Retrieved from http://www.ida.liu.se/~TDDC90/papers/clasp_external.pdf

Serenity Consortium. (2008). *A7.d4.2 - Scenario S&D solutions.* Retrieved from http://www.serenity-project.org

Serenity Consortium. (2008). *A6.D3.2 - Specification of serenity architecture.* Retrieved from http://www.serenity-project.org

Serenity Consortium. (2009). *The final set of S&D patterns at organizational level.* Retrieved from http://www.serenity-project.org

Shiva, S., Stoian, T. R., Satharla, R. R., Ba, E. A., & Hollahan, T. P. (2008). Towards an augmented secure software development lifecycle. In *Proceedings of the Computer Security Conference.*

Sindre, G., & Opdahl, A. L. (2005). Eliciting security requirements with misuse cases. *Requirements Engineering, 10*(1), 34–44. doi:10.1007/s00766-004-0194-4

Sindre, G., & Opdahl, A. L. (2005). Eliciting security requirements with misuse cases. *Requirements Engineering, 10*(1), 34–44. doi:10.1007/s00766-004-0194-4

Singhal, A. (2001). Modern information retrieval: A brief overview. *A Quarterly Bulletin of the Computer Society of the IEEE Technical Committee on Data Engineering, 24*(4), 35–43.

Sinn, R. (2008). *Software security technologies: A programmatic approach.* Australia: Thomson.

Sohr, K., & Berger, B. (2010). Idea: Towards architecture-centric security analysis of software. In F. Massacci, D. Wallach, & N. Zannone (Eds.), *Proceedings of the 2nd International Symposium on Engineering Secure Software and Systems* (LNCS 5965, pp. 70-78).

Soler, E. TruJillo, J., Fernandez-Medina, E., & Piattini, M. (2007). Application of QVT for the development of secure data warehouses: A case study. In *Proceedings of the 2nd International Conference on Availability, Reliability and Security* (pp. 829-836).

Soler, E., Stefanov, V., Mazon, J.-N., Trujillo, J., Fernandez-Madina, E., & Piattini, M. (2008). Towards comprehensive requirement analysis for data warehouses: Considering security requirements. In *Proceedings of the 3rd International Conference on Availability, Reliability and Security* (pp. 104-111).

Soler, E., Trujillo, J., Fernandez-Medina, E., & Piattini, M. (2007b). A framework for the development of secure data warehouses based on MDA and QVT. In *Proceedings of the 2nd International Conference on Availability, Reliability and Security* (pp. 294-300).

Soler, E., Trujillo, J., Fernandez-Medina, E., & Piattini, M. (2007c). A set of QVT relations to transform PIM to PSM in the design of secure data warehouses. In *Proceedings of the 2nd International Conference on Availability, Reliability and Security* (pp. 644-654).

Soler, E., Trujillo, J., Blanco, C., & Fernandez-Medina, E. (2009). Designing secure data warehouses by using MDA and QVT. *Journal of Universal Computer Science, 15*(8), 1607–1641.

Song, D. X., Perrig, A., & Phan, D. (2001). AGVI - Automatic generation, verification, and implementation of security protocols. In *Proceedings of the 13th International Conference on Computer Aided Verification* (pp. 241-245).

SQUALE Consortium. (1999). *SQUALE: Security, safety and quality evaluation for dependable systems.* Retrieved from http://spiderman-2.laas.fr/TSF/cabernet/squale/

Stallings, W. (1999). *Cryptography and network security: Principles and practice* (2nd ed.). Upper Saddle River, NJ: Prentice Hall.

Stamatelatos, M., Vesely, W., Dugan, J., Fragola, J., Minarick, J., & Railsback, J. (2002). *Fault tree handbook with aerospace applications.* Retrieved from http://www.hq.nasa.gov/office/codeq/doctree/fthb.pdf

Steinberg, D., Budinsky, F., Paternostro, M., & Merks, E. (2008). *EMF: Eclipse modeling framework* (2nd ed.). Amsterdam, The Netherlands: Addison-Wesley.

Sun Microsystems Inc. (2000). *RBAC in the Solaris™ operating environment.* Retrieved from http://www.sun.com/software/whitepapers/wp-rbac/wp-rbac.pdf

Swiderski, F., & Snyder, W. (2004). *Threat modeling.* Sebastopol, CA: Microsoft Press.

Sybase Inc. (2005). *System administration guide: Volume 1 - Adaptive server enterprise 15.0.* Retrieved from http://infocenter.sybase.com/help/topic/com.sybase.help.ase_15.0.sag1/sag1.pdf

Thalheim, L., Krissler, J., & Ziegler, P.-M. (2002, November). *Körperkontrolle - Biometrische Zugangssicherung auf die Probe gestellt* (p. 114).

The Apache Foundation. (2011). *Apache Tuscany.* Retrieved September 6, 2011, from http://tuscany.apache.org

The, P. H. P. Group. (2010). *Php: Hypertext preprocessor.* Retrieved from http://www.php.net/

Tøndel, I. A., Jaatun, M. G., & Meland, P. H. (2008). Security requirements for the rest of us: A survey. *IEEE Software, 25*(1), 20–27. doi:10.1109/MS.2008.19

Tran, S., & Mohan, M. (2006). *Security information management challenges and solutions.* Retrieved from http://www.ibm.com/developerworks/db2/library/techarticle/dm-0607tran/index.html

Trujillo, J., Soler, E., Fernández-Medina, E., & Piattini, M. (2009). An engineering process for developing secure data warehouses. *Information and Software Technology, 51*, 1033–1051. doi:10.1016/j.infsof.2008.12.003

Trujillo, J., Soler, E., Fernández-Medina, E., & Piattini, M. (2009). A UML 2.0 profile to define security requirements for data warehouses. *Computer Standards & Interfaces, 31*(5), 969–983. doi:10.1016/j.csi.2008.09.040

Turk, M. A., & Pentland, A. P. (1991). *Face Recognition Using Eigenfaces.*

U. S. Department of Health and Human Services. (1996). *Health insurance portability and accountability act.* Retrieved from http://www.hhs.gov/ocr/privacy/hipaa/understanding/index.html

U. S. Department of Health and Human Services. (2003). *Summary of the HIPAA privacy rule (HIPAA privacy).* Retrieved from http://www.hhs.gov/ocr/privacy/hipaa/understanding/summary/privacysummary.pdf

Van der Putte, T., & Keuning, J. (2002). *Biometrical Fingerprint Recognition: Don't get your fingers burned.* Retrieved from http://cryptome.org/fake-prints.htm

Van Lamsweerde, A., Brohez, S., Landtsheer, R. D., & Janssens, D. (2003). From system goals to intruder anti-goals: Attack generation and resolution for security requirements engineering. In *Proceedings of the International Conference on High Assurance Systems Engineering.*

van Lamsweerde, A. (2009). *Requirements engineering: from system goals to UML models to software specifications.* New York, NY: John Wiley & Sons.

van Lamsweerde, A., & Letier, E. (2000). Handling obstacles in goal-oriented requirements engineering. *IEEE Transactions on Software Engineering, 26*(10), 978–1005. doi:10.1109/32.879820

Vempala, S. S. (2004). *The random projection method.* Providence, RI: American Mathematical Society.

Verhenneman, G. (2010). Consent, an instrument for patient empowerment? In *Proceedings of the 49th FITCE Congress.*

Viega, J. (2005). Building security requirements with CLASP. In *Proceedings of the Workshop on Software Engineering for Secure Systems.*

Viega, J., Bloch, J. T., Kohno, Y., & McGraw, G. (2000). ITS4: A static vulnerability scanner for C and C++ code. In *Proceedings of the 16th Annual Computer Security Applications Conference* (pp. 257-267). Washington, DC: IEEE Computer Society.

Vieira, M., & Madeira, H. (2002). Recovery and performance balance of a COTS DBMS in the presence of operator faults. In *Proceedings of the International Conference on Dependable Systems and Networks* (pp. 615-624).

Vieira, M., & Madeira, H. (2005). Towards a security benchmark for database management systems. In *Proceedings of the International Conference on Dependable Systems and Networks*, Yokohama, Japan (pp. 592-601).

Wahl, M., Howes, T., & Kille, S. (1997). *RFC 2251: Lightweight directory access protocol (v3).* Retrieved from http://www.ietf.org/rfc/rfc2251.txt

Westphall, C. M., & da Silva Fraga, J. (1999, December). A large-scale system authorization scheme proposal integrating Java, CORBA and web security models and a discretionary prototype. In *Proceedings of the Latin American Network Operations and Management Symposium*, Rio de Janeiro, Brazil (pp. 14-25). Washington, DC: IEEE Computer Society.

Westphall, C. M., da Silva Fraga, J., Wangham, M. S., Obelheiro, R. R., & Lung, L. C. (2002). PoliCap - proposal, development and evaluation of a policy service and capabilities for CORBA security. In *Proceedings of the IFIP TC11 17th International Conference on Information Security* (pp. 263-274).

Wikipedia. (2009). *Microsoft Fingerprint Reader.* Retrieved from http://en.wikipedia.org/wiki/Microsoft_Fingerprint_Reader

Wikipedia. (2010). *Biometrics.* Retrieved from http://en.wikipedia.org/wiki/biometrics

Wikipedia. (2010). *Fingerprint.* Retrieved from http://en.wikipedia.org/wiki/Fingerprint

Wikipedia. (2010). *AFIS.* Retrieved from http://en.wikipedia.org/wiki/

Wikipedia. (2010). *Capacitor.* Retrieved from http://en.wikipedia.org/wiki/Capacitor

Wikipedia. (2010). *Electrostatic discharge.* Retrieved from http://en.wikipedia.org/wiki/Electrostatic_discharge

Wikipedia. (2010). *Histogram Equalization.* Retrieved from http://en.wikipedia.org/wiki/Histogram_equalization

Wikipedia. (2010). *Thresholding (image processing).* Retrieved from http://en.wikipedia.org/wiki/Thresholding_%28image_processing%29

Wikipedia. (2010). *Iris Recognition.* Retrieved from http://en.wikipedia.org/wiki/Iris_recognition

Wikipedia. (2010). *Retinal Scan*. Retrieved from http://en.wikipedia.org/wiki/Retinal_scan

Wikipedia. (2010). *Eigenfaces*. Retrieved from http://en.wikipedia.org/wiki/Eigenface

Wikipedia. (2010). *Speaker Recognition*. Retrieved from http://en.wikipedia.org/wiki/Speaker_recognition

Wilhelm, T. (2009). *Professional penetration testing: Creating and operating a formal hacking lab*. Oxford, UK: Syngress.

Wong, R. K. (1997). RBAC support in object-oriented role databases. In *Proceedings of the Second ACM Workshop on Role-Based Access Control* (pp. 109-120). PoliCap - proposal, development and evaluation of a policy service and capabilities for CORBA security.

Wu, B., & Wu, J. (2007). Secure and Efficient Key Management in Mobile Ad Hoc Networks. *Journal of Network and Computer Applications*, *30*, 937–954. doi:10.1016/j.jnca.2005.07.008

Wyk, K. R. v., & McGraw, G. (2005). Bridging the gap between software development and information security. *IEEE Security and Privacy*, *3*, 75–79. doi:10.1109/MSP.2005.118

XStream. (n. d.). *About XStream*. Retrieved from http://xstream.codehaus.org

Yasar, A. U. H., Preuveneers, D., Berbers, Y., & Bhatti, G. (2008). Best practices for software security: An overview. In *Proceedings of the IEEE International Multitopic Conference* (pp. 169-173).

Yi, S., & Kravets, R. (2003). MOCA: Mobile Certificate Authority for Wireless Ad Hoc Networks. In *Proceedings of the Annual PKI Research Workshop Program*, MD (pp. 65-79).

Yi, S., & Kravets, R. (2004). Composite key management for ad hoc networks. In *Proceedings of the First Annual International Conference on Mobile and Ubiquitous Systems: Networking and Services (MOBIQUITOUS 2004)* (pp. 52-61).

Yoder, J., & Barcalow, J. (1997). Architectural patterns for enabling application security. In *Proceedings of the Conference on Pattern Languages of Programs*.

Yu, E. (1995). *Modelling strategic relationships for process reengineering*. Unpublished doctoral dissertation, University of Toronto, Toronto, ON, Canada.

Yuan, E., & Tong, J. (2005). Attributed based access control (ABAC) for web services. In *Proceedings of the IEEE International Conference on web services*. Washington, DC: IEEE Computer Society.

Zhang, F., Sheng, X., Niu, Y., Wang, F., & Zhang, H. (2006). The research and scheme of RBAC using J2EE security mechanisms. In *Proceedings of the SPIE Conference on Broadband Access Communication Technologies, 6390*, 63900L.

Zhang, Y. (2007). Epistemic reasoning in logic programs. In *Proceedings of the 20th International Joint Conference on Artificial Intelligence* (pp. 647-652).

Zhang, Z., Shen, H., Defago, X., & Sang, Y. (2005). A brief comparative study on analytical models of computer system dependability and security. In *Proceedings of the 6th International Conference on Parallel and Distributed Computing Applications and Technologies* (pp. 493-497).

Zhou, W., & Meinel, C. (2004, Feb). Implement role based access control with attribute certificates. In *Proceedings of the 6th International Conference on Advanced Communication Technology* (Vol. 1, pp. 536-541). Washington, DC: IEEE Computer Society.

Zhou, C., & Buttyan, S. L. (2003). Self-Organized Public-Key Management for Mobile Ad Hoc Networks. *IEEE Transactions on Mobile Computing*, *2*(1), 52–64. doi:10.1109/TMC.2003.1195151

Zhou, J., & Alves-Foss, J. (2008). Security policy refinement and enforcement for the design of multi-level secure systems. *Journal of Computer Security*, *16*, 107–131.

Zhou, L., & Haas, Z. (1999). Securing Ad Hoc Networks. *IEEE Network*, *13*(6), 24–30. doi:10.1109/65.806983

Zhu, B., & Bao, F. (2005). Efficient and robust key management for large mobile ad hoc networks. *Computer Networks*, *48*(4), 657–682. doi:10.1016/j.comnet.2004.11.023

Zimmerman, P. (1994). *PGP User's Guide*. Cambridge, MA: MIT.

About the Contributors

Khaled M. Khan is the Graduate Program Coordinator in the department of Computer Science and Engineering at Qatar University. Prior to these, Khaled also served the University of Western Sydney as Head of postgraduate programs in computing. His research interests include secure software engineering, cloud computing, measuring security, trust in computer software, and software evolution. He has taught computing more than twenty years at various universities in Asia, Europe, Africa, and Australia. Khaled received his BS and MS in Computer Science and Informatics from the Norwegian University of Science and Technology. He received his PhD in Computing from Monash University, Australia. He also holds a second Bachelor's degree from the University of Dhaka (Bangladesh). He's the Editor-in-Chief of the *International Journal of Secure Software Engineering*. Khaled has published more than seventy technical papers, and edited four books.

* * *

Walid Al-Ahmad is an associate professor of Computer Science. He obtained his PhD, Masters, and Bachelor degrees from the Catholic University of Leuven in Belgium. He worked on several research projects funded by the European Commission in the area of Medical Informatics. He served at several universities in the Middle East and North Africa. He taught courses both at the undergraduate and graduate levels in different IT disciplines such as Computer Science, MIS, Software Engineering, and Information and Network Security. He is currently teaching at King Saud University in Saudi Arabia. His research interests center around Secure Software, Information Security, Object-Oriented Technology, and Information and Communication Technologies for Development (ICT4D).

Yudistira Asnar received B. Eng. from Bandung Institute of Technology (ITB) in 2002 and PhD in Computer Science and Information Engineering at University of Trento, Italy in 2009. His research interests include the areas of (security) requirement engineering, agent systems, security-dependability risk management, and information assurance. Currently, his main research is on developing methodology and modeling framework for managing governance, risk and compliance of business services. He involves in several R&D EU, National (SERENITY, MASTER), and Local Projects (MOSTRO, TOCAI) on the area security, trust, and compliance.

Travis Atkison is currently an assistant professor in the Computer Science Department at Louisiana Tech University. He received his Ph.D. degree from Mississippi State University in 2009. His current research interests include computer security, computer forensics, software engineering and information retrieval.

Matteo Avalle graduated from the Politecnico di Torino in 2010, and has since been a PhD student in computer engineering, again at the Politecnico di Torino. His research interests include formal methods applied to security protocols and parallel programming applied to network packet processing.

Yun Bai is a senior lecturer in the School of Computing and Mathematics at University of Western Sydney. Her research areas include information security, database security, formal specification and logic reasoning. She is interested in providing a formal specification and reasoning for security policies and rules to protect the information systems. She has published dozens of international conference papers and journal papers and has been served as a program committee member for international conferences such as International Conference on Security and Cryptography, Australasian Joint Conference on Artificial Intelligence, International Conference on Industrial, Engineering and Other Applications of Applied Intelligence Systems.

Konstantin (Kosta) Beznosov is an Associate Professor at the Department of Electrical and Computer Engineering, University of British Columbia, where he directs the Laboratory for Education and Research in Secure Systems Engineering. His research interests are usable security, distributed systems security, secure software engineering, and access control. Prior UBC, he was a Security Architect at Hitachi Computer Products (America) and Concept Five. Besides many academic papers on security engineering in distributed systems, he is also a co-author of "Enterprise Security with EJB and CORBA" and "Mastering Web Services Security" books, as well as XACML and several CORBA security specifications. He has served on program committees and/or helped to organize SOUPS, CCS, NSPW, NDSS, ACSAC, SACMAT, CHIMIT. Prof. Beznosov is an associate editor of ACM Transactions on Information and System Security (TISSEC) and International Journal of Secure Software Engineering (IJSSE).

Wesam Darwish is a software architect with AdvancedIO Systems, Inc. He obtained his Master of Applied Science degree in Electrical and Computer Engineering from the University of British Columbia (UBC) in 2009. He was a member of the Laboratory for Education and Research in Secure Systems Engineering (LERSSE) under the supervision of Professor Konstantin Beznosov. His research interests include distributed systems security, software architecture, and access control architectures.

Jan Durand is currently a graduate student in the Computer Science Department at Louisiana Tech University. He received his B.S. degree in computer science from Grambling State University in 2010. His current research interests include the detection of malicious applications via static analysis and data mining.

Shamal Faily is a post-doctoral researcher at the University of Oxford having recently completed his DPhil at the same university. His main research interests involve examining how the design of secure systems can be better supported with design techniques and tools from HCI and Secure Software Engineering. Shamal is also interested in understanding how entrepreneurship and innovation theories can be used to inform the design of security. Shamal is currently working on the EU EP7 webinos project where he is exploring how the security and privacy expectations of archetypical users can be built into the design of the webinos platform.

Massimo Felici holds a PhD in Informatics from the University of Edinburgh. His main research interests concern the dependability of Information and Communication Technologies within complex organizations. His recent research has focused on dependability, risk and trust.

Ivan Fléchais is a departmental lecturer in the Software Engineering Programme at Oxford University and his main lecturing and research interests are in the area of computer security, in particular, given the important role that people play in secure systems; this involves researching how secure systems can be designed, implemented, and tested to take human factors into account. Prior to this, he graduated with BSc in computer science from University College London (UCL) and then stayed on at UCL to achieve a PhD researching how to design secure and usable systems, which resulted in the creation of the Appropriate and Effective Guidance to Information Security secure system design method.

Juan Carlos Flores is currently a graduate student in the Computer Science Department at Louisiana Tech University. He received his B.S. degree in computer engineering from the University of Houston Clear Lake in 2010. His research interests are in the areas of virtualization technologies, network security and digital forensics.

Martin Gilje Jaatun graduated from the Norwegian Institute of Technology (NTH) in 1992, and has been employed as a research scientist at SINTEF ICT in Trondheim since 2004. His research interests include software security "for the rest of us", information security in process control environments, and security in cloud computing.

Jostein Jensen graduated from the Norwegian University of Science and Technology (NTNU) in 2008, and has since been employed as a research scientist at SINTEF ICT in Trondheim. He is currently pursuing his PhD at NTNU. His research interests include software security, security in Air Traffic Management, and federated identity management systems.

Wouter Joosen is a full professor at the Department of Computer Science of the Katholieke Universiteit Leuven in Belgium, where he teaches course on software architecture and software engineering for secure software, on distributed systems and on the engineering of secure service platforms. His research interests are in security aspects of software, including security in component frameworks, and security architectures. He is member of the steering committee of the international Middleware conference and of the International Symposium on Engineering Secure Software and Systems. He is also part of the steering committee of the ESF scientific programme MINEMA on middleware for network eccentric and mobile applications.

Christian Jung works as a security engineer in the Information Systems Quality Assurance department at the Fraunhofer Institute for Experimental Software Engineering (IESE) in Kaiserslautern. He graduated with a diploma in "Technical Computer Science" from the University of Technology in Kaiserslautern. During his university studies, Christian Jung focused on security in distributed systems. As a member of the security team at the Distributed Computer Systems Lab (disco) at the University of Technology in Kaiserslautern he conducted research in securing wireless networks. At Fraunhofer IESE his working areas include software and system security as well as quality improvements in the software development process. His current research focuses on context-aware and policy-based security concepts for mobile and cloud environments.

Miao Kang is working as a Software Development Manager in Powerchex Ltd since 2009. She obtained her MSc (Distinction) degree in Software Engineering from Bradford University and her PhD degree in Neural Networks from London Metropolitan University. Miao previously worked as a software developer and lecturer before joining Powerchex Ltd. She holds professional memberships with Chartered Management Institute and the British Computer Society, and qualifications of MCSE from Microsoft, Prince2 Practitioner from APM Group and CMI Level5 from Chartered Management institute. Miao's research interests include Artificial Neural Networks, Mobile Agents and Secure Software Development.

Paul El-Khoury holds a Ph.D. in Computer Science from the Université Claude Bernard Lyon1. Currently he is a member of Product Security Response Team mainly focusing on SAP security patches. Prior, he was with SAP Research working on topics in Security Engineering, Web Service Security and Wireless Sensor Networks. He authored various international conference and journal publications in the area of Security Engineering, Web Service Security and Wireless Sensor Networks in addition to several patents. Back in 2004 Paul used to work as a Free Lancer.

Nicholas Kraft is currently an assistant professor in the Department of Computer Science at the University of Alabama. He received his Ph.D. degree from the Clemson University in 2007. His research interests include reverse engineering, program comprehension, grammar engineering and software evolution.

Keqin Li received his Ph.D. in Computer Software and Theory from Peking University, China. Before joining SAP Research, he was a researcher in Bell Labs Research China, Lucent Technologies, and a post-doc in Grenoble Universities. His research interests include security engineering, and software and security testing, and he has published various scientific publications in his area of interest.

Fabio Massacci received a M.Eng. in 1993 and Ph.D. in Computer Science and Engineering at University of Rome "La Sapienza" in 1998. He visited Cambridge University in 1996-1997. He joined University of Siena as Assistant Professor in 1999 and was visiting researcher at IRIT Toulouse in 2000. In 2001 he joined the University of Trento where is now a full professor. In 2001 he received the Intelligenza Artificiale award, a young researchers career award from the Italian Association for Artificial Intelligence. He is member of AAAI, ACM, IEEE Computer society and a chartered engineer. His research interests are in automated reasoning at the crossroads between artificial intelligence and computer security. He has worked on automated deduction for modal and dynamic logics and their application to access control. In 1999 he worked on the encoding of cryptographic algorithms (DES, RSA, etc) into satisfiability problem for verification and cryptanalysis. His interest in protocol verification dates back to 1997 when he proposed to model protocol attacks as a planning problem. His research interests are in security requirements engineering, formal methods and computer security. He is currently scientific coordinator of multimillion Euros industry R&D European projects on security and compliance.

Haralambos Mouratidis is a Principal Lecturer in Secure Systems and Software Development at the School of Computing, IT and Engineering (CITE) at the University of East London (UEL). He holds a B.Eng. (Hons) from the University of Wales, Swansea (UK), and a M.Sc. and PhD from the University of Sheffield (UK). He is also a Fellow of the Higher Education Academy (HEA) and a Professional

Member of the British Computer Society (BCS). Haris is leading the Computer Science Field and he is co-director of the Distributed Software Engineering Research Group. He has published more than 90 papers in the area of secure software engineering and he has secured funding from national – EPSRC, Royal Academy of Engineering- and international funding bodies.

Afonso Araújo Neto has MSc. in Computer Science from the Universidade Federal of Rio Grande do Sul, Brazil, in the field of cryptography and holds a Ph.D. student position at the Department of Informatics Engineering of the University of Coimbra, Portugal, where he is finishing his PhD research in the area of Security Benchmarking of Transactional Systems. He is also an Information Technology Analyst working at *Centro de Processamento de Dados of Universidade Federal do Rio Grande do Sul*. Afonso has a fair amount of research experience and industry experience in the domains of security and databases.

Alastair J Nisbet is a PhD research student at the School of Engineering and Advanced Technology (SEAT) of Massey University New Zealand. His research interest is in the area of MANET key management protocol development and performance studies. Alastair J Nisbet has several publications in journals and refereed international conferences.

Alfredo Pironti received the MS and PhD degrees in computer engineering from Politecnico di Torino, Torino, Italy, in 2006 and 2010 respectively. He is currently a post doctoral researcher at INRIA, France. His main research interests are on formal methods applied to security protocols and security-aware applications, as well as software engineering and model driven development. In 2010, he was post doctoral researcher and teaching assistant at Politecnico di Torino. During winter 2008, he was a visiting PhD student at Open University and Microsoft Research in Cambridge, UK.

Sean Policarpio is a postgraduate student in the School of Computing and Mathematics at the University of Western Sydney, Australia. He obtained his Bachelors of Computer Science (Honours) in 2008 and is currently doing his PhD. His research interests are in the areas of Extensible Markup Language (XML) databases, information access control/security, formal languages, logic programming and knowledge representation (Answer Set Programming). He is a member of the Intelligent Systems Laboratory at UWS, which was established by his supervisor, Prof. Yan Zhang.

Davide Pozza graduated in computer engineering in 2002, and received a PhD degree in computer engineering in 2006, both from Politecnico di Torino, Torino, Italy. He has been a post doctoral researcher at the Department of Computer Engineering at that institution till the end of 2010. He is currently working as a private sector consultant in the field of reliable and secure software engineering. His research interests include: processes, methodologies, and techniques that address software security, reliability, and safety, static analysis techniques to detect software vulnerabilities, formal methods for modelling and analyzing network vulnerability and cryptographic protocols, and automatic code generation of cryptographic protocols by starting from their formal specifications. He taught in the academy, and now he teaches in the private sector, courses on network and distributed programming, and on secure software engineering.

Mohammad Abdur Rashid is a Senior Lecturer of Computer and Communications Engineering at Massey University in New Zealand. He received an MScEng degree in Electronics Engineering specializing in Engineering Cybernetics Systems from the Wroclaw University of Technology in 1978 and a PhD from the University of Strathclyde, UK in 1986. Dr. Rashid is a co-author of two books: *Enterprise Resource Planning: Global Opportunities and Challenges* and *Handbook of Research on Enterprise Systems* published by Information Science Reference, USA. His areas of research interests are Multimedia Communication Networks, Embedded Systems Design, Network Protocols and Performance Studies; Mobile Wireless Multimedia Communication, MANET Key management and ERP/Enterprise Systems.

Carlo Riccucci graduated in Communication Sciences from the University of Siena in June 2004, with a dissertation on educational technologies. Just graduated he worked as usability evaluator in a consultancy firm specialized in human factors and usability services. In September 2004 joined the Research & Development Laboratory at Engineering Ingegneria Informatica S.p.A. as a researcher. He had been involved for over 5 years in Italian and European projects within the sixth and seventh Framework Programme IST concentrating his work on applied research and project management activity for the development of new interaction paradigms through intuitive human-computer interfaces. Since January 2008 he started collaborating on design projects of websites and web portals with a special focus on business analysis, content management, wayfinding structure and information sharing. His research activity started working on the MAIS (Multichannel Adaptive Information Systems) project, funded by Basic Research Funds (FIRB Program) of the Italian Department of Education (MIUR), collaborating at the development of new e-services for the tourist domain through portable devices and of data intensive context aware web applications. In January 2006 he started working on the SERENITY (System Engineering for Security and Dependability) European project, concentrating his research interests on the elicitation of security and dependability patterns at organizational level. In 2008 he began managing as local responsible the DEWS (Distant Early Warning System) European project that is working in order to design and implement an open, standard based early warning system for the Indian Ocean. The last project he joined is MASTER (Managing Assurance Security and Trust for sERvices) in which he researched on visual languages for audit process in complex organizations.

Manuel Rudolph received his Master of Science from the University of Applied Sciences Mannheim in 2009, and has since been employed as an engineer in the Information Systems Quality Assurance department at the Fraunhofer Institute for Experimental Software Engineering IESE in Kaiserslautern. His research interests include the usability and measurability of security as well as Public Key Infrastructures. Currently, he is working on closing the gap between security and usability by developing a methodology for improving and simplifying policy editors in the area of usage control.

Ayda Saidane has PhD in computer systems from INSA Toulouse and M.Eng in computer science from ENSI Tunisia. She prepared her thesis at LAAS-CNRS on intrusion tolerant architectures for Internet servers in the context of collaboration with SRI International. She later participated to the DADi project (Dependable Anomaly Detection with Diagnosis) with SSI team at Supelec Rennes. Between 2007 and 2009, she has been research fellow at University of Trento working in the EU project SERENITY (System Engineering for Security and Dependability). Currently, she is a research scientist at University of Luxembourg, working on SETER project (Security Testing for Resilient Systems).

Riccardo Scandariato obtained his PhD in Computer Science from Politecnico di Torino, Italy, in 2004. Since January 2006, he joined the Distributed Systems and Computer Networks Research Group (DistriNet) at the Katholieke Universiteit Leuven, Belgium. He is a permanent member of the staff and currently leads a team of security researchers in secure software. Dr. Scandariato's main research activities are in the area of secure software engineering, with a particular focus on security in software architecture and empirical methods in securityGriet Verhenneman is Legal researcher at the Faculty of Law at the Katholieke Universiteit Leuven, Belgium, where she is more precisely part of the Interdisciplinary Centre for Law and ICT (ICRI). Her research focuses on the legal aspects of eHealth: the use of information and computer technology in support of health and health care. Within this field she concentrates mainly on privacy, data protection and the rights of the patient. Griet contributes to several Belgian and European research projects and prepares a PhD on the patient's right to privacy and autonomy in a new healthcare environment based on disease management techniques. In 2010 she was awarded the prize for Best Young Presenter at the Fitce Congress in Santiago, Spain for her presentation entitled "Consent, an Instrument for Patient Empowerment?".

Reinhard Schwarz is a senior engineer at Fraunhofer IESE, where he is heading the IT Security group in the Information Systems Quality Assurance department. He has a PhD degree in computer science from the University of Kaiserslautern. His research interests include information security, system security, and software security engineering. He is a founding member of the International Secure Software Engineering Council (ISSECO).

Christian Schwarzl was a master's student at the Vienna University of Technology and focused on information security. The research results of his master's thesis was the starting point of a larger research project involving the combination digitial and biometrics.

Magali Séguran is a researcher at SAP Labs France Sophia-Antipolis in the Security and Trust research program since 2006. She holds a Master degree in computer science from the University of Nice in 1997 and a Doctoral degree in computer science in 2003 from the University of Lyon where she worked as associated researcher. She was involved in the European Project SERENITY (System Engineering For Security and Dependability). Currently she is contributing to the TAS3 (Trusted Architecture for Securely Shared Services) project with the following research areas: Requirements Engineering, Trust and Security for SOA, Business Processes.

Riccardo Sisto graduated in electronic engineering in 1987, and received a PhD degree in computer engineering in 1992, both from Politecnico di Torino, Torino, Italy. Since 1991 he has been working at Politecnico di Torino, in the computer engineering department, first as a researcher, then as an associate professor and, since 2004, as a full professor of computer engineering. Since the beginning of his scientific activity, his main research interests have been in the area of formal methods, applied to software engineering, communication protocol engineering, and computer security. On these and related topics he has authored and co-authored more than 70 scientific papers. Riccardo Sisto has been a member of the ACM (Association for Computing Machinery) since 1999. He is currently senior member of the ACM.

Randy Smith is currently an associate professor in the Department of Computer Science at the University of Alabama. He received his Ph.D. degree from the University of Alabama in 1998. His current research interests include software process measurement and data mining.

Alessandra Tedeschi holds a PhD in Applied Mathematics from the University of L'Aquila and Rome 'La Sapienza'. Her research interests includes the analysis and modeling of Complex Systems with Game Theory techniques . She has been working with Deep Blue since 2007, where she has been involved as Validation expert in EU funded projects, such as SERENITY (2006-2008), ReSIST (2006-2008) and SecureChange (2009-2012).

Marco Vieira is an Assistant Professor at the University of Coimbra, Portugal, and an Adjunct Associate Teaching Professor at the Carnegie Mellon University, USA. Marco Vieira is an expert on dependability benchmarking and is co-author of the first dependability benchmark proposal known – the DBench-OLTP. His research interests also include experimental dependability evaluation, fault injection, security benchmarking, software development processes, and software quality assurance, subjects in which he has authored or co-authored tens of papers in refereed conferences and journals. He has participated in many research projects, both at the national and European level. Marco Vieira has served on program committees of the major conferences of the dependability area and acted as referee for many international conferences and journals in the dependability and databases areas.

Edgar R. Weippl (CISSP, CISA, CISM, CSSLP, CMC) is Research Director of SBA Research and Associate Professor (Privatdozent) at the Vienna University of Technology. His research focuses on applied concepts of IT-security and e-learning. Edgar is member of the editorial board of Computers & Security (COSE), in the steering committee of the ED-MEDIA conference; he organizes the ARES conference (as PC chair 2007, 08; panel and workshop chair 2009). After graduating with a Ph.D. from the Vienna University of Technology, Edgar worked for two years in a research startup. He then spent one year teaching as an assistant professor at Beloit College, WI. From 2002 to 2004, while with the software vendor ISIS Papyrus, he worked as a consultant for an HMO (Empire BlueCross BlueShield) in New York, NY and Albany, NY, and for Deutsche Bank (PWM) in Frankfurt, Germany. In 2004 he joined the Vienna University of Technology and founded together with A Min Tjoa and Markus Klemen the research center SBA Research.

Kim Wuyts is a research assistant at Distributed Systems and Computer Networks Research Group (DistriNet) of the Katholieke Universiteit Leuven in Belgium. She is part of the secure software team and is involved in a number of health-care related projects, both at the regional and European level. Her main research interests are in the area of security and privacy of software, including security and privacy requirements, threat modeling, and secure architectures.

Nicola Zannone received an M.S. degree in computer science at the University of Verona in 2003, and a Ph.D. in computer science at the University of Trento in 2007. He visited the Center for Secure Information Systems at George Mason University in 2005 and the IBM Zurich Research Laboratory in 2006 where he worked on access control and privacy. In 2006-2007, he was a young researcher at CINI in Trento. In 2007 he joined the Department of Computer Science of the University of Toronto as a postdoctoral fellow. Since 2008 he is postdoctoral fellow at the Eindhoven University of Technology. He received the IBM Ph.D. Fellowship Award for the 2006-2007 academic year. His research interests include computer security and formal verification. He is most interested in security requirements engineering, trust management, data protection and privacy.

Yan Zhang obtained his PhD degree in Computer Science from University of Sydney in 1994. He joined University of Western Sydney in 1995, and established the Intelligent Systems Laboratory in the School of Computing and Mathematics. Prof Yan Zhang's research interests include knowledge representation and reasoning, nonmonotonic logic programming, epistemic reasoning for intelligent systems, information security, model checking and modification, and computational complexity for dynamic system modeling. In recent years, he has published significant results in these areas in top international journals and conferences such as journals Artificial Intelligence, ACM Transactions on Computational Logic, Journal of Artificial Intelligence AResearch, and IJCAI, AAAI, ECAI and KR conferences.

Index